Lecture Notes in Computer

T0238045

Commenced Publication in 1973
Founding and Former Series Editors:
Gerhard Goos, Juris Hartmanis, and Jan van Leeuwen

Costas Lambrinoudakis   Günther Pernul
A Min Tjoa (Eds.)

Trust, Privacy and Security in Digital Business

4th International Conference, TrustBus 2007
Regensburg, Germany, September 4-6, 2007
Proceedings

 Springer

Volume Editors

Costas Lambrinoudakis
Department of Information and Communication Systems Engineering
University of the Aegean
Karlovasi, 83200 Samos, Greece
E-mail: clam@aegean.gr

Günther Pernul
Department of Information Systems
University of Regensburg
Universitätsstrasse 31
D-93053 Regensburg, Germany
E-mail: guenther.pernul@wiwi.uni-regensburg.de

A Min Tjoa
Institute for Software Technology and Interactive Systems
Favoritenstrasse 9-11/188
Vienna University of Technology
A-1040 Vienna, Austria
E-mail: amin@ifs.tuwien.ac.at

Library of Congress Control Number: 2007933177

CR Subject Classification (1998): K.4.4, K.4, K.6, E.3, C.2, D.4.6, J.1

LNCS Sublibrary: SL 4 – Security and Cryptology

ISSN   0302-9743
ISBN-10   3-540-74408-8 Springer Berlin Heidelberg New York
ISBN-13   978-3-540-74408-5 Springer Berlin Heidelberg New York

Springer is a part of Springer Science+Business Media

springer.com

© Springer-Verlag Berlin Heidelberg 2007
Printed in Germany

Typesetting: Camera-ready by author, data conversion by Scientific Publishing Services, Chennai, India
Printed on acid-free paper   SPIN: 12112197   06/3180   5 4 3 2 1 0

Preface

This book presents the proceedings of the 4th International Conference on Trust, Privacy and Security in Digital Business (TrustBus 2007), held in Regensburg, Germany September 4–6, 2007. The conference continued from previous events held in Zaragoza (2004), Copenhagen (2005) and Krakow (2006), and maintained the aim of bringing together academic researchers and industry developers to discuss the state of the art in technology for establishing trust, privacy and security in digital business. We thank the attendees for coming to Regensburg to participate and debate the new emerging advances in this area.

The conference program included one keynote presentation, one panel session and eight technical papers sessions. The keynote speech was delivered by Alfred Kobsa from the University of California, Irvine (USA), on the topic of "Privacy-Enhanced Personalization." The subject of the panel discussion was "Managing Digital Identities—Challenges and Opportunities." The participants were Marco Casassa Mont (Hewlett-Packard Laboratories, UK), Eduardo B. Fernandez (Florida Atlantic University, USA), Socratis Katsikas (University of Piraeus, Greece), Alfred Kobsa (University of California, Irvine, USA), and Rolf Oppliger (Informatikstrategieorgan Bund, ISB, Switzerland). The panel was chaired by Günther Pernul (University of Regensburg, Germany). The reviewed paper sessions covered a broad range of topics, from access control models to security and risk management, and from privacy and identity management to security protocols. The conference attracted 80 submissions, each of which was assigned to four referees for review. The Program Committee ultimately accepted 28 papers for inclusion in the proceedings.

We would like to express our thanks to the various people who assisted us in organizing the event and formulating the program. We are very grateful to the Program Committee members and the external reviewers, for their timely and rigorous reviews of the papers. Thanks are also due to the DEXA Organizing Committee for supporting our event, and in particular to Gabriela Wagner for her help with the administrative aspects.

Finally, we would like to thank all of the authors that submitted papers for the event, and contributed to an interesting set of conference proceedings.

September 2007

Costas Lambrinoudakis
Günther Pernul
A Min Tjoa

Program Committee

General Chair

Günther   Pernul   University of Regensburg, Germany

Program Committee Co-chairs

Costas Lambrinoudakis   University of the Aegean, Greece
A Min Tjoa   Vienna University of Technology, Austria

International Program Committee

Acquisti, Alessandro	Carnegie Mellon University (USA)
Atluri, Vijay	Rutgers University (USA)
Casassa Mont, Marco	HP Labs Bristol (UK)
Chadwick, David	University of Kent (UK)
Clarke, Nathan	University of Plymouth (UK)
Clayton, Richard	University of Cambridge (UK)
Cuppens, Frederic	ENST Bretagne (France)
Damiani, Ernesto	Università degli Studi di Milano (Italy)
Dawson, Ed	Queensland University of Technology (Australia)
De Capitani di Vimercati, Sabrina	University of Milan (Italy)
De Meer, Hermann	University of Passau (Germany)
Eckert, Claudia	Technical University Darmstadt (Germany)
Federrath, Hannes	University of Regensburg (Germany)
Fernandez, Eduardo B.	Florida Atlantic University (USA)
Ferrari, Elena	University of Insubria (Italy)
Fischer-Huebner, Simone	University of Karlstad (Sweden)
Flavian, Carlos	University of Zaragoza (Spain)
Furnell, Steven	University of Plymouth (UK)
Gligor, Virgil D.	University of Maryland (USA)
Gonzalez-Nieto, Juan M.	Queensland University of Technology (Australia)
Grimm, Rüdiger	University of Koblenz (Germany)
Gritzalis, Dimitris	Athens University of Economics and Business (Greece)
Gritzalis, Stefanos	University of the Aegean (Greece)
Gudes, Ehud	Ben-Gurion University (Israel)

Gürgens, Sigrid	Fraunhofer Institute for Secure Information Technology (Germany)
Hansen, Marit	Independent Center for Privacy Protection (Germany)
Jøsang, Audun	Queensland University of Technology (Australia)
Karygiannis, Tom	NIST (USA)
Katsikas, Sokratis	University of Piraeus (Greece)
Kesdogan, Dogan	NTNU Trondheim (Norway)
Kikuchi, Hiroaki	Tokai University (Japan)
Kokolakis, Spyros	University of the Aegean (Greece)
Kursawe, Klaus	Philips Research, Eindhoven (The Netherlands)
Lilien, Leszek	Western Michigan University (USA)
Lioy, Antonio	Politecnico di Torino (Italy)
Lopez, Javier	University of Malaga (Spain)
Lory, Peter	University of Regensburg (Germany)
Mana Gomez, Antonio	University of Malaga (Spain)
Markowitch, Olivier	Universite Libre de Bruxelles (Belgium)
Martinelli, Fabio	CNR (Italy)
Mueller, Guenter	University of Freiburg (Germany)
Okamoto, Eiji	University of Tsukuba (Japan)
Olivier, Martin S.	University of Pretoria (South Africa)
Oppliger, Rolf	eSecurity Technologies (Switzerland)
Papadaki, Maria	University of Plymouth (UK)
Patel, Ahmed	Kingston University (UK)
Pfitzmann, Andreas	Dresden University of Technology (Germany)
Piattini, Mario	University of Castilla-La Mancha (Spain)
Pohl, Hartmut	FH Bonn-Rhein-Sieg (Germany)
Posch, Karl	University of Technology Graz (Austria)
Priebe, Torsten	Capgemini (Austria)
Quirchmayr, Gerald	University of Vienna (Austria)
Rannenberg, Kai	Goethe University Frankfurt (Germany)
Ruland, Christoph	University of Siegen (Germany)
Samarati, Pierangela	University of Milan (Italy)
Schunter, Matthias	IBM Zurich Research Lab. (Switzerland)
Siponen, Mikko T.	University of Oulu (Finland)
Spalka, Adrian	University of Bonn (Germany)
Teufel, Stephanie	University of Fribourg (Switzerland)
Tomlinson, Allan	Royal Holloway, University of London (UK)
Varadharajan, Vijay	Macquarie University (Australia)
Zhou, Jianying	I2R (Singapore)

External Reviewers

Andersson, Christer	Karlstad University, Sweden
Antonakakis, Manos	Georgia Tech, USA
Balopoulos, Theodoros	University of the Aegean, Greece
Belsis, Petros	University of the Aegean, Greece
Bergmann, Mike	Dresden University of Technology, Germany
Dritsas, Stelios	Athens University of Economics and Business, Greece
Dürbeck, Stefan	University of Regensburg, Germany
Ekelhart, Andreas	Secure Business Austria, Austria
Fenz, Stefan	Secure Business Austria, Austria
Franz, Elke	Dresden University of Technology, Germany
Galoz, Nurit	Ben-Gurion University, Israel
Gilberg, Jörg	University of Regensburg, Germany
Goluch, Gernot	Secure Business Austria, Austria
Grinshpun, Tal	Ben-Gurion University, Israel
Indrakanti, Sarath	Macquarie University, Australia
Jakoubi, Stefan	Secure Business Austria, Austria
Kambourakis, George	University of the Aegean, Greece
Karjoth, Günter	IBM Research, Switzerland
Karyda, Maria	University of the Aegean, Greece
Kolter, Jan	University of Regensburg, Germany
Konstantinou, Elisavet	University of the Aegean, Greece
Kumaraguru, Ponnurangam	Carnegie Mellon University, USA
Li, Zhuowei	Indiana University, USA
Liu, Joseph	Bristol University, UK
Marias, Giannis	Athens University of Economics and Business, Greece
Martucci, Leonardo	Karlstad University, Sweden
Merten, Patrick	University of Fribourg, Switzerland
Oberender, Jens	University of Passau, Germany
Panchenko, Andriy	RWTH Aachen, Germany
Peng, Kun	Queensland University of Technology, Australia
Perego, Andrea	University of Insubria, Italy
Pham, Vinh D.	RWTH Aachen, Germany
Pimenidis, Alexis	RWTH Aachen, Germany
Pisko, Evgenia	Goethe University Frankfurt, Germany
Reid, Jason	Queensland University of Technology, Australia
Romanosky, Sasha	Carnegie Mellon University, USA
Roßnagel, Heiko	Goethe University Frankfurt, Germany
Rozenberg, Boris	Ben-Gurion University, Israel
Ruan, Chun	University of Western Sydney, Australia
Rudolph, Carsten	Fraunhofer SIT, Germany
Schillinger, Rolf	University of Regensburg, Germany
Schlüter, Jan	University of Fribourg, Switzerland
Steinert, Martin	University of Fribourg, Switzerland
Su, Chunhua	Kyushu University, Japan

Theoharidou, Marianthi	Athens University of Economics and Business, Greece
Tjoa, Simon	Secure Business Austria, Austria
Tsohou, Aggeliki	University of the Aegean, Greece
Tsoumas, Bill	Athens University of Economics and Business, Greece
Tupakula, Uday	Macquarie University, Australia
Volkamer, Melanie	University of Passau, Germany
Weippl, Edgar	Secure Business Austria, Austria
Weiss, Stefan	Goethe University Frankfurt, Germany
Woelfl, Thomas	University of Regensburg, Germany

Table of Contents

Session 4: Authentication and Access Control

Session 5: Compliance and User Privacy

Session 6: Policy Management

Session 7: Security System Management

Session 8: Security and Trust

Trustbus'07 Keynote Talk
Privacy Enhanced Personalization

Alfred Kobsa

University of California,
Irvine, USA
kobsa@uci.edu
http://www.ics.uci.edu/~kobsa

Abstract. Web personalization has demonstrated to be advantageous for both online customers and vendors. However, current personalization methods require considerable amounts of data about users, and the benefits of personalization are therefore counteracted by privacy concerns. Personalized systems need to take these concerns into account, as well as privacy laws and industry self-regulation that may be in effect. Privacy-Enhanced Personalization aims at reconciling the goals and methods of user modeling and personalization with privacy considerations, and to strive for best possible personalization within the boundaries set by privacy. This talk surveys recent research on factors that affect people's personal information disclosure and on personalization methods that bear fewer privacy risks, and presents design recommendations based thereon.

C. Lambrinoudakis, G. Pernul, A M. Tjoa (Eds.): TrustBus 2007, LNCS 4657, p. 1, 2007.
© Springer-Verlag Berlin Heidelberg 2007

Panel Discussion
Managing Digital Identities –
Challenges and Opportunities

Günther Pernul[1], Marco Casassa Mont[2], Eduardo B. Fernandez[3],
Socrates Katsikas[4], Alfred Kobsa[5], and Rolf Oppliger[6]

[1] University of Regensburg, Germany
[2] Hewlett-Packard Laboratories, UK
[3] Florida Atlantic University, USA
[4] University of Piraeus, Greece
[5] University of California, Irvine, USA
[6] Informatikstrategieorgan Bund, ISB, Switzerland

Identity Management (IdM) comes in two dimensions: First, the secure and efficient creation, use, and administration of personal attributes which make up a digital identifier of a human and used in large scale global networks, such as the Internet. Second, as in-house IdM which is a core component of enterprise security management. In this panel we will be focusing on both.

In open networks the major question is how IdM has to be organised to enable efficient user identification (on request) and how it would still be possible at the same time to safeguard privacy by avoiding the scenario of a "transparent system user". The challenges for global IdM are manifold but linked to a basic trade-off-situation: Service providers will only grant electronic access upon successful authentication of a requester, but at the same time users should be able to protect their privacy and transactions shall not be linkable. In addition, in the wake of terrorist threat, the request for global unique electronic identifiers has gained more popularity than ever.

In-house IdM is influenced by organisational and technical drivers. It deals with the management of digital identities during their lifecycle within organisations. Some years ago, technologies like stand-alone Single-Sign-On modules or meta-directories quite often already were branded with the term IdM. Lately researchers as well as software vendors have realised that companies need more than just technical components to solve their identity chaos: Organisations need a comprehensive IdM Infrastructure, bearing in mind technical as well as organisational aspects. In addition to that, the emerging demand for sharing identity information between organisations results in a greater need for standardized data exchange channels.

For IdM on a global as well as on a local scale many technical, organisational and political questions are still to be solved. Data ownership, compliance with laws and regulations, data privacy issues are examples for questions which need to be faced in an efficient way in the future.

C. Lambrinoudakis, G. Pernul, A M. Tjoa (Eds.): TrustBus 2007, LNCS 4657, p. 2, 2007.
© Springer-Verlag Berlin Heidelberg 2007

Recognition of Authority in Virtual Organisations

Tuan-Anh Nguyen, David Chadwick, and Bassem Nasser

University of Kent, Canterbury, England

Abstract. A Virtual Organisation (VO) is a temporary alliance of autonomous, diverse, and geographically dispersed organisations, where the participants pool resources, information and knowledge in order to meet common objectives. This requires dynamic security policy management. We propose an authorisation policy management model called *recognition of authority* (ROA) which allows dynamically trusted authorities to adjust the authorisation policies for VO resources. The model supports dynamic delegation of authority, and the expansion and contraction of organizations in a VO, so that the underlying authorisation system is able to use existing user credentials issued by participating organisations to evaluate the user's access rights to VO resources.

1 Introduction

A Virtual Organisation (VO) is a temporary alliance of autonomous, diverse, and geographically dispersed organisations, where the participants pool resources, information and knowledge in order to meet common objectives. The objectives of an alliance can evolve and the relationships between the different parties may change. Therefore virtual organisations are naturally dynamic. Consequently, management, especially security management in such a dynamic environment must be provided with suitable dynamic mechanisms. There are several areas of security under consideration for VOs but in this paper we are concerned with authorisation and access control.

The behaviour of an organisation's authorisation system is normally governed by an authorisation policy, written by the policy officer (or Source of Authority - SoA). In a dynamic environment like a VO, organisations may continually join or leave the collaboration. When joining a VO, an organisation may need to provide access to its protected resources to users from other organisations in the VO. When the organisation leaves the VO, access rights to its protected resources from users outside the organisation have to be removed. In these cases, the authorisation policy of the organisation has to be *dynamically modified and updated* to cater for these dynamic changes. However,

1. in a VO, which is a pan-organisational system, the number of attributes and users can be in the hundreds or thousands. Managing these attributes and users and their relationships is a formidable task that can not realistically be done by one person ([16]).

C. Lambrinoudakis, G. Pernul, A M. Tjoa (Eds.): TrustBus 2007, LNCS 4657, pp. 3–13, 2007.

2. in reality, an authorisation policy is a set of low-level policies derived from high-level ones and the refinement process requires the involvement of many people, within the same or partner organisations ([6], [11]).
3. the exact form of collaboration between an organisation and a partner in the VO is normally not known beforehand, so the permissions to modify the authorisation policy need to be delegated on demand to the people that deal with the collaboration.

Therefore, the permissions to modify and update the policy may need to be *dynamically delegated* from the SoA to other delegates on demand. Consequently, these delegates are allowed to adjust the organisation's policy, in order to accommodate requirements in the collaborations and to give users in partner organisations access rights to the protected resources of the organisation.

In the RBAC model ([5], [17]), an authorisation policy includes a set of role-permission assignments (RPA), a role hierarchy (optional) and a set of rules that regulate the assignments of roles to users (user-role assignments, URA). In order to avoid policy conflicts, especially when the same organisations are simultaneously members of multiple VOs, we require that each collaboration be independent with its own security objectives and requirements. For example, within one collaboration, a Student role may be considered the subordinate role of a Staff role and the later to inherit the permissions of the former, but within another collaboration, the two roles may be independent with no permission inheritance. If the two collaborations are not independent, it is possible that the requirements of one collaboration cannot be fulfilled or they may conflict with those of the other.

On the other hand, in a VO there may be several organisations that support an inter-organisational workflow and these organisations may need to be changed during the workflow's life cycle. Furthermore, the workflow's requirements (or specification) may also need to be changed. The workflow's security infrastructure should not be tied to users or attributes from any of the partner organisations. Otherwise, if one partner is replaced by another then the workflow security infrastructure would have to be modified to account for this change. Additionally, the partner organisations should not tie permissions used by the workflow to their own users or attributes because if the permissions needed for the workflow change, the partner organisation would need to modify the permissions given to its users or attributes to accommodate these changes. Consequently there needs to be a level of indirection between the workflow's security infrastructure and the organisation's security infrastructure. Since each organisation may support several inter-organisational workflows, it is not realistic for each organisation to restructure its organisational level security infrastructure when workflow security infrastructure changes occur and vice versa. Therefore, the workflow security infrastructure needs to be separated from the organisational-level security infrastructure as stated in [8] and [14]. Our model provides this separation through the dynamic on demand specification of organizational level attributes that grant access to a VO's workflow resources. The organizational level attributes are dynamically mapped into either workflow roles or workflow privileges.

1.1   Objectives and Contribution

In the VO environment, there are issuing domains that issue credentials to users and target domains that consume credentials ([3]). The authorization policy of the target domain decides whether an issued credential is to be trusted or not i.e. is valid or not, and whether it provides sufficient permissions or not to the accessed resource. In an attribute (or role) based authorisation policy, the permission-attribute assignments (or RPA) form the access control policy. The URA form the credential validation policy ([3]). Thus, an authorisation policy includes an access control policy and a credential validation policy.

In this paper, we propose a model called **recognition of authority** which provides the following features for authorisation administration in a virtual organisation:

- Administrative roles are defined which grant permission to dynamically update limited parts of the authorisation policy in the target domain, more specifically, to assign organizational level attributes to a subset of the privileges which grant access to the VO's workflow resources.
- Administrators are dynamically created by assigning these administrative roles to them. These roles can be dynamically delegated, and also dynamically revoked, thereby dynamically adding and removing administrators from the system.
- An administrator can dynamically assign a subset of the permissions granted by the administrative role, to any organizational level user attributes (i.e. perform RPA). In addition, the administrator can provide the policy information for validating the user credentials that contain these attributes (i.e. URA validation).
- Collaborations between organisations are independent of each other, since a VO's workflow privileges are independent of those of other VOs.
- Application-level (workflow) security infrastructures are separated from organisational level security infrastructures since workflow permissions are dynamically assigned to organizational level attributes.

By allowing authorization policies to be dynamically updated as above, our model allows the authorisation system of a target domain to dynamically *recognise* trusted administrators, to dynamically *recognise* the new attributes they are trusted to issue, and to dynamically *recognise* new users of the VO. The initial definition of the administrative roles means that the authorization system knows the limit of their administrative authority in assigning permissions to users.

The rest of this paper is structured as follows: section 2 reviews some related research, section 3 compares and contrasts two approaches for assigning permissions to attributes, section 4 presents our recognition of authority management model in detail and the last section provides a conclusion and indicates where future research is still needed.

2   Related Works

In [7], the authorisation policy in a target domain is only modified and updated by the security officer in that domain, so that the model is not appropriate for dynamic and large environments like VOs. The RT model (Role-based Trust-management – [9], [10]) is a very powerful framework for representing policies and credentials in distributed authorisation system. It provides the capability of role mapping i.e. one role issued in one domain is mapped to another role issued in another domain. In this way, permissions in one organisation are assigned to roles issued in another organisation and users from one organisation can access protected resources in another. The disadvantage of the RT model is that it only supports RT formatted credentials, ignoring the fact that users' credentials in VOs are organisation-dependent. In [14], the policy of an organisation is only updated by its administrator and does not have a mechanism to separate collaborations from each other. Furthermore, the policy for role mapping is statically set by the administrator in a system-site. The current PERMIS infrastructure ([1], [2]) supports the dynamic assignment of roles to users in different domains but does not have the capability of dynamically adjusting the authorisation policy. The CAS model ([15]) is used for authorisation in Grid environments but the policy of a CAS server is only modified and updated by its predefined administrators. Furthermore, it can not separate the workflow security infrastructure from the organisation level security infrastructure or explicitly deal with multiple collaborations. If there is a change of participant in the collaboration, the CAS server has to be re-configured with a new set of users and users' permissions. The framework proposed in [6] does not separate inter-organisational workflows from organisation-level changes because if there is a change in participation, the inter-organisational workflow specification which specifies who can have which permissions will have to be changed. Furthermore, the framework has no mechanism to separate collaborations from each other. In [12], the authors proposed the dynamic coalition-based access control (DCBAC) model that facilitates the formation of dynamic coalitions through the use of a registry service, where available services can be advertised by potential coalition members. This model does not consider the decentralised administration of collaborations, so that only the SoA in an organisation can register the organisation's services to coalitions. Furthermore, the workflow security infrastructures are not separated from the organisation level security infrastructures. The major contribution of our paper is bring together in one model the various advantages of the different models above, by allowing the dynamic update of authorization policies by a dynamically changing decentralized pool of administrators, whilst keeping a tight separation between workflow security infrastructure and organisation level security infrastructure and also between one collaboration and another.

3   Direct Permission Assignment vs. Role Mapping

There are two approaches for assigning permissions in a local organisation to users in partner organisations. The first is to directly assign permissions to remote user attributes ([4], [6], [7], [15]) and the second is to map remote user attributes into local user roles by attribute-role mapping ([9], [14]). Both approaches can facilitate collaboration between organisations. In the attribute-role mapping approach, the permission given to a remote attribute is the permission of the local role, which is fixed. Thus, this approach limits the granularity of delegation to that of the pre-defined local roles (and their subordinate roles), whilst direct permission assignment allows each permission to be delegated or assigned separately. On the other hand, by mapping remote user attributes to local roles (used for workflows), the changes of participants in a workflow are confined to the modification of mappings from an organisation's attributes to the local user roles (it does not affect the workflow's specification) and changes to the specification of local roles do not require modifications to the remote user attribute specifications. Thus, this approach supports the separation of workflows from organisational changes ([8], [14]). Since both approaches have their merits, our model is designed to support both approaches. When an administrative role is defined, its administrative permissions are defined as either an ability to assign permissions to user attributes, or an ability to map user attributes into existing local user roles.

4   Recognition of Authority Management Model

We identify two types of permission: a *normal permission* (or *user permission*) and an *administrative permission*. A user permission is a consent (for a user) to perform an action on a particular resource under certain conditions. An administrative permission is a consent (for an administrator) to perform role permission assignments i.e. to either assign one or more user permissions to a set of (one or more) user attributes, or to perform role mappings between user attributes.

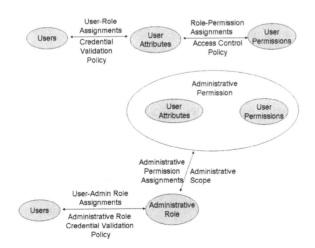

Fig. 1. User Roles and Administrative Roles

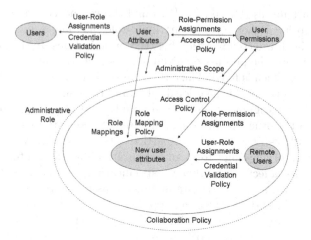

Fig. 2. Collaboration Policy

When a set of user permissions is given to an attribute, we say that the attribute is a *user attribute*. When a set of administrative permissions is given to a role we say the role is an *administrative role*. Someone who holds an administrative role is called an administrator. The set of user permissions and user attributes that an administrator can assign or map to new user attributes is called his *administrative scope*.

The recognition of authority management model for facilitating dynamic collaboration between organisations comprises the following steps:

1. The policy writer (SoA) of the target domain defines a set of administrative roles for the target domain, an administrative role credential validation policy, and the workflow permissions that are attached to these administrative roles (i.e. the administrative scope).
2. The SoA dynamically delegates these administrative roles to trusted people in remote domains with whom there is to be a collaboration, by issuing administrative role credentials to them.
3. To establish a collaboration, one of these administrators must update the SoA's authorisation policy by writing a collaboration policy. The collaboration policy includes an access control policy and/or a role mapping policy, and a user credential validation policy. The latter specifies validation rules for user credentials containing newly defined (organizational level) user attributes, whilst the former specifies either role permission assignments or role mappings for the newly defined user attributes. In this way, users who hold credentials containing these new attributes will gain access to the appropriate target resources.
4. In order to ensure that no administrator can overstep his delegated authority, the authorisation system has to validate that the collaboration policy lies within the the administrative scope specified in Figure 1 above. If it does, it

is accepted, and its policy rules become dynamically incorporated into the SoA's policy. If it does not, it is rejected, and its policy rules will be ignored.

5. When a user from a collaborating domain wants to access a protected resource in the target domain, assuming the collaboration policy has been accepted, the authorisation system retrieves and validates the user's credentials/attributes against the now enlarged credential validation policy. Only valid attributes will then be used by the access control system to make access control decisions for the user's request against the now enlarged access control policy ([3]).

6. An administrator may dynamically delegate his administrative role to another person, providing the delegate falls within the scope of the administrative role credential validation policy set by the resource SoA (see Figure 1). In [13] we have proposed a delegation of authority model that has the capability to further constrain the authority of administrators so that they may not only delegate their administrative roles, but also a subset of them. However, this refined delegation of administrative roles is not considered further in the scope of this paper. We will assume for now that administrators may delegate their (unconstrained) roles to other administrators.

4.1   Administrative Roles

The SoA of a target domain is the person who is fully trusted by the authorisation system to set its authorisation policy. The SoA's administrative scope is all the user permissions that are under his control in the target domain. In our model, we propose that the SoA defines a set of administrative roles which each control either a subset of the user permissions or mappings to subsets of local user attributes. The SoA may then delegate these administrative roles to other people on demand as the need arises, so that the delegates can control subsets of user permissions or role mappings. We express an administrative role as:

– Either a finite set of user permissions p_i which can be assigned to (new or existing) user attributes: $aRole = \{p_1, p_2, \ldots, p_n\}$. The holder of this kind of administrative role is trusted to assign any of the user permissions that comprise the definition of the administrative role, to any set of user attributes provided that the assignments satisfy the restrictions placed on the administrative role.

– Or a set of existing user attributes to which new user attributes can be mapped: $aRole = \{uR_1, uR_2, \ldots, uR_n\}$. The holder of this kind of administrative role is trusted to map any set of new user attributes into any set of existing local user attributes that comprise the definition of the administrative role, provided that the mappings satisfy the restrictions placed on the administrative role.

Note that the remote administrator who deals with a collaboration needs to know either the existing permissions or user attributes in the target domain in order to perform either role permission assignments or role mappings. A DTD for role-permission assignments and attribute-role mappings is provided in the Appendix.

4.2   Validation of an Administrator's Administrative Roles

Validating an administrator's administrative roles is no different to validating a user's credential. The authorisation system validates credentials based on its credential validation policy. We have proposed a model for validating users' credentials, called the Credential Validation Service (CVS) in [3]. In general, the CVS is provided with a trust model that tells it which attribute issuers to trust (roots of trust), and a credential validation policy that provides the rules to control which delegates are allowed to receive which delegated roles.

The formal representation of the CVS's credential validation policy is as follows:

1. a set of attributes $ATTRIBUTES$,
2. a set of attribute hierarchies $S_{RH} = \{RH\}$, RH is a attribute hierarchy,
3. a set of delegation rights $RIGHTS = \{d\}$,
4. a set of trusted root credential issuers or AAs $AAS = \{AA\}$,
5. $HAS \subset AAS{\times}RIGHTS$ is a AA – Delegation Rights table, which says which trusted credential issuers have which delegation rights.

We formulate a delegation right (or the right to delegate or assign an attribute) as $d = d(attr, Q, n, DT)$ where Q is a restriction of the delegation right – the holder of the delegation right can only delegate or assign $attr$ to a user (delegate) that satisfies the restriction Q. Restrictions will be presented shortly. $n > 0$ is the maximum delegation depth of a delegation chain that can be made by the holder. DT is the *maximum validity period* of the delegations that can be made by the holder.

The CVS is able to retrieve (in pull mode) or obtain (in push mode) user credentials, find the delegation chain(s) from a trusted credential issuer to a user's credential and validate the credentials in the delegation chain(s). Trusted credential issuers are only allowed to delegate (or assign) attributes to users who satisfy the restrictions placed on their delegation rights.

For collaborations between organisations, the CVS is able to validate administrative role credentials as well as user attribute credentials. The administrative role credential validation policy provides the rules used to control the validation of administrative role credentials according to the same trust model as user credentials. In this case, the SoA is the only trusted root credential issuer for the delegation of administrative roles.

In our model, Q is an expression of the attributes a user must have in order to become a delegate. Because a user's attributes are the user's properties in his organisation, the expression of user attributes varies between organisations and is application-dependent. User attributes may be the roles of the user in the organisation, the user's age, credit limit, or the domain of the user etc. An example expression of user attributes is (Role = Researcher) $\wedge$ (Age > 35) i.e. i.e. in order to be a delegate, the user must have a "Researcher" role and be aged greater than 35.

4.3   Validation of Collaboration Policies

A collaboration policy made by an administrator includes an access control policy (or role mapping policy) and a credential validation policy. This will control which users are able to access the target resource. The authorisation system in the target domain has to check whether the access control or role mapping policy is within the administrative scope of the administrator, but the credential validation policy does not have any restrictions placed on it, since the administrator is trusted to say which users should have access to the resource. In reality, the VO agreement will state which target resources should be made available to the collaborating organizations, and so the SoA only sets restrictions on which resources can be accessed, via the administrative scope. It is then left up to the various collaborating administrators to decide which of their users should have this access, and to set their credential validation policies accordingly. In this way, the policy that validates the users is delegated to the collaborating administrators, but is enforced by the target resource's PDP.

If we assume that an administrator has a set of valid administrative roles $aRoles = \{aRole^i\}$, $i = 1..n$, where an administrative role has a set of user permissions $aRole^i = \{p_1^i, p_2^i, \ldots, p_{ii}^i\}$ or user attributes $aRole^i = \{uR_1^i, uR_2^i, \ldots, uR_{ii}^i\}$ then a role-permission assignment $attribute \leftarrow \{p_1, p_2, \ldots, p_k\}$ is valid if and only if $\forall p \in \{p_1, p_2, \ldots, p_k\}$, $\exists l, 1 \leq l \leq n$, $p \in aRole^l$ and an attribute-role mapping $uR \leftarrow attribute$ is valid if and only if $\exists aRole^i, uR \in aRole^i$ or uR is a subordinate of uRR in which $\exists aRole^i, uRR \in aRole^i$.

If the above policies are valid, then the target resource will add these policies to its existing ones. The CVS will add the administrator's credential validation policy to its existing ones, and the PDP will add the role-permission assignments to its existing ones. We believe that role mappings are logically part of the CVS's functionality, and that after validating a user's credentials, the CVS should return the mapped roles to the PEP. In this way the PDP can make an access control decision based on its existing rule set.

5   Conclusion

Dynamically decentralising the administration of an authorisation system for a VO's requirements without loosing central control over broad policy is a challenging goal for system designers and architects. Our work provides a significant and practical advance towards this goal by proposing the recognition of authority management model. The ROA model allows dynamically assigned administrators to dynamically adjust the authorisation policy of a target domain. Therefore, our model supports decentralised authorisation administration. By separating authorisation policies created for each collaboration, the collaborations remain independent, so that the policies for one collaboration do not affect other collaborations and the policies can be added and removed independently. By supporting attribute-role mapping, our model can separate workflows from organisational changes. By supporting delegated role-permission assignments we maximize the granularity of administrative delegation. Another benefit of delegated role-permission assignments is that administrators can assign target resource permissions to local organizational level user attributes and it facilitates decentralised management of permissions to VO resources.

Currently, an implementation of the recognition of authority model in the PERMIS authorisation infrastructure is under way. We hope that with the implementation, we can evaluate the usability and performance of the model.

References

1. Chadwick, D., Otenko, S.: The permis x.509 role based privilege management infrastructure. In: Proceedings of 7th ACM Symoisium on Access Control Models and Technologies (SACMAT 2002), ACM Press, New York (2002)
2. Chadwick, D., Zhao, G., Otenko, S., Laborde, R., Su, L., Nguyen, T.A.: Building a modular authorization infrastructure. In: Fifth All Hands Meeting. UK e-science, Achievements, Challenges & New Opportunities (September 2006)
3. Chadwick, D.W, Otenko, S., Nguyen, T.A.: Adding support to xacml for dynamic delegation of authority in multiple domains. In: 10th IFIP Open Conference on Communications and Multimedia Security, Heraklion Crete (2006)
4. Erdos, M., Cantor, S.: Shibboleth-architecture draft v05. Technical report, Internet2 (May 2002)
5. Ferraiolo, D.F., Sandhu, R., Gavrila, S., Kuhn, D.R., Chandramouli, R.: Proposed nist standard for role-based access control. ACM Transactions on Information and System Security 4(3), 224–274 (2001)
6. Firozabadi, B.S., Olsson, O., Rissanen, E.: Managing authorisations in dynamic coalitions. Swedish Institute of Computer Science (2003)
7. Kagal, L., Finin, T., Peng, Y.: A delegation based model for distributed trust. In: Proceedings of the IJCAI01 Workshop on Autonomy, Delegation and Control: Interacting with Autonomous Agent, Seattle, pp. 73–80 (2001)
8. Kang, M.H., Park, J.S., Froscher, J.N.: Access control mechanisms for inter-organizational workflow. In: The sixth ACM symposium on Access control models and technologies, Chantilly, Virginia, United States, pp. 66–74. ACM Press, New York (2001)
9. Li, N., Mitchell, J.C., Winsborough, W.H.: Design of a role-based trust-management framework. In: Proceedings of the 2002 IEEE Symposium on Security and Privacy, pp. 114–130. IEEE Computer Society Press, Los Alamitos (2002)
10. Li, N., Mitchell, J.C., Winsborough, W.H.: Distributed credential chain discovery in trust management. Journal of Computer Security, 35–86 (2003)
11. Moffett, J.D., Sloman, M.S.: Policy hierarchies for distributed systems management. IEEE Journal on Selected Areas in Communications 11(9), 1404–1414 (1993)
12. Mukkamala, R., Atluri, V., Warner, J., Abbadasari, R.: A distributed coalition service registry for ad-hoc dynamic coalitions: A service-oriented approach. In: Damiani, E., Liu, P. (eds.) Data and Applications Security XX. LNCS, vol. 4127, pp. 209–223. Springer, Heidelberg (2006)
13. Nguyen, T.-A., Su, L., Inman, G., Chadwick, D.: Flexible and manageable delegation of authority in rbac. In: Proceedings of The IEEE Ubisafe07, Ontario, Canada, 21-23 May 2007, IEEE Computer Society Press, Los Alamitos (2007)
14. Park, J.S., Costello, K.P., Neven, T.M., Diosomito, J.A.: A composite rbac approach for large, complex organizations. In: ACM SACMAT'04 Yorktown Heights, New York, USA, ACM Press, New York (2004)

15. Pearlman, L., Welch, V., Foster, I., Kesselman, C., Tuecke, S.: Community authorization service for group collaboration. In: IEEE 3rd International Workshop on Policies for Distributed Systems and Networks (2002)
16. Sandhu, R., Bhamidipati, V., Munawer, Q.: The arbac97 model for role-based administration of roles. ACM Transactions on Information and System Security 2(1), 105–135 (1999)
17. Sandhu, R.S., Coyne, E.J., Feinstein, H.L., Youman, C.E.: Role-based access control models, 29(2), 38–47 (1996)

Appendix

A DTD for Attribute-Permission Assignment and Attribute-Role Mapping

```
<!ELEMENT AttributeAssignmentPolicy (AttributeAssignment)+ >
<!ELEMENT AttributeAssignment (SubjectDomain, AttributeList, Delegate, TrustedIssuer, Validity) >
<!ELEMENT SubjectDomain EMPTY>
<!ATTLIST SubjectDomain ID IDREF #REQUIRED>
<!ELEMENT AttributeList (Attribute*) >
<!ELEMENT Attribute EMPTY >
<!ATTLIST Attribute Type IDREF #IMPLIED Value IDREF #IMPLIED >
<!ELEMENT TrustedIssuer EMPTY>
<!ATTLIST TrustedIssuer ID IDREF #REQUIRED>
<!ELEMENT Validity (Absolute?, Age?, Maximum?, Minimum?) >
<!ELEMENT Delegate EMPTY >
<!ATTLIST Delegate Depth CDATA #IMPLIED >
<!ELEMENT TargetPolicy (TargetDomainSpec+) >
<!ELEMENT TargetDomainSpec ((Include, Exclude*)+, ObjectClass* ) >
<!ATTLIST TargetDomainSpec ID IDREF #REQUIRED>
<!ELEMENT ActionPolicy (Action+) >
<!ELEMENT Action EMPTY>
<!ATTLIST Action Name NMTOKEN #REQUIRED Args NMTOKENS #IMPLIED>
<!ELEMENT TargetAccessPolicy (TargetAccess) >
<!ELEMENT TargetAccess ( AttributeList, TargetList, IF?) >
<!ELEMENT TargetList (Target+ ) >
<!ELEMENT Target (TargetName —TargetDomain) >
<!ATTLIST Target Actions NMTOKENS #IMPLIED >
<!ELEMENT TargetName EMPTY>
<!ATTLIST TargetName LDAPDN CDATA #REQUIRED>
<!ELEMENT TargetDomain EMPTY>
<!ATTLIST TargetDomain ID IDREF #REQUIRED>
<!ELEMENT AttributeMappingPolicy (AttributeMapping) >
<!ELEMENT AttributeMapping (Attribute, LocalRole)+ >
<!ELEMENT LocalRole EMPTY >
<!ATTLIST LocalRole Type IDREF #IMPLIED Value IDREF #IMPLIED >
```

Securing VO Management

Florian Kerschbaum[1], Rafael Deitos[2], and Philip Robinson[1]

[1] SAP Research, Karlsruhe, Germany
`firstname.lastname@sap.com`
[2] Automation and Systems Department
Federal University of Santa Catarina, Florianópolis, Brazil
`deitos@das.ufsc.br`

Abstract. In this paper we propose a security architecture and mechanism for Virtual Organizations (VO) for businesses. The VOs we consider are based on web service technology to address interoperability issues and cater for future business software, and are dynamic, i.e. their membership may change frequently throughout their lifetime. We improve over previous approaches in the following aspect: We have designed, implemented and evaluated a comprehensive security mechanism for our architecture that can protect both the web services in the VO and the VO management services. The security policies of VO management are enforced by inspecting the request for the encodings of parameters that are relevant to the policy decision. The basic idea may be applicable to other web service based software with data-dependent security policies, e.g. databases.

1 Introduction

In collaborative world-wide business processes scenarios a large number of organizations interact dynamically sharing their resources. These collaborations can be arranged in Virtual Organizations (VO). A VO consists of a collection of individuals and institutions defined according to a set of resource sharing rules [4]. This definition covers the technical view point favored by the Grid community, while in the business community, the purpose of the VO is emphasized as in the following definition: A VO is a temporary coalition of geographically dispersed individuals, groups, enterprise units or entire organizations that pool resources, facilities, and information to achieve common business objectives [12].

The work in this paper considers VOs with the following properties:

- *dynamic:* VOs evolve during operation, e.g. allowing member replacement.
- *business process driven:* VOs where the interactions are defined by a business process (choreography).
- *web service-based:* VOs where the shared resources are web services.

A (business process) choreography is the description of the flow of visible interactions, i.e. web service calls, of the participating organizations. A standard language for choreography of web services is the Web Services Choreography

C. Lambrinoudakis, G. Pernul, A M. Tjoa (Eds.): TrustBus 2007, LNCS 4657, pp. 14–23, 2007.

Description Language (WS-CDL) [13]. Orchestration based VOs can also be represented by a choreography where the orchestrating party acts a seperate role in the choreography. In this paper choreography is therefore seen as the more general concept encompassing both concepts of regular choreograhpy and orchestration.

A VO management system facilitates the administration and management of such VOs. It enables the creation, deletion and other operations on the state of a VO. This functionality is encapsulated in a component called lifecycle manager. Furthermore, VO management assigns individual organizations roles in the business process thereby implicitly adding, removing and replacing members of the VO. This functionality is encapsulated in a component called membership manager. Each component is a separate web service that can be called by any type of client that wishes to establish or administer a VO. For details of lifecycle and membership management see [12].

Securing VOs (or similar forms of collaborations) has been considered before [2,3,10,16]. The focus of previous work is to secure the interactions of the organizations, i.e. the authentication and access control decision for the web services. The security of the VO management services (referred to as infrastructure services), i.e. the access control policies of the administration interface, are not considered. We propose a security architecture and mechanism that addresses both, the security of the VO operation, as well as its management. The unique outstanding feature is that our architecture uses one security mechanism deployed before resources and VO management services.

The advantages of having one security mechanism are two-fold:

First, there is reduced security engineering effort in implementation and design of security critical components. The number and size of these security critical components decreases by combining the security mechanisms for the resources with those of VO management. Furthermore, the security of VO management services has been externalized to the security mechanism, such that VO management services can now be implemented without security in mind and without embedded security checks. In summary, our overall implementation effort was reduced with this security architecture.

Second, the administration of the overall system becomes easier, since the administrator has to deal with and learn only one security policy language. Instead of a set of heterogeneous policy languages and mechanisms, one mechanism can handle all. This in turn can increase the verifiability and auditability of the system, since consistency check can be performed more easily. In conclusion, our system is more easy to administer and control.

Our particular security mechanism has further advantages:

First, the policy language makes administration of VO management security more flexible. Hard-coded, mandatory security checks have been replaced with configurable, policy-driven checks. Our system can therefore cater for a variety of VO management security requirements.

Second, our security mechanism can be deployed in front of any web service without changes to that web services. Any service implemented according to web service standards can be retrofitted with security and placed into a VO. This makes use and setup of VOs more comfortable and opens it to wider range of legacy services.

The contributions of the paper are

- the design of a VO security architecture and mechanism that allows for distributed control using one security mechanism for VO management services and resources. This includes the design and specification of a set of VO management policies and the security token mechanisms and key distribution to establish trust relations.
- an implementation and an evaluation of the security mechanism. We implemented the security mechanism as part of a larger research project and evaluated its impact on web service invocations.

The remainder of the paper is organized as follows: Section 2 gives an overview of related work, before Section 3 describes the components in the system. Section 4 describes the security components and algorithms and Section 5 summarizes the performance evaluation. Section 6 concludes the paper.

2   Related Work

Other approaches for the authorization challenge in VOs have been proposed in the literature which we will review next. KeyNote and PERMIS do not address the challenge of distributed management of policies, but were rather designed for one trust domain. Akenti focuses on the policy decision as well and leaves the administration question open, but offers the possibility for delegation. CAS and VOMS are designed to be used in distributed administered VOs, but neither considers yet the question of how to secure the infrastructure services themselves.

- **KeyNote:** KeyNote is a trust-management system that defines a language to specify security policies, actions, principals and credentials, and uses a compliance checker to validate access requests [1].
- **Akenti:** The Akenti authorization system [16] is a security model and architecture that uses authenticated X.509 identity certificates and distributed digitally signed authorization policy certificates to make access decisions about distributed resources.
- **PERMIS:** There are three main components to the PERMIS implementation: the authorization policy, the privilege allocator (PA) and the PMI application programming interface (API) - details can be found in [2].
- **CAS:** The Globus team first proposed a security architecture for grids in [5]. This architecture did not yet address the problem of distributed administration of resources, but those of protecting user credentials and identity mapping which are not covered in our architecture. The Community Authorization Service (CAS) proposed as a solution for specifying and enforcing community (VO) policies allows resource owners to grant access to blocks of resources to a community as a whole, and let the community itself manage

fine-grained access control within that framework [10] using capabilities [6]. Granting access to a community gives total control of the local resources to the CAS server administrator [9,10,18]. Furthermore, the problem of securing the infrastructure services, such as the lifecycle and membership manager or the CAS server itself have not been addressed.

- **VOMS:** The Virtual Organization Membership Service (VOMS) can be considered a specialization of CAS [3].

3   System Architecture

Before joining a VO, an organization must obtain a global identity certificate. The certificate authority (CA) issues this certificate to the organization signed with the private key of the trusted root certificate in a public-key infrastructure (PKI).

The VO infrastructure consists of the following components:

- **Web Service** (WS): This is the resource (web service) offered by an organization to other participants in a VO.
- **Policy Enforcement Point** (PEP): The policy enforcement (PEP) is a reference monitor that intercepts every web service call to an organization's web services. The PEP authenticates the caller's identity and verifies all supplied credentials (e.g. in a challenge-response protocol). It then forwards the caller's identity, the attributes of the credentials and the details of the web service call to the policy decision point (PDP). The separation of the access control function into policy enforcement and decision point has been suggested in [11]. After receiving the PDP's access decision it either blocks or forwards the call to the web service (WS). Our security mechanism is a special PEP that not only protects the web services of the VO, but also the VO management web services, i.e. it intercepts calls to both.
- **Policy Decision Point** (PDP): The policy decision point (PDP) receives the caller's identity, attributes and the web service call details from the PEP. It then evaluates the stored policies and returns either a grant or deny

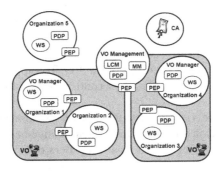

Fig. 1. System Architecture

decision to the PEP. All our policies are implemented using XACML [8] in a role-based access approach [15]. For a good survey of access control see [14]. Access control policies for web services are generated using the approach described in [13].

- **Lifecycle Manager** (LCM): This service is part of the VO management and it allows the creation and deletion of VOs. It also stores the choreography of the VO. The lifecycle manager issues attribute credentials to the creator of a VO.
- **Membership Manager** (MM): The membership manager, as part of the VO Management, assigns organizations to business roles. The security significance of the VO management services are detailed in the next section.

3.1 VO Management Interface

The VO management interface is described only briefly due to space requirements. The lifecycle and membership manager offer methods for VO creation, VO deletion, choreography retrieval, role listing, role assignment (and removal) and member replacement.

4 Security Architecture

4.1 Security Model for VO Management

The current model for security of VO management is simple. Each VO has a VO manager that is responsible for all administration tasks. The VO manager can access all administration services (MM and LCM) and perform the necessary operations. VO members may use the query management services (MM) to get information about the VO they are part of, i.e. the list of the roles, etc. On the other hand, non-members should be prohibited from obtaining any information about the VO. There is a trifold security hierarchy of manager, member, and everybody, similar to UNIX file system access. To ensure the consistency of the VO management model, a set of management policies is generated according in role-based access control.

4.2 Roles

The roles in the policies of the security architecture are the business roles (*BP-ROLE*) as described in the choreography of the VO. To support VO management security, this has to be extended with a second role type for the VO manager (*VOMANAGER*).

In the context of web service security, RBAC policies allow one organization to limit the access to only that role. Compared to capability-based approaches, such as CAS, where the service is exposed to all members of a VO, the organization can now limit the access to a subset of them.

4.3   VO Management Policies

Besides the policies generated for the security of the interactions, there are policies that need to be enforced for the security of the VO management. The security mechanism not only verifies access, but also the content of the web service call, greatly enhancing its capabilities. The set of (allow-)policies derived from our security architecture can be represented as follows in Figure 2.

```
{                                {                                {
  Role: *                          Role: VOMANAGER                  Role: BP-ROLE
  Target: Lifecycle Manager        Target: Lifecycle Manager        Target: Lifecycle Manager
  Operation: createVO()            Operation: deleteVO()            Operation: getChoreography()
}                                }                                }
{                                {                                {
  Role: VOMANAGER                  Role: VOMANAGER                  Role: BP-ROLE
  Target: Membership Manager       Target: Membership Manager       Target: Membership Manager
  Operation: assignRole()          Operation: removeRole()          Operation: getRoles()
}                                }                                }
```

Fig. 2. Policies for VO Management Security

4.4   Role Assignment

This section clarifies the distribution of administration tasks between the different security administrators. The LCM issues an attribute credential attesting the role *VOMANAGER* to the creator of a VO (as a return value of the web service call). This credential can be either signed by a key belonging to the LCM only (with a certificate signed by the CA) or signed by the CA itself. Then the VO manager assigns the roles in the business process choreography (*BP-ROLE*) to specific members. For each assignment the VO manager creates an attribute credential with the *BP-ROLE*, the member's identity and the VO identifier. This credential is issued to the member, i.e. all role assignments are done by the VO manager.

4.5   PEP Implementation

The PEP implementation is able to authenticate the caller's identity, verify all supplied credentials, forward the information to the PDP and grant/deny access. Our implementation is based on the Tomcat server with the Axis web service framework and supporting libraries for XML security and SAML [7]. For encryption, two distinguished methods are used: a symmetric and an asymmetric key algorithm.

The architecture works as an external layer, or module, that can be configured for any web service, setting handlers to intercept all the messages and perform the security tasks. Figure 3 depicts the use of the security layers for a simple echo service. This web service echoes any received message back to the sender. The security layer can be abstracted from the service layer. The service need not know about the security handlers and only care about its own logic, i.e. any

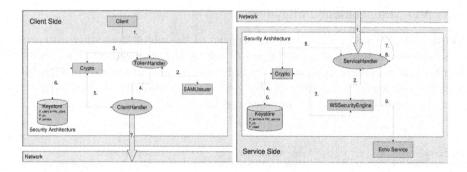

Fig. 3. Overview of the client and server interactions in the implementation

legacy web service can be secured and used in a VO. The implementation of the PEP is divided into three handlers: *TokenHandler* and *ClientHandler* on the client's side and *ServiceHandler* on the server's side.

Outgoing Message. The steps for an outgoing message are depicted with numbers on the left side of Figure 3. Every time a client (using the security mechanism) sends a message to the WS (step 1), the message is intercepted first by the handlers. Two distinct actions take place: first, the token processing, and later, the signature and encryption processes.

Firstly, on step 2, the *TokenHandler* uses a *SAMLIssuer* object to add signed tokens to the header of the message. The tokens (SAML assertions) considered must contain one subject, identified by a X.509 certificate, and, at least, one attribute statement with two attributes: role name and VO identifier (VO–id). It is possible to chain tokens, i.e. the VO manager can be the subject of the token issued by a CA granting the *VOMANAGER* role. Then, the VO manager can issue tokens (signing them with his own key), having others as subjects, granting the businesses roles, creating a chain of tokens.

To prevent unauthorized access to information that only belongs to a specific VO, each VO has an associated symmetric key, shared by the partners. So, after the token insertion, the role name attribute is encrypted (step 3) with the corresponding VO key. This key is currently not being renewed, when the membership of the VO changes, since it is assumed that the party leaving the VO will not receive future messages and therefore encrypted tokens.

After the token processing is completed, the message is intercepted by the *ClientHandler* (step 4) that signs the message's body (steps 5 and 6). Then, the handler encrypts the message's body with the public-key of the recipient before it is sent over the network (step 7).

Incoming Message. The steps for an incoming message are depicted with numbers on the right side of Figure 3. The incoming message is intercepted by the *ServiceHandler* (step 1), which coordinates the verification process. The first verification stage is executed by the *WSSecurityEngine* (step 2). This engine decrypts the message's body with the private key and then verifies the message's body signature (step 3). Next, for each token, the role name attribute is decrypted using the symmetric key associated with the VO–id specified in the corresponding attribute. In case the receiver does not have the key, the attribute is left encrypted.

The next stage is executed by the *ServiceHandler* itself and consists of three major tasks: checking the certificate authenticity (steps 5 and 6), completing verification of the tokens (step 7) and the VO–id parameter verification.

The VO–id parameter verification (step 8) ensures the scope of the message (what VO) and extracts the right permissions (attributes) for the PDP. It is that enables the PEP to secure the VO management services and externalize their security enforcement. Note that there could be more than one VO, and the two partners could be in more than one VO together, i.e. the client could have different permissions in each VO, e.g. in one he is the VO manager and in the other he plays a business role. So it is important to extract the correct attributes for the specific call, in particular for calls to VO management services.

Every message to a VO management service contains the VO–id parameter in the SOAP body element, which is sufficient to detect the scope of the message, although, this information alone is not enough to enforce the policies. The VO–id parameter is the SOAP body is identified by flexible parsing and its special, fixed encoding in its namespace. The VO–id parameter from the SAML assertion (in the SOAP header of the message) is also extracted. The assertion is located and the attribute statement for the VO–id is retrieved. Having both VO–id parameters, it is possible to correlate messages to a VO. By extracting the name of the role from the same assertion, it is possible for the PDP to evaluate the access request against the policies of Figure 2 for this message (in the correct VO scope). If all the verifications are passed successfully, the message reaches the target service (step 9).

5   Performance Evaluation

We measured the overhead created by the insertion of the security mechanism in a web service invocation. The echo service was used for the evaluation and four test cases were defined:

- the message is exchanged with no security
- the message, on both sides, is signed by the sender and then verified by the receiver
- the message, on both sides, is signed and encrypted by the sender, and then verified by the receiver
- a token is added, the attribute statements are encrypted and later, the message is signed and encrypted; at the receiver side, the message is verified.

To compare the different test cases, the round-trip time (RTT) of the messages is used. On each test case, the size of the message's content assumed three different values: empty string, 256 bytes and 64 Kbytes of data. For each size

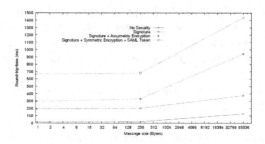

Fig. 4. Graphical representation for time measurement

on each test case, a sample of 110 values (RTT) was gathered. Three rounds of measurements were done. First of all, the size of the resulting *SOAPMessage* at the TCP layer was measured, and is depicted in Table 1.

Table 1. Message size in bytes for the test cases

	Empty String	256B	64KB
No security	371	627	65907
Signature	3163	3426	68707
Signature + Encryption	4777	5127	93311
Signature + Encryption + SAML token	14866	15215	103395

We can conclude that the overhead of the architecture in the size of the message is a linear function, e.g. the size of the message is approximately 1.5 times the size of the content plus a constant overhead. Figure 4 is the graph for time measurement. It represents the average values for the three rounds from the sample. The four different curves represent the four test cases for a different amount of data.

6   Conclusions

We present a security architecture and mechanism for VOs in business. It uses one security mechanism for protecting the VO management services as well as the resources offered in the VO. The advantages of having one security mechanism are reduced implementation effort due the reduction of security critical components and easier administration, since the administrator needs to deal with only one security mechanism. The basic idea of verifying the parameters of a web service call to the supplied credentials may be useful in other data-dependent web services, e.g. databases. Our evaluation of the implementation showed that the overhead introduced by the security architecture is acceptable for practical deployment. Future work is to extend the infrastructure services, e.g. by reputation services, but still secure them with the same security mechanism.

References

1. Blaze, M., Feigenbaum, J., Keromytis, A.D.: Keynote: Trust management for public-key infrastructures. In: 1998 Security Protocols International Workshop (1998)
2. Chadwick, D.W., Otenko, O.: The permis x.509 role based privilege management infrastructure. Future Gener. Comput. Syst. 19(2), 277–289 (2003)
3. Demchenko, Y., Commans, L., de Laat, C., Steenbakkers, M., Ciashini, V., Venturi, V.: Vo-based dynamic security associations in collaborative grid environment. In: Workshop on Collaboration and Security (COLSEC) of The 2006 International Symposium on Collaborative Technologies and Systems (CTS) (2006)
4. Foster, I., Kesselman, C., Tuecke, S.: The anatomy of the grid. International Journal of High Performance Computing Applications 15(3), 200–222 (2001)
5. Foster, I., Kesselman, C., Tsudik, G., Tuecke, S.: A security architecture for computational grids. In: P5th ACM Conference on Computer and Communications Security (1998)
6. Mullender, S., Tanenbaum, A.: The design of a capability-based distributed operating system. The Computer Journal 29(4), 289–299 (1986)
7. OASIS, 2002 Security Assertion Markup Language (SAML) 1.0 Specification (2002)
8. OASIS, 2005 eXtensible Access Control Markup Language 2 (XACML) Version 2.0 Specification (2005)
9. Pearlman, L., Kesselman, C., Welch, V., Foster, I., Tuecke, S.: The community authorization service: Status and future. In: Conference for Computing in High Energy and Nuclear Physics (CHEP) (2003)
10. Pearlman, L., Welch, V., Foster, I., Kesselman, C., Tuecke, S.: A community authorization service for group collaboration. In: IEEE Workshop on Policies for Distributed Systems and Netoworks (2002)
11. Guerin, R., Yavatkar, R., Pendarakis, D.: A framework for policy-based admission control. In: RFC 2753 (2000)
12. Robinson, P., Karabulut, Y., Haller, J.: Dynamic virtual organization management for service oriented enterprise applications. In: 1st International Conference on Collaborative Computing (2005)
13. Robinson, P., Kerschbaum, F., Schaad, A.: From business process choreography to authorization policies. In: 20th Annual IFIP WG 11.3 Working Conference on Data and Applications Security (2006)
14. Samarati, P., De Capitani di Vimercati, S.: Access control: Policies, models, and mechanisms. Foundations of Security Analysis and Design (2001)
15. Sandhu, R., Coyne, E., Feinstein, H., Youman, C.: Role based access control models. IEEE Computer 29(2) (1996)
16. Thompson, M., Essiari, A., Mudumbai, S.: Certificate-based authorization policy in a pki environment. ACM Transactions on Information and System Security 6(4), 566–588 (2003)
17. Thompson, M., Mudumbai, S., Essiari, A., Chin, W.: Authorization policy in a pki environment. In: 1st Annual NIST workshop on PKI (2002)
18. Welch, V., Ananthakrishnan, R., Meder, S., Pearlman, L., Siebenlist, F.: Use of saml in the community authorization service. Computing in High Energy and Nuclear Physics (2003)

Addressing Cultural Dissimilarity in the Information Security Management Outsourcing Relationship

Aggeliki Tsohou[1], Marianthi Theoharidou[2], Spyros Kokolakis[1],
and Dimitris Gritzalis[2]

[1] Dept. of Information and Communication Systems Engineering, University of the Aegean
Karlovassi, Samos GR-83200, Greece
{agt,sak}@aegean.gr
[2] Information Security and Critical Infrastructure Protection Research Group,
Dept. of Informatics, Athens University of Economics and Business,
76 Patission Ave., Athens
GR-10434, Greece
{mtheohar,dgrit}@aueb.gr

Abstract. Organizational culture influences the way a) information security is perceived, b) security countermeasures are adopted, and c) the organization reacts to the cultural changes of a new security program. In Information Security Management Outsourcing (ISMO), cultural differences may arise between the organization and the provider, for example conflict between the countermeasures applied by the provider and the company's internal policies. We propose a conceptual framework of security mechanisms in order organizations that choose ISMO to identify and manage cultural dissimilarity.

Keywords: Information Security Management Outsourcing, Organizational Culture.

1 Introduction

Outsourcing an Information Systems (IS) function is common practice, but, lately, organizations start to outsource IS security function(s), as well. In 2003, Gartner predicted that, for the Western European market, the managed security services would be the fastest-growing service type across all vertical markets in the period 2002-06. Gartner expected outsourced security monitoring and management market to grow at a combined annual rate of 31% through 2005 [8]. According to the three latest CSI/FBI surveys a 37% in 2005 and 39% in 2006 of the respondents outsource, and the percentage of the outsourced security function ranges. In addition, 10% in 2005 and 12% in 2006 outsource more than 20% of the security function; however, "largest firms outsource the highest percentage of their security function" [3]. Nonetheless, Information Security Outsourcing appears to be an emergent issue.

Information Technology (IT) Security Outsourcing is "the transfer of existing in-house IT security function(s) to a third-party provider" [7]. We refer not solely to IT security outsourcing, but to *Information Security Management Outsourcing (ISMO)*, which may include the functions that affect and are affected by cultural, ethical, social

C. Lambrinoudakis, G. Pernul, A M. Tjoa (Eds.): TrustBus 2007, LNCS 4657, pp. 24–33, 2007.

and legal aspects as well [5]. Regarding an Information Security Management System (ISMS), one has to take into account, inter alia, standards, codes-of-practice, regulation, and cultural and ethical issues. In ISMO, then, the MSSP's responsibilities may include risk management, security policy and awareness, regulatory compliance, etc., issues that go beyond the provision and management of physical or technical security. One can assume that the approaches of IT/IS outsourcing are applicable in ISMO, too. Many issues and problems are indeed similar; however, the legal, commercial/organizational and technical elements of ISMO are considerably distinct [7], [15]. Security outsourcing decision-making differs; selecting the functions to be outsourced is complicated, cost and ROI estimation is problematic, and security awareness may be hindered if security services are transparent to the end-users [14].

In IS outsourcing literature [4] two phases are identified: the *decision phase* (e.g. why and what to outsource, what selection criteria exist), and the *implementation one* (e.g. how to select the vendor and structure the relationship, how to negotiate, build and manage the contract, how to evaluate the outcome). We examine ISMO in the implementation phase, meaning best practices, methods, techniques to achieve optimum IS outsourcing outcome and focus on issues that arise due to cultural differences between the organization and the provider. To do so, we examine how organizational culture affects information security, what are cultural dissimilarities and how these affect the ISMO outcome. We also aim at assisting an organization to identify and manage cultural dissimilarities between itself and the Managed Security Services Provider (MSSP). To the best of our knowledge, literature regarding cultural dissimilarity in the ISMO is limited; thus, we draw upon existing IS Outsourcing research, as well as upon social theories (Social Exchange Theory, Power-Political Theory). We identify factors that affect the outsourcing outcome and propose security mechanisms, existing or altered, which may influence these factors positively.

In Section 2, we present our view on organizational culture, how it affects information security, and the emergent security cultural issues. The issue of cultural dissimilarity in the ISMO context is introduced in Section 3. Section 4 describes the need to adopt a social view of the IS outsourcing research, by an outline of two fundamental social theories. Section 5 presents factors that influence the IS outsourcing outcome. We then explore the association of these factors with cultural dissimilarity and the ISMO success. We provide a framework of mechanisms for ISMO (Section 6), which could mitigate problems due to cultural diversity between the outsourcing parties. Finally, we summarize and identify issues of further research.

2 The Role of Organizational Culture in Information Security

Organizational culture is defined by [24] as a three-level model. The first level is organizational *artifacts*; all the phenomena that one sees, hears and feels when encounters the organization. They are visible and easily identified by an outsider (i.e. architecture, language etc.). The second level is the *espoused or shared values*. These are partially visible and reflect the values of a particular group of individuals (i.e. attitudes, policies etc.). The third level is the *basic underlying assumptions*; involves the underlying beliefs and values which are hidden and largely unconscious. Each level influences the other ones; a change in the basic assumptions would alter the shared values of the company and ultimately would affect the artifacts. An example of an information security *artifact* would be the organizational access control means, such as a biometric device. The information security strategy dictated by the senior executives would be considered as the information security organizational *espoused values* [30]; these can be visible in the form of information security policies which constitute another artifact. Finally, the personnel's perceptions of privacy are an example of *underlying beliefs and values* within the organization.

Organizational culture influences information security; it is reflected to the stakeholders' security-related actions, or responses to security incidents. [30] examine the employees' behavior by applying Schein's model, to find alternative methods to auditing and to introduce cultural change in terms of security. [28] also state that culture is one of the determinant factors of employees' security-related behavior. They agree with [30] that cultural change should be initialized at the "basic underlying assumptions" level and, thus, the more visible levels could be affected. Moreover, [13] explore security policy formulation and implementation through organizational context and identify organizational culture as one of its basic elements. [11] identifies the consistency between the ISMS and the organizational culture as a critical success factor. [26] examines the IS security human factors in multi-cultural settings (e.g. attitude to age), and highlights the significance of culture deviations for IS security. In the next section, we study the relation between organizational culture and information security, in the context of ISMO, and define cultural dissimilarity.

3   ISMO Context and the Significance of Cultural Dissimilarity

Organizations outsource security as usually it is not a core competence and they cannot afford to maintain the specialist competency needed [31]. The MSSP provides access to leading edge technology, and warranties for the service level and expertise [2], [6]. The offered services are usually 24x7, which require resources hard to allocate by an organization [1], [25]. ISMO offers just one commercial relationship and places the customer in a much stronger negotiating position [7]. Another merit is the potential cost savings [1], [2], [25], [31], as the security provider benefits from a shallower learning curve, economies of scale, and a potentially more efficient process. Finally, it may cover legal or regulatory requirements, as outsourcing is a way to mitigate legal liability or transfer the risk to a third party [7].

However, the provider imposes its own operational risks [7], since its employees and/or contractors could act unprofessionally or negligently to the detriment of the customer. A MSSP may have access to a company's IT and networks, so as to monitor and manage security; thus, the customer becomes more susceptible to confidentiality breaches and violations of data protection legislation [1], [2]. The provider itself may turn out to be a single point of failure or an appealing target. If the provider's systems suffer an attack, then its customer systems and data are also vulnerable. In addition, as the techniques and methods of a provider are likely to be similar for several customers, a customer security breach may introduce a new risk for the rest. Despite the cost savings of ISMO, any new outsourcing arrangement will require some upfront cost and resources, e.g. new infrastructure or new licenses [6], [7] and may result to the organization's dependency to a single provider.

One also has to consider organizational culture issues, since it affects the way a) information security is perceived, b) security controls are adopted, and c) organization reacts to the cultural changes a security program may introduce [13]. [6] suggests that *cultural differences* between the organization and the MSSP can be an obstacle, as they can introduce conflict between the security controls applied by the MSSP and the company's internal processes and policies. By cultural differences we mean *any dissimilarity that is apparent in the three levels of the company and MSSP's organizational cultures.* This dissimilarity is visible on the artifacts' level and becomes more nebulous to the two underlying levels. Cultural dissimilarity is significant in ISMO, since the security plan is proposed and applied by the MSSP, who remains a third party and does not belong to the organization's inner context. When examining issues of ISMO success, one should consider that the involved organizations may adopt different cultural assumptions, which influence information security.

Consider an ISMO situation where the MSSP must conduct risk management. Although, we recognize that risk analysis methodologies (e.g. CRAMM, OCTAVE) include techniques for observing organizational structure and context, a third party is hard to perceive the lower levels of organizational culture and in sequel reflect the basic underlying assumptions in the risk management procedures. An example of the authors' former experience as security consultants entails performing IS risk management for a Greek public psychiatric clinic. One of the resulting controls was to establish a physical access control scheme in the hospital reception, with physical barriers, because patients' files were stored in the room. The employees consented to a card system and an alarm, but they strongly resisted to physical barriers, as they believed that they needed an easy emergency escape. This underlying assumption was formed based on employees' previous experiences and was not apparent to the risk analysts. In addition, the underlying assumptions of the latter were in contrast to this belief. Next, we will propose a theoretical framework, which can be used to address such cultural diversities and to show how these may influence outsourcing outcome.

4   Social Theories for the Understanding of IS Outsourcing

Information Security is an IS function and, therefore, we draw upon current IS outsourcing literature, which currently suggests a socially-oriented approach. [17], [18] observe a trend towards social theories as opposed to the former economic theoretical models. Recent researchers suggest a social view by incorporating theories such as Social Exchange Theory or Power-Political Theory [10], [19], [27]. [18] propose an integrative view on the issue; an organization can benefit from the competitive advantage goal of the strategic view, the cost efficiency goal of the economic view, and the trust and alliance benefits of the social view. [17] observe a shift from customer-oriented approaches to ones that place emphasis on both customer and provider, and examine the evolving relationship. Outsourcing success does not depend only on the contractual aspects, but also on the relationship between clients and vendors; thus the examination of this relationship is critical [15]. Most of the IS outsourcing approaches rely on transaction cost economics. Researchers argue that the evolving relationship between the provider and the services receiver is changing from a buyer-supplier type, towards a more strategic partnership [10], [15],

[19]. So, this relationship is characterized by: (a) risk and benefit sharing, (b) viewing the relationship as a series of exchanges without a definite endpoint, and (c) establishing a range of mechanisms to monitor and execute its operations [19].

Social Exchange Theory argues that social associations are exchanges of activities between two or more persons; activities that can be tangible or intangible, rewarding or costly [4]. A basic assumption is that the parties of an exchange are involved in a continuous process of activities that reward and activities that compensate the benefit; e.g. a party acts in a beneficial way for the other and obliges him to reciprocate. In IS outsourcing, the theory implies that the acquisition of services or products is achieved through continuous interactions based on mutual benefit [18], and it has been applied to explain and enhance the relationship between the two parties [15], [19], [27].

According to *Power Political Theory*, any relationship is a power-structure; organizations are political entities and people within organizations have different degrees of power. Two major constructs are *power* and *politics*. Power refers to "the potential of a party to influence the behavior of another in a certain manner". Power refers to aspects of authority, recourse allocation, dependency etc. Politics is defined as "the way in which power is exercised". Politics may include the selection of decision criteria and information use, the reliance on outside experts etc. [4], [17]. In IS outsourcing, the outsourcing decision is an outcome of power distribution among stakeholders. The power of the stakeholders affects the decision and the outcome of the outsourcing process influences existing power balances in return. Power-political theory is viewed as an important tool for examining IS outsourcing issues [4], [16], [18], or it is applied in order to explore the power and trust issues that arise [19].

5 A Social View for Managing Cultural Dissimilarity in ISMO

Our research aims at managing cultural dissimilarity between the involved parties in ISMO. We adopt a social view of ISMO, which is in line with the nature of our research questions and the above mentioned shift towards social perspectives. In this section we firstly select factors that determine IS outsourcing success and secondly, we analyze their relationship to organizational culture; cultural dissimilarity is proved to affect all the determinant factors and ultimately the outsourcing success.

In order to apply a social perspective of ISMO we study applications of the above social theories and identify factors that affect the IS outsourcing outcome. The relationship between the interested parties can be viewed as a partnership; *"an interorganizational relationship to achieve the participants' shared goals"* [19]. Four determinants factors positively affect partnership quality: participation, communication quality, information sharing and top management support; thus, these factors influence positively the outsourcing success. The factor of coordination was also identified but was not supported with significant evidence. Since a) we consider it as important for the IS partnership stability and b) it was not proved irrelevant to partnership quality, we choose to include coordination. In addition, [27] identify the factors of communication and mutual understanding. Therefore, the social factors that will be examined regarding their connection with organizational culture are: *Coordination, Communication Quality, Participation, Mutual Understanding, Information Sharing.* We view *Top Management Support* as a prerequisite of ISMO.

[19] did not support the correlation between cultural similarity and outsourcing success, but others argue that cultural dissimilarity affects ISMO success [6]. To support this we reveal the impact of organizational cultural differences on these social factors, and thereby on the ISMO success. *Communication quality* has been connected to partnership quality [19], [27]. In order to achieve internal integration and function as a unit, a group creates a common language - meaning the common use of concepts and words - and a system of communication [24]. A common language is necessary for any kind of consensus or any communication. Disregarding the fact that people may be making different assumptions about the meaning of words results in communication breakdowns. Cultural differences between the provider and the receiver would cause using terms differently or having unlike mental models, without realizing it [23]. Similarly, *mutual understanding*, which empowers trust and ultimately reduces conflicts, is affected by cultural similarity. [24] identifies mutual understanding and trust as a matter of culture; in order to achieve them one has to confront firstly with its own and second with others' assumptions.

Another social factor is the *participation* of the two parties on a common goal. The shared consensus of who is in and who is out of the group or the organization and the criteria that define the group's boundaries is a cultural issue [24]. These rules discriminate people into two categories: the insiders (more trusted) and the outsiders. In ISMO, cultural differences may result in the MSSP's members to be perceived as outsiders; thus, participation will be inhibited. *Information sharing* is also affected by organizational culture (e.g., who is authorized to have access to information, what is considered to be information). A part of the shared assumptions refers to the rules of the organization according to what constitutes data, what information and knowledge are [24]. Therefore, what type of information is considered sensitive, classified or proprietary and what should be the access privileges of the MSSP, are affected. Moreover, power and authority allocation are issues of organizational culture [24]. The ISMO partnership is likely to disturb power distribution or result in power conflicts; e.g. a receiver's member must adhere to security controls that are established by external members. Power allocation is connected to the balanced *coordination* of the two parties. Additionally, the problems of coordination in an organization are ultimately a problem of messing subcultures [23]; organizational cultures deviations will affect the way the two parties coordinate in order to achieve their common goals.

6 Managing ISMO Cultural Dissimilarity: A Framework

In order to manage cultural dissimilarity, one has to seek mechanisms that affect each of the above factors. Our framework consists of mechanisms that influence elements of organizational culture and, therefore, affect the social factors that determine ISMO success (Fig.1). Firstly, we have provided evidence that *communication* is strongly affected by the organizational culture; an impact rooted in the organization members' language and the system of symbols. In the ISMO an example refers to the term of risk - an information security fundamental construct; organizations' members could have different risk perceptions: what is considered as dreadful risk in one organization is not always dreadful for another. This may play an important role on the risk management process and outcome [22]. Managing the different perceptions of risks and creating a common language is important for communication. To do so, we suggest the exploration of the different underlying assumptions about security-related concepts. This can be achieved through a process of *security communication* [29] in order to take under consideration the stakeholders' various risk perceptions in the risk management process. *Security communication is characterized as an interactive one and refers to the exchange of information among individuals, groups and institutions, which involves messages about the nature of security including concerns, opinions or reactions to security messages. These messages may involve reactions to the legal or institutional arrangements for security management* [29]. The purpose of this process is to achieve better understanding of security-related issues amongst stakeholders and, thus, create a common system of symbols. Security management methodologies include some form of communication between security experts and stakeholders, but mostly they involve one-way messages and not an interactive process.

Fig. 1. Managing cultural dissimilarity

Exploring the underlying assumptions of the two organizational cultures is also important for achieving *mutual understanding*. In ISMO, mutual understanding refers to sharing similar assumptions regarding information security; it refers to reaching a consensus towards what is right and wrong regarding IS security. While the communication factor lies on assigning same meanings to words or symbols, mutual understanding refers to stakeholders adopting similar assumptions. Therefore, it can be achieved by exploring own and others' assumptions over information security. The first step towards mutual understanding is confronting with organization's own security assumptions, and second, examining the provider's assumptions; these steps can be achieved by defining and evaluating their security cultures. As information security culture refers to the assumption about which type of security behavior is accepted [20] and defines the way information security is perceived (e.g. what is considered ethical), it affects mutual understanding. We argue that an organization must evaluate its own security culture before selecting an ISMO partner and second, select one that is compatible. Methods of doing so exist in the literature [12], [20].

Participation also poses a positive role in ISMO success. An element of organizational culture is the embraced notions about who belongs in the organizational group. This means that one has to seek ways to redefine and loosen the group boundaries of the members of both organizations, which may hinder the ISMO partnership. We propose employees' exchange between the two parties. When a MSSP employee works and associates within the organizational context of the receiver, he gradually becomes a member of the context, and slowly is not perceived to be an outsider. He also comprehends organizational goals, processes and characteristics of the organization. When a receiver's employee participates in the security management process, or is transferred in the MSSP premises for training, she understands goals and feels that she is part of the security effort, regardless of expertise.

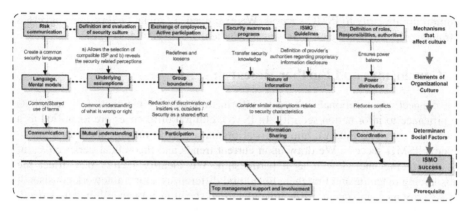

Fig. 2. Managing ISMO cultural dissimilarity framework

In ISMO, *information sharing* refers to the sharing of: a) information from the receiver to the MSSP required by the security management process, or b) security knowledge, security management results, and emergent business changes, towards the receiver. To manage security in a way compatible to the receiver's organizational context, the MSSP must understand its unique characteristics. For example, a hospital and a bank both have security concerns, but the hospital emphasizes on the confidentiality of sensitive medical data, as opposed to the bank where the integrity of the economic transactions is more crucial. This means that the receiver should provide information regarding the internal business objectives and processes. However, the sharing of proprietary information should take place after the employees are guided how to assist the ISMO provider. The second dimension regards the security knowledge sharing, i.e. security awareness programs that communicate the risk management process, the security controls, and responsibilities towards security [21].

We also consider the *coordination* factor to be significant, as it is connected to organizational culture [23] and lies on the element of power distribution. ISMO may contribute to a rearrangement of power and might introduce power conflicts, e.g. employees may resist to security guidelines communicated by of the MSSP. A way to reduce resulting conflicts and maintain power balance is top management timely and clearly to define the roles, responsibilities and authorities that undertake the employees of both organizations. This must be communicated to both involved parties by the early stages of the ISMO in order to avoid possible frustration.

Finally, *top management support and involvement* are significant for achieving security goals [9] and are also important in ISMO. ISO 17799: 2005 states that "*management should actively support security within the organization through clear direction, demonstrated commitment, explicit assignment, and acknowledgment of information security responsibilities*" [11]. The MSSP may propose countermeasures that introduce changes in the standard workflow of a business. To manage these, top management commitment and support are required; otherwise, the proposed security plan may fail and not be embedded in the organizational culture. In any case, top management support is a prerequisite for all the above factors and for undertaking ISMO as a partnership. Summarizing, we have explored the negative influence of cultural dissimilarity to ISMO success. We examined six social factors, and suggested a framework of indicative mechanisms to handle these diversities (Fig.2).

7 Conclusions and Further Research

We connect organizational culture to information security elements and reveal its significance to information security. In ISMO, cultural differences are identified as a negative factor and thus we aim to assist organizations to manage them in order to achieve ISMO success. We draw upon current trends and theoretical perspectives of IS outsourcing and view it as a partnership. We identify factors that affect the outsourcing outcome and link them to cultural differences. Our framework consists of six security mechanisms that affect the identified social factors and ultimately smooth cultural deviations. These are: a) Security communication (affects communication), b) Definition and evaluation of security culture (linked to mutual understanding), c) Employees' exchange and Active participation (influence participation), d) ISMO guidelines and Security awareness programs (affect information sharing), and e) Definition of employee roles, responsibilities and authorities (linked to coordination).

This conceptual framework can be tested either in a longitudinal case study, or in a quantitative survey, since its effectiveness must be explored in an organizational context. In addition, each mechanism can be researched individually, because it either introduces new research questions (i.e. risk management active participation), or it redefines more mature areas of interest (i.e. awareness programs). The framework is significant as it unites and correlates issues of organizational culture under the scope of managing cultural dissimilarity and achieving a fertile ISMO process.

References

1. Alner, M.: The Effects of Outsourcing on Information Security. Information Systems Security 10(2), 35–42 (2001)
2. Bakari, J.K., Magnusson, C., Tarimo, N.C., Yngström, L.: Outsourcing Managed ICT Security Services in the Developing World, Issues and Challenges. In: Proc. of the 6TH Annual ISSA Conference, South Africa (2006)
3. Gordon, L., Loeb, M., Lucyshyn, W., Richardson, R.: CSI/FBI: 2006 Computer Crime and Security Survey, Computer Security Institute (2006)
4. Dibbern, J., Goles, T., Hirschheim, R., Jayatilaka, B.: Information systems outsourcing: a survey and analysis of the literature. ACM SIG on Management Information Systems Database 35(4), 6–102 (2004)
5. Eloff, J., Eloff, M.: Information Security Management - A New Paradigm. In: Proc. of South African Institute of Computer Scientists and Information Technologists, pp. 130–136 (2003)
6. Endorf, C.: Outsourcing Security: The needs, the risks, the providers, and the process. Information Systems Security 12(6), 17–23 (2004)
7. Fenn, C., Shooter, R., Allan, K.: IT Security Outsourcing. Computer Law & Security Report 18(2), 109–111 (2002)
8. Gartner.: European MSSP value trusted relationships not just Technology. Van Mien, A.D., Parveen, K., Research Note No. M-19-2948 (2003)
9. Gonzalez, R., Gasco, J., Llopis, J.: Information systems outsourcing success factors: A review and some results. Information Management & Computer Security 13(5), 399–418 (2005)

10. Grover, V., Cheon, M.J., Teng, J.: The effect of service quality and partnership on the outsourcing of information systems functions. Journal of Management Information Systems 12(4), 89–116 (1996)
11. ISO/IEC 17799:2005.: Information technology - Security techniques - Code of practice for information security management, International Standards Association (2005)
12. Kahraman, E.: Evaluating IT security performance with quantifiable metrics. MSc Thesis, Stockholm University and Royal Institute of Technology, Sweden (2005)
13. Karyda, M., Kiountouzis, E., Kokolakis, S.: Information systems security policies: A contextual perspective. Computers & Security 24(3), 246–260 (2005)
14. Karyda, M., Mitrou, E., Quirchmayr, G.: A framework for outsourcing IS/IT security services. Information Management & Computer Security 14(5), 402–415 (2006)
15. Kern, T., Willcocks, L.: Exploring Information Technology outsourcing relationships: Theory and practice. Journal of Strategic Information Systems 9(4), 321–350 (2000)
16. Lacity, M., Hirschheim, R.: The Information Systems outsourcing bandwagon. Sloan Management Review 35(1), 73–86 (1993)
17. Lee, J.-N., Huynh, M., Chi-wai, K., Pi, S.: The Evolution of outsourcing research: What is the next issue? In: Proc. of the 33rd Annual Hawaii International Conference on System Sciences (2000)
18. Lee, J.-N., Huynh, M.Q., Kwok, R.C., Pi, S.-M.: IT outsourcing evolution - past, present and future. Com. of the ACM 46(5), 84–89 (2003)
19. Lee, J.-N., Kim, Y.-G.: Effect of partnership quality on IS outsourcing success: Conceptual framework and empirical validation. Journal of Management Information Systems 15(4), 29–61 (1999)
20. Martins, A., Eloff, J.: Information Security Culture. In: Proc. of IFIP TC11 17th International Conference on Information Security (SEC2002), Egypt, pp. 535–546 (2002)
21. Peltier, T.: Implementing an Information Security Awareness Program. Information Systems Security 14(2), 37–49 (2005)
22. Renn, O.: The role of risk perception for risk management. Reliability Engineering and System Safety 59(1), 49–62 (1998)
23. Schein, E.: On dialogue, culture, and organizational learning. Organizational Dynamics 22(2), 40–51 (1993)
24. Schein, E.: Organizational culture and leadership, 2nd edn. Jossey-Bass Publishers, San Francisco (1999)
25. Schneier, B.: The case for outsourcing security and privacy: Building confidence in a networked world. Supplement to IEEE Computer Magazine 35(4), 20–26 (2002)
26. Slay, J.: IS security, trust and culture: a theoretical framework for managing IS security in multicultural settings. Campus-Wide Information Systems 20(3), 98–104 (2003)
27. Sun, S.-Y., Lin, T.-C., Sun, P.-C.: The factors influencing information systems outsourcing partnership - A study integrating case study and survey research methods. In: Proc. of the 35th Annual Hawaii International Conference on System Sciences, vol. 8, p. 235b (2002)
28. Thomson, K., von Solms, R.: Information security obedience: A definition. Computers & Security 24(1), 69–75 (2005)
29. US National Research Council Committee on Risk Perception and Communication: Improving risk communication. National Academy Press, Washington, DC (1989)
30. Vroom, C., von Solms, R.: Towards information security behavioral compliance. Computers & Security 23(3), 191–198 (2004)
31. Wilbanks, J.: Outsourcing Internet security: The life you save may be your company's. Information Systems Security 10(2), 28–24 (2001)

Specification of the TrustMan System for Assisting Management of VBEs

Simon Samwel Msanjila and Hamideh Afsarmanesh

University of Amsterdam, Kruislaan 419, 1098VA Amsterdam, The Netherlands
msanjila@science.uva.nl, hamideh@science.uva.nl

Abstract. The establishement of trust relationships among organizations has proved to enhance the cooperation among organizations involved in Virtual organization Breeding Environments (VBEs) and their collaboration within the Virtual Organizations (VOs). Main obstacles to establishing trust relationships however stems from the lack of a common definition for trust and trust parameters. Consequently the assessment of the trust level of organizations as well as the creation of trust among organizations are quite challenging. In practice organizations individually assess the trustworthiness of others both manually and in an ad hoc manner. This paper presents an approach and a system for semi-automatic **Trust Man**agement (TrustMan) in collaborative networks. Based on the multi-criteria and customizable trust model that we have defined in earlier publications, here we define the TrustMan system that on one hand aggregates our previously introduced models and approaches, and on the other hand automates the processes related to management of trust among organizations in VBEs.

Keywords: Trust among organizations, TrustMan system, VBE.

1 Introduction

During the last decade, digital technology has changed the world in profound and exciting ways. Today organizations communicate and interact instantly with others even for sensitive issues, such as for businesses collaborations, without traditional limitations of time and location. Collaborative networks such as global supply chains have enabled industries to manufacture products and deliver them to markets with incredible speed and efficiency. Mobile devices are now facilitating collaborating organizations to be productive no matter where they are.

As more and more of the world's information, commerce, and communications are moving to digital form facilitated with the continuously advancing ICTs, they are opening the door to a new world of connected experiences that link organizations interests and market operations into a seamless whole that extends across local, regional, country, and global markets. An emerging beneficial approach for organizations to co-work in such evolving and expanding market, which has taken advantage of these advanced ICTs, is configuring collaborative networks (CN) [3]. As addressed in section 2, in various forms of CNs, including short term

C. Lambrinoudakis, G. Pernul, A M. Tjoa (Eds.): TrustBus 2007, LNCS 4657, pp. 34–43, 2007.

collaborations, (e.g. in VOs) and long term cooperation, (e.g. in VBEs), organizations can interoperate and co-work with each other while being facilitated by computer networks to achieve some common goals, for example, acquiring and responding to larger, better and more business opportunities.

Of course despite the possibility to collaborate with others, organizations had neither made ful use of the advanced ICTs nor optimally benefited through co-working. But whether they succeed or not is no longer the question of the power of the digital devices (infrastructure) and the speed of network connections. One real challenge today is *trust among organizations needed to smoothen their co-working*. Ultimately, the effectiveness of collaboration among organizations, configured to respond to acquired business opportunities, depends on their ability to quickly create trust to each other and establish trust relationships among them which in turn facilitates sharing of information, resources, costs, etc. [2].

The answer to trust problems had been primarily aligned to security issues-in creating systems and processes that are always secure so that organizations have a high degree of confidence that the technology they use will protect their identity, privacy, and information [9] [15]. However, the creation of trust among organizations, which aims at supporting them to achieve common goals in collaborative business, can hardly be achieved by considering technology only. Some approaches for creating and assessing trust are presented in [4][11].

We address trust as a multi-criteria subject in which the assessment of trust level of organizations can be customized depending on the specific application. In [9]we presented an approach for comprehensively identifying trust elements, which then was applied to identify the main elements. The trust elements are hierarchically categorized from abstract (non-measurable) to measurable ones, addressing trust: objective, perspectives, requirements and criteria.

This paper uses the previous work as the base and presents the specification of the TrustMan system. This system is designed and implemented applying the measurable trust elements, specifically, the trust criteria. It is designed based on service oriented architecture (SOA), thus implemented as web services to enhance its independence from operating environments, and platforms [13]. The remaining part of the paper is organized as follows: section 2 presents the concepts related to trust among organizations in VBEs. Section 3 addresses the specification of the TrustMan system. Finally section 4 concludes the paper.

2   Trust Among Organizations in VBEs

The market is now continuously evolving to match today's connected and digital world. The organizational preparedness necessary to facilitate their collaborative initiatives must match the market's evolution pace. But it has proved hard to individually achieve the required preparedness. Among others the preparedness aspects for configuration of collaborative networks includes: the existence of common operating principles, acquiring interoperable infrastructure, creating trust to other organizations, etc. Previous research on CNs had indicated the importance of the pre-existence of VBEs as facilitating environments for organizations towards their participation in collaborative businesses [3]. The following definitions are adopted in this paper:

- **VO:** A partnership of (legally) independent organizations (e.g. VO partners) that come together and share resources and skills to achieve a common goal, such as acquiring and responding to a market/society opportunity [3].
- **VBE:** An association of organizations and related supporting institutions adhering to a base long term cooperation agreement, and adopting common operating principles and infrastructures, with the main goal of increasing both their chances and preparedness towards collaboration in potential virtual organizations (VO) [1].

A number of concepts constitute the base for modeling trust [8], and are used for the development of TrustMan system. Following are their descriptions [7]:

- **Trust:** is an objective-specific confidence of a trustor organization to a trustee organization based on the results of fact-based trust level assessment of that trustee.
- **Trust objective:** is the purpose for which the trust relationship establishment among the involved organizations is required. Examples of trust objectives include for: inviting an organization to join a VO, selecting an organization as a VO coordinator, an organization to decide joining a VBE, etc.
- **Trust perspective:** represents the specific "point of view" of the trustor on the main aspects that must be considered for assessing the trust level of the trustee. In [6] we presented five trust perspectives for organizations namely: *Technological (Tc), Social (So), Managerial (Mn), Economical (Ec), and Structural (St).*
- **Trust criteria:** represent the measurable trust elements that characterize a respective trust requirement. Therefore, for each organization, the values of its trust criteria can be used to make an objective fact-based judgment on whether the respective requirement is met. Each trust criteria constitutes a value structure, which defines the acceptable structure for its data, such as scalars, vectors, arrays, list of strings, etc. Also it defines the metric applied to scale the data. The comprehensive set of trust criteria for organizations is presented in [7].
- **Trust level:** Refers to the intensity level of trust for a trustee in a trust relationship, based on the assessment of values for a set of necessary trust criteria. The criteria for the trust level assessment are varied and wide in spectrum depending on several issues such as on the objective, perspective, etc. for creating trust. When trust level is evaluated for a specific purpose, such as for inviting a member to a VO, and the evaluation is based on specific trust criteria for that the purpose, we call the results, specific trustworthiness of the trustee.

Some of the most crucial preparedness aspects in the VBE are: making the environment trustworthy enough to convince organizations to join and customers to provide business opportunities, ensuring that all VBE members meet the base trust level, etc. Thus trust levels of members must be assessed, and the results applied for creating trust to each other. The following research questions must be properly addressed to realize trust among organizations in VBEs:

(A) *Can trustworthiness (trust level) of an organization be measured? How complex is it? Does it have quantitative values, and if so, what are the metrics? Furthermore,* *is it one number or a set of numbers? If not quantitative, then does it have qualitative value, such as good or bad, high or low?*

In [7], we presented an approach for trustworthiness of organizations to be measured in terms of quantitative values for a set of trust criteria. We argued that trustworthiness is complex and can neither be measured with a single value nor interpreted with a single metric. The levels upon which several specific metrics are met represent the trust level of an organization. However, it should be noted that the assessed trust level *is not absolute rather comparative* (e.g. as represented in Fig. 1). The trust level of an organization is rated based on its values for the given set of trust criteria as compared to values of others (Fig. 1). To manage trust in VBEs, trust and trust relationships must be properly characterized, and modeled. The modeling of trust and trust relationships among organizations is addressed in [8].

The mechanisms developed for the manipulation of values for trust criteria are based on mathematical equations. The equations are derived based on results from the analysis of causal relations among trust criteria, known factors and intermediate factors. The derivations of equations are beyond the scope of this paper but they are presented in detail in [7]. Below are three general formulas:

$$TL = Avg[(W_{Tc}*S_{Tc}), (W_{So}*S_{So}), (W_{St}*S_{St}), (W_{Mn}*S_{Mn}), (W_{Ec}*S_{Ec})] \quad (1)$$

$$S_{per} = \frac{1}{n}\sum_{i}^{n} W_{IF_i} * S_{IF_i} \quad (2)$$

$S_{IF} = f[trust\_criteria, known\_factors]\ Where 0 < W_i < 1, and \sum_{\forall i} W_i = 1$

TL: trust level, **S**: score, **per**: trust perspective, **IF**: intermediate factor, **W**: weight, **Avg**: average

(B) *How can the TrustMan system assist VBE member to: assess trust level of others in the VBE, foresee their trustworthiness in the coming time, and establish trust relationships with others?*

(C) *How to make TrustMan system replicable, adaptable and sustainable?*

This paper presents the specification of services needed for semi-automatically managing trust among organizations in response to these two questions.

3   Specification of the TrustMan System

In this section we present the specification of users and their requirements, and the functionalities for TrustMan system. We also address the architecture and technical aspects related to the user interface, orchestration and choreography of services, authentication of external access, etc. of TrustMan system.

3.1   The Specification of Users and Their Requirements

There are 3 general trust objectives for creating inter-organizational trust in VBEs [8]: *(1) Trust among VBE member organizations:* Focuses on assessing trust level of organizations, and establishing their trust relationships for different purposes, i.e. smoothing cooperation in the VBE, enhancing collaboration in VOs, etc. *(2) Trust between the VBE member and the VBE administration:* Focuses on creating trust of a VBE member to the VBE administration to enhance the commitment of member to the VBE, to ease the managerial tasks, etc. *(3) Trust between external stakeholders and the VBE:* Focuses on creating trust of external stakeholders to the VBE, i.e. invited organizations to become members or customer to provide opportunities.

Based on these objectives we classified five user groups with their respective requirements as follows: *(i) VBE administrator:* (1)Assesses base trust level of membership applicant and VBE members, (2)Updates the list of trust criteria. *(ii) VO planner:* (1)Selects specific trust criteria for evaluation, (2)Evaluates specific trustworthiness. *(iii) VBE member:* (1)Accesses its base trust level records, (2)Updates the trust related data. *(iv) Membership applicant:* (1)Submits trust related data for base trust level assessment. *(v) External stakeholders:* (1)Supports customer to create trust to the VBE, (2) Supports invited organizations to trust the VBE.

3.2   Specification of Functionalities for TrustMan System

This section addresses the functionalities, input data, output information and their presentation in TrustMan system.

A. Motivation: Assessing organization's trust level has been a challenging task. It is even more challenging when a number of organizations are involved and their trust levels must be *absolutely compared* [6]. Further to addressing the requirements presented in section 3.1, the specification of TrustMan system also addresses the complexity of comparing organization's trustworthiness. If trust level of organizations is properly assessed and compared, and then the results applied to their collaboration establishment, a smooth environment for their interactions will basically be created [7].

B. Functionalities: The TrustMan system implementation adopted the SOA and specifically the web service technology. Thus the specified functionalities are services. The system provides five integrated services as described below:

Service 1: For assessing base trust level of organizations
When customizing the TrustMan system, in a specific VBE, the administrator selects the minimum set of trust criteria provided by TrustMan system that reflects the characteristics and the specific domain/application of the VBE and suits the needs of the environment. This selected minimum set is called the *base trust criteria*. The results of the assessment that applies these base trust criteria are referred to as *base trust level* for organizations. The base trust level provides the threshold for acceptable trustworthiness to keep a member in the VBE. The *service for assessing base trust level* is implemented to support the assessment of trust level for organizations based on these base trust criteria. The kinds of assessment supported by the TrustMan system for the base trust level includes: *periodic assessment of base trust level for members, and one-time assessment of*

base trust level for a membership applicant. This is an administrative service and is accessed by the VBE administrator.

Service 2: For evaluating specific trustworthiness of organizations

This *service* aims at measuring how trustworthy an organization is against a specific trust objective, i.e. inviting a VBE member to participate in a VO, appoint a VBE member to become a VO coordinator or VBE administrator, etc. A priori to the evaluation, the trustor selects the specific set of trust criteria from the general set of trust criteria provided by TrustMan system. Then trustor sets the rating for the values of trust criteria to define different levels of trust for the evaluation. The evaluation of specific trustworthiness can be done at a certain point in time such as current time. Also, the evaluation can be applied to forecast trustworthiness for future collaborations. This is an administrative service and thus it is accessed by the VBE administrator and VO planner.

Service 3: For establishing trust relationships among organizations

The approach suggested to facilitate *establishing trust relationships* among organizations is through measuring their historical data for both their trust records and performance records. While establishing trust relationships among them participating organizations can be provided with relevant information queried from the data stored in the TrustMan system, which will enable them trust others. However, some information stored might be too strategic, and thus owner organizations can hardly allow their information to be publicly accessed. Thus the access is categorized as: *(1) Public access*: Any organization can access the information, *(2) Restricted access*: Only VBE members can access the information, and *(3) Protected access*: The administrator and the owner access the information.

This is a semi-administrative service that can be accessed by the VBE administrator, and VBE members that are permitted for specific reasons.

Service 4: For managing trust related data

This service supports three users of the system, namely: membership applicants, members, and VBE administrator. The applicants will use this service to submit their trust related data to facilite the evaluation towards joining the VBE. The submitted data is used to assess their base trust level to support deciding whether to accept the application. The members will use this service to update their trust related data. And finally, the VBE administrator will use this service to manage all the trust related data in the system i.e. ensuring data is updated, valid and with reliable source.

Service 5: For creating trust to the VBE

This service supports external stakeholders to create trust to the VBE. There are two kinds of external stakeholders: the invited organizations for becoming members, and the customers. These external stakeholders need to access information that will convince them about the trustworthiness of the VBE in relation to their businesses. The service will thus guide respective stakeholder to access specific information based on its purpose or perception of trust.

C. Input data and their sources: The input data applied during the assessment of trust level are the values of trust criteria for organizations. The main sources of data for organizations are twofold: *(1) Data submitted by VBE member*

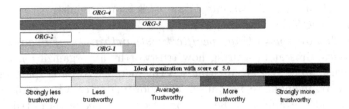

Fig. 1. Trustmetre - Qualitative trust levels of organizations in VBE

applicant, and *(2) Performance data of organizations collected from their participations in VOs.*

D. Output information and presentation: The output from the services for assessing trust level and evaluating specific trustworthiness of organizations is the trust levels expressed qualitatively as indicated in Fig. 1. The resulted trust levels are comparative and thus are valid for the given: values of trust criteria, the selected trust criteria, the involved organizations, and the applied ratings. The qualitative representation of trust levels is based on the interpretations of scores for values of trust criteria for the organizations [7].

3.3   Technical Specification

In this sub-section we address the technical specification of TrustMan system focusing on the general view, interfaces, services' orchestration and choreography.

(i) General aspects of the TrustMan system: The system is made up of three main layers: top, middle and bottom layers. The top layer is the human interface; the middle layer is the orchestration and choreography; and the bottom layer is the invocation interface.

(ii) Human access and interface: The access of the system for human users is controlled by three main parameters: userID, password and user role. The userID refers to the unique identification of the user and specifically for this system, each user is provided with an organization number, which is used as its identification for accessing the system. The password is created by the respective user during the first login. In addition to being an authorized user, their roles are used to identify which information *(public, restricted, and protected)* and services *(assess, or view trust level record)* can be accessed with the current login details. Thus the same user access various parts of the system with different roles, e.g. as a VBE administrator or member. Human access to the system is facilitated by so called *human interface* . It is implemented as a web based interface with various pages accessed by providing authentication information. However, it should be noted that the TrustMan system is a *semi-automatic system* in the sense that the final decision about the trust level of organization is not provided by the system rather is made by the trustor. The interpretation of trust level depends on specific trustor and the TrustMan system only supports trustors by providing them with the assessment results that they can use to make their final decisions related to trust.

(iii) Orchestration and choreography of TrustMan services: In next paragraphs we describe the concepts of orchestration and choreography for services, and provide an example on how we applied them for TrustMan system.

Orchestration refers to the logic (the sequence and flow) for execution of functions within one system process [8]. For example, in java programming this refers to execution of functions within one object. Fig. 2 shows orchestration of several processes integrated in one choreography process, such as system control, access right, base trust level, etc. *Choreography* represents the logic that will be followed to execute various modules including invoking other services in order to provide a single integrated service [12]. Several java web services were choreographed to provide required integrated services including: *for assessing base trust level and evaluating specific trustworthiness of organizations.* To exemplify, we present the service for accessing the base trust level.

Fig. 2 represents the choreography for a set of services constituting the process of base trust level assessment (as explained below) and thus represents a partial processes' architecture of the TrustMan system. Consider a user starting to assess the base trust level of a member in the VBE. The system will first validate whether the user has the right to access the system. Once positively validated

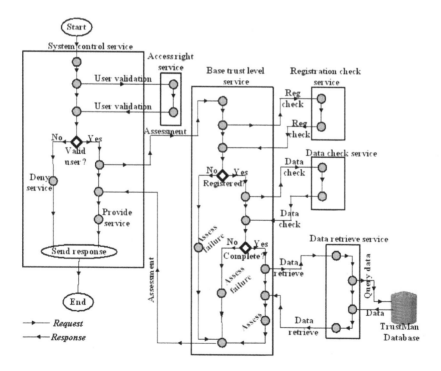

Fig. 2. Choreography of the process for assessing base trust level of an organization

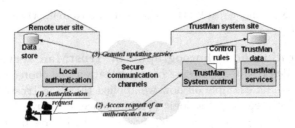

Fig. 3. Authenticated access for TrustMan system from a remote user

the user is granted the access. Then the service for assessing base trust level is invoked. The system checks whether the organization whose trust level need to be assessed is registered and trust data is complete. When positive response is received from the services which check the registration and completeness of data, the data for the organization is retrieved and its base trust level is assessed. Lastly, the response is sent to the user. If at any stage a failure happens then the process is terminated and the user receives a negative response with the right response message, e.g. the organization is not registered (Fig. 2).

(iv) External system access and invocation: TrustMan system provides services to other systems through invocation based on the SOAP protocol. There are several steps that the system should take to verify each specific invocation. Fig. 3 presents a generic invocation design showing interactions needed for an organization to update its trust related data from local repositories. We have applied the security over the network, such as the authentication of source network, as provided by the ECOLEAD ICT infrastructure [14]. It is expected that the request will have a local authentication certificate as shown in step 1 in Fig. 3. If the requested service is granted by the *TrustMan system control* then a positive response is sent otherwise negative response is sent. The only interface for invocation is the *WSDL layer*, which describes the services that can be invoked, and the parameters that must be passed [5].

4   Conclusion

In this paper based on mathematical model addressed in [7], trust elements as presented in [9] and trust models as presented in [8], we have addressed the specification of TrustMan system for the management of trust among organizations in VBEs. The paper presented the main services for assessing trust level of organizations, establishing their trust relationships, creating trust to the VBE and managing trust related data. It has addressed the user categories and their rights for accessing the system through either human or system interface.

The results presented in this paper considered VBEs as reference application domain for which a pilot is now being built and tried in real VBEs. However, these results can also be applied to other collaborative environments and networks whose members involve organizations.

Acknowledgement. This work was supported in part by the ECOLEAD project funded by the European Commission. The authors acknowledge contributions from partners in the ECOLEAD consortium.

References

1. Afsarmanesh, H., Camarinha-Matos, L.: A framework for management of virtual organization breeding environments. In: Collaborative Networks and their Breeding Environments, pp. 35–49. Springer, Heidelberg (2005)
2. Castelfranchi, C., Falcone, R.: Trust is much more than subjective probability: Mental components and sources of trust. In: The proceedings of the 33rd Hawaii International Conference on System Sciences, Hawaii (2000)
3. Camarinha-Matos, L.M., Afsarmanesh, H.: Collaborative Networks: Value creation in a knowledge society. In: knowledge enterprise: Intelligent strategies in product design, manufacturing and management, Springer, Heidelberg (2006)
4. Gambetta, D.: Trust:Making and breaking cooperative relations. Basil Blackwell (1998)
5. Kreger, H.: Fulfilling the web services promise. Communications of ACM 46(6) (2003)
6. Mezgar, I.: Trust Building for Enhancing Collaboration in Virtual Organizations. In: Camarinha-Matos, L., Afsarmanesh, H., Ollus, M. (eds.) IFIP International Federation for Information Processing. Network-Centric Collaboration and Supporting Frameworks, vol. 224, pp. 161–172 (2006)
7. Msanjila, S.S., Afsarmanesh, H.: Trust Analysis and Assessment in Virtual Organizations Breeding Environments. International Journal of Production Research (April 2007)
8. Msanjila, S.S., Afsarmanesh, H.: Modeling Trust Relationships in Collaborative Networked Organizations. The International Journal of Technology Transfer and Commercialisation, Inderscience 6(1), 1470–6075 (to appear, 2007)
9. Msanjila, S.S., Afsarmanesh, H.: HICI: An approach for identifying trust elements – The case of technological perspective in VBEs. In: proceeding of International conference on availability, reliability and security, Vienna (2007)
10. Msanjila, S.S., Tewoldeberhan, T.W., Janssen, M., Block-Bockstel, W., Verbraeck, A.: E-supply chain orchestration using web service technologies: A case using BPEL4WS. In: IRMA (May 2005)
11. Mukherjee, A.: A model of trust in online relationship banking. Journal of Marketing 21 (2003)
12. Papazoglou, M.P, Georgakopoulus, D.: Service-Oriented Computing. Communications of the ACM 46(10) (2003)
13. Peltz, C.: Web services orchestration and choreography. IEEE computer 36(10) (2003)
14. Rabelo, R.J., Gusmeroli, S., Arana, C., Nagellen, C.: The ECOLEAD ICT infrastructure for collaborative networked organizations. In: Camarinha-Matos, L., Afsarmanesh, H., Ollus, M. (eds.) IFIP International Federation for Information Processing. Network-Centric Collaboration and Supporting Frameworks, vol. 224, pp. 161–172 (2006)
15. Weth, C., von der Bohm, K.: A Unifying Framework for Behavior-Based Trust Models. In: Meersman, R., Tari, Z., et al. (eds.) On the Move to Meaningful Internet Systems 2006: CoopIS, DOA, GADA, and ODBASE. LNCS, vol. 4275, pp. 444–461. Springer, Heidelberg (2006)

A Privacy-Preserving Buyer-Seller Watermarking Protocol with Semi-trust Third Party

Min-Hua Shao

Department of Management Information Systems,
National Pingtung University of Science & Technology
1 Hseuh Fu Road, Nei Pu, Pingtung, Taiwan 91201
mhshao@mail.npust.edu.tw

Abstract. Digital watermarking is a value-added technique used in digital rights management systems for the purposes of copy protection and copy deterrence for digital contents, and it has inspired a large variety of work. Unfortunately, much of that work focus mainly on right-holder's security needs rather than those of consumers. This paper proposes a new buyer-seller watermarking protocol for the betterment of consumers' security needs. The key features of our scheme are including of loss-preventing security property ensured, semi-trust third party involved, efficient protection from conspiracy attacks, and lightweight involvement for buyers.

Keywords: Digital commerce, copyright protection, anonymity, conspiracy attacks, security.

1 Introduction

Digital commerce defines a particular subset of electronic commerce which deals only with digital products or digital services, and every auxiliary used for trading is digital [10]. Transferring the traditional business model for selling digital goods linked with physical media to the online world leads to the need for a system to protect digital intellectual property. In order to protect valuable digital content, digital rights management (DRM) is a system that aims at secure distribution and usage of such content and commonly comprises a huge variety of different technologies [14]. Digital watermarking in DRM systems is a technique to bind imperceptible information to digital content for a variety of purposes, i.e., copyright control. The purpose of this service is to trace digital pirates. As soon as the copyright violations are detected, right holders and/or content owners will be notified, and the infringer will likely be sued by the law.

Traditionally, right-holders have a centralized view. They are used to posing as the only victims of trading digital goods online. Therefore, current digital watermarking schemes (and DRM systems) focus chiefly on right-holder's security needs and commonly pass over those of consumers. As the case stands, disputes are inevitable. Memon and Wong [12] indicated an equivocal case that may bring about a fierce debate among the interested parties, especially for buyers and sellers, and will have them mired in difficulties. That is, a content owner (seller) inserts a unique watermark

C. Lambrinoudakis, G. Pernul, A M. Tjoa (Eds.): TrustBus 2007, LNCS 4657, pp. 44–53, 2007.

into a copy of the content before it is sold to the buyer. Once an illegal replica is detected and the responsible distributor (buyer) is determined by extracting the watermark embedded, the original buyer may argue that the unauthorized copy was created or caused by the seller for compensation, a security breach, etc. They proposed a buyer-seller watermarking protocol against the foregoing problem, but not other consumer privacy concerns such as anonymity. Solutions to the problem of anonymity are briefly listed below. Ju et al.'s work [5] is to offer unlinkability of the purchased contents by the same buyer to watermarking protocol with anonymity control. The discussion of collusion attacks against anonymity is considered in Choi et al.'s scheme [6] in which no trusted third party is involved. However, as described by Goi et al. [1], both of the two schemes have more or less weaknesses and/or security flaws with result that they cannot provide the features and security as claimed. In addition, Lei et al.'s effort [2] is to deal with the unbinding problem as well as anonymity appeared in Memon and Wong's scheme.

Early study yielded elegant but typically inefficient solutions to the anonymity problem and the related conspiracy attacks. A key point is how the trusted third party (TTP) involves in the watermarking protocol in order to preserve consumer rights and privacy concerns. Most recent, practical approaches employ one or more TTPs to achieve anonymity. A full trusted watermark certificate authority, which is responsible for the generation of random and valid watermarks upon buyers' requests, is a very common assumption as a base for security services (e.g., [2,5,12]). This work, however, does not consider possible misbehavior by the trusted party, and thus may enable the interested party, that is, the seller, to collude with the third party to gain an advantage. In this paper we propose a different approach to consumer's protection. We use a third party that is "semi-trusted," in the sense of acting as a notary role to provide assurance about the properties of the data (such as its integrity), and then use digital signatures to cryptographically link the buyer's own secret watermark and one-time public key to the purchase order against unbinding problems. In our solutions, no one else but the buyer knows his/her own secret watermark and real identity even though the notary may conspire with either of the main parties. As far as practicability is concerned, the buyer is only required to interact with correspondent certification authorities during the pre-transaction, and with the intended seller during transaction; and further, the buyer is not involved in the procedure of arbitration before he/she is found guilty. The plaintiff (seller) should rightly give proof about the responsible distributor's (buyer) illegality.

The rest of this paper is organized as follows. In Section 2, we discuss preliminary concepts and security properties used in this paper, and Section 3 presents the proposed watermarking protocol in detail. Section 4 gives a security analysis of our new protocol thoroughly. Section 5 then concludes the paper with a summary of our achievements.

2 Preliminaries

Before starting our approach, we set out the requirements that such protocols should meet. Firstly, the detailed treatment of consumer rights and privacy concerns is described in Section 2.1. Then, for completeness and readability, cryptographic primitives used in our scheme are obvious and briefly summarized in Section 2.2.

2.1 Security Properties

Digital watermarks have been proposed for the purposes of copy protection and copy deterrence for multimedia content. In order for on-line business activities with digital content to prosper, there are security requirements that are needed for the correct behavior of the application. As discussed in [1,2,5,6,12], the following set of security properties on a buyer-seller watermarking protocol are incorporated and extended:

- **Accountable Anonymity:** Anonymity refers to the complete absence of identification data in a transaction only if consumers behave correctly.
- **Unlinkability:** The purpose of transaction unlinkability is to prevent linking a customer's transactions to each other [15]. Given two digital contents, anyone, including the sellers, should not be able to determine whether or not these two contents were purchased by the same buyer.
- **Traceability:** The identity of a buyer can be traced and revealed once the buyer has distributed digital contents illegally as with piracy.
- **Binding:** The binding property is to link a chosen watermark to a specific digital content or a specific transaction. The link is needed so that the buyer can prove that this payment is intended for this order and not for some other goods or services. That is, the linkage stops the malicious seller from producing a made-up piracy to get compensated more.
- **Dispute Resolution:** The malicious buyer cannot excuse his/her guilt by claiming that the copy was created by the seller or a security breach of the seller's system. This is a kind of seller's security. The other is a buyer's security that is intended to protect an honest buyer against frame-up of a malicious seller or other buyers.

2.2 Cryptographic Primitives

- **Homomorphic Cryptosystems**

A cryptosystem is required to be privacy homomorphic with respect to the watermark insertion operation $\oplus$ of the underlying watermarking scheme [12]. That is, a homomorphic cryptosystem E^h can be informally stated as follows: $E_K^h(a \oplus b) = E_K^h(a) \oplus E_K^h(b)$ for every a and b in the message space and K is the public (encryption) key. For example, the RSA public-key cryptosystem is a privacy homomorphism with respect to multiplication operation.

- **Anonymous Public-Key Certificates**

An anonymous public-key certificate scheme is originally intended for accountable anonymity and fair document exchange [3]. In order to prevent the recipient from knowing the sender's real identity in the certificate, the scheme is to permit the sender to apply to a certificate authority (CA) for an anonymous public-key certificate, including a new public key and a pseudonym, based on the original certificate [13]. Then, the sender can sign the message with the private key in connection with the new public key without revealing the real identity, and the recipient can still verify the message authenticity by the anonymous certificate. Only the CA issuing the anonymous certificate is able to find a link from the pseudonym to the real identity of the sender, and hold the sender accountable for the message if disputes take place.

- **Verifiable Encryption**

Publicly verifiable encryption is a means to check the correctness of encrypted data without compromising secrecy, and it has been used in applications like digital signature [11], secret sharing [9], or key escrow [4]. Here we give a scenario to depict how a verifiable encryption scheme works in this paper. For anonymity, the buyer (denoted by *B*) generates a one-time key pair randomly in a transaction, and sends the notary (denoted by *NA*) an unavailable but verifiable cipher of the one-time private key using the public key of the arbiter (denoted by *ARB*), who stays off-line. This setting is a kind of fair escrow cryptosystems using off-line escrow agents where the verifiable escrowed cipher convinces *NA* of its validity and that *ARB* is able to recover the key if needed. Normally, the anonymity and privacy concerns of *B* are preserved against the seller.

3 A Privacy-Preserving Buyer-Seller Watermarking Protocol

3.1 Notation and Abbreviations

In the model of the proposed scheme, five different roles involved are as follows.

1. **S:** The seller, who can gain from the sales of digital content. The seller can be in the form of the content provider or the distributor.
2. **B:** The buyer, who wants to consume the digital content from the seller.
3. **CA:** A trusted certification authority, who issues digital certificates and takes responsibility for authentication.
4. **NA:** A notary authority, which assures correctness of data presented and then certifies the validity of watermarks generated by the buyer.
5. **ARB:** An arbiter with the power or influence to make judgements and decide what will be done or accepted for copyright infringement.

The notation used in the scheme description is as follows.

(pk_A, sk_A)	*the identity A is in possession of a pair of keys where pk_A is A's public key and sk_A is A's private key.*
$(\overline{pk}_A, \overline{sk}_A)$	*a public-private key pair, a kind of (pk_A, sk_A), is used for an anonymous certificate.*
(pk_A^*, sk_A^*)	*a one-time public-private key pair, a kind of (pk_A, sk_A), is used for unlinkable serial transactions.*
$Cert_{CA}(pk_A)$	*a public-key certificate associated with subject A is issued by certification authority CA. The format of digital certificates is in accordance with X.509.*
$X' = X \oplus W$	*the watermarked copy X' of digital content X where $\oplus$ denotes the watermark insertion operation and W is the watermark being embedded.*
$E_{pk_A}^h(\cdot)$	*the privacy-homomorphic encryption function using A's public key.*
$Sign_{sk_A}(\cdot)$	*the signature function of entity A with A's private key.*

$D_{sk_A}^h (\cdot)$ *a public-key and privacy-homomorphic decryption function under A's private key with respect to the binary operator $\oplus$.*

$h(\cdot)$ *a collision resistant one-way hash function.*

3.2 The Proposed Scheme

The privacy-preserving buyer-seller watermarking protocol consists of three subprotocols: registration protocol, watermarking generation and insertion protocol, and copyright violator identification and arbitration protocol. The registration protocol is prepared for an online transaction, which can be done before the transaction. The watermarking generation and insertion protocol mainly deals with the matter of digital trading. The copyright violator identification and arbitration protocol is used for a web spider service that routinely searches the Internet and tests for digital files that have been watermarked.

A. Registration protocol

The registration protocol deals with the buyer procedure of acquiring the public-key certificate and its anonymous certificate from **CA** under a secure and trusted communication. First, **B** randomly selects a key pair (pk_B, sk_B) and requests **CA** to issue the public-key certificate $Cert_{CA}(pk_B)$ if the successful verification of **B**'s identification. Due to privacy concerns, **B** randomly generates a key pair $(\overline{pk}_B, \overline{sk}_B)$ and sends **CA** the new public key $\overline{pk}_B$ and the original public-key certificate $Cert_{CA}(pk_B)$ to apply for an anonymous certificate $Cert_{CA}(\overline{pk}_B)$ with the pseudonym of **B**. The above treatment is shown in Figure 1.

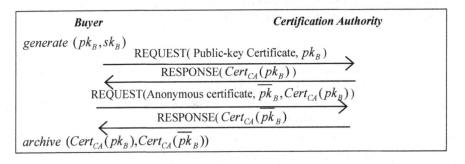

Fig. 1. Registration Protocol

B. Watermarking generation and insertion protocol

This is a three-party protocol among **B**, **S**, and **NA** that describes processes involved in digital trading. To begin with, **B** and **S** should reach an agreement (denoted as ARG) on rights and duties defined during negotiation and written down in a pre-contract in advance. Figure 2 illustrates the details of the following steps.

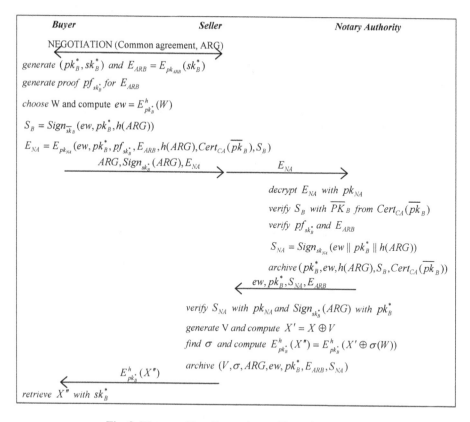

Fig. 2. Watermarking Generation and Insertion Protocol

1. In the cause of transaction unlinkability, **B** randomly selects a key pair (pk_B^*, sk_B^*) used for a single transaction and then generates an escrow cipher E_{ARB} of the new private key sk_B^* by using pk_{ARB}. The ciphertext E_{ARB} is reserved for copyright violator identification and arbitration and its verifiable proof $pf_{sk_B^*}$ is produced by a verifiable encryption scheme. Then, **B** creates a more robust watermark W in compliance with the characteristics of the purchased object X and encrypts it $ew = E_{pk_B^*}^h(W)$. The signature $S_B = Sign_{\overline{sk_B}}(ew, pk_B^*, h(ARG))$ and the ciphertext $E_{NA} = E_{pk_{NA}}(ew, pk_B^*, pf_{sk_B^*}, E_{ARB}, h(ARG), Cert_{CA}(\overline{pk}_B), S_B)$ are made, respectively. Lastly, **B** sends the confirmed agreement $(ARG, Sign_{sk_B^*}(ARG))$ and E_{NA} to S.

2. **S** holds the confirmed agreement and then forwards the ciphertext E_{NA} to **NA** in order to obtain **B**'s one-time public key verified.

3. Upon receiving E_{NA}, **NA** decrypts it and then verifies the validity of S_B and $pf_{sk_B^*}$. If certain well-defined conditions are met, **NA** is assured of sk_B^* escrowed correctly

and generates his/her signature on ew, pk_B^*, and $h(ARG)$ against the unbinding problem. Afterwards, **NA** delivers $ew, pk_B^*, S_{NA}, E_{ARB}$ to **S** and stores $pk_B^*, ew, h(ARG), S_B, Cert_{CA}(\overline{pk}_B)$ in Table$_{NA}$.

4. **S** conducts the verification including S_{NA} and $Sign_{sk_B^*}(ARG)$, and aborts the transaction if any component is invalid. Otherwise, **S** generates a unique watermark V for this particular transaction, produces the watermarked digital content $X' = X \oplus V$. Next, **S** generates a random permutation σ of degree m to permute the encrypted watermark ew by $\sigma(E_{pk_B^*}^h(W)) = E_{pk_B^*}^h(\sigma(W))$. The second-round watermark insertion $E_{pk_B^*}^h(X'') = E_{pk_B^*}^h(X') \oplus E_{pk_B^*}^h(\sigma(W)) = E_{pk_B^*}^h(X' \oplus \sigma(W))$ is performed in the re-permuted and encrypted domain. Obviously, **S** has no idea about X''. After that, $E_{pk_B^*}^h(X'')$ is delivered to **B** and the sales record $(V, \sigma, ARG, ew, pk_B^*, E_{ARB}, S_{NA})$ with respect to X is stored in Table$_X$.

5. After receiving $E_{pk_B^*}^h(X'')$, **B** decrypts it with sk_B^* by computing $X'' = D_{sk_B^*}^h(E_{pk_B^*}^h(X''))$ and obtains the doubly watermarked copy X''. To this end, neither **B** nor **S** can attempt to get X and X'' respectively because of **B**'s lack of the knowledge of σ and V and **S**'s lack of the knowledge of sk_B^*.

C. Copyright violator identification and arbitration protocol

Once an illegal replica Y of certain digital content X is found, **S** will launch the copyright violator identification and arbitration protocol with the help of **ARB**, **NA** and **CA** to extract undeniable evidences, and identify the responsible distributor who was the buyer involved in some earlier transaction. This process is performed by the means of a watermark extraction function $Det(X,Y)$ in compliance with the watermarking algorithm. The protocol is depicted in Fig. 3 and proceeds as follows.

1. On discovering an unauthorized copy Y of X, **S** extracts the unique watermark U in Y. By correlating U with every watermark V stored in Table$_X$, **S** selects the one with the highest correlation beyond a confidence threshold. When a match is found, S collects the relevant data including $V, \sigma, ARG, ew, pk_B^*, E_{ARB}, S_{NA}$ from the matched entry of Table$_X$ and sends them along with Y to **ARB** for arbitration.

2. Upon receiving the arbitration request, **ARB** firstly verifies the validity of **NA**'s signature S_{NA} and rejects the case if the verification doesn't hold. Otherwise, **ARB** decrypts E_{ARB} to obtain **B**'s one-time private key sk_B^* and then retrieves the secret watermark W by computing $D_{sk_B^*}(ew)$. A check on the presence of $\sigma(W)$ in Y can be performed by using the corresponding watermark detection and extraction algorithm. If the verification holds, **ARB** judges the buyer to be guilty and sends pk_B^* to **NA** for extracting **B**'s real identity from the cooperation between **NA** and **CA**. Otherwise, **B** is considered innocent and his/her identity remains unexposed.

3. When receiving pk_B^* from **ARB**, **NA** uses it as the key to retrieve $Cert_{CA}(\overline{pk_B})$ from the matched entry in Table$_{NA}$ and then turns to **CA** to ask for **B**'s real identity by forwarding **B**'s anonymous certificate.

4. After verifying $Cert_{CA}(\overline{pk_B})$, **CA** will disclose and deliver the real identity of the anonymous buyer over to S by **NA** and **ARB**.

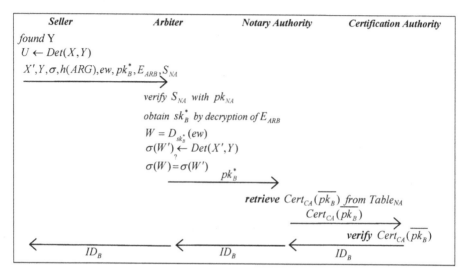

Fig. 3. Copyright Violator Identification and Arbitration Protocol

4 Discussions

A security analysis on the proposed scheme is given in accordance with the list of requirements shown in Section 2.1. Specifically, collusion tolerance to common signal transformations hinges on the security and robustness of the underlying watermarking scheme. We then summarize some features related to practicability and effectiveness in this section.

A. Security analysis

1. Accountable anonymity: Full anonymity may result in security risks such as misuse by anonymous users that are unacceptable in certain applications, most notably in digital commerce. Therefore, we deal with the balance of anonymity versus accountability known as *accountable anonymity*. In our scheme, only the **CA** is in possession of the real identity of an anonymous buyer and cannot violate security agreements to disclose the identification unless **ARB** gives **NA** and **CA** a valid order in a legal procedure.

2. Transaction unlinkability: Only employing anonymous public-key certificates is lacking in privacy protection because sellers are able to protect their interests by maintaining a profile on each anonymous customer. In view of this, we use one-time key pair and verifiable encryption to mask identifications in anonymous public-key certificates even though these certificates are collected by **NA**. To make

privacy protection more secure, a one-time certificate is necessary for unlinkability. The efficient treatment of one-time certificates can be referred to [8].
3. Transaction binding: The unbinding problem takes place for lack of binding a chosen watermark to a specific digital content or a specific transaction [2]. Customers may suffer false accusation from made-up piracy that is the attack of watermark transplantation made from malicious sellers. Due to a similar concern in a credit-card-over-SET transaction, we use the concept of the dual signature that provides a link between two related messages being sent to solve the problem. In protocols two signatures S_B and S_{NA} are designed for the purpose.
4. Dispute resolution: Keeping the buyer own watermark secret is the key to the security of a buyer-seller watermarking protocol. In the proposed scheme, the malicious seller cannot produce a pirated copy X'' for lack of the knowledge of the specific watermark W or the buyer's one-time private key sk_B^*. Similarly, the ill-behaved buyer cannot falsely deny reselling an unauthorized copy and shift the blame onto others, i.e., the seller.

B. Semi-trust third party
In cryptography, a trusted third party (TTP) is an entity which facilitates interactions between two parties who both trust the third party; they use this trust to secure their own interactions. Previous research efforts employ one or more TTPs to ensure security, and thus may enable the third party to learn the contents of documents being exchange, e.g. the buyer's own secret watermark and order information. Here we put an emphasis on reducing the involvement of a TTP, who acts as a semi-trusted third party. That is, the third party **NA** only verifies the validity of the message enclosed in the ciphertext E_{NA} and then sends the endorsed message S_{NA} to the seller if the verification holds. In our scheme, **NA** learns no valuable information about the specific watermark W, and anyone who colludes with **NA** will not gain any useful new information about the buyer.

C. Protection against conspiracy attack
The buyer's secret information could be revealed by a conspiracy between the seller and other participants in a transaction. As described in [12,2], **S** can obtain the specific watermark W in league with **WCA**. Besides, **S** can further know the real identity of **B** and other security properties, including transaction unlikability and dispute resolution, cannot be achieved by a conspiracy in [5,6]. To address the above problem, **B** deals with the generation of the watermark W and one-time key pair (pk_B^*, sk_B^*) for secrecy and anonymity; and further, **B** asks **NA** the endorsement of the related information $(ew, pk_B^*, h(ARG))$ by providing the unavailable but verifiable cipher of sk_B^* encrypted under **ARB**'s public key pk_{ARB}.

D. Lightweight involvement for buyers
Generally, the more consumers need to involve themselves in complicated business activities, the more their reluctance will grow to engage in a transaction. A universal acceptance of SSL-based payment system is an example. For this purpose, **B** is only required to interact with **S** to carry out a transaction in the proposed scheme. Even though the accusation against **B** is in progress, **B** is not involved in criminal investigations conducted by **ARB** unless and until **B** is found guilty.

5 Conclusion

Within digital commerce the buyer-seller watermarking protocol toward consumer rights and privacy concerns is very promising. This is a supplement to current DRM systems and applications, which lay quite a particular stress on right-holder's protection. In this paper, we have shown efficient solutions to consumer's protection in the semi-trusted third-party setting. This option, the notary service, provides a novel type of security from conspiracy attacks since the third party need not be fully trusted.

References

1. Goi, B.M., Phan, R.C.-W., Yang, Y., Bao, F., Deng, R.H., Siddiqi, M.U.: Cryptanalysis of two anonymous buyer-seller watermarking protocols and an improvement for true anonymity. In: Jakobsson, M., Yung, M., Zhou, J. (eds.) ACNS 2004. LNCS, vol. 3089, pp. 369–382. Springer, Heidelberg (2004)
2. Lei, C.L., Yu, P.L., Chan, M.H.: An efficient and anonymous buyer-seller watermarking protocol. IEEE transactions on Image Processing 13(12), 1618–1626 (2004)
3. Critchlow, D., Zhang, N.: Security enhanced accountable anonymous PKI certificates for mobile e-commerce. Computer Networks 45, 483–503 (2004)
4. Poupard, G., Stern, J.: Fair encryption of RSA keys. In: Preneel, B. (ed.) EUROCRYPT 2000. LNCS, vol. 1807, pp. 172–189. Springer, Heidelberg (2000)
5. Ju, H.S., Kim, H.J., Lee, D.H., Lim, J.I.: An anonymous buyer-seller watermarking protocol with anonymity control. In: Lee, P.J., Lim, C.H. (eds.) ICISC 2002. LNCS, vol. 2587, pp. 421–432. Springer, Heidelberg (2003)
6. Choi, J.G., Sakurai, K., Park, J.H.: Does it need trusted third party? Design of buyer-seller watermarking protocol without trusted third party. In: Zhou, J., Yung, M., Han, Y. (eds.) ACNS 2003. LNCS, vol. 2846, pp. 265–279. Springer, Heidelberg (2003)
7. Ortega-Garcia, J., Bigun, J., Reynolds, D., Gonzalez-Rodriguez, J.: Authentication gets personal with biometrics. IEEE Signal Processing Magazine, 50–62 (March 2004)
8. Oishi, K., Mambo, M., Okamoto, E.: Anonymous public key certificates and their applications. IEICE Transactions on Fundamentals of Electronics, Communications and Computer Sciences E81-A(1), 56–64 (1998)
9. Stadler, M.: Public verifiable secret sharing. In: Maurer, U.M. (ed.) EUROCRYPT 1996. LNCS, vol. 1070, pp. 191–199. Springer, Heidelberg (1996)
10. Schmees, M.: Distributed digital commerce. In: the Proceeding of ICEC 2003, pp. 131–137 (2003)
11. Asokan, N., Shoup, V., Waidner, M.: Optimistic fair exchange of digital signatures. IEEE Journal on Selected Areas in Communications 18(4), 591–610 (2000)
12. Memon, N., Wong, P.W.: A buyer-seller watermarking protocol. IEEE transactions on Image Processing 10(4), 643–649 (2001)
13. Zhang, N., Shi, Q., Merabti, M.: Anonymous public-key certificates for anonymous and fair document exchange. IEE Proc.-Commun. 147(6) (December 2000)
14. Liu, Q., Safavi-Naini, R., Sheppard, N.P.: Digital rights management for content distribution. In: the Proceeding of the Australasian Information Security Workshop (2003)
15. Stubblebine, S.G., Syverson, P.F., Goldschlag, D.M.: Unlinkable serial transactions: Protocols and applications. ACM Transactions on Information and System Security 2(4), 354–389 (1999)

Towards Automatic Assembly of Privacy-Preserved Intrusion Signatures

Zhuowei Li[1,2], Amitabha Das[2], and Jianying Zhou[3]

[1] Indiana University at Bloomington
zholi@indiana.edu
[2] Nanyang Technological University, Singapore
asadas@ntu.edu.sg
[3] Institute for Infocomm Research, Singapore
jyzhou@i2r.a-star.edu.sg

Abstract. Intrusion signatures are used to detect and/or prevent fast-spreading worms or exploits, and usually, constructing these signatures is an automatic process without human intervention for the sake of speed. In principle, the automatic signature construction process can produce not only true-positive intrusion signatures but also false-positive ones, the latter of which poses a grave problem because they can be misused to disclose privacy information. Manual signature checking (for a whitelist) can solve the problem, but it slows down the reaction time for an attack dramatically. In this paper, we propose a mechanism to generate signatures automatically while preserving the privacy information. Essentially, we transform the original feature values within an audit trail instance into feature ranges, and then use these feature ranges to construct a privacy-preserved intrusion signature. Our current focus is on the methods constructing feature ranges, and for this purpose, several methods are proposed to discover feature ranges. The experimental results are quite encouraging: the transformation from values to ranges leads not only to the preservation of privacy but also to the enhancement of the detection performance.

1 Introduction

The research on intrusion detection has been intensively pursued in the last 30 years [1], and till now, most successful products (e.g., Snort [15], Bro [12]) are based on a database of intrusion signatures, which consist of characteristic elements of intrusions. Most, if not all, intrusion signatures are mined by security experts after the event using the audit trails left by these intrusions. This manual procedure usually hinders the timely spread of intrusion signatures, making intrusion detection systems useless for detecting worms, especially for fast-spreading worms that can infect most vulnerable computers in the Internet within 30 minutes [17].

For this reason, a lot of solutions have been proposed to mine intrusion signatures automatically. For example, Honeycomb[4], Autograph[3] and EarlyBird[16] used the prevalence of a byte sequence within the worm traffic assuming that the traffic has a large volume, and that there is an invariant bytestring in it. The later assumption could be defeated by polymorphic worms, so PolyGraph[9] is then proposed to alleviate the assumption using the logic relations between several small invariant byte sequences.

C. Lambrinoudakis, G. Pernul, A M. Tjoa (Eds.): TrustBus 2007, LNCS 4657, pp. 54–64, 2007.

However, these systems will generate some false-positive signatures unavoidably [4,3,16,9]. In other words, if these signatures are deployed widely in the Internet, the privacy information within the false-positive signatures will be disclosed. In order to eliminate the possibility, all of them apply the whitelisting strategy based on consensus. In short, the privacy information could be included in such a signature (1) if a sensitive document is intensively circulated in an enterprise, and/or (2) if some 'privacy information' is deliberately inserted to mislead these worm signature generators [13]. The problem becomes worse by the large amplification due to its instant and wide deployment [8]. At present, manually checking on these signatures is the only solution to the problem but it could slow down the reaction time to an intrusion.

In this paper, we present a practical mechanism to generate intrusion signatures automatically while preserving the privacy information within these signatures. Specifically, the feature values in any audit trail are converted into feature ranges to meet the privacy requirement. Since the feature ranges hide the exact sensitive values, the signature after conversion will not disclose any privacy information [19,20]. Furthermore, noise feature ranges could be inserted into the signature to further preserve the privacy information. Xu and Ning [19,20] have shown that the privacy information within values can be preserved using ranges. Therefore, we used their results directly and shifted our efforts to other indispensable parts in the mechanism, where we evaluated several methods in constructing feature ranges from feature values in training audit trails.

The remaining parts of this paper are organized as follows. The design is given in section 2. As an indispensable part in the design, the construction of feature ranges is proposed in Section 3, and we evaluated our proposal in Section 4. Finally, we review the research and conclude the paper.

2   Automatic Assembly of Privacy-Preserved Intrusion Signatures

In this section, using the theoretical framework proposed in [6], we propose a mechanism to automatically build privacy-preserved intrusion signatures.

2.1   Theoretical Basis for Intrusion Detection

In a nutshell, the framework introduces three new concepts to formalize the process of intrusion detection: `feature range`, `NSA label` and `compound feature`. Every instance in a training audit trail can be represented by a feature range of a high-order compound feature, and every feature range has a NSA label, which is used to detect behaviors in test audit trails. In detail, the value of every feature in an instance is first replaced with a feature range, which is gleaned by extending its value so that the extension does not conflict with other existing values. Secondly, the feature ranges of all features are compounded using cartesian products to build a (training or test) behavior signature for intrusion detection.

Within this basis, it is supposed that there are a training audit trail and a feature vector $FV = \{F_1, \ldots, F_n\}$. For every feature F_i, a series of feature ranges $R_{F_i}^1, \ldots, R_{F_i}^m$ is first mined from the training audit trails. Using feature ranges of all features, the behavior signatures $Sig_1, Sig_2 \ldots, Sig_l$ are constructed for intrusion detection. In the

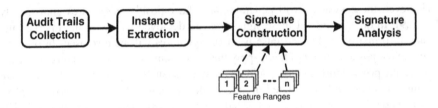

Fig. 1. The design of a signature assembly line

detection phase, a test instance is formalized as a signature Sig_t, and it is detected in accordance with whether it matches any existing behavior signature.

2.2   A Signature Assembly Line

Obviously, in the above theoretical basis, a signature can be constructed automatically provided that the feature ranges of all features are predefined. Using this property, we design a signature assembly line for intrusion detection as illustrated in Figure 1, in which automatic signature assemblers, who have *no knowledge* about intrusions or intrusion detection, construct the signatures automatically and mechanically.

The signature assembly line consists of four modules. The first module collects the audit trails of a computing resource for intrusion detection. For example, Libpcap[7], winpcap[18] etc. The second module extracts an instance from the collected audit trails using a set of predefined features. From the instance, automatic signature assemblers construct a signature by replacing the values of the instance with their corresponding feature ranges. In the last module 'signature analysis', the signatures are post-processed for further detection and/or identification.

Privacy-Preserving Within the Signature Assembly Line. We argue that the privacy information within a signature can be preserved if all of its feature values are replaced by feature ranges, hiding the real values [20,19]. The extent of privacy-preserving can be represented by the extension of a real value to a feature range. In addition, the feature range can be further replaced by an index to provide more privacy-protection.

In the theoretical basis [6], there are two ways to extend a value into a feature range. First, a feature range can be achieved by including the values as well as its neighboring values while such inclusion will not lead to any conflict in the behaviors of a computing resource. By conflict, we mean that, in the collected audit trails, two values falling into the same feature range have different behavior labels (e.g., one is 'normal', another is 'buffer-overflow'). Secondly, we can further extend a feature range in a signature by inserting *noise* if such insertion does not lead to conflicts. For example, suppose that there is a signature "$\{duration = [2s, 5s], protocol = TCP, totalpackets = [100, 300]\}$" with the behavior label 'normal', a non-existing range of *totalpackets* '[1400, 2500]' is considered noise if the behavior label of the extended signature "$\{duration = [2s, 5s], protocol = TCP, totalpackets = [100, 300] \cup [1400, 2500]\}$" is also 'normal'. This is consistent with the fact that there is no behavior from the computing resource matching the signature "$\{duration = [2s, 5s], protocol = TCP, totalpackets = [1400, 2500]\}$". Further study on noise injection is left for our future work.

Our Research Focus. Within the signature assembly line, the first two modules are well-studied in literatures and existing tools [7,18], and the last module can be achieved using several existing work. For example, the signatures can be labeled to fine-tune the behavior models on the fly [5]. These signatures can be correlated to build attack scenarios [11]. In addition, the statistical analysis on signatures was also applied to study the characteristics of the audit trails, and further to identify the anomalies [2].

The signature construction is the most important module in the assembly line because it is critical to guarantee the privacy within the output signatures, and to make the assembly process automatic. Nonetheless, little work has been done on this module. In the following sections, we will solely focus on this module of signature construction.

3   Discovering Feature Ranges

To assemble a signature automatically, it is important to build feature ranges of every feature. Specifically, in order to eliminate uncertainty in the assembly line, the feature ranges of every feature F should be collected in advance such that $R_F^1 \cup R_F^2 \cup \ldots = Dom(F)$. For numerical feature values, only a subset of the possible values are obtained from the training audit trails. The anomalousness of a novel value (i.e., *its NSA label in our framework*) is inferred from existing values. However, for a nominal feature, it is difficult to do such inference since all values are independent. Therefore, each of known nominal feature values is considered as a feature range by itself, and *a special feature range R_F^0 is assigned if a new value occurs*. In other words, our feature range discovery method is mostly applied to discrete and continuous features.

Inferring the NSA label of the new value can be performed using NSA labels of the neighboring values. This, in turn, requires that we should have a clear and unambiguous way to determine whether two values are neighboring. We use the following definition to determine whether two (numerical) values are neighbors.

Definition 1. *Two numerical values v_1 and v_2 are neighbors if there are no value falling between them in the training audit trails.*

Next, we address the question how to assign a NSA label to the new value given its left and right neighbors v_1 and v_2. The answer lies in building the feature ranges in a systematic manner so that the space (v_1, v_2) is completely covered by one or more suitably labeled feature ranges. We first collect all values, $v_1, v_2, \ldots, v_l$, and their NSA labels. Subsequently, the feature ranges are determined and labeled using several different methods as discussed below.

3.1   Methods to Build Feature Ranges

Suppose there are two neighboring values v_i and v_{i+1} ($i < l$), the NSA label of the intervening space (v_i, v_{i+1}) could be determined by $L(v_i)$ and/or $L(v_{i+1})$. If $L(v_i) = L(v_{i+1})$, the space $[v_i, v_{i+1}]$ will be assigned the same NSA label as $L(v_i)$. Otherwise, the space $[v_i, v_{i+1}]$ will be split into two parts, LS_i and US_i, based on different splitting strategies: S1 : *equal splitting*; S2 : *frequency-based splitting*; S3 : *intrusion-constant splitting*.

These splitting strategies are defined below. The NSA label of LS_i is assigned as $L(v_i)$, and the NSA label of US_i is $L(v_{i+1})$. The total size in US_i and LS_i is $v_{i+1} - v_i + \varepsilon$ if these two parts are not overlapping, where ε is the value precision of the feature.

We also evaluated the significance of overlapping feature ranges. This is due to the common argument that overlapping feature ranges could detect more intrusion variations in practice. We use a parameter O_s that determines the amount of overlapping around the splitting boundary between two neighboring feature ranges. A zero value for O_s indicates non-overlapping boundary between neighboring ranges.

S0: No Splitting. For comparison, we will evaluate an extreme scenario when every value is simply considered as a feature range. This scenario is regarded as a baseline for the usefulness of assigning and splitting unknown feature subspace since we have not conducted any generalization in building feature ranges.

S1: Equal Splitting. If $L(v_i) \neq L(v_{i+1})$, the splitting point is $\frac{v_i+v_{i+1}+\varepsilon}{2}$. Splitting with this point, the two parts are $LS_i = [v_i, \frac{v_i+v_{i+1}+\varepsilon+O_s}{2})$ and $US_i = [\frac{v_i+v_{i+1}+\varepsilon-O_s}{2}, v_{i+1}]$.

S2: Frequency-Based Splitting. We also collect the frequency information of all values in the training audit trails, $Fr_{v_1}, Fr_{v_2}, \ldots, Fr_{v_l}$. If $L(v_i) \neq L(v_{i+1})$, the splitting point is $v_i + \varepsilon + (v_{i+1} - v_i - \varepsilon) * \frac{Fr_{v_i}}{Fr_{v_i}+Fr_{v_{i+1}}}$. Splitting with this point, the two parts are $LS_i = [v_i, v_i + \varepsilon + (v_{i+1} - v_i - \varepsilon + O_s) * \frac{Fr_{v_i}}{Fr_{v_i}+Fr_{v_{i+1}}})$ and $US_i = [v_{i+1} - (v_{i+1} - v_i - \varepsilon + O_s) * \frac{Fr_{v_{i+1}}}{Fr_{v_i}+Fr_{v_{i+1}}}, v_{i+1}]$.

S3: Intrusion-constant Splitting. Assume that there is a constant I_c. If $L(v_i) \neq L(v_{i+1})$, it is split and the two parts LS_i and US_i are labeled as follows. (1) $LS_i = [v_i, v_{i+1} - I_c - O_s)$ and $US_i = [v_{i+1} - I_c, v_{i+1}]$ if $L(v_i) = `N'$ and $L(v_{i+1}) = `A'$; and (2) $LS_i = [v_i, v_i + I_c)$ and $US_i = [v_i + I_c - O_s, v_{i+1}]$ if $L(v_i) = `A'$ and $L(v_{i+1}) = `N'$. Otherwise, the unknown part will be split equally as in *S1*.

The overlapping parameter O_s may lead to an incorrect LS_i or US_i whose boundaries are outside the interval $[v_i, v_{i+1}]$. These boundaries are manipulated to make sure that the splitting is applied only to the interval $[v_i, v_{i+1}]$. Figure 2 illustrates one example of splitting an unknown feature subspace using S1, S2 and S3 with $O_s = 0$, $\varepsilon = 1$. There are two feature values $v_1 = 10$ and $v_2 = 15$, and $Fr_{v_1} = 1$, $Fr_{v_2} = 3$, $L(v_1) = `N'$ and $L(v_2) = `A'$. Using S1 in (b), the splitting point is $\frac{v_i+v_{i+1}+1}{2} = 13$, $LS_1 = [10, 13)$ and $US_1 = [13, 15]$. Using S2 in (c), the splitting point is $v_i+\varepsilon+(v_{i+1}-v_i-\varepsilon)*\frac{Fr_{v_i}}{Fr_{v_i}+Fr_{v_{i+1}}} = 12$, $LS_1 = [10, 12)$ and $US_1 = [12, 15]$. Using S3 with $I_c = 1$ in (d), $LS_1 = [10, 14)$ and $US_1 = [14, 15]$.

Furthermore, two feature ranges are merged if they are neighboring with the same NSA label. The merging is used to decrease the number of feature ranges. Specifically,

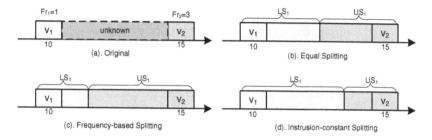

Fig. 2. Splitting strategies for an unknown feature subspace

the two neighboring ranges R_i and R_{i+1}, if $L(R_i) = L(R_{i+1})$, is merged into a feature range. That's also why the unknown subspace is split only if $L(v_i) \neq L(v_{i+1})$.

Finally, we evaluate the different splitting strategies using a labeled test dataset. The test instance in the dataset feeds into the signature assembly line, and the outputted signature will be detected to determine whether it is in the behavior models. Based on the number of instances that are identified correctly, we can determine the usefulness of the splitting strategies.

4   Experiments: A Case Study

In our experiments, we evaluated the effectiveness of the assembly line in two aspects: (1) the influence of feature range conversion on the detection performance, and (2) the difference of our proposed splitting strategies.

We have chosen a typical and widely-used dataset from KDD CUP 1999 contest[1]. The value precision of discrete features is $\varepsilon_d = 1$, and the value precision of continuous features is $\varepsilon_c = 0.01$. We design our experiments in two phases. First, we sample some instances from the training and test datasets. We randomly sample 10000 instances from the total 4898431 training instances and 500 instances from the total 311029 test instances. To make our evaluation results convincing, we give three pairs of such training and test samples. Secondly, we perform the evaluation on the complete datasets.

4.1   Evaluating S0~S3 Splitting Strategies

Table 1 gives the notations used in this section to describe the detection performance.

Table 2 shows the detection performance when there is no label assigning and splitting for unknown feature subspaces. Obviously, most instances in the three test samples as well as the whole test dataset cannot be identified as their original labels, especially for normal behaviors. Specifically, only few normal instances are identified correctly, but more than half intrusive instances can be identified correctly, and there are fewer false negatives in comparison. In S0, an instance will be identified if it is identical to an existing instance in the training audit trails. Thus, the performance in Table 2 indicates that normal behaviors will generate different instances in their audit trails, but for intrusive behaviors, more than half of them will generate known instances.

---

[1] Please refer to http://www-cse.ucsd.edu/users/elkan/clresults.html

Table 1. Notations used in detection results

INDEX	NOTATIONS	ORIGINAL CLASS	DETECTION RESULTS
1	$\#_{NN}$	normal	normal
2	$\#_{NA}$	normal	anomaly
3	$\#_{II}$	intrusion	original intrusion
4	$\#_{IA}$	intrusion	anomaly
5	$\#_{IN}$	intrusion	normal

Table 2. S0: Without Label Assigning and Splitting

Sample Pair	Normal	Intrusion	$\#_{NN}$	$\#_{NA}$	$\#_{II}$	$\#_{IA}$	$\#_{IN}$
Pair 1	103	397	0	103	203	193	1
Pair 2	91	409	0	91	216	193	0
Pair 3	108	392	5	103	193	198	1
Complete	60953	250436	7669	52924	201537	45640	3259

Table 3. Evaluating S1, S2 and S3 Splitting Strategies. To save space, we have merged several rows because they have the same detection performance.

(**Pair 1**) Normal:Intrusion=103:397

S?	I_c	O_s	$\#_{NN}$	$\#_{NA}$	$\#_{II}$	$\#_{IA}$	$\#_{IN}$
S1	-	0	35	68	280	115	2
S1	-	1	35	68	281	114	2
S1	-	2,3,5,10	35	68	281	114	2
S2	-	0,1,2,3,5,10	35	68	280	115	2
S3	0	0	35	68	280	115	2
S3	1	0	35	68	280	115	2
S3	2	0	35	68	281	114	2
S3	3	0	35	68	280	115	2
S3	5	0	35	68	280	115	2
S3	10	0	35	68	281	114	2
S3	0	1,2,3,5,10	35	68	280	115	2

(**Pair 2**) Normal:Intrusion=91:409

S?	I_c	O_s	$\#_{NN}$	$\#_{NA}$	$\#_{II}$	$\#_{IA}$	$\#_{IN}$
S1	-	0,1,2,3	39	52	294	113	2
S1	-	5	39	52	293	114	2
S1	-	10	39	52	292	115	2
S2	-	0,1,2,3,5,10	39	52	292	115	2
S3	0	0	39	52	290	117	2
S3	1	0	39	52	291	116	2
S3	2	0	39	52	291	116	2
S3	3	0	39	52	292	115	2
S3	5	0	39	52	294	113	2
S3	10	0	39	52	294	113	2
S3	0	1,2,3,5,10	39	52	290	117	2

(**Pair 3**) Normal:Intrusion=108:392

S?	I_c	O_s	$\#_{NN}$	$\#_{NA}$	$\#_{II}$	$\#_{IA}$	$\#_{IN}$
S1	-	0,1,2,3,5,10	45	63	273	115	4
S2	-	0,1,2,3,5,10	45	63	273	115	4
S3	0,1,2,3,5,10	0	45	63	273	115	4
S3	0	1,2,3,5,10	45	63	273	115	4

S1,S2,S3 Splitting Strategies. In comparison with Table 2, the overall detection performance has been enhanced after applying S1/S2/S3 splitting strategies in Table 3 and Table 4. For normal behaviors, the performance enhancement is almost the same for different splitting strategies. Although the performance enhancement for intrusive behaviors is a little different, it is small enough to be negligible in comparison with the overall detection performance, especially for the sample pair 3. There are two additional possible reasons for the small difference between S1/S2/S3. First, in the training audit trails, there are very few unknown feature subspaces for these three splitting strategies. Secondly, in the test audit trails, there are few instances whose feature values fall into the unknown feature subspaces. If these *two factors* were not present, we could conclude with certainty that the splitting strategies S1/S2/S3 are indistinguishable in their effectiveness in discovering feature ranges.

Table 4. Evaluating S1, S2 and S3 Splitting Strategies

(**Complete**) Normal:Intrusion=60593:250436

S?	I_c	O_s	$\#_{NN}$	$\#_{NA}$	$\#_{II}$	$\#_{IA}$	$\#_{IN}$
S1	-	0	57102	3491	215834	21636	12966
S1	-	1	57103	3490	215834	21636	12966
S1	-	2	57103	3490	215834	21636	12966
S1	-	3	57103	3490	215834	21636	12966
S1	-	5	57104	3489	215834	21636	12966
S1	-	10	57104	3489	215834	21636	12966
S2	-	0	57104	3489	215832	21638	12966
S2	-	1	57106	3487	215836	21634	12966
S2	-	2	57106	3487	215836	21634	12966
S2	-	3	57106	3487	215836	21634	12966
S2	-	5	57106	3487	215836	21634	12966
S2	-	10	57106	3487	215836	21634	12966
S3	0	0	57106	3487	215829	21641	12966
S3	1	0	57103	3490	215833	21637	12966
S3	2	0	57103	3490	215833	21637	12966
S3	3	0	57103	3490	215833	21637	12966
S3	5	0	57103	3490	215833	21637	12966
S3	10	0	57104	3489	215831	21639	12966
S3	0	1	57106	3487	215829	21641	12966
S3	0	2	57106	3487	215829	21641	12966
S3	0	3	57106	3487	215829	21641	12966
S3	0	5	57106	3487	215829	21641	12966
S3	0	10	57106	3487	215829	21641	12966

Table 5. Detection performance before and after feature range transformation

Sample Pair	Before (%)				After (%)			
	FAR	FPR	DR	IR	FAR	FPR	DR	IR
Pair 1	20.64	100.00	99.75	51.13	14.69	66.02	99.50	70.53
Pair 2	18.20	100.00	100.00	52.81	11.38	57.14	99.51	71.88
Pair 3	20.89	95.37	99.74	49.23	13.97	58.33	98.98	69.64
Complete	17.63	86.83	98.70	80.47	1.45	5.76	94.82	86.18

Comparing the performance enhancement between the test samples in Table 3 and the whole test dataset Table 4, we could make the same conclusion about the usefulness of these splitting strategies in this case study. In other words, the influence of incompleteness in the training audit trails on our conclusions is very small.

4.2 Detection Performance

To explicitly state the usefulness of the signature assembly line, we quantify the detection performance before and after the feature range transformation: false alarm rate $FAR = \frac{\#_{NA}}{\#_{NA}+\#_{IA}+\#_{II}}$, false positive rate $FPR = \frac{\#_{NA}}{\#_{NN}+\#_{NA}}$, detection rate $DR = \frac{\#_{II}+\#_{IA}}{\#_{IN}+\#_{II}+\#_{IA}}$, and intrusion identification rate $IR = \frac{\#_{II}}{\#_{IN}+\#_{II}+\#_{IA}}$.

From Table 5, it is clear that the feature range transformation is effective by lowering false alarm rate FAR, false positive rate FPR and enhancing the intrusion identification capability IR, all of which are desirable for intrusion detection.

In summary, instead of regarding every occurring feature value as a feature range, we should split the unknown feature subspaces to enhance the usefulness of feature ranges for signature assemblers. Thus, we can identify more instances in the detection phase. In our case study, we also found that the overlapping scheme has no use in collecting feature ranges, and that the difference of these three splitting strategies is so insignificant that it can be negligible.

5   Related Work

Our signature assembly line is capable of generating signatures automatically while preserving the privacy information within intrusion signatures. Lincoln et al. [8] has shown the necessity to provide privacy protection in generating alerts. Xu and Ning [19,20] used the feature ranges to protect the privacy in alert correlation. We addressed the privacy information in a signature, which can be spread into the whole Internet while an alert can be contained in several central processing units. Since we have not seen any existing work addressing the privacy problem in intrusion signatures, we review the existing methods for (manual and automatic) signature generation.

Existing Intrusion Signatures. In general, intrusion signatures include the characteristic elements of intrusions/attacks. Existing intrusion detection systems provide different signature languages with varying expressiveness, e.g., Snort[15], RealSecure[14], most of which are only used to express the network-based intrusions. For example, Snort signatures only represent network behaviors, and it is packet-based basically. At present, there is a general lack of systematic and precise definition of intrusion signatures that can be widely applicable in both host-based and network-based scenarios. Furthermore, the creation of these signatures is a tedious, manual process that requires detailed knowledge about software vulnerabilities and the intrusions themselves. Even worse, there does not exist any formal mechanism to guarantee of the quality of the manually constructed signatures. There is no privacy problem because most of these signatures are inspected manually after the event.

Worm Signatures. A lot of work (e.g., Honeycomb[4], Autograph[3], EarlyBird[16] and PolyGraph[9]) has been conducted recently to generate worm signatures automatically. Honeycomb[4] is an automatic tool to generate worm signatures, using pattern detection techniques and packet header conformance tests, from the suspicious traffic captured by honeypots. Autograph[3] tries to automatically detect the signature(s) of any worm that propagates by randomly scanning IP addresses, without knowing the worm's payload or time of introduction in advance. In PolyGraph[9], a series of tokens is first extracted from the suspicious flows. Then, a clustering technique is applied to divide the suspicious flows into several clusters, and for every cluster, a worm signature, which may consist of several disjoint invariants, is generated to match every flow in it. With a specific requirement[16] for high-speed implementation, Earlybird[16] is built in a packet granularity rather than the flow granularity in the above three systems. In summary, these four techniques try to identify *a single contiguous or disjoint invariant pattern* in the worm traffic, which will not lead to false positive in the detection phase. In addition, TaintCheck [10] can further help signature generation systems using information on the vulnerability and how it is exploited.

However, none of the above techniques considered the privacy issue in their signatures and all of them used invariant(s) within the network traffic to build signatures. Our signature assembly line can complement them to preserve the privacy information within the original signature outputted.

6   Conclusions

In this paper, we have proposed a signature assembly line to generate privacy-preserved signatures. It can provide privacy protection for the audit trails by transforming feature values into feature ranges. In our framework, we have proven the feasibility of the transformation, and our experiments have shown its effectiveness in that it not only preserves the privacy, but also enhances the detection performance. Our case study has also shown that though splitting of uncovered feature ranges improve performance, it is relatively insensitive to the particular splitting strategy adopted as well as the allowance of overlapping feature ranges. In our future work, we will further study the effects of noise injection in intrusion signatures.

References

1. Anderson, J.: Computer security threat monitoring and surveillance. Technical report, James P Anderson Co., Fort Washington, Pennsylvania (April 1980)
2. Arshad, D., Chan, P.: Identifying outliers via clustering for anomaly detection. Technical Report CS-2003-19, Computer Science Department, Florida Institute of Technology (2003)
3. Kim, H.-A., Karp, B.: Autograph: Toward automated, distributed worm signature detection. In: USENIX Security Symposium, pp. 271–286 (2004)
4. Kreibich, C., Crowcroft, J.: Honeycomb: creating intrusion detection signatures using honeypots. SIGCOMM Comput. Commun. Rev. 34(1), 51–56 (2004)
5. Li, Z., Das, A.: Visualizing and identifying intrusion context from system calls trace. In: Proceedings of 20th Annual Computer Security Applications Conference (December 2004)
6. Li, Z., Das, A., Zhou, J.: Theoretical Basis for Intrusion Detection. In: Proceedings of 6th IEEE Information Assurance Workshop (IAW) (June 2005)
7. libpcap, http://sourceforge.net/projects/libpcap/
8. Lincoln, P., Porras, P.A., Shmatikov, V.: Privacy-preserving sharing and correlation of security alerts. In: USENIX Security Symposium, pp. 239–254 (2004)
9. Newsome, J., Karp, B., Song, D.: Polygraph: Automatically generating signatures for polymorphic worms. Proceedings of IEEE S&P, 226–241 (2005)
10. Newsome, J., Song, D.: Dynamic taint analysis for automatic detection, analysis, and signature generation of exploits on commodity software. In: Proceedings of the 12th Annual Network and Distributed System Security Symposium (NDSS05) (2005)
11. Ning, P., Xu, D., Healey, C.G., Amant, R.S.: Building attack scenarios through integration of complementary alert correlation method. In: NDSS (2004)
12. Paxon, V.: Bro: A system for detecting network intruders in real-time. In: Proc. 7th USENIX Security Symposium (1998)
13. Perdisci, R., Dagon, D., Lee, W., Fogla, P., Sharif, M.: Misleadingworm signature generators using deliberate noise injection. Proceedings of the 2006 IEEE S&P, 17–31 (2006)
14. RealSecure. http://www.realsecure.com

15. Roesch, M.: Snort - lightweight intrusion detection for networks. In: Proceedings of USENIX LISA (1999)
16. Singh, S., Estan, C., Varghese, G., Savage, S.: Automated worm fingerprinting. In: OSDI, pp. 45–60 (2004)
17. Weaver, N.C.: A warhol worm: An internet plague in 15 minutes!, 2001, http://www.cs.berkeley.edu/ nweaver/warhol.old.html (as of Feburary 2006)
18. winpcap, http://www.winpcap.org/
19. Xu, D., Ning, P.: Privacy-preserving alert correlation: A concept hierarchy based approach. In: Srikanthan, T., Xue, J., Chang, C.-H. (eds.) ACSAC 2005. LNCS, vol. 3740, pp. 537–546. Springer, Heidelberg (2005)
20. Xu, D., Ning, P.: A flexible approach to intrusion alert anonymization and correlation. In: Proceedings of 2nd IEEE Communications Society/CreateNet International Conference on Security and Privacy in Communication Networks, August 2006, IEEE Computer Society Press, Los Alamitos (2006)

Privacy Assurance: Bridging the Gap Between Preference and Practice

Tariq Ehsan Elahi and Siani Pearson

Trusted Systems Laboratory, Hewlett Packard Research Labs, Filton Road, Stoke Gifford,
Bristol, BS34 8QZ, UK
tariq.ee@gmail.com, siani.pearson@hp.com

Abstract. Personal identifying information is released without much control from the end user to service providers. We describe a system to scrutinize the stated claims of a service provider on safeguarding PII by interrogating their infrastructure. We attempt to empower end users by providing means to communicate their privacy concerns in a common language understood by the service provider, allowing them to set baseline privacy practices for service providers to adhere to, and providing a means of retrieving information from the service provider in the common language to base their PII release decisions.

1 Introduction

This paper will describe a system for providing privacy assurance information to end-users so that they can make an informed decision about releasing their PII to others, be they merchants, governments, or business partners. It hopes to be simple to use and deploy, give the end user more control over their PII, and be able to bridge the level of abstraction between high level privacy concerns and technical back-end implementation details.

1.1 Problems and Motivation

PII abuse can come in many shapes, like leaked credit card numbers, email addresses being sold to mailing lists, or search term histories [1]. Granted that the potential for abuse is always present the merchant can take steps to give consumers **assurance** that they can be **trusted** with private information.

Another compelling reason for businesses to take privacy seriously is regulations [2] and laws [3] concerning privacy of consumer records. The penalties are steep and the loss of reputation is unpalatable. Being compliant enhances the business's image with consumers since it shows awareness of privacy issues [4].

Efforts like Trust-e [5], BBBOnLine [6], and Platform for Privacy Preferences (P3P) [7] — amongst other privacy seal programs — help to provide assurance of merchants' willingness to take the issue of privacy seriously, but consumers still express dissatisfaction and want more safeguards for their Personally Identifiable Information (PII) [8,9].

The end user should also be allowed to choose how their PII should be handled [10]. To allow end user participation, unlike privacy seals which have no means of

C. Lambrinoudakis, G. Pernul, A M. Tjoa (Eds.): TrustBus 2007, LNCS 4657, pp. 65–74, 2007.

asking about the end user's choice, P3P, is an effort to give the end user some way of defining their own usage policies for their PII [11].

Unfortunately, neither of the above provide any means to interrogate the business and its processes to see if the promises being made can be fulfilled [12,13,14]. What is needed is for there to be some connection between what is stated on the privacy seal or P3P privacy policy and what really goes on within the business and its privacy capabilities [14].

This brings us to the problem that end users are not privacy experts Instead of discussing privacy at this mind-boggling level it is better to move the discussion to higher and more abstract levels where the business can express their privacy profile in terms that the end user can understand [15].

Another problem is how much information to provide. The right amount of information should be sufficient for end users' needs and also not be too much of a burden for the business in terms of volume and exposure.

1.2 Goals

What is needed is a solution that involves consumers more, is more transparent, and most of all simple [9]. We believe that a privacy assurance solution should allow communication between end-users and service providers in a common language, establish guidelines on levels of assurance information, provide mappings between privacy preferences and the back end, and above all provide trust in these mappings.

2 Our Solution

We will begin by examining how end users and businesses can communicate with each other in ways understandable to both. Then we will see how to reconcile each side's privacy concerns. Afterwards we'll look at how the high level expressions of privacy are mapped to back-end privacy technologies. Then we will consider how privacy information is provisioned on the business side which will lead us, finally, to a discussion of where and how trust fits into the solution.

It should be noted that the term "privacy policies or policy" as used in this paper is different from the typical definition used in privacy and security circles. It is usually used to define a formal means of capturing the privacy characteristics of system in terms of predicates involving rules on how to manipulate the data. In this paper the term is used to define a set of privacy preferences or practices that end users and service providers are interested in which are stated in natural language, and do not have strictly formal underlying semantics. This makes machine processing more difficult but in sections 2.1.1 and 2.2 we give an initial attempt of reconciling our privacy policies with processing systems.

2.1 Clauses: A Vocabulary for Expressing Privacy Policies

Both users and service providers will have the freedom to create policies to suit their needs. In order to bring the two together a common vocabulary is developed. This comes in the form of privacy statements or privacy clauses which are a basic primitive of our solution. A clause is succinct, clear, and unambiguous and clearly communicates its intended purpose at a level that does not require expert knowledge of privacy systems or their implementation. It is expressed in natural language and it is hoped that both clients and services will be able to understand each other more clearly. This empowers an end-user, whom it is assumed has no technically advanced knowledge, to communicate their privacy preferences in a language they understand. In section 5 we discuss how our policies relate to previous work on policy definition.

An important aspect of clauses is that they are standardized. Since the same pool of statements are being used by both the users and service providers it is an easy matter to match up expected policies with actual ones and negotiate the mismatches. At least in this way the glaring omissions in service providers' policies will become obvious and in the same way unrealistic expectations from users will clear up. When there are deficiencies in specific clauses the totality of the policy must be looked at. The set of clauses that form the policy is a stronger indication of the suitability of a policy than the individual clauses of which it is made up. Even if there is disagreement between a user and the service provider at least both know where the other stands on privacy.

A policy is then just a collection of clauses, crafted for a particular purpose depending on the context of the interaction. For the user interacting with a bank they may invoke an "on-line banking" policy; for a service provider interacting with an on-line shopper they may invoke a "website customer" policy.

Templates for policies can provide a set of clauses that adhere to best practices or commonly held standards. To this a user can add or remove clauses depending on their preferences and needs. Templates are especially geared towards end users who may need help creating a privacy policy that would serve the purposes that the end user needed them for.

There is still a problem of where the clauses come from in the first place, and who provides guidance or establishes what is an appropriate policy for a particular purpose and what is not. In order to facilitate both problems it is important that there be some agreement about privacy in general and clauses and policies in particular. A way of doing this is through standardization. Trusted entities, such as governments or standardization bodies such as the W3C, who have experience in this field through efforts like P3P, can be called upon to provide a working pool of clauses and provide guidance on how to go about creating a privacy policy that is appropriate for a particular activity as a template.

We are aware that positive and negative clauses are subjective but it is hoped that through proactive efforts by privacy experts in concert with privacy groups we can arrive at a standard of privacy expectations and conduct.

2.1.1 Matching End User and Service Provider Privacy Policies Using Clauses

During a transaction where PII is to be divulged to the service provider, the end user can conduct a policy matching activity where the system can compare their privacy preferences (as stated in their privacy policy) to that of the service provider's policy.

The trivial case is when both the end user and service provider policies are identical. In this case there would be no warnings. When this is not the case then the system has two scenarios:

- *Missing Clauses*: This occurs when the service provider does not provide a clause(s) present in the end user's policy. This is flagged by the system and reported to the end user.
- *Excess Clause*: This occurs when the service provider's policy has a clause(s) not present in the end user's policy. This is not cause for alarm since all clauses are privacy positive and the additional clause will only strengthen the privacy policy.

After the matching phase the end user can make a decision on whether or not to divulge their PII. or they can then move to the next stage of the process which is validation of the clauses against capabilities of service provider's back-end systems. We talk about this in section 2.2.

2.2 Mapping and Capability Validation

Once a policy has been set by a service provider the onus is upon them to implement the measures to uphold those policies. The fact that clauses only talk about the "what" and not the "how" allows service providers flexibility in choosing the best solution for their particular infrastructure.

To tie together and bridge the "what" to the "how" there has to be some sort of mapping that facilitates this connection. The main job of this mapping is to communicate the back end privacy controls, processes, and other privacy enhancing features implemented by the service provider through the process of verification of clauses in privacy policies.

Our solution allows each clause to be composed of specific tests that query controls and system components on the back end. In this way a suite of tests can be created that inspects the system and reports back the results that can be used to verify clauses.

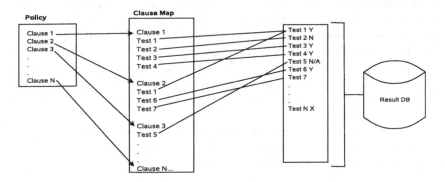

Fig. 1. Mapping clauses to the back end controls through tests

Figure 1 shows how each clause in the privacy policy is mapped to back end tests. A test only validates that the control or feature is in place and working in a known manner. There can be multiple tests on the same control to validate particular attributes, as long as they are relevant to the clause being verified.

Once the proper mapping between clauses and back end controls, via tests, has been established the service provider can now offer the end user a way to verify the claims made on the service provider's privacy policy. This step, called capability checking, is crucial in affording assurance to the end user since it allows the user to see if the service provider is actually able to uphold their promises.

It is important to note that the knowledge of which tests are conducted is security sensitive and it would be a critical weakness against attacks because it would provide information about the nature of the systems on the back end. Therefore, detailed information is filtered out of the transmitted results to the end user. Also no information about the tests to be conducted leaves the service provider. The only information an attacker has is the privacy policy and the clauses. From that the attacker can only make inferences as to the nature of the service provider's back end. The end user does not suffer since all they require is for clauses to be fulfilled, how that is done is beyond their concern, they have the TTP to trust for that.

So far we have assumed that the correct back end controls are in place to ensure the privacy of end users' PII and only those clauses have been put into the privacy policy that are backed up by those controls. This is an obvious area of abuse and so trust has to be introduced here. In our solution trust comes in the form of third parties.

2.3 Trusted Third Parties and the Trust Chain

The missing trust has to come from entities that end users do trust such as trusted third parties (TTPs), like ISO, Trust-e and Verisign [16], or non-government consumer organizations. The way forward is to invite the TTP to scrutinize their back end systems, the mappings and their privacy policies in a compliance verification process similar to ISO 17799 and ISO 27001. If the TTP is satisfied it would issue a trust token that can be presented to the end user at the time of policy matching and verification, thus providing trust in the results and ultimately in the business.

The main concerns of the TTP are:

- Verifying that the controls and privacy enhancing technologies that are implemented by the service provider on their infrastructure are configured and functioning properly
- Verifying that the tests used to interrogate the proper configuration and function of are capturing and analyzing the correct data
- Verifying that the clause-to-test mapping is appropriate and complete
- Maintain the integrity, confidentiality, and availability of trust tokens and service provider data.

It is not the user who is responsible for validating the suitability or appropriateness of the privacy enhancing infrastructure of the service provider, but a trusted third party. The user will only be responsible for checking that third party seals are current and valid and accessing the trustworthiness of the vouching party.

In this way the end user can establish trust based on the reputation of the TTP, while the service provider can benefit from this trust relationship that has already been established, or has a better chance of growing stronger due to the fact that trust is a TTP's business and this shows the good intentions of the business to end users.

In a common usage scenario, the TTP performs its verification of the service provider's back end and how this translates to their privacy policies. It then transfers a trust token to the service provider to display along with their privacy policies as well as with their policy validation results. The TTP will hold a copy of the model, or description, of the service provider's back-end and privacy policy for dispute resolution and as a means of recording the conditions under which the trust token was issued.

After that an end user can ask for privacy policies and/or verification results. The results and the trust token are transmitted back to the end user.

Finally, the end user must now verify that the trust token is valid and intended for this set of results and the privacy policy under scrutiny. The end user can do this via a privacy seal verification scheme, such as one described in [17]. Once the end user has checked the validity of the trust token they can then be assured that the results, whether positive or negative, are correct and worthy of trust.

Also worth noting is the fact that the TTP do not have exclusivity and that both the service provider and end user can utilize any number of TTPs. Situations can arise where no common TTPs are in use between the end user and service provider, at which point the end user can choose to add the TTP and complete or discontinue the transaction.

3 The Implemented System

Now we move on to discuss an implementation of the system described so far. This work is part of an ongoing effort funded by the EU called PRivacy and Identity Management for Europe (PRIME) [18]. This project is a multi-party endeavor with partners across Europe. As such our work is only one component of a large platform and we take for granted work being done by other partners, especially when it provides functionality we can utilize. The system presented has been fully implemented as part of the integrated prototype within PRIME, which is currently at version 2 [18].

The main functionalities provided by the Assurance Control component are to:

- **Compare** privacy polices of the service provider and the privacy preferences of the user and highlight similarities, differences and deficiencies
- **Conduct** capability tests to verify the statements made in the service policy and ensure the service side is capable of fulfilling the promises made in their policy
- **Provide** results of above in a way that allows a user to make informed decisions about releasing their private details, with some guidance built in

For a more in-depth discussion of the specific functions and how the module interacts within the PRIME frame work please refer to [18].

3.1 The End-User Experience

Presenting assurance information in a way that is simple, clutter free, and easily understood is still an area of research. To help direct our interface creation, we have worked in concert with a human computer interface team within PRIME and used their findings from usability tests conducted with end users. The preliminary findings have been published, for further details see [19]. As well, [20] discusses some general guidelines for indicators and their placement that has been incorporated as well in our GUI as well.

Most users claimed that the functionality provided by assurance control was useful and that assurance control features should appear just before release of PII [19].

Although the main purpose of PRIME is to empower individuals in protecting their privacy in customer to business (C2B) scenarios, our system is not limited to this type of usage. With the proper protocols, Businesses to business (B2B) and government to business use cases are also possible.

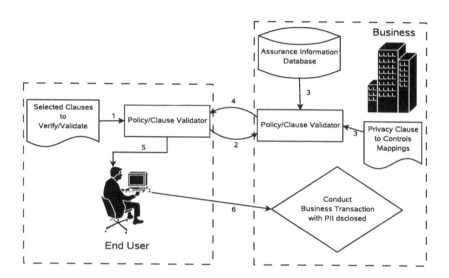

Fig. 2. Capability validation process

A simple walk through is shown in figure 2, corresponding to the following steps:

1. The user, having selecting which clauses they want verified, submits these to his or her capability checking, aka Policy Validator, module.
2. This module communicates this list to its counterpart on the service side and awaits its response.
3. The service-side Policy Validator searches for the clause to test mapping in the mapping file kept on the service side. It then queries the result database for these tests and retrieves their results. It can either aggregate the test results to a level that only verifies that the clause was fulfilled or it can send back more information. This is configurable and left up to service providers to choose how much detail they want to include in test result data.
4. The Policy Validator displays the results to the end user to allow them to make an informed decision about releasing their PII.
5. If the end user is satisfied then they can divulge their PII or if not they can provide feedback to the service provider so that it can make meet user demands in the future.

4 Related Work

There has been a great deal of work done on privacy polices [11,21,22,23,24]. In these policy frameworks the focus has been on access control based on conditional logic. Our polices are just collections or groupings of clauses that serve a particular purpose under a particular context. Since access control plays a big part in the control of PII our solution works in concert with the Access Control Decision Function (ACDF) and Identity Control (IDCTRL) in PRIME, to provide a total privacy package.

P3P is a W3C specification that allows websites and end users to specify their privacy practices and preferences respectively in a standardized way that are easy to retrieve and interpret by end users. There have been many critiques of P3P such as [12,13,21,25]. We shall focus on how our solution differs from P3P, the gaps it fills in, and how P3P could be used within the system we have implemented albeit with changes to its role.

Expressing privacy concerns in P3P is done by defining statements in a machine readable format written in XML [11]. Although there are editors [26] that help with this process, there are two problems that are not yet addressed.

First, end user must know what their privacy vulnerabilities are and how to check if a website will mitigate those risks. Most users are naïve and would not be competent enough to express privacy concerns beyond vague statements.

Second, even with the prerequisite privacy knowledge the definition of privacy polices must be in a language geared towards the facilitation of accessing PII based on conditions. This is a difficult task which our solution simplifies by introducing standardized privacy clauses and templates that are written in human readable form and are unambiguous, concise, and capture privacy concerns based on expert knowledge.

As is also the case with privacy seals, P3P can not link the privacy practices expressed by the website and anything tangible on the back-end. This gap is where our solution introduces mechanisms to check that policies and the technical realities of the website's infrastructure are coherent.

Although P3P has its limitations, its strength as a robust policy definition language and logic model allows it to translate complex privacy clauses into machine readable form. In fact, P3P's strengths could benefit our solution and could be incorporated under the clause layer as the gateway between human readable clauses and service provider result data bases and back end models.

Projects like Privacy Bird [27] from AT&T and Privacy Fox [28] try to bring a simplified and more useful solution to end user by providing a graphical face to P3P. Our solution differs in that instead of just a single aggregate representation embodied by the bird icon we opted to give a more granular output so that the end user could have more context as to exactly what went wrong.

In our solution once the end user divulges their information there is no way for them to sure that the service provider continues to adhere to their privacy practices. One way to combat this is to have a persistent service that monitors the end user's information and checks that the privacy practices are still in place. One such effort is Obligation Manager [29], which is also part of the PRIME framework. Working in concert, they can provide stronger evidence that the service provider is honoring its promises.

5 Future Directions

Since clauses are the central privacy vector they need to be developed further from the select set that are being implemented now. They need to be more complex and recognize complex privacy needs of sophisticated users as well as laws and regulations that businesses must adhere to. They also need to be stated in such a way that is unambiguous in any language. The guidelines for TTP behavior are an open issue that requires research and reflection based on other established TTP standards and the outcome of discussions on privacy.

Presentation of privacy assurance information is an ongoing research effort in concert with the HCI team and efforts will reveal just how much trust can be conveyed between parties and identify the missing pieces in the puzzle.

At the moment the service provider depends on in-house security expertise or third party advice to implement and deploy privacy mechanisms. This dependence on security expertise could be avoided if the clauses themselves provided a set of tests that a service provider had to conduct. It could cut out the third party completely and move the reliance on to the PRIME system itself rather than third parties. The obstacles to resolving this are that service side topologies are not well understood and providing a generic yet robust enough set of tests that would be applicable everywhere is a difficult thing to do at present.

6   Conclusion

We have shown how a common standardized privacy clause pool would help communicate end user concerns as well as service provider promises. With the clauses forming policies we have designed a mapping framework that would allow high level clauses to be mapped to back end technology that would abstract the complexity away for the end user and at the same time allow the service provider flexibility in how they implement and manage their infrastructure. Finally we have shown how trust is injected into this system through trusted third parties and their role in establishing a trust chain. This allows end users to form their own trust relationships with TTPs independent of service providers depending on their preferences and experiences.

In summary, this paper reports work in progress to provide a simple and effective system for providing assurance information and building trust in privacy practices of businesses and other entities whilst being practical for deployment in current infrastructure.

Bibliography

1. AOL Search Data Scandal, http://en.wikipedia.org/wiki/AOL_search_data_scandal
2. Office of the Secretary, Standards for Privacy of Individually Identifiable Health Information, Federal Register, vol. 67–157 (August 2002), http://www.hhs.gov/ocr/ hipaa/ privrulepd.pdf
3. Data Protection Act (1998) - UK, http://www.opsi.gov.uk/ACTS/acts1998/19980029.htm
4. Kobsa, A.: Tailoring Privacy to Users' Needs. In: Bauer, M., Gmytrasiewicz, P.J., Vassileva, J. (eds.) UM 2001. LNCS (LNAI), vol. 2109, pp. 303–313. Springer, Heidelberg (2001)
5. Trust-e Privacy Seal Program, http://www.truste.org/
6. BBBOnLine Privacy Seal Program, http://www.bbbonline.org/privacy/
7. Cranor, L.F., Hogben, G., Langheinrich, M., Marchiori, M., Presler-Marshal, M., Reagle, J., Schunter, M.: The Platform for Privacy Preferences 1.1 (P3P1.1) Specification, W3C Working Draft 10 (February 2006)

8. Berlanger, F., Hiller, J.S., Smith, W.J.: Trustworthiness in electronic commerce: the role of privacy, security, and site attributes. Journal of Strategic Information Systems 11, 245–270 (2002)
9. Shneiderman, B.: Designing Trust Into Online Experiences. Communications of the ACM 43-12, 57–59 (2000)
10. Shneiderman, B.: Designing Trust Into Online Experiences. Communications of the ACM~43-12, 57--59 (2000)
11. Leenes, R., Fischer-Hubner, S. (ed.): Prime Framework version 2, {https://www.prime-project.eu/prime_products/reports/fmwk/pub_del_D14.1.b_ec_wp14.1_V1_final.pdf}
12. Cranor, L.F.: Web Privacy with P3P, O'Reilly and Associates (2002)
13. Clarke, R.: Platform for Privacy Preferences: A Critique, http://www.anu.edu.au/ people/Roger.Clarke/DV/P3PCrit.html
14. Ackerman, M.S.: Privacy in pervasive environments: next generation labelling protocols. In: Personal Ubiquitous Computing 2004, pp. 430–439, Springer, Heidelberg (2004)
15. Pearson, S.: Towards Automated Evaluation of Trust Constraints. In: Stølen, K., Winsborough, W.H., Martinelli, F., Massacci, F. (eds.) iTrust 2006. LNCS, vol. 3986, pp. 252–266. Springer, Heidelberg (2006)
16. PRIME principles, https://www.prime-project.eu/about/principles/
17. VeriSign Identity Protection, http://www.verisign.com/products-services/security-services/identity-protection/index.html
18. Moulinos, K., Iliadis, J., Tsoumas, V.: Towards secure sealing of privacy policies. Information Management & Computer Security 12-4, 350–361 (2004)
19. Sommer, D. (ed.): PRIME Architecture version 2, (will appear mid to late 2007) https://www.primeproject.eu/prime_products/reports/arch/
20. Petterson, J.S.: R1 - First report from the pilot study on privacy technology in the framework of consumer support infrastructure. Working Paper, Department of Information Systems and Centre for HumanIT, Karlstad University, Karlstad (December 2006)
21. Cranor, L.F.: What Do They "Indicate?": Evaluating Security and Privacy Indicators. Interactions, 45–47 (2006)
22. Hogben, G., Jackson, T., Wilikens, M.: A Fully Compliant Research Implementation of the P3P Standard for Privacy Protection: Experiences and Recommendations. In: Gollmann, D., Karjoth, G., Waidner, M. (eds.) ESORICS 2002. LNCS, vol. 2502, pp. 104–125. Springer, Heidelberg (2002)
23. Karjoth, G., Schunter, M., Waidner, M.: Privacy-enabled Services for Enterprise. In: DEXA 2002, IEEE, Los Alamitos (2002)
24. Karjoth, G., Schunter, M., Waidner, M.: Platform for Enterprise Privacy Practices: Privacy-Enabled management of Customer Data. In: Dingledine, R., Syverson, P.F. (eds.) PET 2002. LNCS, vol. 2482, pp. 69–84. Springer, Heidelberg (2003)
25. Backes, M., Pfitzmann, B., Schunter, M.: A Toolkit for Managing Enterprise Privacy Policies. In: Snekkenes, E., Gollmann, D. (eds.) ESORICS 2003. LNCS, vol. 2808, pp. 162–180. Springer, Heidelberg (2003)
26. Clarke, R.: P3P Re-visited, http://www.anu.edu.au/people/Roger.Clarke/DV/P3PRev.html
27. P3P 1.0 Implementation Report, http://www.w3.org/P3P/implementation-report.html
28. AT&T, AT&T Privacy Bird, http://www.privacybird.com
29. Arshad, F.: Privacy Fox – A JavaScript-based P3P Agent for Mozilla Firefox, http://privacyfox.mozdev.org/PaperFinal.pdf
30. Casassa Mont, M.: Dealing with privacy obligations: Important aspects and technical approaches. In: Katsikas, S.K., Lopez, J., Pernul, G. (eds.) TrustBus 2004. LNCS, vol. 3184,Springer, Heidelberg (2004)

Enhancing Optimistic Access Controls with Usage Control

Keshnee Padayachee[1] and J.H.P. Eloff[2]

[1] University of South Africa, School of Computing,
PO Box 392, Pretoria 0002
padayk@unisa.ac.za
[2] Information & Computer Security Architectures Research Group,
Department of Computer Science, University of Pretoria, Pretoria 0002
eloff@cs.up.ac.za

Abstract. With the advent of agile programming, lightweight software processes are being favoured over the highly formalised approaches of the past. Likewise, access control may benefit from a less prescriptive approach with an increasing reliance on users to behave ethically. These ideals correlate with optimistic access controls. However, ensuring that users behave in a trustworthy manner may require more than optimistic access controls. This paper investigates the possibility of enhancing optimistic access controls with usage control to ensure that users conduct themselves in a trustworthy manner. Usage control enables finer-grained control over the usage of digital objects than do traditional access control policies and models. Further to ease the development and maintenance of usage control measures, it is posited that it is completely separated from the application logic by using aspect-oriented programming.

1 Introduction

With the advent of agile programming, lightweight software processes are being favoured over the highly formalised approaches of the 80s and 90s, where the emphasis is on "people not processes". Likewise, access control may benefit from a less prescriptive approach with an increasing reliance on users to behave ethically. These ideals correlate with optimistic access controls which were first advocated by Povey [9]. However, optimistic access controls alone may not be enough to ensure that users behave in a trustworthy manner. This paper firstly investigates the possibility of enhancing optimistic access controls with usage control to ensure that users conduct themselves in a trustworthy manner. Usage control enables finer-grained control over the usage of digital objects than do traditional access control policies and models, as trust management concerns are also given consideration.

It is evidently difficult to implement access control and often in dynamic environments preconfigured access control policies may change dramatically depending on the context. Often in unpredicted circumstances users that are denied access could have prevented a catastrophe had they been allowed access. Consider as an example a nurse – at a hospital that been isolated during a tornado – who needs access to a patient's records but cannot access them as nurses are not authorised to access this

C. Lambrinoudakis, G. Pernul, A M. Tjoa (Eds.): TrustBus 2007, LNCS 4657, pp. 75–82, 2007.

information [9]. The costs of implementing and maintaining complex preconfigured access control policies sometimes far outweigh the benefits. Optimistic controls are retrospective and allow users to exceed their normal privileges. However, if a user accesses information unethically, the consequences could be disastrous. Hence this paper proposes that optimistic access control be enhanced with some form of usage control which may prevent the user from engaging in risky behaviour.

The next section of this paper discusses typical access control methods, while Section 3 presents the concept of optimistic access control. Section 4 describes the concept of usage control as a means to enhance optimistic access control, while the discourse in Section 5 focuses on a possible technique to implement the model proposed using aspect-oriented programming. Section 6 concludes with directions for future work.

2   Background Work on Access Control

Discretionary access control is an access policy that restricts access to files and other system objects such as directories and devices on the basis of the identity of the users and/or the groups to which they belong [12]. With discretionary access control, no control is enforced on the use or dissemination of the information once this information has been released to an authorized user [8]. Discretionary access control is very flexible but highly vulnerable to Trojan Horses. As a result of this inadequacy, mandatory access policies are proposed.

Mandatory access control [11] refers to access control policy decisions that are made beyond the control of the individual owner of the object. A central authority determines what information is to be accessible by whom, and the user cannot change access rights [8]. Mandatory access control is deemed to be superior to discretionary access control as it is not vulnerable to illegal information flows. An illegal flow arises when information is transmitted from one object to another object in violation of the information flow security policy [13]. Even the most dominant model of recent times, the role-based access control model, is vulnerable to illegal information flows, as demonstrated by Chon et al.[1]. Within role-based access control (RBAC), system administrators create roles according to the job functions performed in a company or organization, grant permissions (access authorization) to those roles, and then assign users to the roles on the basis of their specific job responsibilities and qualifications [15].

These models often assume that users want and are able to determine permissions before the actual access is made. These mechanisms require a priori setting of permissions that are difficult to specify and maintain in highly dynamic environments. In other words, these models assume that human beings cannot behave in a trustworthy manner and the system has to prevent them from behaving in an undesirable manner. Human trust is subjective and context specific and therefore it is difficult to form a definition that incorporates all views and types of trusts [4]. Integrating trust/distrust into the computing world requires transforming a complex social concept into an easy-to-use technical product that embodies the basic principles of trust/distrust [3]. Human beings make decisions based on the circumstances of a particular situation. For example, within a typical mandatory access control model, *doctors* may have the privilege to view sensitive information but *nurses* and *clerks* would not. With role-based access control, the role could be based on job responsibilities. For instance, a patient's record can be written by any health professional assigned to the role of ward physician [10]. However, this does not guarantee that a valid user demonstrates integrity or acts professionally.

Hence, if software systems could trust humans to decide how and when they can access information, this would be a more accurate assessment of trust. Trust on a humanistic level is highly complex and there are a variety of factors that influence trust. The emergence of trust-based access control frameworks is largely due to communications occurring among parties where each party is unknown. This communication is typically decentralised. A new type of access control is needed where the access is not preconfigured and the user is essentially trusted to behave ethically. If it is left to humans to make that judgement and not to the information system, then the complexity of the system is shifted to allow all the users to interact with the system.

While pessimistic access controls such as DAC, MAC and RBAC maybe highly appropriate in certain contexts, optimistic access controls may be more appropriate in other circumstances. For instance, Stevens and Wulf [16] considered an actual interorganizational co-operation scenario where it was found that traditional access control did not comply with the organization's requirements and that co-operation and competitive reasons motivate the use of interactive and optimistic access controls. Hong and Landany [5] also established that there is a need for privacy-sensitive systems to have a range of control and feedback mechanisms for building pessimistic, optimistic and mixed-initiative applications.

3 Optimistic Access Control

Optimistic access control is useful in cases where openness and availability are more important than complete confidentiality. Optimistic access control also has the advantage that it is far easier for people to use, since it is rather difficult for individuals to predict all of the possible usage scenarios and thus all of the necessary permissions. Optimistic access control is based on the assumption that most access control processes will be legitimate, and it relies on controls external to the system to ensure that the organization's security policy is maintained. The scheme allows users to exceed their normal privileges in a way which is constrained so that it is securely audited and may be rolled back [9].

According to Povey [9] the optimistic enforcement of security policies is retrospective and relies on administrators to detect unreasonable access and take steps to compensate for the action. Such steps might include the following:

- Undoing illegitimate modifications
- Taking punitive action (e.g. firing or prosecuting individuals)
- Removing privileges

Most access control methods require setting of permissions that are difficult to specify and maintain in highly dynamic environments. Optimistic access controls trust human beings to perform legitimate accesses and take retrospective action after such trust is breached. The initial costs of implementing optimistic access control methods are minimal. However, the consequences of a breach in trust could be disastrous. If such a breach is discovered, it could involve prosecution or require the performing of a roll-back procedure. Although the roll-back procedure may be able to restore the system to its original state prior to the breach, it is highly likely that it may not be able to undo the damage done. This paper proposes that this type of access control should be augmented with some sort of control to ensure that humans behave ethically. It is proposed that optimistic access control be complemented with usage control.

4   Enhancing Optimistic Access Control with Usage Control

Sandhu and Park [14], recognizing the inadequacy of traditional access control models, propose a new approach to access control called usage control (UCON). Consequently, there has been a trend towards complementing access control methods such as role-based access control with usage control (see [7] and [19]). The UCON model encompasses emerging applications such as trust management in a unified framework. They claim that the missing components of traditional access control involve the concepts of *obligations* and *conditions*. *Obligations* require some action by the subject (user) so as to gain or sustain access, e.g. by clicking the ACCEPT button on a license agreement or agreeing not to distribute the document. *Conditions* represent system-oriented factors such as time-of-day, where subjects are allowed access only within a specific time period.

Sandhu and Park [14] expanded usage control into a family of models for usage control, involving pre-authorizations and ongoing authorizations. The implementation of pre-authorization is relatively simple as it warrants checking the conditions and obligations before the user may proceed. The implementation of ongoing authorization is, however, non-trivial. Furthermore, Sandhu and Park [14] do not propose how ongoing authorizations may be implemented. We propose using multithreading to implement ongoing authorizations (see Fig. 1). If a subject (user) requests an object (such as a file), the pre-conditions and pre-obligations are checked, then two separate threads are invoked representing ongoing conditions and the ongoing obligations respectively. During the access, the ongoing conditions and ongoing obligations are tested intermittently. As this model is based on optimistic access control, it will allow the user to proceed even if either the pre-conditions, pre-obligations, ongoing conditions or the ongoing obligations are invalid. However, the system will advise the user that this access is invalid and the user has to accept responsibility for this illegitimate access. The illicit access will be red-flagged and logged. Perhaps the user will be asked to justify his or her actions to the system administer at a later stage.

In terms of the enforcement of security policies, it is imperative that it is centrally located and enforced uniformly. Accordingly, the same notion would apply to the implementation of such policies in terms of application logic [17]. This type of deployment may be achieved though the use of aspect-oriented methodologies. The premise of the model is to create an aspect that will intercept calls when a subject requests access to an object and enhance optimistic access control with usage control. A significant amount of work has been conducted in aspect-oriented security in respect of access control. It has been shown that the implementation of access control using aspect-oriented programming eases the implementation of security type concerns such as access control [2]. It results in an implementation that is easier to maintain and port to different environments. Many recent systems are based on a three-tier architecture – access is via the web, the application programs reside within an application server,

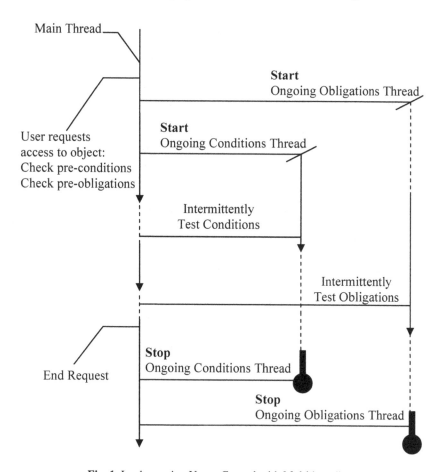

Fig. 1. Implementing Usage Control with Multithreading

and the data is stored within a database system [7]. However, only the application layer is considered in the next section.

5 An Aspect-Oriented Approach to Usage Control

Aspect-orientation provides explicit language support for modularising design decisions that cross-cut a functionally-decomposed program [18]. An aspect is a modular unit of a crosscutting implementation that is provided in terms of pointcuts and advices and that specifies what (advice) and when (pointcut) its code is going to be executed. While aspects are similar to objects, aspects observe objects and react to their behavior. An aspect describes a recurring property of a program and can span multiple classes, interfaces or aspects. Unlike a class though, aspects are injected into other types. They also allow programmers to write, view and edit a crosscutting concern as a separate entity. The application code and aspectual code will be combined at compile time by invoking a special tool called a weaver [6].

In the next elucidation, a generic aspect to facilitate the non-intrusive implementation of usage control to enhance optimistic access control measures is presented. The operations relating to optimistic access control are not included in the aspect as this depends on the system design. Optimistic access control may be assimilated into the object-oriented design or it may be separated as an aspectual concern. If optimistic access control is treated as a separate concern then measures such as the roll back procedures may be invoked within the generic aspect.

The generic aspect to enhance optimistic access control with usage control, defines three pointcuts. The first pointcut intercepts those calls where a subject requests access to an object. The *around* advice defines code that is executed before the request is granted. This advice contains operations to test the pre-Obligations and the pre-Conditions. If the pre-Conditions and pre-Obligations are not satisfied, warnings are issued. Additionally the aspect should contain operations to log all accesses. It is important to note that an aspect cannot capture two join points running in two different threads concurrently. Therefore we have to pass the context of this access to the threads via the `AccessObject` object. This contextual information will be required when ongoing conditions and obligations are no longer satisfied. Note that once the `request` method of the `Access` class is allowed to *proceed* it will have to pause periodically to allow the other threads to execute.

```
pointcut Intercept_Request(Access AccessObject):
execution(* *.request(..)) &&
!within(OngoingConditions) && target(AccessObject);
void around(Access AccessObject):
Intercept_Request(AccessObject){
    pre_Conditions();
    pre_Obligations();
    Conditions conditions = new
    Conditions(AccessObject);
    Thread conditionsthread = new Thread(conditions);
    conditionsthread.start();
    Obligations obligations =
    new Obligations(AccessObject);
    Thread obligationsthread = new Thread(obligations);
    obligationsthread.start();
    proceed(AccessObject);

    obligationsthread.stop();
    conditionsthread.stop();
}
```

The next two pointcuts intercept execution points which indicate that the ongoing conditions and ongoing obligations are no longer satisfied. The *after* advice defines code that is executed after such an irregularity is detected. Here this is represented by the `stop` method. If some action results in the `stop` method being called on either the `conditions` object or the `obligations` object, then this call will be intercepted by the aspect. In either case, with optimistic access control, a warning is issued. Perhaps in other contexts the access could be terminated immediately. The `getState( )` method gives contextual information about the access – such as whether the access is sustained despite the illegitimacy of the access.

```
pointcut OngoingConditions(Conditions conditions):
call(* *.stop() ) && target(conditions);
after(Conditions conditions):
OngoingConditions(conditions){
    if (conditions.getState()){
        //Warning Issued
    }
}

pointcut OngoingObligations(Obligations obligations):
call(* *.stop() ) && target(obligations);
after(Obligations obligations):
 OngoingObligations(obligations){
    if (obligations.getState()){
        //Warning Issued
    }
}
```

All the pointcuts and advices defined above will be encapsulated within a single aspect. In terms of this generic aspect a request could be either *read* or *write* access. Hence this generic aspect has to be re-specified according to the application's naming.

6 Conclusions and Future Work

The element of trust within optimistic access control requires an investigation into human behaviours and responses to its application. It would be pragmatic to investigate whether the model presented here does in fact result in human beings behaving in a trustworthy manner. The aspect designed for the enhancement of optimistic access control has not been tested within a real world context. However, confining all the operations relating to usage control to a single modular structure will ease both development and maintenance costs. This paper furthermore explored the relationship between multithreading and crosscutting behaviour and demonstrated how ongoing authorisations may be maintained with multithreading.

The proposed solution to access control draws inspiration from some of the principles advocated by agile methods. For examples, consider the agile principles relating to embracing change and maintaining simplicity. Here access control was implemented in its most rudimentary form – as with agile methods, the reliance was on people rather than on complicated processes to maintain control. The use of aspect-oriented programming contributed to the principles of embracing change and maintaining simplicity.

References

1. Chon, R., Enokido, T., Wietrzsk, V.: Role Locks to Prevent Illegal Information Flow among Objects. In: 18th International Conference on Advanced Information Networking and Applications (AINA'04), Fukuoka, Japan, 29-31 March, 2004, vol. 1, pp. 196–201 (2004)
2. De Win, B., Vanhaute, B., Decker, B.: Security Through Aspect-Oriented Programming. In Advances in Network and Distributed Systems Security. IFIP TC11 WG11.4 First Working Conference on Network Security, Leuven, Belgium, November 2001, pp. 125–138. Kluwer Academic Publishers, Boston (2001)

3. English, C., Nixon, P., Terzis, S., McGettrick, A., Lowe, H.: Security Models for Trusting Network Appliances. In: 5th Annual Workshop on Networked Appliances, October 2002, Liverpool, England (2002)
4. Grandison, T.W.A.: Trust Management for Internet Applications (PhD thesis), in Department of Computing, University of London (2003)
5. Hong, J.I., Landay, J.A.: MobiSys' 04, Boston, Massachusetts, USA, pp. 177–189 (2004)
6. Kiczales, G., Hilsdale, E., Hugunin, J., Kersten, M., Palm, J.: Getting Started with AspectJ. Communications of the ACM 44(10), 59–65 (2001)
7. Li, X., Naeem, N.A., Kemme, B.: Fine-Granularity Access Control in 3-tier Laboratory Information Systems. In: Database Engineering and Application Symposium, IDEAS, Montreal, Canada, 25-27 July, 2005, pp. 391–397 (2005)
8. Pfleeger, C.P.: Security in Computing, 2nd edn. Prentice Hall, United States of America (1997)
9. Povey, D.: Optimistic Security: A New Access Control Paradigm. In: Proceedings of the 1999 workshop on New security paradigms, September 22 - 24, 1999, Caledon Hills, Ontario, Canada (1999)
10. Pudney, P.: e-Consent in consumer health & telemedicine. Telemedicine Research Center, University of South Australia (2003), http://www.pudney.net.au/ phillip/papers/ econsent.pdf
11. Ramachandran, R., Pearce, D.J., Welch, I.: AspectJ for Multilevel Security. In: The 5th AOSD Workshop on Aspects, Components, and Patterns for Infrastructure Software (ACP4IS), Bonn, Germany, 21 March, 2006, pp. 1–5 (2006)
12. Russell, D., Gangemi, G.T.: Computer Security Basics, Sebastopol, O'Reilly and Associate, California (1991)
13. Samarati, P., Bertino, E., Ciampichetti, A., Jajodia, S.: Information Flow Control in Object-Oriented Systems. IEEE Transactions on Knowledge and Data Engineering 9(4), 624–538 (1997)
14. Sandhu, R., Park, J.: Usage Control: A Vision for Next Generation Access Control. In: The Second International Workshop on Mathematical Methods, Models and Architectures for Computer Networks Security, St Petersburg, Russia, pp. 17–31 (2003)
15. Sandhu, R.S., Coyne, E.J., Feinstein, H.L., Youman, C.E.: Role-Based Access Control Models. IEEE COMPUTER 29(2), 38–47 (1996)
16. Stevens, G., Wulf, V.: A New Dimension in Access Control: Studying Maintenance Engineering across Organizational Boundaries. In: Proceedings of the ACM conference on Computer Supported Cooperative Work (CSCW), New Orleans, Louisiana, USA (2002)
17. Verhanneman, T., Piessens, F., De Win, B., Joosen, W.: Uniform Application-level Access Control Enforcement of Organizationwide Policies. In: Srikanthan, T., Xue, J., Chang, C.-H. (eds.) ACSAC 2005. LNCS, vol. 3740, Springer, Heidelberg (2005)
18. Walker, R.J., Baniassad, E.L.A., Murphy, G.C.: An initial assessment of aspect-oriented programming. In: Proceedings of the 21st international conference on Software engineering, Los Angeles, California, May 1999, pp. 120–130 (1999)
19. Xu, Z., Feng, D., Li, L., Chen, H.: UC-RBAC: A Usage Constrained Role-Based Access Control Model. In: Qing, S., Gollmann, D., Zhou, J. (eds.) ICICS 2003. LNCS, vol. 2836, pp. 337–347. Springer, Heidelberg (2003)

Usage Control in Service-Oriented Architectures*

Alexander Pretschner[1], Fabio Massacci[2], and Manuel Hilty[1]

[1] Information Security, ETH Zürich, Switzerland
[2] Dept. of Information and Communication Technology,
Università degli Studi di Trento, Italy

Abstract. Usage control governs the handling of sensitive data after it has been given away. The enforcement of usage control requirements is a challenge because the service requester in general has no control over the service provider's information processing devices. We analyze applicable trust models, conclude that observation-based enforcement is often more appropriate than enforcement by direct control over the service provider's actions, and present a logical architecture that blends both forms of enforcement with the business logics of service-oriented architectures.

1 Introduction

The past few years have seen major technological and business trends that are reshaping software technology and business processes. These trends have a profound impact on the trust models, security policies, security procedures, and security infrastructures that companies need to develop and maintain [1,2]. From a technological perspective, service-oriented architectures (SOA) and business process management platforms have emerged as the architectures and technologies of choice for structuring and integrating applications within and across enterprises. From a business perspective, companies and institutions have increasingly outsourced the non-core parts of their business processes. Outsourcing is the ongoing administration, management, and possibly subcontracting of specific IT processes by external parties to enhance efficiency and effectiveness of those processes (cited after [2]). Outsourcing is sometimes iterated, so that the service provider (SP) itself outsources some functions to third parties [3]. In this way a company can concentrate on its core business rather than on peripheral tasks. Outsourcing often involves sensitive data such as trade secrets or the personal data of customers. Data owners (i.e., the companies who own the trade secrets) and data subjects (i.e., the customers to whom (personal) data is related) are interested in governing how that data may be used by the SPs. Further, regulatory frameworks such as the Sarbanes-Oxley act also impose technical and governance restrictions on how business-relevant data may or must be processed.

There is a long history of security research concerned with the protection of data. *Access control* (AC for short) addresses the question of who may access which data

---

* This work was done while A. Pretschner was on leave at the universities of Trento and Innsbruck—support by the Bolzano Innsbruck Trento Joint School for Information Technology is gratefully acknowledged. F. Massacci was supported by the EU-funded S3MS project.

C. Lambrinoudakis, G. Pernul, A M. Tjoa (Eds.): TrustBus 2007, LNCS 4657, pp. 83–93, 2007.

under which circumstances. Those decisions are taken with information that relates to the present and the past. More recent work has extended the concept to *usage control* (UC for short; [4,5,6,7]) that is concerned with what may happen with data once a *data provider* has given it to a *data consumer*. In service-oriented settings, the data consumers are typically the SPs. Requirements about the future handling of data are called *obligations*. Examples include "delete the document within thirty days", "notify the data owner whenever the data is accessed", "log every access to the document", and "the data must be stored in an encrypted manner" [8]. Obligations are also studied in the areas of privacy (e.g., [9,10,11]) and digital rights management (DRM, e.g., [12,13]).

In this paper, we tackle the problem of enforcing obligations in SOAs. Because of the special trust relationships in service-based business processes, it might be sufficient not to *ensure* the adherence to obligations—which is what is needed in DRM contexts—but rather to *observe and react* to violations in hindsight. Based on these considerations, we present a logical architecture that identifies the necessary core functionalities for enforcing UC. We show how to connect the UC logic to the business logic(s) of a SOA. We make the assumptions explicit, discuss the crucial aspect of trust, and demonstrate the limitations of the architecture. Implementing the architecture is a next step.

Problem Statement and Contribution. To summarize, the *problem* that we study is whether and how UC requirements can be enforced in SOAs and which enforcement strategies are appropriate in which scenarios. Our *solution* is the analysis of different trust models in usage control scenarios and the specification of functional components that can enforce UC requirements. The *contribution* of this paper is, to our knowledge, the first explicit conceptual treatment of security and trust requirements for UC in outsourced SOAs and the first logical architecture addressing it.

Overview. In §2, we discuss the fundamentally different UC-related trust models in the areas of DRM and service-based business processes. This analysis leads us to two different kinds of enforcement of UC requirements in §3, detective and preventive enforcement. We present the logical architecture in §4 and sketch two different deployment schemes in §5. Finally, in §6, we put our work in context and conclude.

2   Usage Control and Trust in Different Domains

Different stakeholders have different interests in UC. Human data subjects are interested in their privacy being respected. To keep their competitive advantage, companies want to prevent their trade secrets from falling into the hands of competitors. Similarly, artists and distributors of artworks and software are interested in receiving royalty payments for their intellectual property. Finally, shareholders and other parties are interested in compliance with governance rules such as the Sarbanes-Oxley act. In contrast to this perspective of the *data provider*, data consumers (or SPs, respectively) have different interests with regard to whether and how obligations are enforced.

In the DRM (B2C) area, the data consumer has in general no interest in adapting its computing infrastructure to meet the more or less prying needs of a data provider. The data consumers' well-being does not depend on whether or not they receive a movie. Furthermore, limitations imposed by DRM are often seen as a nuisance by the data consumers because DRM may also prevent playing data on several devices or making backup copies. Legal restrictions are often not taken seriously by the data consumers because the enforcement of the law in this area is nearly impossible. In terms of UC enforcement mechanisms, the data consumers have an interest in data protection as many DRM mechanisms send information back to central servers that may be of privacy-sensitive nature.

This is in contrast to the relationship between a company and an outsourced SP (B2B). SPs are interested in adhering to the stipulated terms and conditions for two reasons. Firstly, maintaining a high reputation is important in competitive markets. Loosing one customer translates into considerable losses (compare the value of an outsourcing contract and the value of an mp3 song). Depending on the level of customization, a company using, e.g., the SAP R/3 business suite, might quickly move from one SP to another; and SPs with a low reputation have difficulties of finding new customers. Secondly, the legal implications of not adhering to the terms and conditions may be severe. The penalties stipulated in the outsourcing contracts act as a deterrence for the SP to handle the customer's data in unintended ways.

Finally, public administrations, seen as SPs, have in general no direct economic relationship with businesses (A2B) or citizens (A2C) who send them sensitive data. However, most processes in administrations are strictly governed and public administrations usually have no particular interest in breaking the respective laws and regulations. We may conclude that these administrations are inherently honest and that violations of usage control requirements tend to happen unintentionally rather than deliberately.

The relationship between SPs and service requesters often is subject to regulatory demands. These may include the requirement that a company provide evidence to regulators, auditors and finally its customers that it is delivering a secure, privacy-respecting, trustworthy service. Yet, regulators might not consider sophisticated outsourcing structures and may only hold one of the parties accountable to the end user. Similarly, even if contractual protection and deterrence can help avoid problems with regulators and law enforcement, they are not sufficient to mitigate the rage of customers whose pressure might force a global brand to take responsibility for outsourced services.

In sum, service requesters (data providers) must trust the SPs (data consumers) to handle the received sensitive data in accordance with stipulated terms. To achieve this trust, secure service-oriented infrastructures must be developed so that data providers can *specify* security policies for services and the infrastructure can *enforce* such policies, *monitor and detect* violations, and diagnose the root causes for violations in order to take appropriate actions. However, SPs may be reluctant to give the service requesters too much control over their IT infrastructures. Even giving away information about the internal behavior may be critical to the SP; but it is generally more acceptable than giving control to the service requester.

3   Enforcement of Usage Control

In DRM, data providers are interested in gaining enough control over the data consumers' IT infrastructures so that they can make sure that UC requirements are adhered to. This is a consequence of the trust relationship described in §2. In contrast, in the domain of business IT it may be impossible, not practical, too costly, or simply not necessary to fully control the IT infrastructure of the service that receives sensitive data. This is equally a consequence of the respective trust relationship discussed in §2. SPs may, however, agree to present some (trustworthy—cf. §5) information about their actions. The original senders of the data can then, in hindsight, decide whether previously stipulated obligations have been adhered to. If not, they can penalize the receiver, e.g., by lowering trust ratings. The idea is that of deterrence: potential delinquents are aware that their wrongdoings may be detected and that they may be held accountable. In the following, we will refer to the first kind of enforcement as *preventive enforcement* and to the second kind as *detective enforcement*.

The functionality of mechanisms for *preventive enforcement* can be broken down into the fundamental strategies of inhibition, modification, execution, and finite delay [8,14]. Mechanisms for preventive enforcement are mostly developed in the DRM area and usually perform enforcement by inhibition, with a few exceptions that support enforcement by modification [15]. *Detective enforcement* does not require direct influence on the actions performed by the SP but relies on signaling mechanisms that *inform* about actions of the SP. As a consequence, the original requirement (e.g., "delete the data item within thirty days") is transformed into a combined statement that consists of an observable requirement ("the execution of the deletion command within thirty days must be confirmed") and a compensating action that is executed in case of violation (e.g., "lower the SP's trust rating") [7]. We require that a violation of the observable requirement implies a violation of the original requirement. Ideally, one would like the opposite direction to hold as well, but this is in general not possible—this is the cost for using the weaker observation-based kind of enforcement. Detective enforcement involves both *signaling* and *monitoring* components. Typically, signalers reside at the SP's side (or at some distributed parts of the service requester infrastructure such as SAP R/3 clients). They send (partial) information about the provider's internal state or actions to the service requester. Monitors predominantly reside at the requester's side. They receive signals from the signalers and verify if these signals conform with applicable UC policies. Obviously, a monitor must trust the information that is sent by signaling components; the latter must be correct and complete: notifications are sent whenever necessary, and there must not be any "spurious" notifications (§5).

4   A Logical Architecture for Usage Control in SOAs

We now describe an architecture for UC in SOAs. It is logical in the sense that it is completely independent of any implementation. Later, in §5, we sketch two deployment schemes for integrating UC with an existing SOA.

Abstractly, a service is a functional entity with an internal state that receives and sends messages under well-defined conditions (contracts). A service S sends a request to another service S'; if there is a result of the computation that S may be interested in, S' can send a response message. Messages consist of a command that the requester wants the receiver to execute, possibly including references to the receiver's state (e.g., a data base), data that the receiver needs to perform its task and that might have to be usage-controlled, and UC policies for that data.

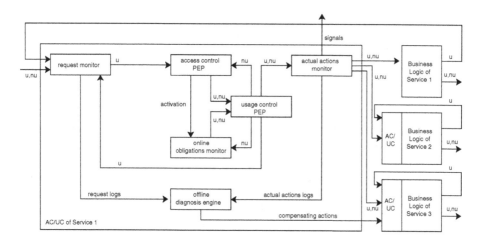

Fig. 1. Services with access and usage control

Fig. 1 schematically shows how to incorporate enforcement mechanisms for AC and UC into this simple service model. Labeled arrows represent the main data flows (messages) and boxes represent functional components; we will convey the meaning of the labels later. A request enters the system from the left hand side. Rather than passing it directly to the business logic of the receiving service (say, service 1, to which the request was directed), we first make the message enter the hierarchically decomposed box labeled "AC/UC". Once this box has performed its tasks, messages are sent to other services. These messages may be identical to those originally received, and the receiving services may be identical to the original receiver (service 1), but they need not, because the AC/UC enforcement mechanisms may have decided otherwise. The idea is that an AC/UC component resides within each communication channel between two services; it intercepts requests and performs its tasks.

We distinguish between messages that directly relate to usages (label u) and those that do not (label nu). Usage always relates to data for which UC policies exist. It can be classified into management, distribution to other parties, rendering, data processing, and execution of programs [15]. Usages can be combined; editing a document with a word processor, for instance, usually involves rendering, processing, and management usages. Messages that do not relate to usage include notifications, status reports, payments, fines, etc. In Fig. 1, we make the following assumption. All usage-related actions that the business logic of a service undertakes (manage, render, process, execute) as the result of processing a request (that is, usages that are not *directly* mentioned in the original request) are *not directly executed* but rather encoded as an explicit request and fed back to the AC/UC component of the service (uppermost arrow and feed-back data flows for services 2 and 3). In this way, we make sure that *all* usage-related actions (messages) always pass the AC/UC component of a service and are hence subject to UC. This is of course a strong assumption. However, it can be justified by the logical nature of the architecture: UC need not necessarily be implemented by dedicated software components (§5).

The main functional components of the AC/UC component are three monitoring components (request, actual actions, and obligations monitor), the AC policy enforcement point (PEP), a UC PEP that takes policy-defined actions should this be necessary (e.g., delete a file after thirty days, notify the data owner, spell out a fine), and a component that can be used to analyze system executions w.r.t. a set of policies in an off-line manner and to analyze existing logs for business decisions.

The *request monitor* does nothing but log incoming requests. The main requirement is to be sufficiently fast and to scale. Some requests may not be allowed to be logged; this is stipulated by monitoring policies. The logs of all requests can later be used for offline analysis purposes. Incoming requests are forwarded to the AC PEP.

The *AC PEP* decides whether a request can be granted, that is, if the command in the (command, data, UC policy) triple of the message can be executed w.r.t. the applicable AC policies. These policies can reflect both the AC functionality of the business logic of the service itself and AC functionality that reflects requirements on the entire system rather than a single service (e.g., chinese wall policies). In addition to AC policies, UC policies may be applicable. These UC policies are defined system-wide (reflecting legal frameworks), on a per-service, or a per-data item basis. How these policies are retrieved and how the system knows when to activate them is outside the scope of the logical architecture. If any UC policies are applicable to the data that is part of the data in the request, they must be tied to the data object in question and then be activated. Activated obligations are handled by the *obligations monitor* discussed below. If the AC PEP decides that a request can be granted, it forwards it to the *UC PEP*. The reason for not directly sending the request to the service's business logic is that even at the moment of granting access, UC requirements may have to be enforced—e.g., a notification may have to be sent, or a policy that was activated earlier prohibits the current request from being forwarded to the service's business logic.

The online *obligations monitor* monitors requirements on the future of a data item that was previously sent to the service and for which an applicable UC policy exists. The monitor keeps track of the actions of the service. If specific policy-defined conditions are met (or violated), it makes the *UC PEP* perform specific tasks.

The *UC PEP* enforces UC requirements based on the four classes of enforcement defined in §3. For instance, the execution of action conditions with an executor mechanism can be done by spelling out fines—i.e., sending the respective message to a respective service—notifying a data owner, or automatically issuing a payment. Note that the execution of actions may also be delayed as demonstrated by the above example of deletion in thirty days (this is different from delaying enforcement mechanisms which simply wait to see if certain favorable conditions have, by virtue of actions the requester may have taken in the meantime, become true). As a second example, the obligations monitor can also tell the UC PEP *not* to forward a request to the service's business logic, i.e., inhibit it. For instance, a UC policy might state that some action must not be executed more than three times. When the fourth request arrives, then the obligations monitor will notify the UC PEP that this fourth request must not be forwarded to the service's business logic. The other forms of enforcement can be achieved in a similar manner. If the result of the UC PEP is different from the original request yet itself a usage (an action for which UC policies may be applicable), then this result must be enveloped into a request and fed back to the request monitor: similar to actions that the business logic of a service may want to execute, UC policies may be applicable.

If according to the obligations monitor, the UC PEP has nothing to do, then the latter forwards the input received from the AC PEP, and possibly also that of the obligations monitor. The actions of the UC PEP may affect the AC PEP and the obligations monitor, e.g., if any policy stipulates actions to be taken after three fines were spelled out. These components hence get fed back with the actions executed by the UC PEP.

The *actual actions monitor* logs all messages that the UC PEP has deemed appropriate (or modified into something appropriate) for being executed by the service. Furthermore, it forwards the requests that it receives to the service's business logic (or to another service, if this is applicable—for instance, a penalty service). The actual actions monitor also serves as the signaling component for other services, as discussed in §3. The actual actions monitor does not need to send its data to the UC PEP and the obligations monitor because this has already been achieved by the UC PEP. The monitoring activity is governed by a monitoring policy, similar to the monitoring policy that governs the request monitor.

Finally, an *offline diagnosis engine* analyzes activities in the logs. Data mining techniques can be performed for risk analysis, or it might be decided that online detection of UC policy violations is not really an issue and that offline detection—e.g., once a week—is fully appropriate for a given business scenario.

In addition to trust issues that we will discuss in §5, this perspective on UC involves a constraint that relates to side effects. A UC policy may depend on the *output* of a service. For instance, a policy may state that if the *result* of the service's computation includes specific names, then it must not be distributed to specific parties. This means that the UC PEP must first trigger the service's business logic, then retrieve the result, and check it w.r.t. its UC policies. The problem then obviously is that the service's computation may have side effects that cannot be undone.

5 Engineering Usage Control in SOAs

We now describe the mapping of this functionality to a technical architecture and to the implementation.

Dedicated Services. One approach to implementing the above functionality implements dedicated software components for each functionality of one of the logical entities. AC and UC are hence enforced at the interface level of a service. The challenge with this approach is twofold. Firstly, preventive enforcement requires that *all* actions of a service are initiated by requests that pass through the respective AC/UC component. In other words, there must be no other way for a service to receive requests, and the service exclusively performs actions that are initiated by an external request. Proactive behavior of a service—that is not initiated by sending explicit messages to itself—is obviously prohibited by this approach. Secondly, detective enforcement requires all consumer-side events that are relevant for checking compliance with a policy to be (1) generated by the signaling components and (2) received and appropriately interpreted by the monitoring components. In particular, signaling components must not miss any events that they should inform the monitoring components about (completeness) and the signaling components must not notify the monitors of actions that have not taken place (correctness). As an example for a possible technical infrastructure, Apache Axis (ws.apache.org/axis), a development framework for Java web services, allows the definition of request handlers and handler chains. These handlers intercept requests, perform specific actions, and then send requests to the business logic (and all requests necessarily pass the handlers). The AC and UC PEPs can be implemented as part of these handlers. Because the online obligations monitor must take into account information that is not exclusively related to requests that are sent to the business logic (e.g., time or notification messages), it cannot in general be integrated into the handlers. Checking the conditions of a UC requirement must be done by a dedicated component.

Weaving. The approach of implementing the enforcement infrastructure along the lines of the functional entities is appealing because of its modular nature: AC/UC components can be added to any communication channel in a system. However, we have seen that it relies on a set of rather strong assumptions on the deployment of the services. A further possibility consists of compiling the AC/UC functionality directly into the service. This scenario is attractive when a SP is tailoring services to customer's needs anyway, as it happens in several outsourcing scenarios. We would argue that when the service binary is built, one could also alter the source code so as to incorporate some functionalities of the logical architecture. In this scenario, generic AC PEPs, online obligation monitors, and UC PEPs could be interwoven with the service's business logic at compile time, similarly to what aspect weavers do in aspect-oriented programming [16], how monitors can be interwoven with object code [17], and to what modified Java virtual machine class loaders do at runtime to implement security requirements [18].

Parsimonious Trusted Computing. Both approaches to implementing UC enforcement mechanisms rely on assumptions that relate to trust at different levels. How can it be ensured that the only way for services to receive requests is after they have passed the respective AC/UC component? The system must be trusted that there are no other ways to request actions from a service. Similarly, how can the (currently deployed) business logic of a service itself be trusted? How can signalers provide monitors with the correct and complete information that these monitors need for assessing adherence to policies? How can it be ensured that a service reacts to a message in the specified way, i.e., how can input messages and internal actions be linked? And how can it be ensured that the components of AC and UC mechanisms have been implemented correctly and may not be tampered with? These difficult questions are relevant in both deployment scenarios.

At least some technological help can be expected here. First, with trusted computing technology, hardware-based solutions for restricting the actions of an IT system and making sure that a certain configuration of a service is running on a specific host (remote attestation) are becoming increasingly powerful. For example, trusted computing technology could be used to make signaling mechanisms more tamper-resistant. Approaches in this direction have been presented in the literature [19,20]. Second, data caging at the level of hardware (e.g., Intel's LaGrande Technology) and operating systems (e.g., Symbian OS v9) can also be implemented for general business information systems and protect both program code and cryptographic keys. These cryptographic keys can be used to restrict access to data to those who possess the respective key (which of course implies that decrypted data must not be publicly accessible). Third, there exist approaches for securing software that cannot rely on trusted hardware [21,22]. However, these approaches are often considered weaker than hardware-based approaches. Finally, off-the shelf components such as databases can be equipped with built-in mechanisms for increasing trust (e.g., Hippocratic databases [9]).

6 Related Work and Conclusions

UC has been discussed by several authors [5,6,7], with few researchers explicitly catering to the notion of distribution in UC, i.e., the loss of control over a data item after giving it away. Several policy languages for UC have been proposed [23,24,13,12,8]. Enforcement by observation and penalties has been documented [25,5,26]; and preventive control mechanisms have been surveyed and characterized [15,8,14]. All this work does not relate to the specifics of loosely-coupled software architectures for business information systems (in the P2P context, related work was mentioned earlier [20,19]). To our knowledge, this paper constitutes the first treatment of UC in SOAs.

Distributed UC is concerned with requirements on data after this data has left the data provider's scope of influence. Sources for the respective requirements are the data owners' interests but also governance rules and regulations. Some of these requirements can be controlled. For other requirements, enforcement by observation and compensation is a suitable solution. Whether or not preventive or detective control mechanisms are applied depends on the underlying business and trust models. Enforcement by observation and compensation seems to be applicable in outsourced business service scenarios rather than in DRM (§2). In SOAs, the data consumer (SP) may not want the data provider (service requester) to be so powerful; full control may also be technically impossible, inappropriate because of the wrong trust model, or too costly. In the DRM scenario, the trust model is fundamentally different. Furthermore, in the area of DRM for handheld devices, we would argue that if there is sufficient control over the handheld's operations for *observation purposes*, then there should be sufficient control to directly enforce by *control* as well.

The contributions of this paper are technical and conceptual. *Technically*, we have identified the main functional components for enforcing UC policies. We have defined a logical architecture and presented two different deployment schemes, one relying on dedicated SW components, and one relying on weaving the functionality with the service's business logic at compile-time. *Conceptually*, we have shown how the appropriateness of different enforcement schemes (preventive or detective control) depends on the business model of the SP and the applicable trust model. In other words, we have shown that UC in SOAs and UC in DRM are fundamentally different. While trust is a huge technological and also organizational problem, we have hinted at first building blocks for respective solutions. We are aware that a logical architecture is only a first step and that we will face many challenges when implementing it.

In addition to scalability issues that we did not scrutinize in this paper, we did not mention two further technical challenges. Firstly, when instantiating the abstract notions of usages with actual usages, then the question about their semantics arises: if a policy specifies that a data item has to be "deleted", does this mean that all copies have to be deleted, that the data has to be physically over-written several times, or that in case of encrypted storage the key is deleted? At the level of business processes, however, policies may directly relate to (standardized) messages exchanged between services, which means that this problem may be less relevant. Secondly, we did not touch the problem of rights delegation and propagation in iterative outsourcing scenarios.

Open research and engineering problems relate to all of the above. We need to better understand how hardware-based trusted computing technology, secure storage of keys, application-specific enforcement schemes, modern operating systems and middleware can help establish the necessary trust.

Acknowledgments. We would like to thank F. Casati and B. Crispo for contributing to and discussing the architecture as well as V. Lotz for many useful comments on the business side of SOAs.

References

1. Karjoth, G., Pfitzmann, B., Schunter, M., Waidner, M.: Service-oriented Assurance - Comprehensive Security by Explicit Assurances. In: Proc. of QoP'05 (2005)
2. Karabulut, Y., Kerschbaum, F., Massacci, F., Robinson, P., Yautsiukhin, A.: Security and Trust in IT Business Outsourcing: a Manifesto. In: Proc. STM. ENTCS (2006)
3. Goth, G.: The ins and outs of it outsourcing. IT Professional 1, 11–14 (1999)
4. Schaad, A., Moffett, J.: Delegation of Obligations. In: Proc. POLICY, pp. 25–35 (2002)
5. Bettini, C., Jajodia, S., Wang, X.S., Wijesekera, D.: Provisions and obligations in policy rule management. J. Network and System Mgmt. 11(3), 351–372 (2003)
6. Park, J., Sandhu, R.: The UCON ABC Usage Control Model. ACM Transactions on Information and Systems Security 7, 128–174 (2004)
7. Pretschner, A., Hilty, M., Basin, D.: Distributed Usage Control. CACM 49(9), 39–44 (2006)
8. Hilty, M., Pretschner, A., Schaefer, C., Walter, T.: A System Model and a Policy Language for Distributed Usage Control. Technical Report I-ST-20, DoCoMo (2006)
9. Agrawal, R., Kiernan, J., Srikant, R., Xu, Y.: Hippocratic DBs. In: VLDB, pp. 143–154 (2002)
10. Karjoth, G., Schunter, M., Waidner, M.: Platform for Enterprise Privacy Practices: Privacy-enabled Management of Customer Data. In: Proc. PET, pp. 69–84 (2002)
11. W3C: The Platform for Privacy Preferences 1.1 (P3P1.1) Spec., Working Draft (2005)
12. Wang, X., Lao, G., DeMartini, T., Reddy, H., Nguyen, M., Valenzuela, E.: XrML–eXtensible rights Markup Language. In: Proc. XMLSEC, pp. 71–79 (2002)
13. Iannella, R.: Open Digital Rights Language - Version 1.1 (2002), odrl.net/1.1/ODRL-11.pdf
14. Ligatti, J., Bauer, L., Walker, D.: Edit Automata: Enforcement Mechanisms for Run-time Security Policies. International Journal of Information Security 4(1-2), 2–16 (2005)
15. Hilty, M., Pretschner, A., Schaefer, C., Walter, T.: Enforcement for Usage Control—An Overview of Control Mechanisms. Technical Report I-ST-18, DoCoMo EuroLabs (2006)
16. Filman, R., Elrad, T., Clarke, S., Aksit, M.: Aspect-Oriented SW Development (2004)
17. Erlingsson, U., Schneider, F.: SASI enforcement of security policies: A retrospective. In: Proc. New Security Paradigms Workshop, pp. 87–95 (1999)
18. Bauer, L., Ligatti, J., Walker, D.: Composing Security Policies with Polymer. In: Proc. ACM SIGPLAN Conf. on Programming Language Design and Implementation, pp. 305–314. ACM Press, New York (2005)

19. Zhang, X., Chen, S., Sandhu, R.: Enhancing Data Authentity and Integrity in P2P Systems. IEEE Internet Computing 9(6), 18–25 (2005)
20. Sandhu, R., Zhang, X.: Peer-to-peer access control architecture using trusted computing technology. In: SACMAT, pp. 147–158 (2005)
21. van Oorschot, P.: Revisiting software protection. In: Proc. IST, pp. 1–13 (2003)
22. van Oorschot, P.: SW protection and application security: understanding the battleground. In: State of the art and evolution of computer security and industrial cryptography (2003)
23. W3C: A P3P Preference Exchange Language 1.0 (APPEL1.0) (2002)
24. Backes, M., Pfitzmann, B., Schunter, M.: A toolkit for managing enterprise privacy policies. In: Snekkenes, E., Gollmann, D. (eds.) ESORICS 2003. LNCS, vol. 2808, pp. 162–180. Springer, Heidelberg (2003)
25. Povey, D.: Optimistic security: a new access control paradigm. In: Proc. workshop on new security paradigms, pp. 40–45 (1999)
26. Hilty, M., Basin, D., Pretschner, A.: On obligations. In: Proc. ESORICS, pp. 98–117 (2005)

On Device-Based Identity Management in Enterprises

Marco Casassa Mont and Boris Balacheff

Hewlett-Packard Labs, Trusted Systems Lab, Bristol, UK
{marco.casassa-mont, boris.balacheff}@hp.com

Abstract. This paper focuses on the management of device-based identities within enterprises. This is a key requirement in enterprises where the identities of devices have become as important as the identities of humans (users) to grant access to enterprise resources. In this context, access control systems need to understand which devices are being used to access resources, by whom and in which contexts. Trust in managed devices' identities is an important first step to enable this. Most related commercial solutions are deployed at the network level. Instead, we focus at the application/service level to leverage current enterprise identity management solutions, used to manage users' identities. We investigate requirements and related issues. We introduce an initial approach and describe our related solution. A working prototype (proof-of concept) has been fully implemented by extending HP OpenView Identity Management solutions and using trusted computing-enabled devices. This is work in progress: we aim at setting the context and discussing our current status and next steps.

1 Introduction

Devices are becoming more and more pervasive in today's society. Laptops, PDAs, mobile phones, etc. are used by employees in enterprises to fulfill their jobs and sometimes also for personal matters. From a user (individual) perspective, this further simplifies their day-to-day life by avoiding any unnecessary duplication of devices and tools. From an enterprise perspective, the fact that devices are used by employees for a variety of purposes, introduces additional risks and threats, in particular about the integrity of these devices and their trustworthiness to access enterprise intranets and networked resources. Private devices (e.g. personal laptops, etc.) could also be used at work - with potential risks due to lower security and assurance (e.g. about installed software, patch control, local access control settings, etc.) than the ones mandated by the enterprise.

This paper specifically focuses on devices (e.g. laptops) owned by enterprises and used by employees to carry out their daily work (and potentially their private activities). Current enterprise services, applications and information are mainly protected by traditional access control systems (within enterprise identity management solutions) that usually only take into account human-based identities (via login/passwords, digital certificates, etc.) or human-based identities that are strongly bound to a given device. To have better control of resources, it is becoming more and more important for enterprises also to explicitly identify devices and their properties i.e. consider the identity of a device as a self-standing entity or as one of a group of known entities.

C. Lambrinoudakis, G. Pernul, A M. Tjoa (Eds.): TrustBus 2007, LNCS 4657, pp. 94–103, 2007.
© Springer-Verlag Berlin Heidelberg 2007

Furthermore, trust and assurance are required about the authenticity and validity of a device's identity. Dealing with devices' identities and their associations to human identities is not trivial. The goal of this paper is to explore this space and propose an initial approach and solution to address (aspects of) the management of devices' identities in enterprises. This is work in progress, involving ongoing R&D activities at HP Labs, in collaboration also with HP business groups.

2 Enterprise Scenario

An enterprise scenario is considered, where users (i.e. employees, business partners, other workers, etc.) use enterprise devices to access enterprise resources, e.g. web services, shared file systems, document repositories, legacy applications/services. Users authenticate to their devices via their login and password: their "identities" are known by the enterprise. In this scenario, the identity of a device is also taken into account. A user can be granted access to a resource purely based on the identity of a device (it is using) and its properties (e.g. if it has been checked and vouched by enterprise IT administrators). In this case the user could be anonymous or authenticated. Alternatively, access could be granted only if a specific combination/association of user identity and device identity is available. The same device could be shared by multiple users, at different times and for different purposes. In this scenario, enterprise IT and security administrators protect enterprise resources by defining appropriate fine-grained access control policies that are derived from business and security needs and can be based on any combination of devices' identities, users' identities, device properties and other contextual information. Trusted computing components, such as Trusted Computing Group (TCG) modules [1], are deployed within devices and leveraged to strongly protect identities (that can be encrypted before being locally stored) and provide mechanisms to check for the integrity of these identities and their installed software.

3 Problem Space and Important Requirements

Our work aims at addressing the problem of the management of device-based identities in enterprises. Most of current solutions focus on devices' identities at the network level, not really at an application/service level (see "Related Work" Section). Whilst the former approach is definitely important, the latter approach enables enterprises to leverage their "middleware" identity management solutions (e.g. [3,9], that handle users' identities at the application/service level) also to manage devices' identities. The remaining part of this paper focuses at this level, by setting the context and suggesting an initial approach to deal with it.

A few important requirements have been identified by investigating our enterprise scenario and by focusing on aspects and processes involved in device-based identity management: (1) define a model and explicitly represent a device identity; (2) be able to "assess" and "certify" a device identity to deal with trust issues; (3) securely store and protect a device identity; (4) be able to associate users' identities to devices' identities; (5) be able to provision devices' identities (along with users' identities) within enterprise systems and IT security systems, such as access control systems; (6) deal with the lifecycle management (inclusive of modification and disposal) of devices' identities, in addition to the lifecycle management of traditional users' identities; (7) define and manage fine-grained access control policies to keep into account any combination of users' identities, devices' identities, device properties and other contextual information.

All these requirements have an impact on current devices, on how enterprises assess, manage and use identities, their lifecycle and how resources are protected.

4 Our Analysis of Device-Based Identity Management

This section further analyses the stated problem, by taking into account requirements and current enterprise identity management solutions. This analysis focuses on three key aspects: (A) processes that an enterprise needs to put in place to deal with device-based identities; (B) modelling and storage of a device identity; (C) definition of fine-grained access control policies involving devices' and users' identities.

A) **Enterprise Processes for Device-based Identity Management**. The management of devices' identities in enterprises has to comply with enterprises' current identity management processes, in particular the ones that have already been deployed to deal with users' identities [2]. These processes usually are automated by identity management solutions that operate at an enterprise "middleware" level. A more detailed description of these processes and related implications for devices' identities follows:

- **Identity creation and certification.** identity information is collected by an enterprise, its provenance is checked and verified. An identity can be certified and potentially vouched by another entity (e.g. a trusted third party). In case of a device's identity, this stage requires collecting properties and information about the device itself and the definition of what its unique identity is. This might require as well a certification of this information, according to Enterprise IT security standards. An additional step, also related to devices' identities, consists in storing these identities (in a secure and safe way) directly on the devices, for their future usage. As anticipated, trusted computing features can be leveraged to securely achieve this goal. Point B) further expands on this point;
- **Identity provisioning.** once an identity (of a user or a device) has been created, it has to be "provisioned" within enterprise systems, by: (1) processing and storing identity attributes in relevant enterprise data repositories (e.g. databases, LDAP directories, etc.); (2) creating user accounts; (3) setting and configuring applications and services to recognise these new identities. Current Identity Management enterprise solutions (e.g. [3]) provide these provisioning and account management features but mainly focus on users' identities. These steps are also required for devices' identities;
- **Access control setting and policy definition.** fine-grained access control policies are defined and deployed (by security administrators) to protect enterprise resources and allow/disallow accesses based on rights and credentials. The introduction of devices' identities increases the degree of control and richness of

access control policies but, at the same time, poses problems on how to effectively capture all these aspects within access control policies. Point C) further expands on this aspect;

- **Identity lifecycle management.** once identities are provisioned and access control policies are in place, they can be subject to modification, updates and – eventually deletion. The lifecycle of devices' identities (and related policies) not only has implications on enterprise resources but also on the affected devices. This introduces further complexity to the lifecycle management that needs to be addressed.

B) Modelling, Representation and Storage of Device Identity. A device identity consists of a set of information (attributes) that uniquely identifies a device and describes its properties in a given context – in this case an enterprise context. In general a device identity can include: device unique identifier; logical name of the device; product properties of the device (including manufacturer, production date, etc.); expected "location" of the device (in case of static device); intended usage of the device/business purposes of the device; potential list of device's owners, etc. The list of attributes composing a device identity can vary depending on the context. There is currently no agreement in the industry on exactly what a device identity (i.e. which attributes) consists of. There are a few initiatives carried on in this space to further explore this aspect, including the one mentioned in [4].

Key requirements for device identity (as well as for user identity) include being able to explicitly represent it, safely store it and then use it, for example for authentication and authorization purposes. At the current stage there are two main options for representing devices' identities, reflecting what happens for users' identities:

- **"Uncertified" device identity.** this is a collection of identity attributes, with no certification or assessment made by any party (if not the device itself, its owner or its manufacturer). The main disadvantage of this approach is that this type of identity can be easily modified and tampered with;
- **"Certified" device identity.** this identity is still a collection of attributes, however it is "certified", for example by using digital certificates, XML-based signature schemas, etc. By leveraging public-key cryptographic schemas, e.g. [5], a "private key" and a correspondent "public key" are associated to a device. A certified device identity (e.g. signed XML digital credentials [6] or an X509 identity/attribute certificate [5]) contains a statement about the device's public key and it is signed, to check for the integrity of identity attributes. Further trust on an asserted device identity can be provided if the certification of this identity is made by a "trusted" party. In the case of the enterprise scenario, the enterprise itself can vouch for and issue these certificates: this simplifies the overall certification process and avoids dependencies on third parties. However a certification infrastructure has to be put in place within enterprises to deal with the lifecycle management of these certificates.

In both cases (uncertified and certified identities) there is the issue of safely storing a device identity on the device itself and to strongly associate this identity to the device and (potentially) to a user. In case of "certified device identity" this is typically done by protecting the secret (cryptographic private key) associated to the device identity.

To address these issues, help can be provided by trusted computing technologies [1] that are more and more pervasive in business computing systems. Specifically Trusted Platform Modules (TPM) are currently available on a broad range of devices including laptops and PCs. Typically, a TPM is a tamper-resistant cryptographic module and ships with a built in endorsement (cryptographic) credential installed by its manufacturer. This endorsement credential can be used to implement a device identity provisioning solution that can remotely identify that a device has the appropriate trusted computing capabilities to protect the device identity with hardware and to bind it physically to the device via the TPM. More generally, TPM will be used to generate a cryptographic key in a secure way, with the assurance that this cryptographic key can only be used on the device where it was provisioned to represent the device's identity. Details of the use of state-of-the-art TPM mechanisms and protocols can be found in TCG specifications [1] and in literature on this topic such as [15].

C) Fine-grained Access Control Policies involving Device Identity and User Identity. Devices' identities provisioned in enterprises can be used by enterprise security administrators to define access control policies. These policies involve authentications and authorization aspects.

At a "conceptual level", traditional user-based access control policies can be represented via a "*Resources x Users*" access control matrix [7] - for a given set of resources and users. This matrix describes - for each protected resource and for each user - which access rights a user has on a given resource. This conceptual approach allows discriminating between *known* and *unknown* (anonymous) users, based on the knowledge of their identities. These access rights could be as simple as allowing/disallowing particular operations (read/write/execute, etc.) or include more complex policy constraints, dictating for example levels of required authentication, time-based constraints, conditions on specific (contextual) attributes, etc. This is a good starting point also to explore how to factor in devices' identities. Two related models of access control policies have been analysed by leveraging the matrix model:

- **Representation of devices as a "special type" of Users.** this involves their classification as either "*Unknown Devices*" or "*Known Devices*", based on the fact their identity is unknown/known – in the context of the classification of "*Known/Unknown*" users - see Figure 1. Hierarchies of groups of known devices can be provided. Access control on resources can be expressed by keeping into account either users' identities or devices' identities. This representation constrains administrators to represent devices in the context of (known, unknown) users that might use/be associated to these devices.

  Fine-grained access control rules/constraints can be defined in the intersection of a user/device with a resource. Rules in the access control matrix can be used to deal with joint authentication (*AND*) of both a user and a device and related access constraints. This includes: constraints for authenticating users with traditional authentication mechanisms (e.g. login/password, credentials); constraints for authenticating devices, for example by requiring certified identities; check properties of the involved user and device and impose additional constraints on other contextual information. This approach allows enterprise security administrator to express a policy such as "*only a known user using a specific known device, with, for example, an identity underpinned by a TPM module, can access the specified resource".*

- **Representation of devices (along with their identities) as resources**. In this approach, devices are listed (either separately or within hierarchies) as "Resources". A device can authenticate itself with its own identity. A negative aspect of this approach is that it is not clear how to deal with unknown devices and, in general, how to associate overall access control rights. In this model devices are just represented as resources: we still want to enable their access to other resources purely based on their identities.

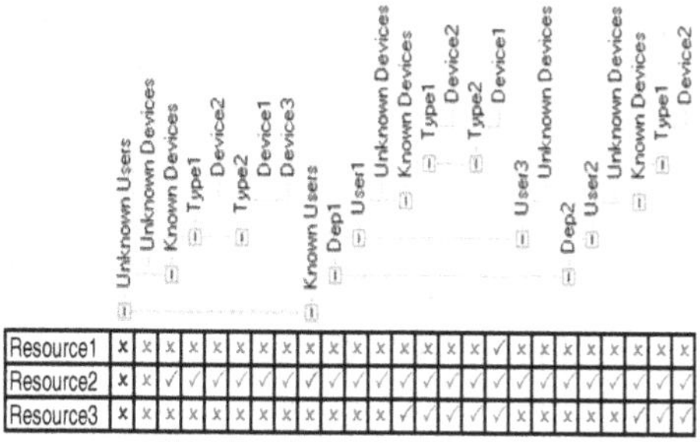

Fig. 1. Representing devices as a "special type" of users

The main limitation of the above two approaches is that users and devices are classified in the same matrix – hence constraints applies to the identity of a user AND the identity of a device (unless one of the two or both are unknown). In our analysis additional technical approaches have been explored to deal with access control involving constraints on "users AND devices" and "users OR devices". These alternative approaches include [16]: (1) usage of multiple matrices, including a "Resources x Users" matrix and a "Resources x Devices" matrices; (2) usage of three-dimensional matrix; (3) usage of a "Tree of Matrices". They all have limitations, mainly in terms of complexity in defining and managing them [16].

At the current stage, the most realistic and feasible approach (based also on current enterprise identity management solutions for users' identities) consists of representing devices as a "special type" of users, by using a *"Resources x Users"* matrix, as shown in Figure 1. In this context, *Allow/Deny* policies or fine-grained access control policies can be set at the intersections of managed resources and users/devices, to obtain the required level of control.

5 Our Current Approach

Our current approach to device-based identity management is pragmatic: to move towards its adoption, it leverages as much as possible state-of-the-art enterprise identity provisioning and access control solutions (used to protect applications and services) and extends them to manage devices' identities. In this context it is important to recognise the role that trusted computing components play to protect devices' identities and the need for certification and trust assurance of these identities.

Based on key requirements and our analysis, a solution is proposed, consisting of a system and related mechanisms to: (a) explicitly certify and protect devices' identities by leveraging (when available) trusted computing capabilities [1] of a device (e.g. its TPM module) and an enterprise "Identity Certification Service"; (b) allow for a flexible association of human identities to device-identities, when this is required; (c) provision and manage the lifecycle of device identities (and other associated information) into enterprise management systems; (d) support fine-grained, policy-driven access control on enterprise resources taking into account different types of identities (device and/or human-based) and contextual information.

The significant case where enterprise devices are configured by enterprise administrators is considered. In the proposed model, a "self-registration" web service is used to authenticate administrators, before starting the process of registering and provisioning a device identity. Attributes qualifying a device identity (e.g. name, manufacturer, configuration attributes, etc.) are inserted by an administrator via a related web form. An optional approach for the "self-registration" service is to allow individual users to register a device and provision a device identity within the enterprise infrastructure.

Managed devices may or may not have trusted computing capabilities e.g. TPM modules. In either case, a unique (cryptographic) private key is associated to a device and a device identity is "certified" for that key via the "Identity Certification Service". Specifically, a device identity is in the form of a signed certificate. In case of a device being TPM enabled, further cryptographic strength and security is introduced as the private key associated to the "device identity" certificate is generated by using TPM cryptographic capabilities.

The "Identity Certification Service" is a "Certification Authority" specialised in handling and certifying devices' identities with a format that can be configured by the enterprise: current formats (we experimented with) are based on X.509 certificates and digital-signed XML credentials. Importantly the "Identity Certification Service" will be able to identify in the device identity certificates it issues whether those are issued to (1) strong device identities rooted in hardware TPM, or (2) to software-protected device identities protected by a user credential. In the case where the user "self-registration" option is used for the provisioning service, identifying whether a device identity is appropriately protected by a TPM hardware or not cannot be verified by an administrator. In this case it is possible to take advantage of the TPM endorsement credentials for the web service to identify remotely that the device identity to be certified is indeed related to a cryptographic key generated by a hardware TPM module - produced by a known manufacturer. Details of these mechanisms are not discussed in this paper as they are standard applications of TPM technology. This "Identity Certification Service" can be operated by either the enterprise or a trusted third party. If required, the "Identity Certification Service" also allows an administrator to associate a human-based identity (e.g. his/her login name or his/her identity certificate) to the device identity and certifies this binding. Certified devices' identities are then provisioned to enterprise systems via existing enterprise identity provisioning solutions (e.g. [3]). In our approach, the same identity provisioning solution is used to provision both "human-based identities" and their associations to "device-identities".

This phase includes configuring an access control system to be aware that a new device identity has been provisioned so that access control policies can be set: alternatively, if the device identity is part of an existing hierarchy of devices, it will obey to the associated policies. Our access control system leverages existing access control solutions (e.g. [8]): it is driven by fine-grained access control policies, targeting enterprise resources (e.g. systems, web services, applications, etc.). It consists of: (a) a Policy Authoring Point (PAP) to author fine-grained access policies keeping into account the nature of the remote device (e.g. with or without TPM), different types of identities (including "devices' identities", "users' identities", association of devices to users), their hierarchical organisation, etc; (b) a Policy Decision Point (PDP) to make decisions based on the context and the above policies; (c) a Policy Enforcement Point (PEP) to intercept runtime attempts to access enterprise resources, gather contextual information (such as a device identity) and enforce decisions made by the PDP component. The significant case of an enforcement point deployed within a web server (providing enterprise web services/applications) has been considered. It uses an access control "*matrix*" model described in section 4 based on a "*Representation of devices as a "special types" of Users*" and shown in Figure 1. This matrix represents (a) *controlled resources* and (b) all combination of *Known/Unknown "entities"* that can (or cannot) access resources. Entities can be devices, users and any grouping of them based on their identities. The intersection in the matrix of a resource with an entity (or a set of hierarchical entities) can be set to allow/disallow accesses via fine-grained rules (based on time, contextual parameters, certificate properties, TPM-based device authentication, etc.). Hierarchies of groups of devices are supported. In this context, a device can authenticate itself with its own identity, potentially underpinned by its TPM (when present). A full working prototype has been implemented. Figure 2 illustrates the main components and steps involved in our prototype.

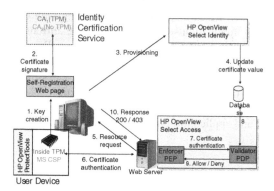

Fig. 2. Device-identity Management Demonstrator

This prototype leverages and extends three HP Identity Management solutions: HP ProtectTools Security Manager [8]; HP OpenView Select Identity [3]; .HP OpenView Select Access [9]. More details are available in [16].

6   Related Work, Current Status and Next Steps

The idea of being able to identify devices is not new and has been pursued extensively with weakly bound identifiers such as software protected cryptographic identities, MAC addresses, or even statically allocated IP addresses. There are currently multiple initiatives to standardise device identities [4] but it is not clear how they will evolve and if they will converge.

A few solutions (e.g. [17]) provide software mechanisms to protect data (via encryption) stored in (mobile) devices at different levels of abstraction. Additional relevant work on security solutions to protect data on mobile devices and deal with authentication aspects can be found at [18]. The idea of using a Hardware Security Module to strongly protect device identities is described in [10]. Also the idea of using TPM modules to protect confidential information stored on a device (including identity information) is not new. However, most of current solutions mainly address the problem of how to protect the identity of a device and how to use it, not really how to manage this identity in enterprises, consistently with enterprise "middleware" identity management processes (e.g. provisioning, configuration and access control). This is a key contribution of our work.

Relevant work is going on in the context of Liberty Alliance [13] in terms of *Identity Capable Devices*: this involves provisioning devices (potentially using trusted computing devices) with "identity tokens" and autonomously using them in federated identity management context [14]. This work can influence the way devices' identities are certified and locally associated/stored to devices. We are currently involved in this initiative and related activities.

Device identities have primarily been used in the network infrastructure, such as in [11,12], rather than to protect access to application-level resources in the enterprise. Most of the existing enterprise identity and access control management solutions do not include features to support device identities and authentication: our work aims at addressing this issue. Our prototype (integrated with HP OpenView Identity Management solutions) demonstrates the feasibility of dealing with device-based identity management also at an application/service level. We are currently refining our technology by adding further expressiveness to access control policies.

Next steps include further research in this space, in particular with regards to the representation of devices in access control policies (by analysing additional models) and the full lifecycle management of devices' identities. This will also include researching additional aspects of the usage of "device" authentication, such as reconciling network-based and application-based access control management.

7   Conclusions

This paper focused on the problem of dealing with device-based identity management in enterprises. Most of related solutions address this problem at the network level. However, current enterprise identity management solutions operate at the "middleware" level and lack support for integrated management of devices' identities and users' identities - in terms of provisioning, access control policies and authentications. Our work aimed at leveraging and extending these identity management solutions to deal also with device-based identity management. We explored requirements and introduced our approach. A full working prototype has been implemented along with a related demonstrator, leveraging TPM-enabled devices and state-of-the-art HP Identity Management solutions. This is work in progress: further research is required to fully explore the implications of devices' identities on access control policies and how to deal with their overall lifecycle management in enterprises.

Acknowledgements

We would like to thank Xavier Chassagneux for his hard work and key contributions made to this R&D project whilst he was an HP Labs intern.

References

1. TCG: TCG TPM Specification, Version 1.2 (2003), http://www. trustedcomputinggroup.org
2. Casassa Mont, M., Bramhall, P., Pato, J.: On Adaptive Identity Management: The Next Generation of Identity Management Technologies, HPL-2003-149 (2003)
3. Hewlett-Packard (HP): HP OpenView Select Identity: Overview and Features (2007), http://www.openview.hp.com/products/slctid/index.html
4. Wills, T.: The Identities of Electronic Devices, Digital ID World article (2002), http://www.digitalidworld.com/modules.php?op=modload&name=News&file=article&sid=96
5. IETF: IETF PKIX Working Group (2005), http://www.ietf.org/html.charters/pkix-charter.html
6. W3C: XML Signature WG (2003), http://www.w3.org/Signature/
7. Lampson, B.W.: Protection. In: Proc. 5th Princeton Symposium on Information Sciences and Systems, pp. 18–24. Princeton University (1974)
8. Hewlett-Packard (HP): HP ProtectTools Security Manager (2007) http://www.hp.com/sbso/ security/protecttools.html
9. Hewlett-Packard (HP): HP Openview Select Access: Overview and Features (2005), http://www.openview.hp.com/products/select/
10. Baldwin, A., Shiu, S.: Hardware Encapsulation of Security Services. In: Snekkenes, E., Gollmann, D. (eds.) ESORICS 2003. LNCS, vol. 2808, Springer, Heidelberg (2003)
11. iPass: DeviceID (2007), http://www.ipass.com/services/services_deviceid.html
12. INTEL: Network Access Control: User and Device Authentication (2005), http://www. intel.com/it/pdf/network-access-control.pdf
13. Liberty Alliance: The Liberty Alliance Project (2007), http://www.projectliberty.org/
14. Liberty Alliance: ID-WSF Advanced Client 1.0 DRAFT Specifications (2007)
15. Pearson, S. (ed.): Trusted Computing Platforms. Prentice Hall, Englewood Cliffs (2002)
16. Casassa Mont, M., Balacheff, B.: On Device-based Identity Management in Enterprises, HP Labs Technical Report, HPL-2007-53 (2007)
17. Bluefire: Mobile Security Enterprise solutions (2007), http://www.bluefiresecurity.com/
18. NIST: Mobile Device Security (2007), http://csrc.nist.gov/mobilesecurity/ publications.html

Analysis-Level Classes from Secure Business Processes Through Model Transformations

Alfonso Rodríguez[1], Eduardo Fernández-Medina[2], and Mario Piattini[2]

[1] Departamento de Auditoría e Informática, Universidad del Bio Bio Chillán, Chile
alfonso@ubiobio.cl
[2] ALARCOS Research Group, Information Systems and Technologies Department,
UCLM-Soluziona Research and Development Institute, University of Castilla-La Mancha,
Ciudad Real, Spain
{Eduardo.FdezMedina,Mario.Piattini}@uclm.es

Abstract. Nowadays, business processes (BP) are important in the maintenance of competitiveness within enterprises. Moreover, security is a crucial issue in business performance. In the last few years, the languages used for BP representation have been improved and new notations have appeared. Proposals for security requirement specifications at this high level of abstraction have also appeared. Nevertheless, these models have not been transformed into concrete models that can be used in a software development process. In our proposal, we will obtain analysis-level classes from a business process specification in which security requirements are included. Model transformations are within the scope of MDA and they are specified by using the QVT standard. Finally, we shall apply this approach to a typical health-care business process.

1 Introduction

In recent years, enterprise performance has been linked to the capability that they have to adapt themselves to the changes that arise in the market. In this context, business processes have become valuable resources that have been used to maintain competitiveness since they are the means through which an enterprise describes, standardizes, and adapts the way it reacts to certain types of business events, and how it interacts with suppliers, partners, competitors, and customers [19].

On the other hand, economic globalization, along with the intensive use of communications and information technologies, have caused enterprises to not only expand their businesses but also to increase their vulnerability. As a consequence, and with the increase in the number of attacks on systems, it is highly probable that sooner or later an intrusion may be successful [14].

Although the importance of business process security is widely accepted, the business analyst perspective in relation to security has hardly been dealt with to date. In [17] we introduced security representation into business processes. To do so, we extended the UML 2.0 Activity Diagram [13] by creating the BPSec profile, which allows us to capture security requirements expressed by the business analyst. Such a specification gives origin to a Secure Business Process.

Nowadays, model transformation has come under the scrutiny of the community of researchers and practitioners since it focuses upon solving the problems of time, cost

C. Lambrinoudakis, G. Pernul, A M. Tjoa (Eds.): TrustBus 2007, LNCS 4657, pp. 104–114, 2007.
© Springer-Verlag Berlin Heidelberg 2007

and quality associated with software creation. The OMG (Object Management Group) proposal in relation to this fact is called MDA (Model-Driven Architecture) [12]. MDA is a framework for software development that allows the creation of models which are independent of technological implementation and QVT (Query/View/Transformation) [15], a standard for model transformation.

The MDA approach is composed of the following perspectives: (i) the Computation Independent viewpoint which focuses on the environment of the system, (ii) the Platform Independent viewpoint which focuses on the operation of a system whilst concealing the details necessary for a particular platform, and (iii) the Platform Specific viewpoint which combines the platform independent viewpoint with an additional focus on the detail of the use of a specific platform by a system [12].

In our proposal, we consider that an SBP (Secure Business Process) is a CIM (Computation Independent Model) that can be transformed into a PIM (Platform Independent Model). This transformation, carried out with QVT, leads to the generation of UML artifacts that can be used in a systematic and ordered process in software development. We have chosen the UP (Unified Process) [8, 16], which is composed of a set of activities necessary for transforming user requirements into a software system, due to the fact that it is a consolidated and successful software construction method [5].

The structure of the remainder of the paper is as follows: in Section 2, we will summarize the main issues concerning security in business processes together with our profile of a security requirement specification in business processes. In Section 3, we will present our proposal. Finally, in Section 4, we will put forward an example and in Section 5 our conclusions will be drawn.

2 Security in Business Process

In business process modeling, the main objective is to produce a description of reality, for example, the way in which a commercial transaction is carried out, in order to understand and eventually modify it with the aim of incorporating improvements into it. As a consequence, a notation must allow us to incorporate different perspectives which give place to various diagrams in which the rules, goals, objectives of the business and not only relationships but also interactions are shown [3].

In spite of the importance of security within business processes, the research works related to the security specifications carried out by business domain experts are; (i) scarce [1, 6, 7, 10], (ii) orientated towards transaction security [18], (iii) directly orientated towards information systems in general [21] or (iv) intended for security and software engineers [11].

However, at the present it is possible to capture security requirements at a high level, which are easily identifiable by those who model business processes, because: (i) the business process representation has improved in the UML 2.0 version, (ii) the security requirement will tend to have the same basic kinds of valuable and potentially vulnerable assets [4], and (iii) empirical studies show that it is common at the business process level for customers and end users to be able to express their security needs [9].

Therefore, we have approached the problem of including security in business processes [17] by extending the UML 2.0 Activity Diagram (UML 2.0-AD) which allows business analysts to specify security requirements. The proposed extension, which we have called BPSec, basically considers the graphical representation of security requirements, a non-limited list (see Figure 1) taken from the taxonomy proposed in [4].

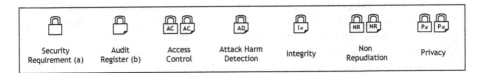

| Security Requirement (a) | Audit Register (b) | Access Control | Attack Harm Detection | Integrity | Non Repudiation | Privacy |

Fig. 1. Icons to represent security requirements in BPSec

In our proposal we have used a padlock (Figure 1a) to represent security requirements in a standard way. The same symbol, the padlock, but with a twisted edge (Figure 1b) is used to represent a Security Requirement with Audit Register.

The relation between security requirement (dark-coloured) and the UML 2.0-AD is shown in Figure 2. «SecurityRole», «SecurityPermission», «G-AuditRegister», «NR-AuditRegister» and «SP-AuditRegister» stereotypes have been added with the purpose of complementing the security requirements specification.

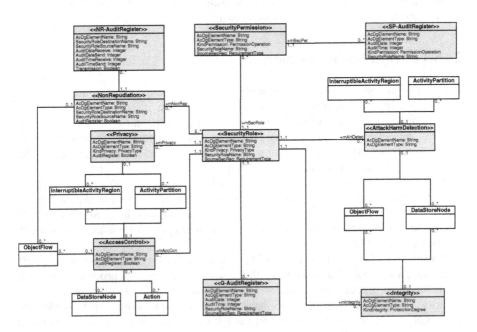

Fig. 2. BPSec and UML 2.0-AD Elements Model

Table 1. Security Requirements and UML 2.0-AD elements

Access Control: This corresponds to the limitation of access to resources by authorized users only. It implies the limitation of access to a set of resources that are considered important enough to be protected in a special way
– Action: This implies the definition of a secure role and security permissions associated with the action. The possible permissions are: Execution (default value) and CheckExecution.
– ActivityPartition: This implies the creation of a secure role and security permissions associated with actions, data store and data flows contained in the partition
– DataStoreNode: This implies the definition of a secure role and security permissions associated with the data store: The possible permissions are: Create, Delete, Read, and Update (default value)
– InterruptibleActivityRegion: This implies the creation of a secure role and security permissions associated with actions, data stores, and data flows contained in the region
– ObjectFlow: This implies the definition of a secure role and of security permissions associated with the object flow: The possible permissions are: SendReceive (default value) and CheckSendRecieve
Attack Harm Detection: This is defined as the detection, register and notification of an attempted attack or threat, whether it is successful or not. This requirement represents an attention signal covering the elements which are indicated.
– ActivityPartition: This implies the identification of a security role associated with the partition and the registration of the date and time of the produced accesses to the partition
– DataStoreNode: This implies the identification of a security role and the registration of the date and time of the accesses produced upon the data store
– InterruptibleActivityRegion: This implies the identification of a security role and the registration of the date and time when the accesses are produced in the region
– ObjectFlow: This implies the identification of the security roles (sender and receiver) related to the object flow and the registration of the date and time of the sending and reception of the flow
Integrity: This is related to the protection of components from intentional and non-authorized corruption. The integrity specification is valued as low, medium, and high. An integrity specification (at any degree) is related to the importance of the information contained in the data store or data flow
– DataStoreNode: This implies the protection of the data store content. Together with this, the security role, date and time of all accesses to the data store are registered
– ObjectFlow: This implies the protection of the data contained in the object flow. Additionally, security roles involved in the flow, date and time of sending and reception are registered
Non Repudiation: This establishes the need to avoid the denial of any aspect of the interaction (e.g. message, transaction, transmission of data) so that any future problems (e.g. legal and liability) can be avoided.
– ObjectFlow: This implies flow protection. Additionally, the date and time of the sending and reception of the flow involved in the interaction are registered.
Privacy: This is related to conditions of information protection concerning a determined individual or entity, thus limiting access to sensitive information by non-authorized parties. From the point of view of the business analyst, the privacy specification implies the non-revelation (confidentiality) and non-storage (anonymity) of the information regarding a determined role.
– ActivityPartition: This implies the creation of a secure role associated with the partition
– InterruptibleActivityRegion: This implies the creation of a secure role associated with the region

---

The set of security requirements, which is not exclusive, is described in Table 1. The meaning of the relationship between each security requirement and UML 2.0-AD element is also described.

As a result of BPSec application, a Secure Business Process is obtained. The SBP description is used to obtain the analysis-level classes.

3   Analysis-Level Classes from Secure Business Processes

A business process built by a business analyst is not only useful in the specific business field, but is also very useful in a process of software construction, and can be used to obtain numerous kinds of system requirements. In our proposal, CIM2PIM transformations are aimed at obtaining useful artifacts in software development in such a way that automatically obtained analysis-level classes become part of an ordered and systematic process of software development.

In Figure 3, the basic aspects of our proposal are shown. At the top, we can see UML 2.0-AD and BPSec. In an MDA approach, an SBP description corresponds to a

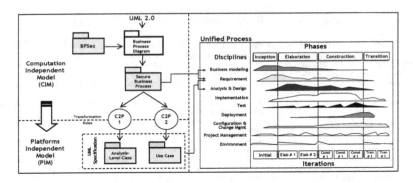

Fig. 3. An overview of our proposal

computation independent model (left-hand side). Through the application of a set of transformation rules, C2P_1, applied to SBP, it is possible to obtain a subset of the security analysis-level classes that facilitate the understanding of the problem. UP (right-hand side) is considered because the SBP description will be useful in the "Business Modeling" and "Requirement" disciplines, and the analysis-level classes complement the "Requirement" and "Analysis & Design" disciplines.

In our review of related literature, ranging from business processes to analysis-level class transformations, we have found two works that deal directly with this type of transformations. In the first [2], activity diagrams are transformed into analysis classes. This transformation is not performed automatically, and a previous version of UML 2.0 is used. In the second work [20], the software designer studies the business process model described with BPMN by extracting the UML classes which are later refined. The differences between these proposals and ours are that, firstly we use QVT for transformation specifications, secondly we pay special attention to security requirements, and finally we connect the result of transformations with a software development process.

In order to obtain a clearer view of the transformation rules, we shall present them in the following order: (i) QVT rules mapping general aspects of SBP which are not related to security specifications, (ii) QVT rules directly related to security specifications and finally, (iii) refinement rules that must be applied once analysis-level classes have been obtained as a consequence of QVT rule application.

QVT rules that are not related to security specifications can be used to obtain analysis-level classes derived from partitions, regions and the operations associated with the classes obtained. The QVT rules are described in Table 2.

If the QVT rules are applied to the security requirements described with BPSec, we can directly obtain analysis-level classes that have the requirement name. Indirectly, a class called SecurityRole is created and eventually SecurityPermission. The specification of audit register gives place to classes of the AuditRegister type associated with SecurityRole, SecurityPermission or a particular security requirement. The QVT specifications for these rules are described in Table 3.

Table 2. Mapping between Activity Diagrams and Class Diagrams elements

```
transformation ActivityDiagram2ClassDiagram
  top relation R1   // from Activity Partition to Analysis-Level Class
  {
    checkonly domain uml_ActivityDiagram ap:ActivityPartition {name = n}
    enforce domain uml_ClassDiagram c:Class {name = n}
    where { ap.containedNode → forAll(cn:Action|R4(cn))}
  }
  top relation R2   // from Interruptible Activity Region to Analysis-Level Class
  {
    checkonly domain uml_ActivityDiagram iar:InterruptibleActivityRegion {name = n}
    enforce domain uml_ClassDiagram c:Class {name = n}
    where { ap.containedNode → forAll(cn:Action|R4(cn))}
  }
  top relation R3   // from Data Store Node to Analysis-Level Class
  {
    checkonly domain uml_ActivityDiagram dsn:DataStoreNode {name = n}
    enforce domain uml_ClassDiagram c:Class {name = n}
  }
  relation R4 // from Action to Operation in Analysis-Level Class
  {
    checkonly domain uml_ActivityDiagram ac:Action {name = n, inPartition=ap}
    enforce domain uml_ClassDiagram op:Operation {name = n, ownerClass=c:Class{name=ap.name}}
  }
```

Table 3. Mapping between BPSec and Class Diagrams elements

```
transformation BPSec2ClassDiagram
top relation R5    // from Security Requirement to Analysis-Level Class
 {
  checkonly domain bpmn_BPSec sr:SecurityRequirement {requirementtype = n}
  enforce domain uml_ClassDiagram c:Class {name = n}
 }
top relation R6    // from Security Requirement to specific Analysis-Level Class
 {
  checkonly domain bpmn_BPSec sr:SecurityRequirement {requirementtype = n}
  enforce domain uml_ClassDiagram c:Class {name ="SecurityRole"}
 }
top relation R7    // Access Control to specific Analysis-Level Class
 {
  checkonly domain bpmn_BPSec ac:AccessControl {name = n}
  enforce domain uml_ClassDiagram c:Class {name ="SecurityPermission"}
 }
top relation R8    // from AccessControl to audit register Class
 {
  checkonly domain bpmn_BPSec ar:AuditRegister {requirementtype = n}
  enforce domain uml_ClassDiagram c:Class {name =nc}
     where { nc= if (n="AC") then "SP_AuditRegister" endif;}
 }
top relation R9    // from Integrity to generic audit register Class
 {
  checkonly domain bpmn_BPSec In:Integrity {name = n}
  enforce domain uml_ClassDiagram c:Class {name ="G_AuditRegister"}
 }
top relation R10    // from AttackHarmDetection to generic audit register Class
 {
  checkonly domain bpmn_BPSec Ad:AttackHarmDetection {name=n}
  enforce domain uml_ClassDiagram c:Class {name ="G_AuditRegister"}
 }
top relation R11    // from Privacy to generic audit register Class
 {
  checkonly domain bpmn_BPSec ar:AuditRegister {requirementtype = n}
  enforce domain uml_ClassDiagram c:Class {name =nc}
     where {nc= if (n="P") then "G_AuditRegister" endif;}
 }
top relation R12    // from NonRepudiation to audit register Class
 {
  checkonly domain bpmn_BPSec ar:AuditRegister {requirementtype = n}
  enforce domain uml_ClassDiagram c:Class {name =nc}
     where {nc= if (n="NR") then "NR_AuditRegister" endif;}
 }
```

Table 4. Refinement Rules for Analysis-Level Classes

```
RR1: InterruptibleActivityRegion Name is obtained by linking the ActivityPartition names in
     which the Region is contained
RR2: Composition relationships are obtained from top and middle ActivityPartitions
RR3: Relationships between classes derived from security requirements and the activity
     diagram element are obtained from the "BPSec and AD-UML 2.0-AD Elements Model" (Figure
     2)
RR4: Relationships between classes derived from security requirements are obtained from
     "BPSec and AD-UML 2.0-AD Elements Model" (Figure 2)
RR5: Redundant specifications must be eliminated
```

4 Example

Our illustrative example (see Figure 4) describes a typical business process for the admission of patients to a health-care institution. In this case, the business analyst identified the following Activity Partitions: Patient, Administration Area (a top partition which is divided into the Admission and Accounting central partitions), and the Medical Area (divided into Medical Evaluation and Examination).

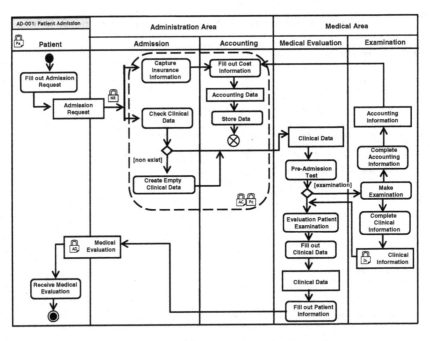

Fig. 4. Admission of Patients in a Medical Institution

The business analyst has considered several aspects of security. He/she has specified «Privacy» (anonymity) for the "Patient" Activity Partition, with the aim of preventing the disclosure and storage of sensitive information about Patients. «Nonrepudiation» has been defined for the control flow which goes from the action "Fill out Admission Request" to the actions "Capture Insurance Information" and "Check Clinical Data" with the aim of avoiding the denial of the "Admission

Table 5. QVT and refinement rules applied to Patient Admnission Business Process

R1:	Patient, Administration Area, Admission, Accounting, Medical Area, Medical Evaluation, and Examinations
R2:	Region 01 (from InterruptibleActivityRegion)
R3:	Admission Request, Accounting Data, Clinical Data, Accounting Information, Medical Evaluation and Clinical Information
R4:	Patient [Fill out Admission Request and Receive Medical Evaluation]; Admission [Capture Insurance Information, Check Clinical Data, and Create Empty Clinical Data]; Accounting [Fill out Cost Information, and Store Data]; Administration Area [Capture Insurance Information, Check Clinical Data, Create Empty Clinical Data, Fill out Cost Information, and Store Data]; Medical Evaluation [Pre-Admission Test, Evaluation Patient Examinations, Fill out Clinical Data, and Fill out Patient Information]; Examinations [Complete Accounting Information, Carry out Examinations, and Complete Clinical information]; Medical Area [Pre-Admission Test, Evaluation Patient Examinations, Fill out Clinical Data, Fill out Patient Information, Complete Accounting Information, Carry out Examinations, and Complete Clinical information]; Region 01 [Capture Insurance Information, Check Clinical Data, Create Empty Clinical Data, Fill out Cost Information, and Store Data]
R5:	Privacy (anonymity), NonRepudiation, Access Control and Privacy (confidentiality), Integrity (high), and AttackHarmDetection
R6:	SecurityRole
R7:	G-AuditRegister
R8:	SP-AuditRegister
R9:	G-AuditRegister
R10:	G-AuditRegister
R11:	NR-AuditRegister
RR1:	AdmissionAccounting (name assigned to Region 01)
RR2:	Administration Area composed of Admission and Accounting; Medical Area composed of Medical Evaluation and Examinations
RR3:	Privacy → Patient ; Privacy → AdmissionAccounting; NonRepudiation → Admission Request; AccessControl → AdmissionAccounting; Integrity → Clinical Information; AttackHarmDetection → Medical Evaluation
RR4:	Privacy → SecurityRole; AccessControl → SecurityRole → SecurityPermission → SP-AuditRegister; Integrity → SecurityRole → G-AuditRegister; AttackHarmDetection → SecurityRole → G-AuditRegister
RR5:	SecurityRole → G-AuditRegister redundancies must be eliminated

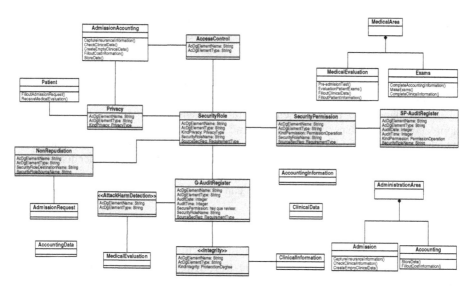

Fig. 5. Analysis-Level Class from Patient Admission

Request" reception. «AccessControl» and «Privacy» (confidentiality) has been defined for the Interruptible Activity Region. A «SecurityRole» can be derived from this specification. Admission/Accounting will be one role. All objects in an interruptible region must be considered for permission specification. The Access Control specification has been complemented with an audit requirement. This implies that it must register information about the security role and security permissions.

Integrity requirement (high) has been specified for the "Clinical Information" Data Store and finally, the business analyst has specified Attack Harm Detection for the "Medical Evaluation" Data Store, so that all events related to the attempt or success of attacks or damages are registered.

The attainment of analysis-level classes through the application of the transformations defined with the QVT rules (R) and the Refinement Rules (RR) are described in Table 5.

Figure 5 shows a graphical representation of the analysis-level classes which are presented in Table 5. This figure is enriched since, after the application of the QVT rules, we have named the region, we have incorporated the relationship between the elements in the class diagrams and we have eliminated the redundancies. In addition, the analysis-level class derived from the security requirement specification is shown in the dark-coloured areas.

5 Conclusion and Ongoing Work

One way in which to confront the problem of security consists of incorporating it into the business process specifications at an early stage. At that level, it is possible to capture security requirements which take into account the business analyst's viewpoint. In previous works, we have proposed an extension of the UML 2.0 Activity Diagram through which it is possible to specify security requirements at a high level of abstraction.

In addition, models transformation has come to the attention of the community of researchers and practitioners owing to the fact that it has the aim of solving the problems of time, cost and quality associated with software creation.

In this paper, we have presented a model transformation by using the MDA approach with QVT specification. By using a Secure Business Process specification, which is considered to be a Computation Independent Model, we have obtained a set of analysis-level classes, which are considered to be a Platform Independent Model. The analysis-level class obtains a subset of all classes which are necessary for describing a problem, and the SBP can be used in a well-known software development process.

Ongoing work is orientated towards enriching transformations in order to make it possible to obtain more complete models of analysis-level classes. Together with this, our future work also has the purpose of optimizing the prototype that we have created to carry out the transformations with the aim of improving specification reuse and documentation.

Acknowledgments. This research is part of the following projects: DIMENSIONS (PBC-05-012-1), and MISTICO (PBC06-0082) both partiality supported by the FEDER and the "Consejería de Ciencia y Tecnología de la Junta de Comunidades de Castilla-La Mancha", Spain, COMPETISOFT (506PI287), granted by CYTED and ESFINGE (TIN2006-15175-C05-05/) granted by the "Dirección General de Investigación del Ministerio de Ciencia y Tecnología", Spain.

References

1. Backes, M., Pfitzmann, B., Waider, M.: Security in Business Process Engineering, International Conference on Business Process Management (BPM). In: van der Aalst, W.M.P., ter Hofstede, A.H.M., Weske, M. (eds.) BPM 2003. LNCS, vol. 2678, pp. 168–183. Springer, Heidelberg (2003)
2. Barros, J.P., Gomes, L.: From Activity Diagrams to Class Diagrams. In: Workshop Dynamic Behaviour in UML Models: Semantic Questions In conjunction with Third International Conference on UML, York, UK (2000)
3. Castela, N., Tribolet, J., Silva, A., Guerra, A.: Business Process Modeling with UML. In: 3st. International Conference on Enterprise Information Systems, Setubal, Portugal, vol. 2, pp. 679–685 (2001)
4. Firesmith, D.: Specifying Reusable Security Requirements. Journal of Object Technology 3(1), 61–75 (2004)
5. Fuggetta, A.: Software process: a roadmap. In: ICSE 2000, 22nd International Conference on Software Engineering, Future of Software Engineering, Limerick Ireland pp. 25–34 (2000)
6. Herrmann, G., Pernul, G.: Viewing Business Process Security from Different Perspectives. In: 11th International Bled Electronic Commerce Conference, 1998, Slovenia, pp. 89–103 (1998)
7. Herrmann, P., Herrmann, G.: Security requirement analysis of business processes. Electronic Commerce Research 6(3-4), 305–335 (2006)
8. Jacobson, I., Booch, G., Rumbaugh, J.: El proceso unificado de desarrollo de software, p. 464 (2000)
9. Lopez, J., Montenegro, J.A., Vivas, J.L., Okamoto, E., Dawson, E.: Specification and design of advanced authentication and authorization services. Computer Standards & Interfaces 27(5), 467–478 (2005)
10. Maña, A., Montenegro, J.A., Rudolph, C., Vivas, J.L.: A business process-driven approach to security engineering. In: 14th. International Workshop on Database and Expert Systems Applications (DEXA), Prague, Czech Republic, pp. 477–481 (2003)
11. Maña, A., Ray, D., Sánchez, F., Yagüe, M. I.: Integrando la Ingeniería de Seguridad en un Proceso de Ingeniería Software, VIII Reunión Española de Criptología y Seguridad de la Información, RECSI, Madrid. Españ, pp. 383–392 (2004)
12. Object Management Group; MDA Guide Version 1.0.1. (2003), http://www.omg.org/docs/omg/03-06-01.pdf
13. Object Management Group; Unified Modeling Language: Superstructure, version 2.0, formal/05-07-04 (2005), http://www.omg.org/docs/formal/05-07-04.pdf
14. Quirchmayr, G.: Survivability and Business Continuity Management. In: ACSW Frontiers 2004 Workshops, Dunedin, New Zealand, pp. 3–6 (2004)
15. QVT, Meta Object Facility (MOF) 2.0 Query/View/Transformation Specification, OMG Adopted Specification ptc/05-11-01, p. 204 (2005)
16. Rational Software, Rational Unified Process, Best Practices for Software Development Teams, p. 21 (2001)
17. Rodríguez, A., Fernández-Medina, E., Piattini, M.: Towards a UML 2.0 Extension for the Modeling of Security Requirements in Business Processes. In: Fischer-Hübner, S., Furnell, S., Lambrinoudakis, C. (eds.) TrustBus 2006. LNCS, vol. 4083, pp. 51–61. Springer, Heidelberg (2006)

18. Röhm, A.W., Herrmann, G., Pernul, G.: A Language for Modelling Secure Business Transactions. In: 15th. Annual Computer Security Applications Conference, Phoenix, Arizona, pp. 22–31 (1999)
19. Roser, S., Bauer, B.: A Categorization of Collaborative Business Process Modeling Techniques. In: 7th IEEE International Conference on E-Commerce Technology Workshops (CEC 2005), Munchen, Germany, pp. 43–54 (2005)
20. Rungworawut, W., Senivongse, T.: Using Ontology Search in the Design of Class Diagram from Business Process Model, Enformatika, Transactions on Engineering. Computing and Technology 12, 165–170 (2006)
21. Tryfonas, T., Kiountouzis, E.A.: Perceptions of Security Contributing to the Implementation of Secure IS, Security and Privacy in the Age of Uncertainty, IFIP TC11 18th International Conference on Information Security (SEC2003), Athens, Greece, vol. 250, pp. 313–324 (2003)

A Trust and Context Aware Access Control Model for Web Services Conversations

Marijke Coetzee[1] and J.H.P. Eloff[2]

[1] Academy for Information Technology, University of Johannesburg,
Johannesburg, South-Africa
marijkec@uj.ac.za
[2] Information and Computer Security Architecture research group,
Department of Computer Science, University of Pretoria,
Pretoria, South-Africa
eloff@cs.up.ac.za

Abstract. The design of effective access control models, to meet the unique challenges posed by the web services paradigm, is a current research focus. Despite recent advances in this field, solutions are generally limited to controlling access to single operations of request-response nature. To ensure that a service is used appropriately, message exchanges can be grouped into conversations consisting of related messages that are governed by sequence constraints. Towards addressing the security of message exchanges, this paper describes an access control model for web services conversations. A trust and context aware access control model is presented that promotes the seamless execution of operations contained by web services conversations.

1 Introduction

The emergence and continued development of web services currently sustains the creation of e-business applications. Web services technology [16] has however not reached its full potential, as Internet invocations are generally limited to simple request-response exchanges. The development of protocols for web service conversations is being addressed by current research [20], [4]. For instance, a Travel service exposes several operations in a conversation to allow users to book flights, reserve hotel rooms, view and cancel bookings and make payments. Considering access control, it would be important to ensure that users starting conversations can successfully conclude them, and that conversations are not terminated for the lack of authorisation.

Widespread acceptance of conversational web services will not become a reality if effective security solutions are not found, as web services allow greater availability and access to information, thereby introducing the possibility of more malicious attacks. Vendor-driven specifications that address security are focused around WS-Security [2] that enables the exchange of secure messages between web services requestors and providers. WS-Trust [13] extends WS-Security to establish trust relationships between web services requestors and providers. WS-SecureConversation [1] describes how web services requestors and providers establish a security context with credentials before commencing with message exchanges. Thereafter, a security

C. Lambrinoudakis, G. Pernul, A M. Tjoa (Eds.): TrustBus 2007, LNCS 4657, pp. 115–124, 2007.
© Springer-Verlag Berlin Heidelberg 2007

token accompanies all subsequent messages to increase the overall performance and security of all subsequent messages. Access control rules are defined in XACML to protect web services resources. The use of XACML is limited for conversations, as its profile for RBAC does not address basic requirements such as session-based authorisation management [6].

Several web services access control schemes have been suggested in the past. Research has steadily progressed by suggesting the use of mechanisms such as access control lists [12], role-based access control [22], attribute based access control [21], trust management [19] and context information [5]. Often mechanisms are used in conjunction with each other to enhance flexibility [5], [9], [18]. This research builds upon previous approaches to define an access control model for web services conversations. A contribution is made by illustrating how a trust relationship and related trust context information can be used to manage access control throughout the progression of a conversation.

The paper is structured as follows: Section 2 provides a background on web services conversations, and employs an example to highlight access control requirements. Section 3 describes the approach to trust and trust context information for this research. Section 4 describes all features of the model, and section 5 concludes the paper.

2 Background

A conversation is a sequence of operations aimed at the completion of a general goal, such the fulfillment of an order. A conversation can be supported by a specification such as the Web Services Conversation Language (WSCL) [3], [20] that describes a web service's external behavior. A conversation is maintained by tracking the series of messages going backward and forward between two endpoints with a unique conversation identifier, and demarcated by start and end tags. The conversational nature of web services interactions is now illustrated by means of an example that will be referred to throughout the paper.

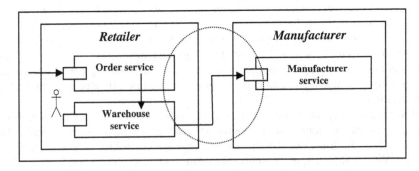

Fig. 1. Web services conversation

The application being modeled is that of a Retailer offering consumer goods, depicted in figure 1. Interactions between the Retailer and Manufacturer services represent automated B2B (Business-to-Business) interactions that take place in a conversational manner. For this paper, a subset of Manufacturer operations is considered such as *SubmitOrder*, *CancelOrder*, *NotifyShipment* and *ReturnGoods*. When requests are made to execute these operations by Warehouse services, the access control policy of the Manufacturer service needs to consider the trust relationship with each of these services. For instance, access to the *SubmitOrder* operation should only be granted to Warehouse services that are trusted, as they would probably pay their orders at a later stage. The context of the trust relationship also influences access control decisions. For instance, the Manufacturer service should only be able to send a shipment notification to a Warehouse service, if it has already paid its order, or is know to pay orders on time. In this case the Warehouse service's payment history, which is context information relating to the Warehouse service's behavior, can ensure that the request is granted.

The Manufacturer service interacts with the Warehouse application, the manager of the warehouse, or the Warehouse web service to where notifications are sent. For example, a Warehouse application automatically invokes the *SubmitOrder* operation of the Manufacturer service when items fall below stock. If necessary, a designated employee such as a warehouse manager can invoke the *CancelOrder* operation within 24 hours. This is only allowed if the manager presents a digital credential stating his authority as an employee designated to this task.

The case study identifies access control requirements for web services conversations namely: trust, trust context information and participants, which need to be dealt with in the access control policy of the web services provider. The next section highlights related research, supporting our approach to access control for web services conversations.

3 Related Work

To address the openness of the environment, researchers in web services and other distributed system technologies employ trust as mechanism to allow cross-domain movement of users and application entities, represented by digital credentials [7], [15], [19]. The enforcement of access control for web services conversations has been addressed by considering the release of policies during trust negotiation [17]. To ensure that a conversation can be concluded successfully, all policies that relate to the conversation are released to users, so that they can provide required credentials.

Web services access control based on trust and context constraints is described by Bhatti et al [5]. A user is assigned to a role, based on the trust in the certified attributes the user presents. In this case, trust is of binary nature and is based on cryptographic controls. Context constraints, such as time and location, are further used to ensure fine-grained access to resources. The concept of access control based on a trust level was discussed by Chakraborty and Ray [8], who described a role-based access control model that assigns roles to users based on their trust level. A consequence of computing a trust level for individual users accessing a system is that it may result in excessive overheads.

In line with current research, the authors of this paper have defined a trust formation framework that determines trust levels for web services entities [10], [11].

The reader is referred to [11] for a discussion of this work. A trust level for each web services requestor is determined by a trust component. Information is stored in memory and can dynamically be requested by the access control policy to adapt the assignment of permissions. Trust context information, over which trust is defined is for instance the identity of the web services requestor; security and privacy policies that regulate the environment between the web services requestor and provider; the past history and experiences associated with the web services requestor; and service level agreements that exist between the web services requestor and the web services provider. Such trust context information is hierarchically structured and evaluated by means of a fuzzy mathematical model to obtain the resultant trust level intuitively.

Based on the well-known definition of context by Dey and Abowd [14], trust context in the realm of a web services trust relationship is defined as the information that characterises the trust in the web services requestor, the web services provider and the external environment that they share, which is considered relevant to the conversation taking place between them. At the next level of this hierarchy, the trust in the web services requestor is for instance determined by four trust context categories namely *Compliance to agreements*, *Competence*, *Predictability* and *Goodwill*. Each represent summarized trust context information, determined by fuzzy techniques and indicates the degree to which the trust context information is realised. The trust level, inferred from trust context categories, represents the degree to which a trust relationship exists.

Such trust levels therefore do not reflect the trust held towards individuals, but rather the trust held towards organisational entities, represented by web service requestors such as Warehouse services. These trust level enables the construction of rules which can be included in access control policies to treat trusted web services requestors differently from those in whom there is little or no trust. Trust levels also influence permissions that are assigned to respective users operating within the domain of web services requestors.

The current research proposes that a trust level and its related context information are employed to support access control decision-making during web services conversations. The rationale behind this statement is that if the trust level of a web services requestor is not sufficient to access an operation, there may be cases where relevant trust context information, representing specific conditions which are related to the state of the conversation can be used, enabling the conversation to conclude successfully.

The next section describes a trust and context aware access control model for web services conversations that illustrates the how trust context information, identified in this section, can be used by access control decisions of a web services conversation.

4   Access Control Model for Web Services Conversations

The access control model presented in this paper is based on the trust relationship that exists between a web services provider and web services requestor. At the same time, the access control model is in line with current developments in attribute-based access control, as access is granted to users, such as the warehouse manager, based on their abilities, expressed as sets of attributes. As the trust relationship between a web services provider and its web services requestors dominates all interactions, it is possible that a user may be granted access to a particular operation from one domain, but users from another domain may be denied access even though they possess similar credentials. Finally, the context of the trust relationship is used to compensate for potential lack of available trust information, to allow a conversation to complete successfully. Important features of the proposed model are defined next, followed by a definition of rules and facts which should be part of the access control policy. A high-level view of the access control model is given in figure 2.

CSession. A conversation session is defined as a set of messages, identified by start, continue and end message tags. A csession $\in$ CSESSION is identified by a unique identifier. There can only be one web services requestor that participates in a conversation session, but a web services providers can participate in many conversation sessions.

WSObject is the set of all web services objects that require protection in the domain of a web services provider. A web service object is an expression of the form wsobject = value, where wsobject $\in$ WSOBJECT and value is a variable, and wsobject is a web service operation, a collection of operations, a web service or a collection of web services that are exposed by the web services provider. Such relationships introduce a partial order $\subseteq_{wsobj}$ on the set of web service objects, where operations are the minimal elements of the partial order.

SAction is the set of all signed actions. A signed action is an expression of the form saction = value. Given a set of actions A, a set of values saction $\in$ SACTION is defined as $\{+a, -a \mid a \in A\}$. An example of a signed action would be saction = "+exe".

AccessDecision is the set of all access decisions that can be made by the system of the web services provider. Permissions, defined by the set WSOBJECT x SACTION, are assigned to either roles or user attributes, and are used to derive access decisions.

WSRequestor is the set of all web services requestors who require access to operations and services provided by web services providers. A web services requestor is an expression of the form wsrequestor = value, where wsrequestor $\in$ WSREQUESTOR, wsrequestor is the identifier of a web services requestor, and value is a variable.

TrustLevel is the set of all trust levels, defined as $\{ignorance, low, moderate, high\}$. Trust levels are defined in a hierarchy where $ignorance \subseteq low \subseteq moderate \subseteq good \subseteq high$. The trust level is an expression of the form trustlevel = value, where trustlevel $\in$ TRUSTLEVEL, and value is a variable. During a conversation, a web services requestor is assigned to a role or a set of roles based on its trust level.

CxtConstraint is an expression in the form cxtconstraint(wsrequestor, $attr_i$, $attr_j$), where cxtconstraint $\in$ *CXTCONSTRAINT*, cxtconstraint is the name of the constraint, and $attr_1..attr_j$ is the list of elements. For each $0 < i \leq j$, $attr_i$=value, where value is a variable.

ReqRole is the set of all roles assigned to web services requestors. The role reflects the relationship that the web services provider has with the web services requestor. A reqrole is an expression of the form reqrole = value, where reqrole ∈ REQROLE, and value is a variable. Examples of roles are guest, associate, and partner that are defined in a role hierarchy.

UsrAttr are sets of attributes representing users and is an expression in the form UsrAttr(attr$_1$, attr$_j$), where usrattr ∈ *USRATTR*, usrattr is the name of the assertion, and attr$_1$, . . attr$_j$ is the list of elements. For each $0 < i \leq j$, attr$_i$=value, where value is a variable.

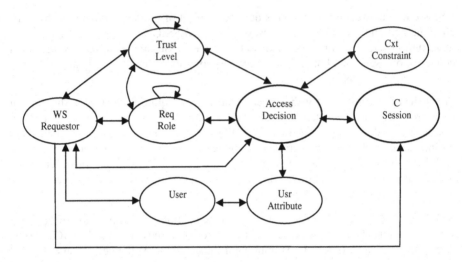

Fig. 2. Access control model

4.1 Access Control Policy Rules

Access control rules are represented as logical expressions in Datalog [23], [24]. To make an access control decision, a query ?*dercando*(wsobject, wsrequestor, +saction) is answered by a process of inference. For example, the query *dercando*(submitorder, abcretail, +exe) determines if web services requestor ABCRetail can execute the *SubmitOrder* operation. Access control rules and facts are described next, where variables are defined in uppercase and constants in lowercase.

Assume that **moderately** trusted web service requestors may be granted access to the *SubmitOrder, CancelOrder, NotifyShipment* operations. *ReturnGoods* is an operation granted only to **highly** trusted web services requestors. Assume there is a retailer named ABCRetail who is moderately trusted. Roles are defined in the systems as follows: the associate role has a moderate (moderate = 2) trust level and the partner role has a high   (high = 3) trust level. Next, three different cases, identified by the case study, are considered to illustrate the operation of the access control model.

Case 1: Access decision based on the trust level of a web services requestor
First, access granted to web services requestors, automatically invoking operations, is discussed. In this case, a web services requestor may access an operation, if the web services requestor is active in the role to which the permission has been assigned,

shown by rule 1. Rule 2 determines this role activation by comparing the trust levels of the web service requestor and roles. Trust levels are retrieved from the trust component when facts are instantiated. The *cando* predicate defines a permission to access the object.

```
dercando(WSOBJECT, WSREQUESTOR, +SACTION) :-
  cando(WSOBJECT,REQROLE,+SACTION) ∧ active(WSREQUESTOR, REQROLE).(1)
active(WSREQUESTOR, REQROLE) :-
  (reqtl(WSREQUESTOR, TLREQUESTOR), roletl(REQROLE, TLROLE) ∧
    ((TLREQUESTOR > TLROLE) ∨ (TLREQUESTOR = TLROLE)).          (2)
```

For example, assume ABCRetail needs to execute the *SubmitOrder* operation. Facts instantiated in the access control policy are:

```
cando(submitorder, associate, +exe).   - permission   (associate = 2)
reqtl(abcretail, 2).                    - trust level of service requestor
roletl(associate, 2).                   - trust level of role
```

Permission is thus granted to ABCRetail to execute the *SubmitOrder* operation as permission exist for web services requestors active in the associate role to execute the *SubmitOrder* operation. ABCRetail activates this role since its trust level is moderate.

Case 2: Access decision based the context of the trust relationship
Secondly, access granted to web services requestors who have made progress in a conversation, but who do not have an adequate trust level to access an operation is considered. In order to support the continuation of the conversation, trust context is used where possible, to compensate for the lack of trust, as indicated by the trust level of the web services requestor. The trust level of the web services requestor can be one level lower that what is required, determined by the *below* predicate. The *canaccess* predicate defines a permission to access the object. Rule 3 extends rule 1 to include these features.

```
dercando(WSOBJECT, WSREQUESTOR, +SACTION) :-
  (cando(WSOBJECT, REQROLE, +SACTION) ∧ active(WSREQUESTOR, REQROLE)) ∨
  (below(WSREQUESTOR ∧ canaccess(WSOBJECT, +SACTION) ∧
  cxtconstraint(WSREQUESTOR, ATTR .. ATTRⱼ)).                  (3)

below(WSREQUESTOR) :-
  (reqtl(WSREQUESTOR, TLREQUESTOR), roletl(REQROLE, TLROLE) ∧
  (diff is TLROLE - TLREQUESTOR) ∧ (diff = 1)).                (4)
```

For example, access to the *ReturnGoods* operation is granted to web services requestors in whom there is **high** trust. To allow the conversation to proceed at this point, relevant trust context that can be considered are *predictability* and *creditworthiness*, in conjunction with a *moderate* trust level. Creditworthiness is a trust context category found under competence, described earlier. This information is used in conjunction with good trust in the environment between the web services provider and web services requestor, another trust context category. By granting web services requestors with a **moderate** trust level access to the *ReturnGoods* operation, organisational trust relationships are cultivated with those who have potential to become highly trusted partners in the future. Rule 4 specifies trust context constraints for the *ReturnGoods* operation if the trust level is insufficient.

```
canaccess(returngoods, +exe) ∧ trustenvironment(WSREQUESTOR, TV = good) ∧
predictable(WSREQUESTOR, PR = high) ∧ creditrec(WSREQUESTOR,
                                      CR = good).                        (4)
```

For example, assume ABCRetail needs to execute the *ReturnGoods* operation. Its trust level is moderate, and it has progressed to the last point of the order conversation. The following facts exist in the access control policy:

```
canaccess(returngoods, +exe).          - permission
reqtl(abcretail, 2).                    - trust level of service requestor
roletl(partner, 3).                     - trust level of role
trustenvironment(abcretail, good).      - trust in environment is good
predictable(abcretail, high).           - predictability is high
creditrec(abcretail, good).             - creditrecord is good
```

ABCRetail, a web services requestor with a moderate trust level, is thus granted access to the *ReturnGoods* operation, as the trust in the environment with the web services provider is good, its predictability is high, and its credit record is good. Each of these trust context categories is retrieved from the trust component, where they are stored in memory.

Case 3: Access decision based on the attributes of a user

Finally, access granted to the user making a request from within the domain of the web services requestor is considered. The manager is not considered as an individual acting on his/her own authority, but rather as a member of a trusted partner, acting on its behalf. The level of trust in the web services requestor influences the access granted to the user. The user must present a credential containing required attributes, over and above conditions stated in rule 3. The *usrcando* predicate defines a permission to access the object.

```
dercando(WSOBJECT, WSREQUESTOR, +SACTION) :-
 (cando(WSOBJECT, REQROLE, +SACTION) ∧ active(WSREQUESTOR, REQROLE) ∧
   usrcando(WSOBJECT, +SACTION)) ∨
 (below(WSREQUESTOR ∧ canaccess(WSOBJECT, +SACTION) ∧
   cxtconstraint(WSREQUESTOR, ATTR .. ATTRⱼ) ∧
   usrcando(WSOBJECT, +SACTION)).                                     (5)

usrcando(WSOBJECT, +SACTION) :- attr(ATTR₁ ,… ATTRⱼ).                 (6)
```

Consider the case where the *CancelOrder* operation is executed by a warehouse manager, of ABCRetailer. The access control rule specifies that ABCRetailer application must be active in the associate role, and that the user making the request must present a digital credential stating his title and permission for the operation.

```
cando(cancelorder, associate, +exe).    - permission
reqtl(abcretail, 2).                     - trust level of service requestor
roletl(associate, 2).                    - trust level of role
attr(title = senior manager,
     permit = may-cancel-orders).        - user attributes
```

The manager is granted access to invoke the CancelOrder operation, because ABCRetailer is a moderately trusted web services requestor, and trusted attributes are presented stating the ability of the manager. If there was low trust in the web services requestor, the manager would not have been able to invoke this operation, even if he/she presents valid credentials.

5 Conclusion

This paper presented a trust and context aware access control model for web services conversations that grants and adapts permissions assigned to both web services requestors and their respective users based on the current context of the trust relationship that exists. The paper proposes that access control for web services conversations can only be implemented meaningfully if the trust context over which decisions are made is firmly entrenched in the decision-making process. The paper highlights that an access decision is made based on the evaluation of different types of permissions, defined for different types of entities making requests to the web service, in conjunction with trust and context restrictions. The paper does not address context information relating to aspects such as time and location. Next research will address reasoning over hierarchical trust context information by means of logical rules.

Acknowledgement

This material is supported by the NRF in South Africa under Grant Number 2054024 and TTK2006061500002, as well as by Telkom and the IST through THRIP.

References

1. Anderson, S., Bohren, J., Boubez, T., Chanliau, M., Della-Libera, G., Dixon, B.: Web Services Secure Conversation Language (WS-SecureConversation) (February 2005)
2. Atkinson, B., et al.: Web Services Security (WS-Security), Version 1.0 (5 April 2002), http://www.verisign.com/wss/wss.pdf
3. Banerji, A., Bartolini, C., Beringer, D., Chopella, V., Govindarajan, K., Karp, A.: Web Services Conversation Language (WSCL) (2002), http://www.w3.org/TR/wscl10/
4. Benatallah, B., Casati, F., Toumani, F., Hamadi, R.: Conceptual Modeling of Web Service Conversations. In: Eder, J., Missikoff, M. (eds.) CAiSE 2003. LNCS, vol. 2681, pp. 449–467. Springer, Heidelberg (2003)
5. Bhatti, R., Bertino, E., Ghafoor, A.: A Trust-Based Context-Aware Access Control Model for Web-Services. Distributed and Parallel Databases archive 18(1), 83–105 (2005)

6. Bhatti, R., Bertino, E., Ghafoor, A.: An integrated approach to federated identity and privilege management in open systems. Commun. ACM 50(2), 81–87 (2007)
7. Blaze, M., Feigenbaum, J., Ioannidis, J., Keromytis, A.D.: The role of trust management in distributed systems security. In Proceedings of Fourth International Workshop on Mobile Object Systems: Secure Internet Mobile Computations. In: Vitek, J. (ed.) Secure Internet Programming. LNCS, vol. 1603, pp. 185–210. Springer, Heidelberg (1999)
8. Chakraborty, S., Ray, I.: TrustBAC: integrating trust relationships into the RBAC model for access control in open systems. In: SACMAT 2006, pp. 49–58 (2006)
9. Coetzee, M., Eloff, J.H.P.: Towards Web Services access control. Computers and Security 23(7) (2004)
10. Coetzee, M., Eloff, J.H.P.: Autonomous trust for Web Services. Internet Research 15(5) (2005)
11. Coetzee, M., Eloff, J.H.P.: A Framework for Web Services Trust. In: 21st IFIP International Information Security Conference, Security and Privacy in Dynamic Environments, Karlstad University, 22 - 24 May, 2006, Karlstad, Sweden (2006)
12. Damiani, E., De Capitani Di Vimercati, S., Paraboschi, S., Samarati, P.: Fine-grained access control for SOAP e-services. In: Proceedings of the 10th International World Wide Web Conference (WWW10), May 1-5, 2001, Hong Kong (2001)
13. Della-Libera, G., et al.: Web Services Trust Language (WS-Trust) (2003), http://www.ibm.com/developerworks/library/ws-trust/index.html
14. Dey, A., Abowd, G.D.: Towards a Better Understanding of Context and Context-Awareness. In: the Workshop on The What, Who, Where, When, and How of Context-Awareness, 2000 Conference on Human Factors in Computing Systems, The Hague, The Netherlands (2000)
15. Dimitrakos, T.: A service-oriented trust management framework. In: Falcone, R., Barber, S., Korba, L., Singh, M.P. (eds.) AAMAS 2002. LNCS (LNAI), vol. 2631, pp. 53–72. Springer, Heidelberg (2003)
16. Gottschalk, K., Graham, S., Kreger, H., Snell, J.: Introduction to web services architecture. IBM Systems Journal 41(2) (2002)
17. Mecella, M., Ouzzani, M., Paci, F., Bertino, E.: Access control enforcement for conversation-based web services. In: WWW 2006, pp. 257–266 (2006)
18. Miao, L., He-Qing, G., Jin-Dian, S.: An attribute and role based access control model for Web services. In: International Conference on Machine Learning and Cybernetics, vol. 2, pp. 1302–1306 (2005)
19. Olson, L., Winslett, M., Tonti, G., Seeley, N., Uszok, A., Bradshaw, J.M.: Trust Negotiation as an Authorization Service for Web Services. In: ICDE Workshops, vol. 21 (2006)
20. Paurobally, S., Jennings, N.R.: Protocol engineering for web services conversations. Engineering Applications of Artificial Intelligence 18(2), 237–254 (2005)
21. Shen, H., Hong, F.: An Attribute-Based Access Control Model for Web Services. In: Proceedings of the Seventh International Conference on Parallel and Distributed Computing, Applications and Technologies, pp. 74–79 (2006)
22. Wonohoesodo, R., Tari, Z.: A Role based Access Control for Web Services, Services Computing. In: IEEE International Conference on (SCC'04), pp. 49–56 (2004)
23. Jajodia, S., Samarati, P., Subramanian, V.S.: A logical language for expressing authorisations. In: Proceedings of the 1997 IEEE Symposium on Security and Privacy, Oakland, CA, IEEE Computer Society Press, Los Alamitos (1997)
24. Li, N., Mitchell, J.C.: Datalog with constraints: A foundation for trust-management languages. In: Dahl, V., Wadler, P. (eds.) PADL 2003. LNCS, vol. 2562, pp. 58–73. Springer, Heidelberg (2002)

Design and Implementation of Distributed Access Control Infrastructures for Federations of Autonomous Domains

Petros Belsis[1], Stefanos Gritzalis[1], Christos Skourlas[3], and Vassillis Tsoukalas[2]

[1] Department of Information and Communication Systems Engineering University of the
Aegean, Karlovassi, Samos, Greece
{pbelsis,sgritz}@aegean.gr
[2] Department of Informatics, Technological Education Institute, Athens, Greece
cskourlas@teiath.gr
[3] Department of Industrial Informatics, Technological Education Institute, Kavala, Greece
vtsouk@teikav.edu.gr

Abstract. Federations of autonomous domains allow resource sharing in a highly dynamic manner, improving organizational response times and facilitating cooperation between different information systems. To accomplish this, it is essential to provide a scalable and flexible mechanism that allows security management and acts at application level independently of operating system or platform. In this paper we present a scalable solution that enables interoperation between different systems participating in a dynamic federation, while it also allows the participating systems to retain their autonomy; we present the software architecture of this distributed access control enforcement mechanism and describe our implementation choices.

1 Introduction

Over the last decades we have experienced a major shift towards the decentralized, distributed computing paradigm. The benefits from the realization of distributed infrastructures are manifold; among else, many challenges have attracted considerable attention in distributed computing, such as: implementation of sophisticated knowledge extraction techniques that enable utilization of assets from different domains; achievement of interoperability between different platforms; performance issues and last but not least, advances in distributed security models. Most of the developed security techniques apply at operating system level; other solutions apply by embedding at each application a customized security mechanism that enables access to authorized users, before logging in. As a consequence, in order to utilize resources in distributed infrastructures, a user has to undergo several independent authorization procedures. This task creates a considerable overhead on each domain, while it also makes more difficult any attempt for Information System's integration. Another parameter that has to be considered is the immediate drop in the degree of user satisfaction, which can prove to be detrimental in business application scenarios.

While decentralization of administrative control requires that all participating domains specify their policies in an interoperable manner, there are a number of challenges related with the ability to transfer the credentials of users in the federated

C. Lambrinoudakis, G. Pernul, A M. Tjoa (Eds.): TrustBus 2007, LNCS 4657, pp. 125–134, 2007.

environment across organizational boundaries [1]. In order to achieve this, there is a requirement to establish interoperable protocols and to provide support for composite policy evaluation.

One additional concern regarding the management of distributed systems is related to heterogeneity, due to the presence of resources of diverse nature. In this paper we describe a distributed infrastructure utilizing XML technologies for access control enforcement. The system's modular components communicate using the Java Remote Method Invocation (RMI) model. The developed prototype is characterized by its scalability potential and its platform independency. The contribution of this paper relies on the following: (i) We present a technique that enables cooperation and resource sharing between multiple autonomous domains; (ii) we present techniques that enable user authentication through a single sign-on procedure for all domains, simplifying thus the authentication procedures to a high degree; (iii) We enable ease of integration of our access control mechanism with existing platforms, while we retain platform and operating system independency.

The remainder of the paper is organized as follows. After the brief introduction, we present the motivation for our research in Section 1; related work and background literature is studied in Section 2. Section 3 analyses the requirements placed on the system design and Section 4 raises and discusses issues related to the system's design and provides example usage scenarios; Section 5 provides concluding remarks and directions for future work.

2 Related Work

The problem of defining access control models for multi-domain environments has recently attracted considerable interest. A number of solutions have been proposed towards this direction. So far, more emphasis has been placed on implementing models, than for creating mechanisms that enable secure interoperation between different domains. In [2] the notion of secure virtual enclaves is being introduced, where domains complying with the Role Based Access Control (RBAC) model share resources. In this work the roles and shared resources are specified in advance and agreed without using technological means, providing thus little support towards the formation of dynamic coalitions.

Bonatti et al [3], propose an algebra for the synthesis of an access control policy out of simpler policies. In their model their language's expressiveness is analyzed with respect to first order logic. They show that their language's formal semantics are equivalent to first order logic formulations. Even though this work provides a tool for preliminary feasibility analysis, the exact implementation details to provide support for coalition formation are missing [3].

Khurana et al [4], define a model for the dynamic management of coalitions based on a Restricted First Order Predicate Logic (RFOPL) RBAC compliant language RCL 2000. In their model, domains take turns in making proposals about the management of shared coalition assets resources. A coalition access control matrix is being formulated keeping records of allowed accesses, while the matrix is being modified during the negotiation process and as intermediate system states are formed. Their work also builds upon a negotiation process that defines membership upon roles with predefined access permissions instead of negotiating the permissions according to the role classified for every specific user, as defined instead in our work.

Another notable approach that builds upon an XML policy language is the X-GTRBAC framework [1]. This framework provides support for most of the RBAC concepts, such as Separation of Duty Constraints; it also has an integrated mechanism for resolving conflicts emerging from ambiguities or conflicting requirements from the domain specific policies. Unfortunately there are no supporting software tools for this framework so far. Instead of defining a new language, we have decided to utilize evolving standards in access controls and extend them appropriately and develop suitable software tools for multi-domain environments security management. Our work in addition develops a scalable infrastructure built upon independent modules that interoperate using evolving standards in access control.

3 Requirements Analysis

Among the basic requirements when developing distributed access control enforcement infrastructures is the preservation of autonomy. The requirement for decentralization of administrative control in multi-domain environments poses major challenges when specifying the framework for access control policy definition. Decentralization in our framework is achieved by implementing multiple autonomous domains each one of which is responsible for enforcing local access control policies. Each policy enables determination of access privileges for role-access-object pairs, in accordance to the generic Role Based Access Control Model (RBAC) compliant policy definition.

Our framework builds upon the main principles of the XACML [6] policy framework which focuses on enabling distributed management of resources. XACML is an XML based framework for specifying and applying access control for Web-based resources that supports prohibitions, obligations, and resolution of conflicts. Our extended authorization framework has the following strong points:

- It is built using standardized technologies, thus providing support for extensions and enables interoperation between various platforms
- It allows extensions as to support the needs for a variety of environments.
- It allows context-based authorization, by enabling authorization upon examination of domain related predicates (see also section 4).

Our work extends this single-domain authorization framework to provide support for role and privilege assignment for users belonging to remote domains. This is necessary when users from one domain need to be assigned privileges to access data from other federated domains. In order to achieve this interconnection between different domains, several issues need to be taken under consideration:

- Access to data should be regulated by specific generic guidelines, applicable for all the cooperating environments.
- While the data access guidelines should be uniform, enforcement points should be autonomous and have a large degree of freedom in managing their IT infrastructure.

- Dynamic nature of the coalition. The number of units who participate in the cooperating schema is not stable. Units can join or depart at any time, increasing thus the complexity of the overall management.
- Absence of centralized authorization architecture. Security policies can be defined locally without the necessity for central management which would endanger the system's performance by introducing a single point of failure. It would also not be consistent to the distributed nature of the system.
- Transparency to the users. The procedures for retrieving i.e. medical-record details, whether retrieved locally or from a remote domain should be of no difference to the user.

3.1 Generic Access Control Enforcement Model

The basic operational principles of our framework can be divided in two major categories: authentication-related and authorization-specific. Authentication is performed by implementing a mechanism that allows interpretation using SAML [7] compliant assertions for authenticating credentials. The SAML standard provides support for various types of authentication information; a SAML assertion provides information that the requester's credentials match predefined policy requirements. In order to provide an efficient and robust mechanism to verify the user's identity we have utilised X.509 certificates. Thus, the first task for a user is to provide appropriate credentials that will allow him/her identification within the domain he/she belongs to. The SAML assertion issued by the authentication module can be further used by the access control framework in the presence of multiple policies, eliminating the necessity for a user to undergo multiple authentication procedures within the context of the federated environment.

Every solution attempting to enable intra-domain communication should be characterized by its interoperability and scalability features. Our approach in order to enable cooperation between different access policies, builds upon a policy mapping process, which enables roles from one domain to be mapped to another domain [1][9]. In a multi-domain environment, a requester usually originates from a different domain than the one that the requested resource belongs to. As we already stated in the previous paragraphs, a basic requirement is related with the credential management in the federated environment in such a manner that a single sign-on (SSO) mechanism is provided [12]. By integrating in our authentication mechanism SSO capabilities through signed SAML statements, different domains in the federated environment identify authorization decisions already issued by other domains. In addition, our framework provides support for context-enabled authorization and authentication; this is achieved by incorporating context related environmental attributes in role definitions (for example the domain where a user belongs, such as medical.administration.gov). In cases where a request does not originate from the same domain with the PDP, the PDP communicates with the coalition registry which stores information about the available mappings for the requester's role. Each PDP contains information about in-mappings consisting information about roles from remote domains associated with roles to its own jurisdiction and out-mappings for roles in other domains that its policy is associated with. Our approach thus results in a distributed implementation of the coalition registry, which only stores information on a domain-pair basis.

Table 1. Xpath based role mapping between roles in two domains

DOMAIN A	DOMAIN B
Minister/GenSecretaryB/SectorB2Manager	Minister/GenSecretary/SectorBDirector

Typically if we consider that the policy is encoded in XML compatible form, the coalition registry contains information about role equivalences between different role hierarchies, which can be encoded by means of XPath expressions [8]. XPath aims at addressing parts of XML documents. It represents location of data in an XML document correctly and efficiently, which makes it a suitable language for both XML query and access control [11]. An example mapping based on XPath is presented in Table 1. This provides an example of a mapping codification example, where the XPath expressions identify role equivalences between different role hierarchies. Therefore we define paths that allow the mapping of roles between different role schemata. Notice that due to the expressiveness of XPath, one can represent more complex role mappings in a very compact way, by grouping together equivalent roles in one XPath expression, without having to write separate rules for each role. The applicability of such a solution is apparent in case of organizations which operate under a common framework (example medical organizations, ministries in e-Government environments, etc).

We enable role mapping to be performed on single-direction basis i.e. a role in one organization could acquire the permissions of another role on the target domain, without the opposite being necessary valid. The next section discusses in detail our proposed approach and we underline the design decisions we undertook in respect to the system design issues raised in this section.

Upon authentication of the requester, the authorization framework works as follows: The administrator edits the policy in appropriate format and makes it available to the PDP. Each request is directed to the Policy Enforcement Point (PEP) which constructs a XACML request message and directs it to the Policy Decision Point (PDP). The PDP proceeds by loading the policy from the policy repository and evaluating the request according to the loaded policy. Accordingly the response is formulated in an XACML response message and is directed to the PEP which finally enforces the decision, authorizing or rejecting the request.

4 System Architecture and Implementation

The distributed policy authorization module is realized by means of object-oriented software architecture, using Java. The system design can be represented using UML class diagrams. Figure 2 depicts a UML based representation of the software architecture meta-model, which extends the single-domain XACML's generic model by introducing the multi-domain management classes.

The main classes of the model include the following: Rule, Policy and PolicySet. The Policy class manages those policies which refer to shared target objects. A target refers to a set of resources under request (Objects requested), the subject (requestor's role) and the action intended to be performed over the shared objects.

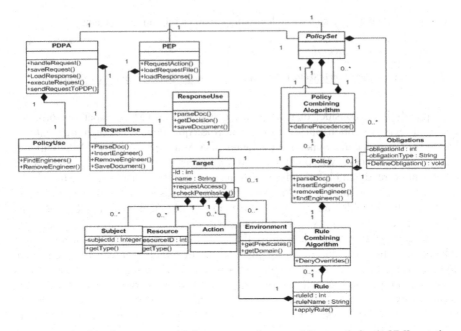

Fig. 1. The distributed access control infrastructure software architecture design in UML notation

The effect of a Rule indicates the result of a logical (i.e. true or false) evaluation of the rule. The allowed actions we have provisioned for are "Permit" and "Deny". A policy <Target> element specifies the subsets resources, actions and environment to which the policy applies. Obligation policies may be supported but their existence is not deemed as necessary, considering our requirements. Obligation policies are likely to be defined by administrators and their characteristic is that there may be less strict controls on modifying an obligation policy. For example, a negative obligation policy may act as a restraining guideline in cases where it is not practical or feasible to issue a negative authorization policy. Policy interoperation is ruled by a Policy combining algorithm, implemented by an appropriate class, responsible for resolving conflicts and ambiguities; depending on the criticality of shared resources, a deny overrides mechanism specifies the priority of access denial criterion in case of a conflict. Subject and Resource classes enable including constraint determination and manipulation in the role-specification schema; for example temporal constraints (determination of activating and deactivating times for a session) or environmental constraints that facilitate role management and enable defining a set of actions for a group of users characterized by common attributes. The distributed PEP and PDP which enable interoperation in a federated environment have been implemented by means of appropriate classes.

The PEP handles authorization enforcement and is responsible for formulating the request for a resource in a XACML compliant message and subsequently forwarding it to the PDP. Furthermore, the PDP except from reasoning over a specific access request provides through its interface the ability to edit and load available policies

Table 2a (left). An Excerpt from an XACML request. The requester's attribute is highlighted, as well as the requested resource. **Table 2b (right)** XACML response message.

<Request> <Subject> <Attribute > <AttributeValue>secretary@nsf.gov</AttributeValue> </Attribute></Subject> <Resource><Attribute><AttributeValue> file://record/ResearcherlRecords/PeterDoe </AttributeValue></Attribute></Resource> <Action><Attribute><AttributeValue>read </AttributeValue></Attribute></Action> </Request>	<Response> <Result> <Decision>NotApplicable </Decision> </Result> </Response>

from the domain's policy repository. Our PDP's interface allows loading policies from the policy repository and editing them invoking the PolicyUse class. In a similar manner, the PEP constructs the XACML compatible request (Table 2a) and also extracts the response from the XACML response (Table 2b) by invoking the ResponseUse class. All the main modules of the developed prototype represented in UML notation are represented in Figure 2.

4.1 System Usage Scenario - Implementation Details

When a request for a resource appears, it is directed towards the PEP of the domain that contains the requested objects. The request includes the requested object, the subject (requester) and the action (permission) over that resource. Imagine the following scenario: a doctor who works as a general practitioner in two different hospitals while located in hospital B, wants to access some files that he/she has created in hospital A. Since there is a request for files to a remote domain, the authorization process works as follows: the authentication server issues a signed credential which will be also recognized by the corresponding module in hospital B; thus domain B's authentication module is invoked, evaluating the provided by domain A's SAML assertions, allowing a single sign-on procedure for all the participating domains in the coalition. Accordingly domain A's PEP identifies the address of all the cooperating PDP's and forwards the request to them. Each PDP maintains records of

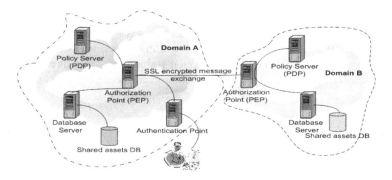

Fig. 3. Multi-domain access control enforcement

the role equivalences from other domains in its coalition registry; thus hospital's B PDP will identify the doctor as one of the roles that should be authorized to access hospital B resources. The invocation also of the context handler integrated in the authentication module and using XACML's context enabled role definition, allows easily authentication evaluating domain specific attributes for a role (such as the domain that the request originates from; for example we authenticate all users that originate from a specific domain like: medical.admin.gov). These attributes can be easily included in the generic XML-based role definition schema. The issued credential along with the request is directed to the domain's PEP which upon receiving an access request, formulates a XACML compliant message indicating the requester, the object to be accessed and the permission under request and directs it to the PDP.

From a technical perspective, there were several issues to consider: first, the need to provide a means to authenticate all users with a single sign-on mechanism; second, the necessity to provide a technique to allow efficiently a mechanism for policy interoperation; third, to provide a technique to reflect easily policy updates, while retaining the security features of the system.

Communication between the different modules from the remote domains is achieved using Java's Remote Method Invocation Model; the reason for selecting this is that it allows to reflect easily updates in both domains authentication-authorization models and to reflect also easily policy updates. Figure 3 gives an overview of the generic architecture of the distributed access control framework. The authenticating module functions in a way that was presented in the beginning of the current section. The authorization framework implemented for our experimental federated environment which consisted of 3 subnets, functions as follows: Each PDP (one for each domain) through the developed for our evaluation purposes prototype interface provides the ability to edit and modify policies. The PEP provides through the interface the ability to formulate requests, and then constructs an appropriate message in XACML format. Through an RMI call the PEP identifies the PDPs of the cooperating domains and directs an XACML message. Accordingly the message is parsed by the parsing module and the original request is identified from the message's payload. Then the policy is loaded from the policy repository and finally the request is evaluated against the available policies. Finally a response message is sent to the PEP which enforces the decision. For the overall system, the potential impact on the PEP's performance is small since there is absence of a centralized PEP; on the contrary, the PEP is implemented in a distributed manner. We have implemented an experimental topology comprising of three different domains with different role hierarchies. Each domain comprises of a different sub-network each one with its own PEP and PDP; these independent modules communicate using Java RMI. For our evaluation scenario we have directed several concurrent requests from each domain towards the other, measuring the capability of our prototype to correctly evaluate those different access requests.

5 Conclusions

In this paper we presented a distributed authorization framework that supports federated autonomous environments. Among its more distinctive features are: (i) its distributed nature that allows maintenance of autonomy of participating domains; (ii) credential management using single authentication procedures by means of SAML assertions (iii) incorporation of context-related parameters in role specification schemas that effortlessly allow for context-based authentication and authorization. Moreover we can distinguish its scalability support due to the low complexity of the role mapping mechanism; we presented its salient features that support interoperability, since it utilizes XML-based technologies for role specification and role mapping codification. The fact that the coalition registry is also implemented in a distributed manner facilitates its deployment as it demands fewer resources and avoids the existence of a single point of failure as in the case of deploying it in a centralized manner.

We have presented a prototype implementation as part of an ongoing research work; throughout the paper we have presented a generic software architecture using UML notation as well as an operation scenario explaining in detail the role of each module. So far we have tested our prototype using an experimental setting of three different domains and the initial findings are promising. Our framework provides the possibility to apply access controls at application level, providing platform and operating system independency.

Our architecture supports the satisfaction of the requirements recorded in section 3 by: a) providing access to data for users in the federated domain using the presented architecture which applies the policy rules for each domain, while it facilitates autonomy maintenance for all the participating domains; b) by not restricting the number of domains that join or leave the federation since maintenance of coalition related information adds only a small amount of information overhead to the coalition registry; c) there is absence of centralized management. Each domain may cooperate with each other without intermediate management.

One of the main limitations of our approach is the fact that policy mappings have to be agreed by means of bilateral service level agreements between domain administrators; such a limitation though may not always be restrictive, since it is the case for most federated frameworks [10] such as e-Government alliances, or e-healthcare coalitions, to regulate under a common framework; moreover, the legal implications of an inappropriate access to sensitive personal data make automated coalition formation a risky process. In addition, it has been proved that the problem of automated negotiation for more than two policies is intractable [5]. In cases also that there is no direct equivalency in between the different role hierarchies, it is easy to create a new role on one of the hierarchies so as to provide support for a remote domain to access only specific shared resources. In addition the complexity of the approach is by far less than that of creating a global policy out of the component policies of the individual domains and requires less time to integrate a new role equivalency in the coalition registry.

The technical challenges that had to be overcome by the proposed approach are manifold: the architecture of the platform allows ease integration of a large number of domains, supporting thus scalability to a high extent; in addition the policy mappings have been implemented using a low cost technique by both means of technical feasibility and information overhead, something that makes it possible to integrate the platform over wireless infrastructures that lack hardware resources.

Our future work focuses on providing an automated framework to facilitate conflict resolution for the participating domains and on testing the validity of our framework by extensive experimentation for a large number of domains.

References

1. Bhatti, E., Bertino, E., Ghafoor, A.: A Policy framework for Access Management in Federated Information Sharing. In: IFIP Joint Working Conference on Security Management, Integrity, and Internal Control in Information systems, Fairfax USA, December 2005, pp. 95–120. Springer, Heidelberg (2005)
2. Shands, D., Yee, R., Jacobs, J.: Secure Virtual Enclaves: Supporting Coalition Use of Distributed Application Technologies. In: proceedings of the Network and Distributed System Security Symposium, NDSS 2000, San Diego, California, USA (2000)
3. Bonatti, P., De Capitani di Vimercati, S., Samarati, P.: An algebra for composing access control policies. In: ACM Tranactions on Inormation Systems Security (TISSEC) 5, 1, 1–35 (2002)
4. Khurana, H., Gligor, V.D., Linn, J.: Reasoning about Joint Administration of Coalition Resources. In: Proc. of IEEE International Conference on Distributed Computing Systems (ICDCS), Vienna, Austria, July 2002, pp. 429–439. IEEE press, Los Alamitos (2002)
5. Bharadwaj, V., Baras, J.: Towards automated negotiation of access control policies. In: Proc. of the 4th IEEE International workshop on Policies for distributed Systems and Networks (POLICY 03), pp. 77–86. IEEE press, Los Alamitos (2003)
6. Moses et al.: eXtensible Access Control Markup Language specification, v.2 Technical Overview (May 2004) Available: XACML Oasis TC Homepage, http://www.oasis-open.org/committees/tc_home.php?wg_abbrev=xacml
7. Hughes et al.: Technical Overview of the OASIS Security Assertion Markup Language (SAML) V1.1. OASIS (May 2004) http://xml.coverpages.org/saml.html
8. http://www.w3.org/TR/xpath (Accessed May 2006)
9. Belsis, P., Gritzalis, S., Katsikas, S.: A Scalable Security Architecture enabling Coalition Formation between Autonomous Domains. In: Proceedings of the 5th IEEE International Symposium on Signal Processing and Information Technology (ISSPIT'05), Athens, Greece, December 2005, pp. 560–565. IEEE Computer Society Press, Los Alamitos (2005)
10. Ao, X., Minsky, N.H.: Flexible regulation of distributed coalitions. In: Snekkenes, E., Gollmann, D. (eds.) ESORICS 2003. LNCS, vol. 2808, Springer, Heidelberg (2003)
11. Malatras, A., Pavlou, G., Belsis, P., Grtizalis, S., Skourlas, C., Chalaris, I.: Deploying Pervasive Secure Knowledge Management Infrastructures. International Journal of Pervasive Computing and Communications, Troubador Pub 1(4), 265–276
12. Mukkamala, R., Atluri, V., Warner, J.: A Distributed Service Registry for Resource Sharing among Ad-hoc Dynamic Coalitions. In: Proc. of IFIP Joint Working Conference on Security Management, Integrity, and Internal Control in Information Systems, December 2005, Springer, Heidelberg (2005)

On Device Authentication in Wireless Networks: Present Issues and Future Challenges

Georgios Kambourakis and Stefanos Gritzalis

Laboratory of Information and Communication Systems Security
Department of Information and Communication Systems Engineering
University of the Aegean, Karlovassi, GR-83200 Samos, Greece
{gkamb,sgritz}@aegean.gr

Abstract. Whilst device authentication must be considered as a cardinal security issue, complementary and of equal importance to user authentication, in today's wireless networks, only a few papers address it patchily. This paper identifies and analyses possible major solutions towards solving the device authentication problem. We discuss key issues and future challenges that characterize each solution examining its pros and cons. We also offer a short qualitative comparative analysis for the device authentication schemes in question, examining its applicability for both infrastructure and ad-hoc deployments.

Keywords: Device authentication, 802.1X, TCG, Wireless security.

1 Introduction and Problem Statement

Today, networks face many security risks, whether wired or wireless. One of the most common is unauthorized network access by an unknown device that connects to a network. From the one hand, wired devices like routers and switches are considered to be "locked-in-the-rack" and therefore under the supervision of an administrator. In contrast, one of the most important problems in today's deployment of infrastructure IEEE 802.11 wireless LANs, Mobile Ad-hoc Networks (MANET) and Wireless Sensor Networks (WSN) is that of the rogue device problem. In many installations, anything plugged in is given access to the network. Devices can almost immediately begin broadcasting data and reading information, regardless of what they are or come from. These systems can be difficult to scan, patch, or control. Furthermore, an unauthorized device is difficult to identify, locate and repel, when on the move, in an emergency situation. For instance, this refers to the situation in which an insider connects an unauthorized IEEE 802.11 device, say an Access Point (AP), to the corporate LAN, thus creating a security hole in the company network. Whether this sort of attack is most common to infrastructure IEEE 802.11 networks, similar problems may easily arise to MANETs, WSNs and even Radio Frequency Identification (RFID) tags where a rogue or even a compromised or cloned device can be fatal for the overall network trustworthiness. For instance, at present, most RFID devices promiscuously broadcast their static identifier with no explicit authentication procedure. This gives the opportunity to attackers to passively scan identifying data

C. Lambrinoudakis, G. Pernul, A M. Tjoa (Eds.): TrustBus 2007, LNCS 4657, pp. 135–144, 2007.

performing a *skimming attack*. Additionally, skimmed data may be used to fabricate cloned tags, thus giving more opportunities to attackers. In a *swapping attack*, for example, the adversary fabricates cloned tags, seals them inside a decoy container and quickly swaps the fake container with the original. Having the ability to clone a tag and prepare the decoy in advance, the adversary is able to carry out the physical swap very quickly. Furthermore, it is well known that erratic behaviours in sensors networks seeking physical access to sensor devices are difficult to be repelled due to the anonymous and (semi)uncontrolled terrain in most cases. At best, physical access to a certain sensor enables the aggressor to obtain sensor's secret keys. According to [1] a competent attacker equipped with a laptop is able to retrieve sensor keys in less than a minute given that he/she has physical access to it. Once these keys are compromised the attacker has access to the communications of the whole network.

In all cases, the heart of the problem is the lack of any mutual device-to-device authentication procedure or mechanism when a certain device attempts to join the network. Also, there are many cases where an identified device may not be allowed on the network; for example, if it was reported as stolen, the metadata in the device identity or policy store would indicate that it should not be allowed. Device authentication mechanisms enable an organization to manage both users and devices, thus it is considered as a second layer of authentication, ensuring that only specific authorized devices operated by authorized users can access the organization's network. Separately, neither one can have access. This means that even in case passwords, credentials or tokens are stolen or compromised, the network will still be well protected as long as the authorized device is not employed. It also assures that private data stored across network resources are never exposed because unauthorized devices cannot access the network, even when operated by an authorized person. Moreover, in case of infrastructure devices (e.g. Access Points, switches, etc) and other hardware that is not operated directly by humans, (like sensors) device authentication can guarantee to a great deal that a device is genuine and has not been somehow compromised. Therefore, device authentication effectively enforces network access control policies in a proactive manner, that is, before they connect to the network.

Currently, the most usual practice to protect against unauthorized access is to perform device identification by maintaining a list of MAC addresses that are allowed to access the network. However, today, this solution is considered ineffective as the majority of end-user devices allow the user to configure its MAC address at will. As a result, an insider can modify the MAC address of his rogue AP to match an existing authorized device and connect to the network without detection. In this paper we survey all major potential solutions and trends to the device authentication issue and examine its pros and cons. Each option is further analyzed and compared with the others based on some indicative qualitative criteria giving a comprehensive view about its applicability and robustness in terms of security. The remainder of the paper is structured as follows: the next section identifies and analyses possible solutions to the device authentication problem so far. Section 3 gives a qualitative analysis for the device authentication schemes in question. Finally, Section 4 offers some concluding thoughts and future directions of this work.

2 Identification of Possible Solutions

2.1 The IEEE 802.1X Framework

With the advent of the IEEE 802.11i specification [2] the 802.1X [3] framework provides various Extensible Authentication Protocol (EAP)-based and certificate-oriented mechanisms that can be employed both for user as well as for device authentication. Towards this direction every device must afford a device certificate bound to it to be able to prove its identity prior acquiring an IP address and joining the network. The uniqueness of each network device can be determined by a combination of its hardware and software characteristics. For example, hardware parameters may be the device's serial number, hard disk or other components serial codes and manufacturer identities, MAC address, processor type, memory capacity, etc, while as software parameters may use a hash of some driver codes, start/end memory address of software portions stored in ROM and other similar attributes. A careful choice of this kind of characteristics is enough to uniquely identify each network device even those of the same model and type. Note however that these attributes must be static in the long run as they comprise the identity of each particular device.

Once a collection of such parameters has been decided, e.g. by the network operator, a hash of the concatenated sequence (charact_1∥ charac_2 ∥...∥ charact_n) is calculated to serve as the mid or long-term identity of the device. As a result, a device certificate must bind a combination, say a hash of various physical properties of the device (MAC address, serial number, driver versions, etc), to a private key in the form of a X.509 certificate. After that, device-to-device authentication can be effectively exercised utilizing EAP methods (EAP-TLS, EAP-TTLS, PEAP, etc), before any user authentication takes place. It is stressed that the private key of the device must be stored securely in the device in the form of a tamper resistant memory, therefore not accessible by human users or applications. By this scheme, the authentication server can utilize the same identity certificate that is always used when being authenticated by other network nodes.

However, at least for IEEE 802.11 infrastructure mode, 802.1X-based device authentication mandates several modifications concerning the current communication procedures between the AP and the authentication (usually RADIUS) server. Specifically, all APs must act as supplicants when booting-up (before acquiring an IP address) to be able to be authenticated as devices to the corresponding RADIUS server. Moreover, all network devices, including APs, must support e.g. EAP-TLS protocol functionality to support certificate based authentication at the data link layer. In addition, a well-defined and scalable (re)keying mechanism between the AP and the authentication server to encrypt the traffic between them must be somehow automated and not rely on administrators to configure it manually. This is especially true for remote network devices. Currently however, no standard automated session key derivation procedure between an AP and the authentication server exists. Furthermore, to thwart clever attackers any solution applied must support periodic re-authentication at regular intervals, thus ensuring session freshness. Additionally, periodic session validation may presume the derivation of a session key between the involved devices during initial device authentication phase. After that, it is not possible to substitute a legitimate device, since the rogue one does not know the current session parameters, including the key. Apart from all previously discussed issues the 802.1X approach: (a) cannot straightforwardly be accommodated to ad-hoc network configurations as it requires infrastructure mode, (b) mandates some sort of Public Key Infrastructure (PKI) and some rather sophisticated and maybe costly hardware and software components to be implemented, (c) in most cases requires expensive public key operations and protocols, that lightweight mobile devices is difficult to afford. Therefore, it is only appropriate for medium to large organizations rather than for Small Office/Home Office (SOHO) environments, MANETs, or WSNs. Concluding this subsection, we can say that 802.1X-oriented device authentication, if refined and standardized sometime in the future, can provide a promising avenue towards solving the device authentication problem.

2.2 The IEEE 802.16 Case

When Device authentication through corresponding device (manufacturer) certificates is already part of the IEEE 802.16 standard, namely the Privacy Key Management (PKM) protocol [4]. The PKM RSA authentication protocol employs X.509 digital certificates and the RSA public key encryption algorithm that binds public RSA encryption keys to MAC addresses of MSs. Under this context, a Base Station (BS) authenticates a client Mobile Station (MS) during the initial authorization exchange. Each MS must incorporate a unique X.509 digital certificate issued by the MS's manufacturer. The digital certificate among other contains the MS's Public Key and serial number and the MS's MAC address. When requesting an Authorization Key (AK), an MS presents its X.509 certificate to the BS. Upon reception, the BS verifies the MS's certificate, and then uses the public key that it contains to encrypt an AK, which then sends back to the corresponding MS. Under this scheme MAC spoofing attacks can be effectively repelled considering that only the legitimate MS device has the matching private key to decrypt AK and join the network. Briefly, the specification mandates that all MSs using RSA authentication shall have factory-installed RSA private/public key pairs or provide an internal algorithm to generate such key pairs dynamically. All MSs with factory-installed RSA key pairs shall also have factory-installed X.509 certificates. All MSs that rely on internal algorithms to generate an RSA key pair must offer a mechanism for installing a manufacturer-issued X.509 certificate after key generation. For mutual authentication each BS is also equipped with a digital certificate that binds its hardware characteristics with the corresponding public key as described in [4].

Note that the newest PKM version 2 protocol specification [4] supports 802.1X/EAP authentication too. This is of course a movement towards providing a unified 802.11/802.16 authentication framework, but in our case device authentication services to heterogeneous 802.11/802.16 contexts may also be applied as discussed earlier in the previous subsection. Generally, the PKM's authentication protocol establishes a shared secret (AK) between the MS and the BS. The shared secret is then used to secure subsequent PKM exchanges of temporary keys. PKM also supports periodic re-authentication / re-authorization and key refresh. Although, the 802.16 approach is effective as far as the device authentication problem is concerned, it suffers from the same problems discussed in Section 2.1.

2.3 The Trusted Computing Solution

A different hardware oriented solution towards solving the device authentication problem has been examined in the means of trusted computing. Considering this option a number of hardware and software manufacturers have cooperated forming the non-profit Trusted Computing Group (TCG). The main aim of TCG is to develop trusted platforms by utilizing Trusted Platform Module (TPM) chips and novel hardware architectures. The TPM chip [5], also referred to as the "Fritz chip", is responsible for a number of basic functions including integrity measurement, integrity storage and integrity reporting of all critical events occurring in the trusted platform. This chip can be either embedded in a smartcard or dongle soldered onto the motherboard or will be integrated in the main processor. The latter approach offers better security because the data is not transferred on motherboard buses between the TPM and the CPU. Very recently [6], TCG formed the Mobile Phone Work Group focusing on the adoption of TCG concepts for mobile devices. This work group will enhance TCG as needed to address specific features of mobile devices like their connectivity and limited capability.

The specification defined by the TCG [7] states that Trusted Platforms (TPs) are computing platforms that add to themselves the property of trust. In other words, they provide proper mechanisms to verify, in a secure way, that the data yielded by them is not tampered with. When a manipulation is performed, a security discrepancy is detected and reported to the user who will decide whether or not to trust the data provided by the TPs. More specifically, on booting up, the TPM takes over inspecting the integrity of boot ROM, then loading and executing it, and finally, verifying the overall system's state. It then verifies the first portion of the operating system, loads and executes it, and again attests the system's state. This procedure repeats several times for all protected software modules which in the end are loaded and become available to the system upon booting up. Moreover, the TCG-enabled system preserves and maintains a list of approved hardware and software components. For each of them, the system must confirm whether it is approved and not revoked and whether it is digitally signed in case of software. Meanwhile, e.g. in case that some components have been upgraded and therefore the system's configuration has changed, it must go online to be recertified. In this context, trusted computing can contribute a great deal to the vision of the "self authenticated, self protecting network" where every wireless or wired network entity that contains a TPM is self and cross authenticated before entering the network. As a result, rogue components either hardware or software can be repelled from joining the network. Nevertheless, currently the level of security provided by TPM modules highly depends on the details of design and implementation, which are not clear yet for almost all trusted computing manufacturers. Moreover, the TCG specifications has to cover some distance until it reaches a mature state and proved to be secure and trustworthy enough (not simply trusted) in the long run [8,9,12].

2.4 Other Approaches

In this subsection we shall briefly survey other research works dealing diametrically or partly with device authentication.

In NIST report 7206 [10] the authors employ smart cards to support user and mobile devices authentication. They state that smart card authentication is perhaps the best-known example of a proof by possession mechanism when compared to other more traditional categories of authentication, including proof by knowledge (e.g. passwords) and proof by property (e.g. fingerprints). Towards this direction the report provides an overview of two novel types of smart card that use standard interfaces supported by most handheld devices. Without doubt, when used for user authentication, smart cards can improve the security of a device and provide additional security services too. Device authentication can also be seconded considering that it is generally more difficult to operate a rogue (compromised or stolen legitimate) device without the proper smart card. On the other hand, cloning an existing device and its matching smart card is not exactly an easy task for the attacker to accomplish. On the contrary though, standard size smart cards are generally not suitable for handheld devices due to the relatively large size of the card, the need for a proper card reader, and the difficulty and cumbersomeness of embedding a reader to the device. Putting aside these obstacles, by e.g. utilizing interfaces found today in most smart card readers (as in the aforementioned report), smart card authentication may prove very profitable. Some difficulties remain however including the increased acquisition and administrative cost for the users and the organizations themselves and the fact that this solution is not suitable for small wireless devices like sensors and RFIDs.

In another work [11] that partly deals with device authentication the authors examine location-based access control mechanisms. They propose a new protocol for location verification, called the Echo protocol and they prove its security. Location verification enables location-based access control. This means that a person carrying a specific device can be granted access to particular resources only if his/her location has been confirmed by employing a corresponding protocol. Naturally, when this approach is combined with physical security e.g. who's entering the building, then location verification can be used to allow wireless access to all those inside. It is true that location-based access control has several pros. Among others, it is natural for various applications. While one simple security policy might permit wireless access of only the printers installed in the office you are in, on the other hand might force that a wireless device must cease operating if it is detected operating outside the company building or being moved to another room. By this means, stolen, compromised or rogue devices not operated in certain premises, where they are supposed to operate according to the current policy, will be proved useless to malevolent individuals. Though, while location-based access control in human terms is straightforward, e.g. turning on the TV set in a particular room needs to have a physical presence in the room, achieving the same kind of guarantee with wireless networks, is not so easy. Location-based access control policies on networks and information resources by extension, requires a method to perform location verification, where an entity's location is securely verified to meet certain criteria: e.g. being inside a particular room. In practice, while this approach may be effective if implemented properly (guarantee in-region verification for a high rate of legitimate location claims), requires significant administrative costs in terms of configuring and maintaining proper and strict policies for every network entity involved. On the top of that, as with 802.1X, location-based access control adapts better with infrastructure wireless networks having some sort of administrative authority to define policies rather than ad-hoc pervasive mode and nomadic computing.

A different approach that examines the feasibility of identifying wireless nodes in a network by measuring distinctive electromagnetic characteristics or "signatures" of Wireless Local Area Network (WLAN) cards is presented in [13,14]. There the authors focus and perform preliminary experiments with IEEE 802.11 compatible cards but their conclusions can be applicable to other wireless technologies as well. Their idea originates from the remark that the physical layer of 802.11 wireless communications cannot effectively protect the identities of the communication endpoints. Specifically, any electromagnetic signal transmitted over the air can be passively or actively monitored, captured and analyzed at will by any properly equipped adversary located within the wireless device's transmission range. This physical layer "vulnerability" is also under investigation by several researchers in the context of the so called template attacks. Therefore, users' anonymity and privacy can be in danger if their device can be uniquely identified, through the measurement of distinctive radio-frequency electrical characteristics or electromagnetic signatures that it emits. The attacker's aim in this case is to correctly relate a received electromagnetic emission with a specific transmitter (device). At frequencies, such as 2.4 GHz or 5.2 GHz, used in 802.11 networks even minor component variations in a transmitting circuit may result to a significant effect on the emitted signal. Given that we are able to detect and record distinctive electromagnetic signatures, a wireless device and its user can not only be monitored, but when combined with visual identification, can also be identified. Due to these qualities, devices' electromagnetic emissions are worth being further investigated in the context of effective device identification / authentication. Rogue, compromised and even cloned devices can be differentiated from the legitimate ones through their electromagnetic signature that they emit. However, this must be proven so, not only in sporadic experiments, but also in large scale, where many types and access technologies of wireless devices are employed. On the other hand, device authentication based on this scheme may be practical in corporate networks - by constructing beforehand a database of all authorized devices' electromagnetic signatures (metadata describing the asset) and putting it in a corresponding authentication server - but seems rather unpractical for ad-hoc deployments.

The last one but lightweight category of solutions has been proposed in [15] and redefined later in under a three party (proxy assisted) setting[1]. The authors analyze a particular human-to-computer authentication protocol designed by Hopper and Blum (HB), and demonstrate by using RFID tags that it is practical for authenticating low-cost pervasive devices as well. The outcome of their work is a new symmetric authentication protocol, namely HB+ that is appropriate to securely identify and authenticate wireless devices with limited power and processing capabilities. The motivation here is that low-end RFID tags and other similar pervasive devices share many limitations with human beings. For instance, just like people, RFID tags can neither remember long passwords nor keep long calculations in their working memory. In this context, well-studied human authentication and identification

---

[1] We selected these works among others in the literature [17] as the most representative for low-end, low-cost wireless devices.

protocols utilized for proving human's identity to a machine, can also be applied in low-cost wireless devices. It is true that securing low-end wireless devices is a challenging issue because of their limited resources and small physical form. Towards this direction the HB+ and other analogous protocols [17] can contribute to the problem of secure device authentication. Nevertheless, while theoretically the HB+ protocol is secure against both passive and active aggressors and should be realizable for implementation in current RFID tags, a number of open questions remain before the HB+ can see practical realization [15]. Moreover, do not neglect that HB+ and alike protocols proposed both for RFIDs and sensors devices lean against symmetric secrets stored inside the device, which in turn can be entirely revealed through active or physical attacks, such as electron microscope probing as discussed in [16].

3 Discussion

Currently, there exist several software-based ways to safeguard mobile devices Virtual Private Networks (VPNs), firewalls, upper layer data encryption software, device management solutions, to name just a few. These types of solutions typically protect the data and or operating systems of the devices from attacks, but cannot guarantee the integrity and authenticity of the hardware platform on which they are running. For example, while SIM or UICC are employed in the wireless cellular networks to authenticate users, they cannot ensure the computing platform on the mobile equipment is trustworthy too. Also, many applications of cryptographic identification protocols are vulnerable against adversaries who perform real time active attacks. For instance, when identifying a physical device like a wireless AP, common identification schemes can be by-passed by faithfully relaying all messages between the communicating participants. This attack is well known in the literature as mafia fraud. Furthermore, this sort of solutions does not contribute much in protecting the unique identity of a handheld device such as a mobile phone. When intercepted, these identities can be further utilised to install rogue network components in absence of effective access control mechanisms. However, device authentication is a hard problem to deal with, as it involves some sort of bootstrapping trust between the access control mechanism and the stranger device or between several stranger devices in ad-hoc mode. This becomes even more complicated considering (a) the heterogeneity of the wireless access technologies that currently exist and (b) the diversity of network providers reflected in their security policies. In the previous section we investigated several device authentication schemes and discussed its pros and cons. Generally, schemes based on symmetric cryptography have obvious performance advantages over public-key cryptography; they fit much better to low-end wireless devices and ad-hoc modes, but usually suffer from complex key management. They also mandate some sort of trust in the entire network as a device moves from one wireless domain to another. Admittedly, schemes based on public-key technology offer less computation for more communication rounds, but are still too costly to be practical for at least non-infrastructure wireless networks that involve low-power computing devices.

Table 1. Device authentication schemes comparison (Mod.=Moderate, P=Partly, NA=Not Applicable, S=Symmetric, A= Asymmetric, Inf.=Infrastructure)

Scheme Description	Inf. /Ad-Hoc	S/A key	Effectiveness/ Robustness	Scal- ability	Prac- ticability	Heterog. Env.
IEEE 802.1X	Inf.	A	High	High	Mod.	Partly
IEEE 802.16	Inf.	A	High	High	Mod.	Partly
Trusted Comp.	Mainly Inf.	Both	High	High	Mod.	Mostly
Smart Cards	Mainly Inf.	Both	High	Mod.	Fair	Partly
Location-based Access Control	Mainly Inf.	NA	Mod.	Mod.	Mod.	Partly
Electromagnetic Signatures	Mainly Inf.	NA	Mod.	Mod.	Mod.	Partly
HB+ and other similar protocols	Both	S	Mod.	Fair	High	Partly

Table 1 depicts an aggregate comparative view of all the anticipated schemes considering six basic criteria: (a) supports infrastructure and/or ad-hoc deployments, that is, centralized and/or distributed, (b) requires symmetric or/and asymmetric key technology, (c) effectiveness and robustness in terms of security, (d) scalability, (e) practicability to implement, (f) supports heterogeneity in terms of access technologies and trust relations between network providers. As a general remark it seems that the trade-offs between security robustness and lightness in terms of processing power and accompanying infrastructures and between ad-hoc and infrastructure modes are not easy to fulfil. More specifically, the trusted computing approach and the 802.1X authentication framework seem to be the most promising solutions towards solving the device authentication problem. On the downside, these options are rather impractical for nomadic users and ad-hoc deployments, due to the PKI and Authorization, Authentication, Accounting (AAA) entities that they mandate and the associated cost that goes with them. The IEEE 802.16 solution although based on 802.1X principles is more or less custom-tailored to Wi-Max networks. All the other approaches are very interesting still, they have to prove their effectiveness in terms of security robustness, scalability, key administration and ease of materialisation. In our opinion one global universal solution is at present difficult to form. It is better to orientate ourselves in choosing one of the aforementioned schemes, according to our particular needs and interest or alternatively develop a custom-made hybrid solution.

4 Conclusions and Future Work

In this work we define device authentication (or identification) as the entity authentication in which the objective is to identify and further authenticate a physical device possibly at a specific location. In this paper a constructive analysis of the current potential solutions and trends to the device authentication issue have been given. Each scheme was briefly presented and some comments including implementation problems and research challenges have been provided. Finally, a comparison of the schemes was conducted based on several criteria. As a statement of direction, we are currently working on expanding this work by proposing a new optimized hybrid device authentication method, which exploits the advantages of the presented mechanisms, while at the same time minimizes the drawbacks pointed out throughout this paper. Another important issue worthy of investigation is how to preserve privacy, that is, logically disassociate the user from the device that they operate; in other words how to correctly identify a device without disclosing user's private information, thus preserving anonymity, context privacy, location identity, etc.

References

1. Hartung, C., Balasalle, J., Han, R.: Node Compromise in Sensor Networks: The Need for Secure Systems, T.R. CU-CS-990-05, Department of C.S. Univ. of Colorado (January 2005)
2. IEEE Std. 802.11i-2004, Amendment to IEEE Std. 802.11, 1999 Edition, Amendment 6: Medium Access Control (MAC) Security Enhancements, Part 11, IEEE Press, Los Alamitos (June 2004)
3. IEEE 802.1X-2004 IEEE Standards for Local and metropolitan area networks - Port-Based Network Access Control (December 2004)
4. IEEE P802.16e/Draft12, IEEE Standard for Local and metropolitan area networks, Amendment for Physical and Medium Access Control Layers (published October 2005)
5. TCG, TPM Main Part 1 Design Principles Spec. Version 1.2 Revision 85 (February 2005)
6. TCG Mobile Trusted Module Spec., version 0.9, Revision 1, DRAFT (September 2006)
7. TCG, Spec. Architecture Overview, Specification Revision 1.2 (April 2004)
8. Bruschi, D., Cavallaro, L., Lanzi, A., Monga, M.: Attacking a Trusted Computing Platform, Improving the Security of the TCG Specification, Tech. Report RT (June 2005)
9. Hendricks, J., van Doorn, L.: Secure Bootstrap is Not Enough: Shoring up the Trusted Computing Base. In: Proc. of the 11th ACM SIGOPS, September 2004, ACM, New York (2004)
10. Jansen, W., Gavrila, S., Séveillac, C., Korolev, V.: Smart Cards and Mobile Device Authentication: An Overview and Implementation, NIST, NISTIR 7206 (July 2005)
11. Sastry, N., Shankar, U., Wagner, D.: Secure Verification of Location Claims. In: ACM WiSE'03, September 19, 2003, California, USA, pp. 1–10 (2003)
12. Zheng, Y., He, D., Yu, W., Tang, X.: Trusted Computing-Based Security Architecture For 4G Mobile Networks. In: Proc. of PDCAT '05, pp. 251–255 (2005)
13. Remley, K., et al.: Electromagnetic Signatures of WLAN Cards and Network Security. In: IEEE Int'l Symposium on Signal Processing and Information Technology, pp. 484–488 (2005)
14. Henrici, D., Muller, P.: Hash-based Enhancement of Location Privacy for Radio-Frequency Identification Devices using Varying Ident. In: IEEE PerCom, pp. 149–153, 04
15. Juels, A., Weis, A.: Authenticating Pervasive Devices with Human Protocols. In: Boyd, C. (ed.) ASIACRYPT 2001. LNCS, vol. 2248, pp. 149–153. Springer, Heidelberg (2001)
16. Anderson, R., Kuhn, M.: Low Cost Attacks on Tamper Resistant Devices. In: Christianson, B., Lomas, M. (eds.) Security Protocols. LNCS, vol. 1361, pp. 125–136. Springer, Heidelberg (1997)
17. Wen, H.-A., et al.: Provably secure authenticated key exchange protocols for low power computing clients. Computers & Security 25, 106–113 (2006)

The Meaning of Logs[*]

Sandro Etalle[1,2], Fabio Massacci[1], and Artsiom Yautsiukhin[1]

[1] University of Trento, DIT
[2] University of Twente, The Netherlands
sandro.etalle@utwente.nl, {evtiukhi,massacci}@dit.unitn.it

Abstract. While logging events is becoming increasingly common in computing, in communication and in collaborative environments, log systems need to satisfy increasingly challenging (if not conflicting) requirements. In this paper we propose a high-level framework for modeling log systems, and reasoning about them. This framework allows one to give a high-level representation of a log system and to check whether it satisfies given audit and privacy properties which in turn can be expressed in standard logic. In particular, the framework can be used for comparing and assessing log systems. We validate our proposal by formalizing a number of standard log properties and by using it to review a number of existing systems. Despite the growing pervasiveness of log systems, we believe this is the first framework of this sort.

1 Introduction

In the past few years we have witnessed a struggle between two competing forces: privacy protection and fight against cyber-crime. Privacy protection has called for new regulations [15,5], new technological solutions [2,4] and re-thinking of business interactions [8]. On the other hand, efforts in countering cyber-crime, have led to increasingly invasive laws [13] and new auditing techniques [24,3,1].

Such clash is most evident in the realm of auditing in general, and in the regulations on how logs should be taken, maintained and deleted in particular. A folklore pun well describes the problem as follows: if logs mention private information they are forbidden and if they do not - they are useless. For instance, an important privacy requirement for log systems is the compliance with the maximal retention period (the time after which a company has to delete user's data) which in some cases must be determined on a need basis [2,4,12] (e.g. service providers have to delete logged data when they do not need it any longer to offer their services). On the other hand, logs have to be kept for audit purpose or for computer forensics. This problem goes beyond privacy in databases: Internet Service Providers (ISPs) have similar regulations [10,27]. A recent amendment to EU Directive N 2002/58/EC [13] requires service providers (i.e. ISPs, e-mail services, communication providers) to store their logs for not less than 6 months to help law enforcement agencies. Consequently, sensitive information about a user may be in the system after the user's own account has been deleted.

[*] This work is partly supported by the project EU-IST-IP-SERENITY.

C. Lambrinoudakis, G. Pernul, A M. Tjoa (Eds.): TrustBus 2007, LNCS 4657, pp. 145–154, 2007.
© Springer-Verlag Berlin Heidelberg 2007

We notice that even though logs are ubiquitous in computing and telecommunication security and there is a significant amount of work on *analyzing logs*[1], we find relatively few papers on *design and analysis of log systems* [28,22,14] and on what security properties a log system may or should exhibit [17]. This is somehow striking in comparison with the large body of work on security properties for e.g. security protocols or security models for access control.

In this paper we define a formal framework for modeling and analyzing log systems, which allows one to provide a high level specification of a log system, thereby allowing her to check whether it has the expected properties (e.g., if it meets given privacy or audit requirements). in particular, our framework can be used to compare different log systems with each other.

To validate our proposal, we include a survey of the requirements that are applicable to log systems, and we show how to represent them formally. In addition, we have considered a number of log systems taken from the literature and we show how they compare to each other when modeled in our framework.

2   Log Requirements

First we need to specify some notation: here we talk about (real world) *events* and call *trace* a sequence of events. In turn, a trace may be logged in a *log*; by *recovering a trace* we indicate the action of associating to a given log the trace(s) of events that could have generated it. To be useful, logs often have to meet various requirements. Here we list the most common of them (collected from various papers in the literature: ISO17799 [16], CC [17], [6]); later, we will be able to give a precise formalization of these properties.

– *Completeness*: All events in a trace of events can be recovered from its log.
– *Partial Completeness*: All events in a trace of events matching a given property (relevant events) can be recovered from its log.
– *Past Independence*: In a trace, older events have no influence on the log and recovery of newer events.
– *Future Independence*: In a trace, newer events have no influence on the log entries of older events, nor on their recovery.
– *Context Independence*: The conjunction of past and future independence.
– *Chaining*: Valid logs become invalid if an intermediate record is altered.
– *Exactness*: The recovery of a log of a trace is unambiguous: given a log there is a unique trace of events which could have generated it.

These notions allow one to characterize the precision and completeness of the audit.

Events in a trace usually have attributes (e.g. date, user name, address); the following properties concern whether a given log system allows or not to recover a certain attributes. This is particularly important for privacy protection.

– *Complete Anonymity (w.r.t. attribute A)*: The recovery of an event does not give any information on the value of its attribute *A*.

- *Ambiguity (w.r.t. attribute A)*: The recovery of an event does not allow one to establish the value of its attribute A.
- *Linkability (w.r.t. attribute A)*: It is possible to determine whether two recovered events had the same value for attribute A (notice that the system could still be ambiguous w.r.t. A).
- *Positive/Negative Monotonicity*: Newer events do not introduce/reduce anonymity in older events.

These notions allow one to characterize the extent to which a log system protects private information. Linkability is common because it allows precise auditing even if some information is hidden.

An example of a log system which is not past independent is e.g. the log system in Linux, which records a user's name together with the assigned pseudonym[2]. An example of a system which does not satisfy future independence is one in which log entries are destroyed after a given retention time. Such system is not complete either. Positive monotonicity is important when we do not want to lose information we logged. Negative monotonicity is important from the privacy perspective.

3   A Formal Model of Logs

To introduce our framework we give the definition of the world model, which is the environment where logging takes place. Here and in the sequel, given a set X we denote by 2^X its powerset and by X^* the set of sequences of elements from X.

Definition 1. *A* World Model *is a tuple* $\langle E, T, AD, \{AF_i\}_{i \in I} \rangle$; *where: E is a set of real world events; $T \subseteq 2^{E^*}$ is a set of valid traces; AD is a general attribute domain which includes all possible dimensions (e.g. strings, real, data, etc.); $\{AF_i\}_{i \in I}$ is a set of attribute functions, which given a sequence of events return the corresponding sequence of attribute values: $E^* \mapsto (2^{AD})^*$ (e.g. user(), date()).*

Now we can define a log system which records events from the world model.

Definition 2. *Let* $WM = \langle E, T, AD, \{AF_i\}_{i \in I} \rangle$ *be a world model, then a* Log System *for WM is a tuple* $\langle R, L, Log(), Rec() \rangle$; *where: R is a set of records; $L \subseteq 2^{R^*}$ is a set of valid logs in the system. Log: $E^* \mapsto R^*$ is a function mapping a trace of events into the corresponding log. Rec: $R^* \mapsto 2^{E^*}$ is the function which given a log returns the corresponding set of traces (of events).*

In other words, the recovery function *Rec()* maps a log into the set of traces of events that could have originated the log. Considering that some information might be lost during the logging process (e.g., in the case of anonymous systems), it can well be the case that the *Rec(l)* contains more than one trace. We denote events by e and records by r. A trace is represented by $t = \langle e_1, e_2...e_n \rangle$. Similarly, a log is denoted by $l = \langle r_1, r_2...r_n \rangle$. In the sequel, $x \circ x'$ means that sequence x' is appended to (after) sequence x preserving elements order.

---

[2] In Linux pseudonyms are used for convenience, and not to preserve users' privacy.

Example. Let us describe a log system using pseudonyms (as in [18]). Consider a hospital-based database containing medical and personal data of patients. The hospital keeps track of all accesses to the database both to prevent data linkage (privacy) and for accountability purposes. To define the World Model, we introduce the following domains: *Time* is a set of positive integer values which denote time; *Operator* is a set of users (represented by strings) who have access to patient data; *Patient* is a set of all possible patients of the hospital (represented by strings); *Status* is the set: {successful, failed} used to denote whether an action was carried out successfully or not. The general attribute-domain is $AD = Time \bigcup Operator \bigcup Patient \bigcup Status$. Finally, attribute functions are defined and named according to the domains above $AF = \{Time(), Operator(), Patient(), Status(), Data()\}$. In the world model, there are six types of events (here, $\tau \in Time$; $o \in Operator$; $p \in Patient$; $s \in Status$):

$$E = \{ \quad login(\tau, o, s) \qquad \text{(Operator) } o \text{ logged-in at time } \tau;$$
$$logoff(\tau, o, s) \qquad o \text{ logged-off at time } \tau;$$
$$add(\tau, o, p, s) \qquad o \text{ added the record of } p \text{ to the system at time } \tau;$$
$$read(\tau, o, p, s) \qquad o \text{ read the record of } p \text{ at time } \tau;$$
$$update(\tau, o, p, s) \qquad o \text{ updated the record of } p \text{ at time } \tau;$$
$$delete(\tau, o, p, s) \qquad o \text{ deleted } p \text{ from the system at time } \tau\}$$

Having defined the set of possible events, a valid trace is any ordered (in time) sequence of such events. $T = \{t \in E^* |$ if $\forall e_i \in t \wedge \forall e_j \in t \,.\, i < j \implies Time(e_i) < Time(e_j)\}$. We can now move on to the definition of the log system. Let us first define some additional domains: *Patient_id* is a set of all possible identifiers (strings) of all patients; *Record_id* is a set of integers which unambiguously point to a log record. Note that the *Patient* domain from the world model differs from *Patient_id*, as the real names of patients are substituted with pseudonyms. We underline the identifier to refer to the pseudonym, so $\underline{p}$ is the pseudonym of patient p. We also underline the records to distinguish between records and events. The log system has four types of records (here: $j \in Record\_id$; $\tau \in Time$; $o \in Operator$; $\underline{p} \in Patient\_id$; $s \in Status$;):

$$R = \{ \quad \underline{add}(j, \tau, o, \underline{p}, s) \qquad o \text{ added the record of } \underline{p} \text{ to the system at time } \tau;$$
$$\underline{read}(j, \tau, o, \underline{p}, s) \qquad o \text{ read record of } \underline{p} \text{ at time } \tau;$$
$$\underline{update}(j, \tau, o, \underline{p}, s) \quad o \text{ changed record of } \underline{p} \text{ at time } \tau;$$
$$\underline{delete}(j, \tau, o, \underline{p}, s) \quad o \text{ deleted } \underline{p} \text{ from the system at time } \tau \}$$

Record identifiers (j) are assigned incrementally. We can now define the *Log()* function:

$$Log(t) = \begin{cases} \underline{add}(j, \tau, o, \underline{p}, s) \circ Log(t') \text{ if } t = e \circ t' \text{ and } e = add(\tau, o, p, s); \\ \underline{read}(j, \tau, o, \underline{p}, s) \circ Log(t') \text{ if } t = e \circ t' \text{ and } e = read(\tau, o, p, s); \\ \underline{update}(j, \tau, o, \underline{p}, s) \circ Log(t') \text{ if } t = e \circ t' \text{ and } e = update(\tau, o, p, s); \\ \underline{delete}(j, \tau, o, \underline{p}, s) \circ Log(t') \text{ if } t = e \circ t' \text{ and } e = delete(\tau, o, p, s); \\ Log(t') \text{ if } t = e \circ t' \text{ and none of the above applies;} \\ \varepsilon \text{ otherwise.} \end{cases}$$

The mapping between a patient and his pseudonym is done with a special binding table to which access is restricted. We assume that *login* and *logoff* events are not logged. For the recovery function, let M be the set of bijective mappings *Patient_id* $\mapsto$ *Patient*; given $m \in M$ we define R_m as follows:

$$R_m(l \circ \underline{add}(j, \tau, o, \underline{p}, s)) = R_m(l) \circ add(j, \tau, o, m(\underline{p}), s)$$
$$R_m(l \circ \underline{read}(j, \tau, o, \underline{p}, s)) = R_m(l) \circ read(j, \tau, o, m(\underline{p}), s)$$
$$R_m(l \circ \underline{update}(j, \tau, o, \underline{p}, s)) = R_m(l) \circ update(j, \tau, o, m(\underline{p}), s)$$
$$R_m(l \circ \underline{delete}(j, \tau, o, \underline{p}, s)) = R_m(l) \circ delete(j, \tau, o, m(\underline{p}), s)$$

(where $R_m(\varepsilon) = \varepsilon$); the recovery function is: $Rec(l) = \{t|\ t = R_m(l)$ for some $m \in M\}$.

Notice that the recovery function maps a log into a set of traces. Consider the following list of events: *Login(8:58 21/10/2006,[3],Edward Green,successful) Add(10:30 21/10/2006,Edward Green,Mackle Daniels,successful) Login(12:00 21/10/2006,Suzi Wallach,successful) Changed(12:21 21/10/2006,Suzi Wallach, Paul Anderson,failed) Changed(12:22 21/10/2006,Suzi Wallach,Mackle Daniels, successful)* Then the corresponding log is:

Record ID	Cause	Time	Operator	Patient	Status
1	Add	10:30 21/10/2006	Edward Green	102	successful
2	Update	12:21 21/10/2006	Suzi Wallach	101	failed
3	Update	12:22 21/10/2006	Suzi Wallach	102	successful

As one can see the log file itself (without knowledge of the bijection mapping) does not disclose any information about the patients of the hospital other than the fact that records 1 and 3 concern the same patient. If an operator who has no access to the private data tries to recover the log he obtains six possible traces: one for each pseudonym-user assignment.

4   Properties

The formal log system allows us to give a precise definition of the informal properties stated in Section 2, providing us with a basis for assessing and comparing different log systems.

Having a formal definition of these properties is very important to make them precise, which is a less trivial task than it may seem at first. If one argues that a log system where i) everything is logged but ii) old records are deleted is complete then we need to change both the informal and the formal definitions. Let WM=$\langle E, T, AD, \{AF_i\}_{i \in I}\rangle$ be a world model, and $\langle R, L, Log(), Rec()\rangle$ be a log system for WM:

---

[3] Time is stored as an integer value, but for the sake of simplicity it is represented as usual.

Definition 3 (Properties)

- *Trace Completeness:* $\forall t \in T \; t \in Rec(Log(t))$.
- *Partial Trace Completeness (w.r.t. a property P. Here we simply indicate by $P(t)$ the subsequence of t consisting of all and only events satisfying property P).* $\forall t \in T \; . \; P(t) \in Rec(Log(t))$.
- *Future Independence:* $\forall t, t' \in T \; . \; t' \in Rec(Log(t)) \iff \forall t_1 \in T \; \exists t'_1 \in T \; . \; t' \circ t'_1 \in Rec(Log(t \circ t_1))$
- *Past Independence:* $\forall t, t' \in T \; . \; t' \in Rec(Log(t)) \iff \forall t_1 \in T \; \exists t'_1 \in T \; . \; t'_1 \circ t' \in Rec(Log(t_1 \circ t))$.
- *Context Independence: conjunction of future and past independence.*
- *Chaining:* $l \circ \langle r \rangle \circ l' \in L \implies \forall r' \neq r \;\; l \circ \langle r' \rangle \circ l' \notin L$.
- *Exactness:* $\forall t \in T \; \{t\} = Rec(Log(t))$

To express most privacy-related properties we need to be able to make the correspondence between single events and single log entries. In particular, if e is an event in a trace t and $t' \in Rec(Log(t))$ we have to be able to tell which event in t' corresponds to the original e. We denote this event by $t' \downarrow e$. In most cases, the correspondence function $\downarrow$ is realized quite simply by assigning consecutive numbers to events and log entries.

Definition 4 (Privacy Properties). *Let AF be an attribute function.*

- *Complete Anonymity (w.r.t. AF):* $\forall t \in T \; \forall t' \in Rec(Log(t)) \; \forall e_1, e_2 \in t', AF(e_1) = AF(e_2)$.
- *Ambiguity (w.r.t. AF):* $\forall t \in T \; \forall e \in t \; |AF(Rec(Log(t)) \downarrow e)| > 1$.
- *Linkability (w.r.t. AF):* $\forall t \in T \; \forall e_i, e_j \in t \; . \; AF(Rec(Log(t)) \downarrow e_i) = AF(Rec(Log(t)) \downarrow e_j) \iff AF(e_i) = AF(e_j)$.
- *Positive Monotonicity (w.r.t. AF):* $\forall t, t' \in T \; \forall e \in t \; AF(Rec(Log(t)) \downarrow e) \subseteq AF(Rec(Log(t \circ t')) \downarrow e)$
- *Negative Monotonicity (w.r.t. AF):* $\forall t, t' \in T \; \forall e \in t \; AF(Rec(Log(t)) \downarrow e) \supseteq AF(Rec(Log(t \circ t')) \downarrow e)$

We have now the formal machinery to relate some of these properties to each other and these relations are shown in Figure 1 (see [11] for the proof).

Example. Consider again the system shown in the Section 3. The system is not complete since exist events (e.g., $t'=Login(t,o,s)$) that are not logged corresponding logs; it is partially complete w.r.t. the property P which is true for all events except for *login* and *logoff*. The system in our example is context independent because the recovery of a record does not depend on other records; it is not chained since changes in the log are not noticeable by the system since by definition of L any sequence of records from R is valid; it is not exact because pseudonyms are mapped back (by the recovery function) to any person belonging to the set of patients; for the same reason, it is completely anonymous. Notice however that the system is still linkable: it allows us to see if two events pertain to the same patient (though the presence of the pseudonym does not allow to see which patient it is) as every user has only one identifier and visa versa. It is monotonic since it is context independent.

Theorem 1

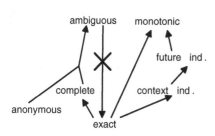

1. *Every exact system is complete.*
2. *Every ambiguous system is not exact.*
3. *Every exact system is context independent.*
4. *Every exact system is (positively and negatively) monotonic.*
5. *Every future independent system is (positively and negatively) monotonic.*
6. *Every complete and anonymous system is ambiguous.*

Fig. 1. Relationships among properties

Other examples. We now use the properties just defined to assess and compare some existing logging systems.

Pseudonyms based systems [18,19,20]. These systems use pseudonyms to hide user identities to regular log users while allowing special authorized parties (who have access to the pseudonymization function) carry out precise auditing, The basic idea is to substitute private information with an arbitrary string (the pseudonym). The correspondence between pseudonyms and user identifiers is stored in some binding database with restricted access (here we should mention that even the use of pseudonyms does not guarantee complete protection from the use of statistical methods to reconstruct the behavior of user [9,20]).

Linux logs. Sometimes pseudonyms are used for convenience rather than for privacy reasons. The Linux log system is an example of such pseudonymization ante-literam: here, user identities are partially hidden using group and user identifiers which can be considered as pseudonyms (e.g. user "grayyoga" has pseudonym 1001:100). The binding between user and her pseudonym is stored in the */etc/passwd* file. All kernel audit information contains no references to the username but only to the user id[4]. On the other hand, when a new user is added in the system his identity and pseudonym are stored in a log file. This means that even if access to the */etc/passwd* file is denied it is possible to recover a user identity by consulting the log file.

Buschkes-Kesdogan system [7]. Buschkes and Kesdogan proposes a log system which uses group pseudonyms (e.g. for access right management). Before logging into a server a user receives from a Trusted Third Party (TTP) a credential containing a Group Reference Pseudonym (GRP). When she connects to the server, she reveals her credential and the server authenticates the user as a member of a group according to the GRP. The main peculiarity of the log system is that a pseudonym id corresponds to a *set* of user identifiers.

---

[4] See http://www.die.net/doc/linux/man/man8/auditctl.8.html

IDA system [25]. The IDA log system uses pseudonyms as well, but instead of substituting the private information with a pseudonym encrypts data. The main advantage is that for re-identification of logs no binding database is required: only the decryption key is needed for full recovery.

Waters et al. [28]. Our last example is to the system of Waters et al., where log entries are encrypted as a whole. This solution eliminates the need to store the correspondence between users and their pseudonyms. The disadvantage of this approach is that – in general – searching in encrypted logs is difficult. To overcome this problem the system stores a separate list of keywords for each log entry encrypted with a unique key. This allows the system to carry out limited search actions while offering good data protection. The authors also use a hash function to preserve the order and integrity of the log.

We can now compare these systems along our classification.

	Context Independence	Complete Anonymity	Ambiguity	Monotonicity	Linkability	Exactness [5]	Chaining
Linux logs	–	–	–	√	√	–	–
Lundin–Johnnson [18]	√	√	√	√	√	–	–
Buschkes–Kesdogan [7]	√	–	√	√	–	–	–
IDA [25]	√	√	√	√	√	–	–
Waters et al. [28]	√	√	√	√	–	–	√

5   Related Works and Conclusion

There are a few works focusing on audit log properties. Billable and Yee in [6] introduce forward integrity property and propose a system enforcing it. The well-known Common Criteria security standard [17] reports some requirements which we have referred to as properties. The audit requirements specify what should be stored in the logs and how to use the logs collected.

Most log formalizations have been developed for monitoring purposes [23,21,26]. Roger and Goubauld-Larrecq [23] investigate linear time logic for log auditing and propose another logic consisting of Wolper-style linear-time formulae which make auditing more efficient. Spanoudakis et al. [26] propose a formal description of compliance checking for web-service based systems. Mansouri-Samani and Sloman [21] present GEM (generalized event monitoring language) which is used for monitoring networks and distributed systems. B. Waters et al. [28] provide a formal description of a searchable temper-resistant log model.

---

[5] Note, that all these systems except [7] become exact if the operator has access to the inverse mapping from pseudonyms to user names. Also note, that in contrast to the system shown in our example, the system in [18] is complete.

In this paper we propose an abstract framework for formalizing and reasoning about log systems. Our framework allows one to model a concrete log system and to check whether it satisfies certain properties; in particular it allows one to check whether the system meets various requirements such as the one we have collected from the literature [6,17,25,7].

The practical motivation for realizing this framework is given by the need compare and assess precisely different log systems against the properties they have to satisfy, which in our system can be expressed in a precise way using a simple logic formalism. To validate our framework, we have encoded in it a number of different systems ([18,7,25,28]). To the best of our knowledge, this is the first framework of this kind.

References

1. Agrawal, R., Bayardo, R.J., Faloutsos, C., Kiernan, J., Rantzau, R., Srikant, R.: Auditing compliance with a hippocratic database. In: Nascimento, M.A., Özsu, M.T., Kossmann, D., Miller, R.J., Blakeley, J.A., Schiefer, K.B. (eds.) Proceedings of the 30th International Conference on Very Large Data Bases (VLDB'04), pp. 516–527. Morgan Kaufmann, San Francisco (2004)
2. Agrawal, R., Kiernan, J., Srikant, R., Xu, Y.: Hippocratic databases. In: Bernstein,P.A., Ioannidis, Y.E., Ramakrishnan, R., Papadias, D. (eds.): Proceedings of the 28th International Conference on Very Large Data Bases (VLDB'02). Morgan Kaufmann (2002)
3. Allen, J., Christie, A., Fithen, W., McHugh, J., Pickel, J., Stoner, E.: State of the practice of intrusion detection technologies. Technical Report CMU/SEI-99-TR-028, Carnegie Mellon, SEI (January 2000)
4. Ashley, P., Hada, S., Karjoth, G., Powers, C., Schunter, M.: Enterprise privacy authorization language (EPAL 1.1). Technical report, IBM (October 2003)
5. Baumer, D.L., Earp, J.B., Poindexter, J.: Internet privacy law: a comparison between the united states and the european union. Computers & Security 23(5), 400–412 (2004)
6. Bellare, M., Yee, B.: Forward integrity for secure audit logs. Technical report, University of California at San Diego (1997)
7. Buschkes, R., Kesdogan, D.: Privacy enhanced intrusion detection. In: Mueller, G., Rannenberg, K. (eds.) Proceedings of the Conference on Multilateral Security for Global Communication, pp. 187–207. Addison-Wesley-Longman (1999)
8. Cranor, L., Langheinrich, M., Marchiori, M., Presler-Marshall, M., Reagle, J.: The Platform for Privacy Preferences 1.0 (P3P1.0) Specification. W3C, 1.0 edn. (April 2002)
9. Domingo-Ferrer, J., Torra, V.: Disclosure risk assessment in statistical microdata protection via advanced record linkage. Statistics and Computing 13, 343–354 (2003)
10. Electronic Privacy Information Center. Data retention (23/05/2007) Available at http://www.epic.org/privacy/intl/data%5Fretention.html
11. Etalle, S., Massacci, F., Yautsiukhin, A.: The meaning of logs. Technical Report TR-CTIT-07-24, Centre for Telematics and Information Technology, University of Twente (2007)
12. EU. Directive 95/46/EC of the european parliament and of the council (1995)

13. EU. Directive 2006/24/EC of the european parliament and of the council. Official Journal of the European Union, 105/54 (2006)
14. Hansen, J.V.: Audit considerations in distributed processing systems. Communications of the ACM 26(8), 562–569 (1983)
15. HIPAA.: Health insurance reform: Security standards; final rule. Federal Register 68(34), 8333–8381 (2003)
16. ISO/IEC. Information technology–Security techniques–Evaluation criteria for IT security (November 2001)
17. ISO/IEC. Common Criteria for Information Technology Security Evaluation. Common Criteria Project Sponsoring Organisations, 2.2 edn. (January 2004)
18. Lundin, E., Jonnson, E.: Privacy vs. intrusion detection analysis. In: Proceedings of the 2nd International Symposium on Recent Advances in Intrusion Detection (1999)
19. Lundin, E., Jonsson, E.: Anomaly-based intrusion detection: privacy concerns and other problems. Computer Networks 34(4), 623–640 (2000)
20. Malin, B., Sweeney, L.: How (Not) to Protect Genomic Data Privacy in a Distributed Network: Using Trail Re-identification to Evaluate and Design Anonymity Protection Systems. Journal of Biomedical Informatics 37(3), 179–192 (2004)
21. Mansouri-Samani, M., Sloman, M.: GEM: a generalized event monitoring language for distributed systems. Distributed Systems Engineering Journal 4, 96–108 (1995)
22. Ohtaki, Y., Kamada, M., Kurosawa, K.: A scheme for partial disclosure of transaction log. IRICE Transaction on Fundamentals of Electronics Communications and Computer Sciences E88(1), 222–229 (2005)
23. Roger, M., Goubault-Larrecq, J.: Log auditing through model checking. In: Young, D.C. (ed.) Proceedings of the 2001 IEEE Computer Society Security Foundations Workshop, pp. 220–236. IEEE Computer Society Press, Los Alamitos (2001)
24. Schneier, B., Kelsy, J.: Secure audit logs to support computer forensics. ACM Transactions on Information and System Security 2(2), 159–176 (1999)
25. Sobirey, M., Fischer-Hoebner, S., Rannenberg, K.: Pseudonymous audit for privacy enhanced intrusion detection. In: Yngstroem, L., Carlsen, J. (eds.) Proceedings of the IFIP TC11 13 international conference on Information Security (SEC '97) on Information security in research and business, London, UK, 1997, pp. 151–163. Chapman & Hall, Ltd (1997)
26. Spanoudakis, G., Mahbub, K.: Non intrusive monitoring of service based systems. International Journal of Cooperative Information Systems 15(3), 325–358 (2006)
27. Statewatch. UK-EU call for mandatory data retention of all telecommunications (2005), Available at http://www.statewatch.org/news/2005/jul/05eu-data-retention.htm
28. Waters, B.R., Balfanz, D., Durfee, G., Smetters, D.K.: Building an encrypted and searchable audit log. In: Proceedings of the 11th Annual Symposium on Network and Distributed System Security, San Diego (2004)

Data Protection and Privacy Laws in the Light of RFID and Emerging Technologies

Gerald Quirchmayr[1,2] and Christopher C. Wills[3]

[1] University of Vienna Faculty of Computer Science
Department of Distributed and Multimedia Systems
Liebiggasse 4, A-1010 Wien, Austria
Gerald.Quirchmayr@univie.ac.at
[2] University of South Australia Division of Information Technology,
Engineering and the Environment
School of Computer and Information Science
Mawson Lakes, SA 5095, Australia
Gerald.Quirchmayr@unisa.edu.au
[3] Kingston University Faculty of Computing Information Systems and Mathematics
Penrhyn Road, Kingston Upon Thames, KT1 2EE
ccwills@kingston.ac.uk

Abstract. This paper investigates the effect of new technologies and new systems on data protection and privacy. It attempts to give an overview of the major issues resulting form the introduction of new systems, mainly those based on RFID and ubiquitous/pervasive computing technology and discusses the consequences of increased efficiency and improved security in relation to privacy protection. Most of the legally-oriented analysis carried out in this paper is primarily grounded in the current European data and privacy protection legislation.

1 Privacy Protection in a Changing World

Privacy protection has not been exempted from recent developments in which increasing organized crime and the fear of terrorism have led to a substantial push towards more, tighter and better surveillance. It is difficult to argue that an individual's right to privacy protection has to be respected when at the same time this protection of privacy is abused by criminals to harm the public. At the same time when terrorism and organized crime are starting to force governments all over the world to cut back on all sorts of freedoms, the pressure on the economy to continuously improve efficiency to remain competitive and to turn out innovative products is also mounting.

It is therefore predictable that in the name of safety, security and competitiveness new technology will quickly be introduced, some of it probably without having properly reflected the consequences for privacy. From smart phones to smart homes and smart production, the effort to increase efficiency and comfort comes at a price: the growing volumes of person-related data being collected. While the nightmarish Orwellian scenarios described in several books ring an alarm with the public, it is

C. Lambrinoudakis, G. Pernul, A M. Tjoa (Eds.): TrustBus 2007, LNCS 4657, pp. 155–164, 2007.
© Springer-Verlag Berlin Heidelberg 2007

smart technology invading every corner of life that goes virtually unnoticed. Nice gadgets added to mobile phones and PDA's have been accepted and the applications coming with the new devices have quickly been embraced by users. Location based services, the first widely spreading form of context aware services, are highly helpful, while at the same time revealing a lot of information about the mostly unaware user. Questions such as "Which information about a certain location is the user interested in?" and "What are the typical movements of users at a certain time of day?" will be easy to answer once the user is forced to be online permanently. As long as the paradigm remains that the user is logging on to a system via a device and not a system logging on to a device operated by the user, the control is at least with the user. Ubiquitous / pervasive computing is beginning to change this in a drastic way. Questions such as "Which level of control should the user have in the future?" and "Which level of privacy should the user be granted?" are already starting to dominate the privacy protection discussion.

As comfortable as it is to walk into an area covered by a system and automatically be recognized and provided with the full spectrum of services, this comfort comes at a very high price. These services only work if the system has sufficient information about a user meaning that the more a system "knows" about a person the better it can tailor the service offered to the user. However, it should still be up to the user to decide which information a system should be allowed to hold and not the system operators who make this decision. With selling products or services being the focus of this operation it is of course in the best interest of business to move as far as possible towards complete customer profiles and push technology. How wrong this approach can go ubiquitously can be felt by the pervasiveness of spam. The nuisance that has so far been limited to electronic mail now is starting to spread to other devices with SMS spam being the second wave users are suffering from. In a world where technology is pervasive, i.e. computers can be found as part of almost everything we use, this flood of information will continue to increase and might, if not controlled, render certain technology useless. The developers of IT solutions also have to be increasingly careful not to lose the trust of consumers. Smart phone technology and RFID, both technologies which may substantially contribute to the desperately needed turnaround of the telecommunications and IT industries, are already perceived as invaders of privacy, facing users and providers of the technology with how to retain consumer trust and prevent the consumer from switching over to competitors products because of the justified or non-justified feeling to be spied on [rfidjournal March 12, 2003], [boycottbenetton 2003].

It is therefore in the interest of consumers, users and technology providers to start an open discussion in order to create an environment of trust in which technology will again be viewed as helping friend instead of the surveillance and "enemy of the state" image it has acquired over the past view years. Data and privacy protection legislation can play a decisive role in achieving this goal.

2   Selected New Systems and Technologies

Some of the new systems and technologies beginning to be used in either defense and law enforcement environments or in commercial contexts are bound to cause a controversy from a privacy perspective. As necessary as the introduction of this technology may be, the way in which it was handled has in several cases provoked the outcry of privacy advocates. The technologies under scrutiny from privacy groups today are primarily databases and information systems operated by law enforcement and other governmental agencies for the prevention and investigation of serious crime, location-based and other context aware services aimed at users of mobile equipment, customer cards and the RFID. It was initially not so much the technology itself that provoked the adverse reactions, but the envisaged and in some cases already practiced uncritical and uncontrolled use of person-related information collected through the application of this technology has already given some of the technology a very bad name. An envisaged data exchange that has initially been aimed at increasing the security of airline passengers has for example sparked a completely unnecessary conflict between the US and the European Union, finally resulting in the European Parliament taking the EU Commission to court over an alleged breach of data protection legislation (cf. background information on [EPIC 2004], [EU-US 2003]). Privacy advocates all over the European Union and safety fears in the US have contributed their share in escalating the situation and damaging the relationship. RFID has led to similarly strong emotional reactions which the discussions accompanying the planned use of the technology by companies in California [rfidjournal March 1, 2004] and by the clothing industry in Europe [boycottbenetton 2003] frequently being quoted as reference points for the growing fear of consumers.

The recent European proposal to store basic data about phone calls for a length of up to three years in case this information should be needed for the investigation and prosecution of serious crime, has immediately resulted in very critical reactions from privacy advocates in Europe. In this context the ability of telecommunications operators to collect an increasing amount of customer-related information which is generated from location-based services and from payments made via the mobile phones becomes problematic. There is no doubt that in the cases of serious organized crime and terrorism it would be very beneficial to have all this information, but the question arises who else than law enforcement officers might be given access to this customer history once the data has been collected. It is this basic uneasiness among customers which has led to very useful services, such as "mobile friend finders" not being greeted with the level of acceptance expected by service providers [Datenschutz versus Bequemlichkeit 2004].

The ongoing reports and discussions linked to identity theft as well as the recent legislative efforts made by governments around the world indicate the level of threat being perceived when it comes to "electronic identities". Thousands of customer records have not only being stolen or lost from the sites of e-commerce operators, but have also disappeared without trace from such highly regarded institutions as leading banks. These cases have initiated a level of loss of trust that has very rarely been seen with any major technology in the past. Identity theft has for example reached a level at which even the US Federal Trade Commission has decided to become active [FTC 2005], [ABA 2005].

It is obvious that the more complete and comprehensive a customer or citizen profile is, the more dangerous its theft becomes. In this atmosphere of fear of identity theft, abuse of information and increasing surveillance a hostile reaction towards technology is inevitable.

3 Efficiency and Better Security vs. Privacy

The underlying assumption of this section of the paper is that the drive towards introducing new technology primarily stems from the desire to improve the security and safety of the public and to increase the efficiency of a wide range of operations in order to cut costs. While the growing amount of technology use by law enforcement and other agencies can be viewed as a temporary development that will last as long as the dangers persist, there is no such corrective in sight for steadily increasing use of technology in a commercial context. With users and consumers demanding an ever increasing level of service and quality, supply chains being under growing pressure to perform more cost-efficiently and the competition not hesitating to introduce available cost cutting measures, including technology, the only alternative companies are left with is to embark on technology that gives them a competitive edge. As problematic as this ever stronger dependence on IT systems is, it seems to be the only alternative to completely losing whole industry sectors to countries that do not care too much about social and environmental standards. It is therefore natural that governments back the use of innovative technology by local industry. Better customer services and in general services that are better suited for the customer have led to the introduction of substantial information technology on the customer service side. Loyalty programs and the IT infrastructure behind them are only part of the new environment in which companies are trying to continuously collect and mine data about customers. Technology aimed at collecting data of all sorts is gradually being sneaked into products and services, the best example being all sorts of personalized and location based services for smart phones.

The growing number of arising data security and privacy concerns do however slow the potential market growth. Consumers worrying about the safety of their Internet banking accounts, the security of their financial data, ongoing trading of their profiles and the potential abuse of collected data by government, have recently been very reluctant to accept new technology. The benefit of the technology for them is now carefully weighed against the potential risk it is associated with. Remote data collection and monitoring systems for vehicles are a major benefit when it comes to the prevention of theft and to the support of maintenance. They do on the other hand give a full movement profile of the owner of a monitored vehicle. As long as the prevention of abuse of this data cannot be guaranteed, consumers will be very reluctant to have this technology installed. The major problem is that in a situation in which potential abuse and lack of knowledge combine, the resulting confusion of the consumer can lead to a complete loss of trust. The best examples of such a development are the use of the Bluetooth technology in mobile phones and the use of RFID chips to tag consumer products (for an overview of ongoing debates cf. [Surden 2005] and [SOLOVE 2005]). Handled carefully and properly, none of these technologies can do any harm, but an improperly configured Bluetooth connection can easily lead to the leakage of information from mobile devices. RFID tags can in theory communicate with their environment, but do need a reader in the close vicinity. That certain variations can be and in fact are already implanted in humans has certainly not helped to calm down the ongoing emotional debate [RFID Chips Implanted in Mexican Law-Enforcement Workers 2005]. Realistically viewing the technology, RFID tags can send information to nearby readers and Bluetooth equipped devices can communicate with other such devices. In reality RFID tags will be used to replace the existing barcode giving the carrying product the ability to provide information stored on the tag. Unless deliberately stored on the tag, it will not contain any information about the user. In some situations such information can even be life saving, e.g. in the case of patients suffering from critical allergies. The danger is that such highly beneficial use might get blocked by the fear of potential abuse of information, e.g. by suppliers of medical products and services.

In a work environment the increasing use of technology can lead to an increasing amount of surveillance. As long as this surveillance is carried out to assure the safety of employees and to enhance the quality of products and services, it is justified under the condition that it does not violate existing privacy legislation. The temptation to fully monitor a production line or a supply chain, including the continuous surveillance of involved humans is always there and might in some exceptional situations be justified, such as in today's airport operations [Qantas baggage security 2005]. Non-intrusiveness with respect to the production process and non-violation of privacy should be primary goals. Ubiquitous and pervasive computing technology offer the possibility for people to carry information about themselves with them and to communicate this information when entering or approaching a suitably equipped area, e.g. a production line. From a convenience as well as a security perspective it is a dream that once the employee enters a room, the equipment needed to perform a certain role automatically starts up and logs on the user. The obvious drawback is that every move of the user can now also be recorded, making it possible to carry out a detailed analysis of the user's behavior patterns. This might in turn be beneficial for better adapting the surrounding equipment to the user's needs, but it also is very easy to abuse such information. If this technology is combined with systems automatically logging on to mobile or wearable computers, the consequence could easily be an almost continuous surveillance. Such systems might be justifiable in dangerous work environments where this technology can substantially contribute to reducing the risk of accidents, but in an average office environment it will certainly provoke adverse reactions from employees. Privacy protection legislation will in most cases prevent the creation of such surveillance-oriented environments anyway, but previous scandals have shown that in the name of safety and security some companies could in the opinion of privacy advocates and the public easily go too far, as the use of simple video surveillance equipment has shown [Boston Magazine 2003].

Countless previously documented attempts to use new technology to circumvent privacy legislation have however raised the level of suspicion among customers and employees.

The major problem however is the rather careless use of technology whenever it becomes available. This has again been documented by the analysis of WLAN and Bluetooth connections all over Europe. Safe in theory and equipped with technology that can block out an intruder, the equipment usually comes with a standard configuration that is not aimed at security, but at the ease of use. Unaware users installing WLAN access points with standard configurations, turning on Bluetooth enabled mobile phones without checking the status of the Bluetooth connection all too often find themselves in a situation where they openly invite access to their devices and the connected networks without even realizing the potential dangers they create. In spite of legal regulations (cf. [§ 14 Austrian DSG 2000]) requesting that all necessary and financially justifiable measures be taken to keep person-related data safe, unaware users continue to ignore even the elementary basics of data and privacy protection.

Movement tracking, combined with increasingly complete consumer behavior profiles, gives companies the possibility to deliver the right product or service at the right time in the right place. As is well known, the position of mobile equipment, typically a mobile phone, being identified by either GPS or location services implemented through provider base stations, can today be quite exactly. Future systems will allow the calculation of a position within some centimeters. The core legal question is to which extent this data can be used by applications. The push towards storing more and more information over longer periods to have it available in case it is needed for business evaluations or for the future prosecution and prevention of crime, is in direct contradiction to the aim of privacy protection to have only the minimal amount of data stored and to grant access only for predefined applications. The second problem is that the more data we collect about a person, the more sensitive this data becomes, because the increasing amount of available data allow to construct an increasingly complete profile.

The scale and potential implications of identity theft scandals have reached a frightening dimension, which one of the most recent scandals amply documents: "The numbers and the names associated with approximately 1.4 million credit and debit cards used at 108 of our stores primarily during a 90 day period between mid-November 2004 and mid-February 2005 were stolen from DSW ... In addition, checking account information was stolen for around 96,000 checks used to make purchases at these same stores. This included the bank account numbers located on checks that were provided to DSW (the "Magnetic Ink Character Recognition" or "MICR" numbers) and the drivers' license numbers provided when paying by check." [DSW 2005]. Especially when cases like these emerge, the appropriateness of data protection measures taken by companies handling such large amounts of sensitive financial data needs to be investigated. For a recent example of work on privacy ands risk perception frameworks in the context of RFID see [Thiesse 2007].

The results of several war drives carried out in past years in major cities, showing that a vast number of networks even today still remain completely unprotected, indicates the size of the problem. The current situation can be attributed to a mixture of missing awareness and negligence, both on the system administrator and on the end user side. PIN codes being written on the back of ATM and credit cards in spite of all warnings, completely unprotected WLAN's, and PIN codes on mobile phones being turned off show that many users are at least as careless as some of the worst companies operating the IT systems. Intruders therefore see "phishing" and similar attacks, the intrusion in unprotected or only weakly protected systems and different forms of identity theft as an easy way to commit crime. With the possibility of organized crime getting involved as well, commercial IT infrastructures might soon become so vulnerable that they become unusable for business purposes. Legal frameworks, as well developed as they might be, will therefore have to be complemented with the necessary technological defenses and an according legal obligation to implement them. This legislation partially already exists on a European scale (see Article 17 of [EUDPG 1995]).

4   Can Existing Legal Frameworks Cope?

Existing legal frameworks can in some parts of the world cope very well with challenges to privacy. The European Data Protection Directive [EUDPG 1995], which has been in effect since the 1990's has widely been viewed as one of the landmark agreements in privacy protection. As one of the core underlying assumptions of modern privacy protection is that it covers all forms of automated and non-automated processing of data, the change of technology cannot result in the successful circumvention of privacy protection legislation. Debates such as the one on RFID tags in California in 2004 [RFID California 2004] occurring inside the European Union would therefore see European privacy advocates being able to argue on the basis of an already existing and comparatively comprehensive legislation. The major remaining problem from a privacy perspective would be the use of the technology under one of the exemptions regulated in Article 13 or the Directive [EUDPG 1995].

Article 13

1. Member States may adopt legislative measures to restrict the scope of the obligations and rights provided for in Articles 6 (1), 10, 11 (1), 12 and 21 when such a restriction constitutes a necessary measure to safeguard:
   (a) national security;
   (b) defence;
   (c) public security;
   (d) the prevention, investigation, detection and prosecution of criminal offences, or of breaches of ethics for regulated professions;
   (e) an important economic or financial interest of a Member State or of the European Union, including monetary, budgetary and taxation matters;
   (f) a monitoring, inspection or regulatory function connected, even occasionally, with the exercise of official authority in cases referred to in (c), (d) and (e);
   (g) the protection of the data subject or of the rights and freedoms of others.
2. Subject to adequate legal safeguards, in particular that the data are not used for taking measures or decisions regarding any particular individual, Member States may, where there is clearly no risk of breaching the privacy of the data subject, restrict by a legislative measure the rights provided for in Article 12 when data are processed solely for purposes of scientific research or are kept in personal form for a period which does not exceed the period necessary for the sole purpose of creating statistics.

These exemptions, when closely looked at, are very similar with the exemptions regulated in many other countries, including the US. That is why some of the highly emotional discussions around the exchange of passenger data in the interest of aviation security could have been approached in a more constructive way from the beginning, as discussed in the first section of this paper. One of the major benefits of the existence of the Directive is that all major changes affecting the level of protection of privacy have to be discussed in the light of this Directive. In case the suggested change is not covered by one the exemptions in Article 13, a change to the Directive has to be proposed, which in turn will almost automatically lead to a public debate about the envisaged measure. It is then up to the democratically elected representatives to vote on the suggested change. In an extreme case the initiated debate might even lead to an EU-wide referendum.

Nationally introduced legislation can at this stage, at least inside the European Union, in principle cope with newly introduced technology, such as RFID tags. The trickiest issue is the use of new technology in the workplace. It is on one hand essential in order to continuously increase the competitiveness of a company, but does on the other hand occasionally lead to experiments that result in outcomes which cannot be implemented due to a possible violation of existing legislation. Ubiquitous / pervasive computing, the tagging of equipment and in an extreme case of humans, has also launched a widespread discussion among data protection activists in Europe, because the growing amount of data collected about individuals increases the possibility of abuse by criminals getting hold of the data. Mechanisms for securing data are therefore dominating the European discussion. More and more single points of attack created by infrastructure designers increase the level of risk and the potential damage that can be done by an intruder. At the same time the virtually uncontrollable number of mobile equipment on which sometimes highly sensitive data is stored, leads to growing vulnerability. Inside the European Union it is therefore not so much the legislative side which makes data protection advocates worry, it is more the careless use of technology and in several cases unfortunately the outright incompetence of systems administrators and users that are viewed as major threats.

The really alarming problem associated with the new technology is its use in cooperation with companies located outside the European Union. Unless covered by international treaties and agreements, such as the Safe Harbor Agreement between the US and the EU [Safe Harbor Website 2005], problems will doubtlessly occur as soon as any person-related data is exported outside the EU. This may, if not properly taken care of, become a serious obstacle to free trade, especially whenever customer-related information is to be stored in information systems located outside the European Union.

The fundamental guidelines set out in the European Data Protection Directive are, where necessary, complemented by other European legislation on specialized areas, such as digital signatures, telecommunications, electronic commerce. Privacy legislation is also backed by European Human Rights legislation which has over the years been embedded in the constitutions of Member States of the European Union.

Privacy protection on a purely abstract level would still leave too many holes. That is why, in Article 17 of the relevant EU Directive [EUDPG 1995], the obligation of the technological level of protection to be achieved is so explicitly stated:

Article 17 - Security of Processing

1. Member States shall provide that the controller must implement appropriate technical and organizational measures to protect personal data against accidental or unlawful destruction or accidental loss, alteration, unauthorized disclosure or access, in particular where the processing involves the transmission of data over a network, and against all other unlawful forms of processing.

Having regard to the state of the art and the cost of their implementation, such measures shall ensure a level of security appropriate to the risks represented by the processing and the nature of the data to be protected.

National legislators in Member States of the European Union have in many cases directly or almost directly translated this regulation to implement it (see the example of [§ 14 Austrian DSG 2000]). If found guilty of not having taking the necessary technologically feasible and economically justifiable privacy protection measures, companies and organizations not only face penalties, but are also open to a series of potential law suits if victims of the privacy violation suffer any damages which are directly attributable to a successful intrusion.

5 Conclusion

While new technology, such as RFID and ubiquitous/pervasive computing, doubtlessly has a lot of potential benefits which industry and consumers are eager to see delivered, the question of how to assure privacy is looming over the new systems. Having a modern legal framework that is able to cope with the new technological developments will be essential for assuring continued economic growth. Adequate legislation also gives users of the technology and consumers the much needed safety net which ultimately makes a new technology trustworthy and therefore acceptable. The possibility of abuse by criminals will always be there with every new technology. That is why legislation has to be accompanied by two other safeguards, trustworthy safety and security mechanisms and organizational arrangements that can prevent the careless and improper use of the new technology. As experience especially in the field of information technology shows, it is only if all three areas are covered, that users and consumers will be prepared to widely accept the new technology. With advanced business strategies being highly dependent on information technology, this combination of safeguards becomes essential not only for the protection of privacy, but also for our economy to be able to successfully continue to develop. The avoidance of a worst case scenario, a public that aggressively rejects information technology as unsafe and insecure, therefore justifies substantial investment in the development of adequate legislation and in the technologically sound implementation of the fulfillment of requests made by this legislation. Information technology legislation and associated privacy protection technology come at a considerable cost, but not making this investment might lead to short term savings only to cause a very expensive catastrophe later.

References

[ABA 2005] http://www.aba.com/Industry+Issues/ealert412.htm
[Boston Magazine 2003] http://www.bostonmagazine.com/ArticleDisplay.php?id=283
[boycottbenetton 2003] http://www.boycottbenetton.com/
[Datenschutz versus Bequemlichkeit 2004] http://www.ftw.at/ftw/press_news/ pressespiegel/ PressespiegelFolder/DerStandard FSp_20040719/DerStandard_20040719.pdf
[§ 14 Austrian DSG 2000] Bundesgesetz: Datenschutzgesetz 2000 - DSG 2000 (NR: GP XX RV 1613 AB 2028 S. 179. BR: 5992 AB 6034 S. 657.) (CELEX-Nr.: 395L0046)
[DSW 2005] http://www.dswshoe.com/credit_card_faq.jsp
[EPIC 2004] http://www.epic.org/privacy/intl/passenger_data.html
[EUDGP 1995] Directive 95/46/EC of the European Parliament and of the Council of 24 October 1995 on the protection of individuals with regard to the processing of personal data and on the free movement of such data; Official Journal L 281 , 23/11/1995 P. 0031 - 0050 (1995)

[EU-US 2003] http://europa.eu.int/comm/external_relations/us/intro/pnrmem03_53.htm

[FTC 2005] http://www.consumer.gov/idtheft/

[RFID California 2004] http://www.computerweekly.com/Article131982.htm

[RFID Chips Implanted in Mexican Law-Enforcement Workers 2005] http://www. techweb. com/ wire/26805353

[Qantas baggage security 2005] http://www.qantas.com.au/regions/ dyn/au/ publicaffairs/ details?ArticleID=2005/apr05/3255

[rfidjournal March 12, 2003] http://www.rfidjournal.com/article/articleview/344/1/1/

[rfidjournal March 1, 2004] http://www.rfidjournal.com/article/articleview/812/1/1/

[Safe Harbor Website 2005] http://www.export.gov/safeharbor/

[Surden 2005] http://www.stanford.edu/ĥsurden/RFID_Privacy_Law.htm

[SOLOVE 2005] http://ncvhs.hhs.gov/050111p4.pdf

[Thiesse 2007] Thiesse, F.: RFID, Privacy and the Perception of Risk: A strategic Framework. Journal of Strategic Information Systems (2007) (See http://www.alexandria.unisg.ch/ Publikationen/31815)

Consistency of User Attribute in Federated Systems

Quan Pham, Adrian McCullagh, and Ed Dawson

Information Security Institute,
Queensland University of Technology,
126 Margaret Street, Brisbane, QLD 4001, Australia
{q.pham,a.mccullagh}@isi.qut.edu.au,
e.dawson@qut.edu.au
http://www.isi.qut.edu.au/

Abstract. In a federated system, it is not uncommon for a user profile registered to a particular system to contain enough attributes to request services from that system. Other attributes may be missing from that profile when services are requested from another system. The problem is that currently, when a change in user attributes happens, it is very difficult for the federation to incorporate the changes in order to resolve the conflict of attributes and maintain the consistency of attributes of users between different systems. Currently ready-for-deploy systems such as Liberty Alliance, Microsoft Windows CardSpace (formerly InfoCard) and Shibboleth do not address this issue efficiently. In general, consistency issues of user attributes in federated system via a 2-dimentional view: consistency between member systems (horizontal consistency) and consistency between federation and local system (vertical consistency). In this paper, we discuss the issue of horizontal consistency to achieve better interoperability and fine-granularity for access control decisions in a federated system by analysing the two approaches to achieve the consistency of user attributes: attribute synchronisation and delegation.

Keywords: Access Control, Role Based Access Control, Identity Management, Federation, Federated System, Attribute Synchronisation, Delegation.

1 Introduction

Modern enterprises are now pervaded by information systems. There are stronger demands for industrial vendors to provide increasingly general-purpose solutions that must be configurable so that they can be deployed in a wide range of solutions. This leads to an increasing demand to federate existing systems to achieve certain objectives, especially to address the *complexity*, *flexibility* and *scalability* which the traditional distributed architectures are unable to cope with.

It is not uncommon that most enterprises are facing demands to integrate and incorporate together the many different, possibly heterogeneous systems, which have been independently designed and developed, to allow synchronised access so

C. Lambrinoudakis, G. Pernul, A M. Tjoa (Eds.): TrustBus 2007, LNCS 4657, pp. 165–177, 2007.

as to emulate one large unified system. At the same time, these data bases have to be able to maintain local autonomy and be able to continue working as an independent entity. This problem has introduced a new distributed architecture known as federated systems [9,14].

In this context, federated identity management has recently emerged as a potential solution for user management across the federation. The main motivation of federated identity management is to provide a mechanism to enhance convenience via a single sign on capability and user privacy as well as to decrease the identity data-store overload via decentralisation. However, a non-trivial problem has been identified, the problem of managing user profiles across a federated system [15]. Every new addition to a federated system is subject to incorporating a new user identity entity within the user database. It can be a costly and complex approach for the creation, maintenance and termination of user identities. Identity management across a federated system can result in over-burden tasks that must span the entire federated system.

Due to the distributed and autonomous nature of the federation, consistency between the federal and local and inter-domain environments has proved to be one of the major issues for the research community to explore. Consistency of access control in a federated system can be considered in a 2-dimentional view: consistency between member systems (*horizontal consistency*) and consistency between federation and local system (*vertical consistency*).

Ideally, access is only allowed when there is no conflict of policies and/or attributes of users. Furthermore, user profiles registered to a particular domain may contain enough attributes to request services from that domain but other attributes may be needed from that profile when services are requested from another domain.

The problem is that currently, when a change in user attribute happens, it can be very difficult for the federation to incorporate the changes to resolve the conflict of attributes and maintain the consistency of attributes of users between the different domains to make the access control decision. Currently ready-for-deploy systems such as Liberty Alliance, Microsoft Windows CardSpace (formerly Info-Card) and Shibboleth do not address this issue efficiently [4,7,16]. So it is difficult to make an access control decision due to the lack of a mechanism to maintain the consistency of user attributes across the federation.

This paper discusses the issue of horizontal consistency to achieve better interoperability and fine-granularity for access control decisions in a federated system by analysing the two approaches to achieve the consistency in user attributes: attribute synchronisation and delegation. In this paper, an attribute is defined as any characteristic related to an identity such as location, organisation, role, privileges, etc.

Section 2 briefly reviews federated identity management. The remainder of this paper will concentrate on the substantial issue of maintaining consistency of user attribute profile across federated system. Section 3 presents the study about the impacts of consistency on access control decisions. Sections 4 and 5 provide an overview about the Federated Identity Profiling and the attribute synchronisation approach to maintain consistency. Section 6 shows how delegation can be used as a better alternative to achieve the consistency in attributes of the same user across federated domains in the federation. Section 7 concludes the paper.

2 Federated Identity Management

In general, there are three types of identity management approaches: isolated, centralised federated, and distributed federated identity management [15].

The isolated identity management model is the most conservative and primitive of the three approaches. Each member system of the federation governs absolute authority and its own security framework, identity management domain, as well as its own way of maintaining the identities and the attributes of identities. Thus, this model is simple to implement and provides tight control on users via its own security framework. However, this model puts a significant burden on users as users have to manage multiple identities and so it degrades user convenience.

In the centralised federated identity model, all members of the federation must be in the circle of trust. There is only a single identity provider and manager in this model. The single identity provider will be the sole authenticator which has central authority over the identity management task. This approach provides simple and easy access for users to service providers. This model also reduces the management load but still be able to maintain a tight control over the security framework and user identities. This approach is well suited for large organisations under the umbrella of a single authority such as branches or members of a multinational company or agencies of a government. The main problem of this model is that the single identity manager can be a single point of failure.

The distributed federated identity management model provides a promising solution for identity management [15,18]. In this model, a set of common agreements, standards and technologies must be utilised to enable service providers the ability to verify identities issued by other identity providers in the federation. Authentication, thus, becomes a distributed task as each member in the federation will take part in the authentication process. This model increases the flexibility and availability as well as overcoming the single point of failure issue identified in the centralised federated identity management model. However, the cross recognition issue (policies, risk profile or user attributes) make distributed identity management a complex task. An example of distributed federated identity management is Liberty Alliance. Table 1 provides a comparison between the three models.

Among these three models, the distributed federated identity management model has the most potential with the high flexibility, usability and low management cost for user as identified in Table 1. That is, the distributed federated identity management model meets the objectives noted in Section 1 concerning complexity, flexibility and scalability. Therefore, the high flexibility and low user cost are a substantial advantage over the other two models. The complexity issue

Table 1. A comparison between 3 identity management models

Characteristic	Isolated Model	Centralised Model	Distributed Models
Flexibility	Low	Medium	High
Complexity	Low due to the ease to implement as each service provider has its own security framework.	Medium due to the difficulty to achieve the common agreement between service providers.	High due to the high trust requirements, technical and legal issues.
Usability	High but only well suited for users with small number of identities otherwise the usability is low when then number of service providers increases.	High. Well suite for service providers under single managements.	High as the ability, in theory, to incorporate any large number of service providers.
Management Cost for Service Provider	Low due to the simplicity in architecture.	Medium	High due to the management issues in cross-recognition of user identity and attribute, risk profile and security policy as well as efforts in maintaining consistency but this needs to be counterbalanced that the cost per user is actually reduced across the federated system.
Management Cost for User	High when user must manage a large number of identities.	Low as management task is partially distributed.	Low as management task is totally distributed.

is manageable and as such it is not such a disadvantage in the whole scheme. The rest of this paper will focus on the consistency issue on the distributed federated identity management model.

3   Consistency and Access Control in Federated Systems

In a federated system, consistency of user attributes plays a very important role. In some cases, the authorisation decision is made and derived by the combined effort of both federation and local authority. Basically, there are two approaches to derive final authorisation: top-down and bottom-up [18].

The top-down approach is designed for the authorisation at the local level. The local authorisation decision is derived from the authorisation policy and user attributes defined by the federation authority. After being authenticated at the federation level, if a user initialises an access request to a member system's resource, this request will be passed to the local authority. This local authorisation decision is made based on the federation level identity of users and the consistency of the federal and the local authorisation policies and user attributes. In this approach, it is mandatory for the federation to ensure that if a user has appropriate attributes (privileges, etc.) at the federation level, that user should also have appropriate attributes at the local member system. Otherwise there will be no federated activities allowed to be executed at member system level (vertical inconsistencies). This approach is faced with a difficulty in matching a local authorisation policy to a federal one and matching the attributes of a user in local domain to the federal domain. This problem could be solved by building information mapping mechanism between two types of policies and attributes but it is still very complex and costly to deploy and maintain.

On the other hand, the bottom-up approach is designed for the authorisation at the federation level. In this case, the federation level authorisation decision is derived from the access control policy and user attributes defined by the local member system authority. If the federation activity involves many member systems, the final authorisation is a combination of all those local authorisation policies. This approach contains a potential problem that if one member system rejects the access request, the activity will be denied. In addition, any inconsistencies (horizontal inconsistencies) between the member systems' authorisation policies will lead to the denial of the federation level access request. This approach also has problems in synchronising the changes in component systems' authorisation policies.

As mention above, in either approach, there will be some problems in maintaining the consistencies of user attributes when a change occurs. Several propagation strategies could be applied [5,17,18]:

i. Changes should be applied immediately: This strategy provides full consistency of access control policies for the whole federation and allows the change to take effect immediately after the change happens. However, this strategy increases the administrative cost for monitoring, maintaining and synchronising all changes. More seriously, if the federation fails to synchronise the changes, the access control process could be severely degraded.

ii. Changes should be applied periodically: This strategy allows for a period of temporary inconsistency. This helps in saving administrative costs. However, this strategy does not have enough flexibility for high-demand access and critical applications. This approach could be found in some commercial applications today such as elevator access control, etc. as when a change in access control happens; the user needs to allow a certain period of time for the change to take effect. However, until the change is effective, a user will not have access to the resource. Thus any delay in taking account of the changes can cause a follow on effect of denying rightful access to the system.

iii. Changes should be applied at the access time: This strategy also allows temporary inconsistency. However, this strategy overcomes the disadvantage of the approach above as when the system receives a request from a user, the system will check for the change and if applicable, the new change will take effect at the time of access request. This strategy provides high flexibility and fine-grained synchronisation ability while still being able to maintain the lost administrative costs.

iv. Changes should be applied on demand (only upon request): This strategy also allows temporary inconsistency. However, this strategy allows the change to take effect only when the authority, who could be owner or administrator, explicitly states so. This strategy puts substantial power on the authority and somehow, looses the necessary flexibility and the mandatory autonomy nature.

After such changes, when a user requests access permissions on a certain resource, it is important for the federation to recognise the updates, verify the consistency of user attributes and effectively granting the necessary permissions. All the cases above show a strong demand for a mechanism to maintain the consistency of user attributes across the federation.

4   Federated Identity Profiling and Attribute Consistency

Under the umbrella of a federated system, user attributes can be defined at its home system and theoretically, can be recognised by other members in the federation. However, with current approaches, in order to allow attribute exchange to happen, the exchange process may be required to follow common representation syntax which is not always feasible. Benantar (2005) [3] has clearly pointed out that the lack of a common set of attributes and a common interpretation of attributes is an impediment for making access control decisions in federated systems. Figure 1 presents a high level concept of federated identity profiling.

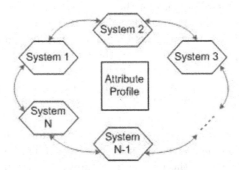

Fig. 1. A high-level concept of federated identity and attribute synchronisation issue

Overall, there are three solution approaches for this problem namely: local profiling, distributed profiling, and third party profiling [3].

In local profiling, a user is registered with its home system and so the profile attributes of user are totally under the control of and maintained by the local system. All other member systems will not have knowledge about such attributes until the attributes are exchanged under the trust relationship defined by the federation. This approach is well suited for federated systems with a common attribute representation and interpretation in which the attribute data is well defined and understood by all members of the federation. However, this is also a drawback as it is difficult to achieve such common agreements and the cost for maintaining the agreement can be high.

In distributed profiling, a user can initially register with its home system. Then if necessary, this user can further expand and acquire a new profile with a different system. As mentioned above, one of the reasons for having additional registrations is the need for new attributes that are specific to a particular system. By doing this, the attribute profile of a user is distributed across multiple member system of the federation. However, this poses a risk in which the definition of the same attribute may be duplicated and thus synchronisation may become an issue. In the context of federated system, this scheme offers the advantage of scalability and flexibility and somewhat leads to separation of concerns when it comes to managing user attributes among systems. Thus this approach is suitable for large and disparate federated systems.

Unlike the previous two approaches, in third party profiling, a designated third party within the established federation is responsible for the management of users' attribute profile. So member systems are effectively removed from this task. The third party may distinguish among profile information that is common to all or to a subset of the member systems as well as those that are pertinent to specific ones [3]. This approach offers the advantage of having to manage trust establishment with the third party only. However, to some extent, this approach utilise a kind of central point of authority which can turn to the single point of failure. Moreover, scalability can also be an issue as race condition, which can lead to dead-lock, can happen when member systems may contend over the single third party for retrieval and update profile information. The replication of the third party may be needed to address such a problem. When that happens, the replicas are required to be kept synchronised. Attribute synchronisation problem will be limited to the confines of the single third party where attribute profile information of a specific system may be duplicated for two or more target systems [3]. Table 2 provides a comparative overview about three approaches in some key characteristics.

Based upon the above Table 2, the profiling method selected will depend upon the situation at hand and thus should be selected on a case by case basis.

5 Attribute Synchronisation and Consistency Issue

Currently, attribute synchronisation can be done via meta-directories [4] and affiliate networks [3,11].

The meta-directory approach federates multiple systems by exposing the user identity to a higher level while retaining its relationship to various participating systems in which the identity is known [3,4]. The relationships of the global identity to the corresponding local level identities are formed by the links binding meta-directory information to the directories of the member systems. So, in this approach, common user attributes are maintained by the meta-directory. Updating

Table 2. Some characteristics of the 3 profiling approaches

Characteristic	Local Profiling	Distributing Profiling	Third-party Profiling
Flexibility	Low due to the need of a common and well defined profile by all member systems.	High due to the ability to expand and incorporate new profile.	Low due to the central role of the third party.
Complexity	Low. Simple to manage with low trust requirements.	High but difficult to manage with high trust requirements. Profile may be duplicated.	Low. Simple to manage due to the central role of the third party. Low trust requirements (only need to trust the third party). No duplicated profile.
Scalability	Low. Scalability is not a matter here as each member system in the federation maintains their own profile information and does not need to worry about the others.	High but again high scalability comes at a price of maintaining attribute consistency.	High as any addition of new member system to the federation is not a simple matter (third party control the profile).
Feasibility	Low due to the low interoperability.	High but comes at a price of maintaining attribute consistency.	High due to the substantial cost of maintaining attribute consistency.

these attributes is centrally undertaken and synchronisation is performed automatically which enables seamless sharing and maintenance of identity information.

Affiliate networks provides a tightly coupled structure by directly mapping an identity defined in one system onto a corresponding identity in another system [3,11]. Updating user identity information requires updating all involved systems. It is important to note that mapping an identity is not simply about associating names from one system to another. The mapping applies to the attributes associated with an identity. Updating such attributes in one directory requires the consistency of user attributes to be maintained across multiple directories. Figure 3 depicts the 3-way identity mapping problem presented by the affiliate networks architecture.

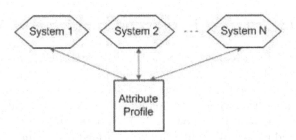

Fig. 2. Joining multiple systems via a meta-directory

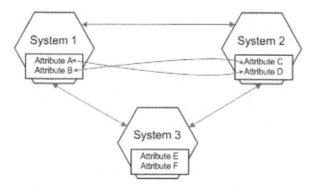

Fig. 3. Joining 3 systems via affiliate networks and its mapping problem

The meta-directory approach provides a low-cost and simple management mechanism. Due to the implementation of the central meta-directory, this approach is suitable for systems under a single authority. However, the key drawback of this approach is that it is not scalable enough to accommodate a potentially large number of identity domains as the management cost for maintaining large attribute profile storage will be too high. In contrast, the affiliate network is more complex and comes at a higher management cost. The main difference between this mapping approach and that enabled by meta-directories is that here the mapping is achieved without actually having to create an additional join in directory. So the affiliate network approach has better flexibility and scalability over meta-directories. Mapping users across all directories, however, creates management complexities associated with the n-wise problem, in which the number of mappings grows exponentially as the number of nodes increases [3]. Hence, the flexibility and scalability of the affiliate network make it a better solution than the meta-directory approach.

6   Delegation for Consistency

Preliminaries. Delegation is a mechanism of assigning attributes to a user which can be categorised in two forms: administrative delegation and user delegation [8]. In administrative delegation, the administrator such as security officer, with or without the delegating attributes, will conduct the delegating operations. In contrast, user delegation is conducted by user and such delegation requires the user possesses the delegating attributes. User delegation is believed short-lived (temporary) and intended for a specific purpose or activity [13]. The user who performs the delegation is referred to as a "delegator" and the user who receives a delegation is referred to as a "delegatee" [8,12].

Attributes can be delegated in two ways: by delegating the whole identity or by delegating some specific attributes. Delegating an attribute such as name or permission gives the delegatee the ability to use delegated attributes. However, delegating the whole identity gives the delegatee the ability to impersonate the delegator with its newly delegated identity. That is, the delegatee is authenticated and authorized for the new identity and thereby gains the ability to use attributes associated with this identity.

In general, delegation may be classified into (at least) two kinds: grant and transfer [2,8]. In grant delegation model, a successful delegation operation allows a delegated attribute to be available to both the delegator and delegatee. So after a grant delegation, both delegatee and delegator will share a common set of attributes. However, in transfer delegation model; following a successful delegation operation, the ability to use delegated attributes is transferred to the delegatee and the delegated attributes are no longer available to the delegator. Grant delegation model makes the availability of attributes increases monotonically with delegations [8]. Grant delegation model is, primarily, concerned with allowing the delegatee to use the delegated attributes. On the other hand, in transfer delegation models, besides allowing the delegatee to use the delegated attributes, the mechanism must be able to prevent the use of the delegated attributes by the delegator. This requirement makes transfer delegation policy enforcement more difficult [1,8,13].

Attribute Delegation. Initially, when a user, with multiple accounts on multiple systems, wants to take the advantage of federation, the user has to choose one of the systems as its home system. This system will become the identity provider for this user and other systems, as service providers, rely upon this identity provider (Figure 4). Then the user must link its account on the home system to other system to initialise the federation. By doing this, the user maintains a link between the account on the home system to other accounts on service providers.

As discussed above, when roles or permissions, or generally, attributes of the user are changed; the changes must be recognised by the federation. In the attribute synchronisation approach, the problem of n-wise combination results in a significant overhead and management complexity. It is submitted that delegation is a more robust means to achieve the same object.

Delegation for maintaining attribute consistency can come up with the predefined superset of attributes [3]. The superset can be defined as the common agreement of the members of the federation and could be considered as the sum of all necessary attributes. A member system of the federation can contribute to this overall superset of attributes by introducing attributes of their own. A member system therefore may be aware of only a subset of the overall attributes. In a particular member system, some attributes for a certain user may not necessarily have values assigned to them. For example, a user who does not have an account on a particular service will not require values for any of the attributes that are specific to that service. Multi-valued attributes are used to maintain the fact that the same attribute is assigned different values depending on the target service in which the user has an account. For example, due to conflicting identity management policies, a user may be required to have different values on each target service where the user maintains an account [2,6,10]. This approach offers the advantage of scalability via distributing user attribute profiles.

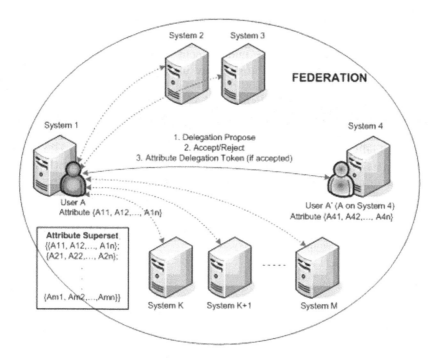

Fig. 4. High level architecture of attribute delegation mechanism

Table 3. Attribute Synchronisation Vs Delegation

Characteristic	Attribute Synchronisation	Attribute Delegation
Attribute Consistency	High but costly and hard to manage	High
Complexity	High due to n-wise problem	Medium
Flexibility	Low	High due to the self-control of the delegation process and the ability to delegate and revoke the delegated attributes on demand.
Scalability	Medium. Scalability dramatically decreases when the number of systems increases.	High
Others	Simple for implementation.	Quite complex for implementation but good for accounting and auditing.

The use of delegation for maintaining attribute consistency allows the dynamic definition of identity attribute. This allows the superset of attributes that can be dynamically redefined and potentially be incorporated for more attributes. Table 3 compares the two approaches in some key characteristics.

Primarily, delegation eases the management overheads and provides better scalability, flexibility as well as granularity in maintaining consistency. With delegation, the federation does not really need to incorporate the changes of attribute immediately when it happens, but it can use delegation to achieve consistency only when necessary. Furthermore, such an approach employs separation of tasks, thus, making the process less error prone while updating attributes. Finally, unlike the synchronisation approach, delegation is a duplex mechanism as delegation provides revocation functionality to efficiently remove the delegated attributes if necessary. Thus, in general, delegation offers several advantages in comparing with the attribute synchronisation approach. Despite of the complexity in management and implementation, the advantage of scalability and flexibility a make delegation an ideal solution for maintaining attribute consistency in large scale federated systems.

7   Conclusion

In this paper, we have studied and analysed the two approaches to provide horizontal consistency of user attributes across the federation. In particular, profiling scheme, attribute synchronisation and delegation are discussed and analysed as schemes for maintaining consistency. Meta-directory and affiliate network are evaluated as two main attribute synchronisation approaches in which affiliate network is proved to be more flexible and scalable. We have also shown that the concept of delegation can be used to provide consistency for user attribute and is more effective than the current attribute synchronisation approaches as discussed in Section 6.

This research is the first step in a series of investigations to explore the consistency issue in user attributes across federation to provide a better scalability, flexibility and granularity in making access control decision in federation systems. An immediate priority in future work is to investigate the delegation mechanism to see how far delegation can be fit into the federated access control mechanisms. Furthermore, the vertical consistency as well as the administration of authorisation will be studies to how these factors affect the consistency between federal and local access control. A long term goal is to develop a proof of concept that implements the studies.

Acknowledgments. The research is funded by the Smart Services CRC, Australia (formerely Smart Internet Technology CRC). The research is also supported by the Information Queensland, Queensland State Government, Australia.

References

1. Aura, T.: Distributed access-rights management with delegation certificate. In: Vitek, J. (ed.) Secure Internet Programming. LNCS, vol. 1603, pp. 211–235. Springer, Heidelberg (1999)

2. Barka, E., Sandhu, R.: Framework for role-based delegation models. In: Proceedings of the 16th Annual Conference Computer Security Applications (ACSAC '00), pp. 168–176 (2000)

3. Benantar, M.: Access Control Systems - Security. In: Identity Management and Trust Model, Springer, New York (2006)

4. Brown, K.: Security Briefs: A First Look at InfoCard. MSDN Magazine 21 (2006)

5. Bullock, A., Benford, S.: An access control framework for multi-user collaborative environments. In: ACM SIGGROUP Conference on Supporting Group Work, pp. 140–149 (1999)

6. Canovas, O., Gomez, A.F.: Delegation in distributed systems: challenges and open issues. In: 14th International Workshop on Database and Expert Systems Applications, pp. 499–503 (2003)

7. Chappell, D.: Introducing Windows CardSpace, Microsoft Corporation, Available: http://msdn.microsoft.com/windowsvista/default.aspx?pull= /library/en-us/dnlong/html/IntroInfoCard.asp (4th September 2006)

8. Crampton, J., Khambhammettu, H.: Delegation in Role-Based Access Control. In: Gollmann, D., Meier, J., Sabelfeld, A. (eds.) ESORICS 2006. LNCS, vol. 4189, pp. 174–191. Springer, Heidelberg (2006)

9. Heimbigner, D., McLeod, D.: A federated architecture for information management. ACM Transactions on Information Systems (TOIS) 3(3), 253–278 (1985)

10. Joshi, J.B.D., Bertino, E.: Fine-grained role-based delegation in presence of the hybrid role hierarchy. In: Proceedings of the 7th ACM symposium on Access control models and technologies, Lake Tahoe, California, USA, pp. 81–90 (2006)

11. Park, J.S., Sandhu, R., Ahn, G.J.: Role-based access control on the web. ACM Transactions on Information and System Security (TISSEC) 1(4) (2001)

12. Sandhu, R.:Role Usage and Activation Hierarchies (2005), Available: http://www.list.gmu.edu/it862/it862s05/Role_Activation_Hierarchies.ppt (16th February 2007)

13. Schaad, A.: A Framework for Organisational Control Principles, PhD Thesis, The University of York, York, England (2003)

14. Sheth, A.P., Larson, J.: Federated database systems for managing distributed, heterogeneous, and autonomous databases. ACM Computing Surveys (CSUR) 22(3), 183–236 (1990)

15. Shin, D., Ahn, G.J., Shenoy, P.: Ensuring information assurance in federated identity management. In: Proceedings of the 2004 IEEE International Conference on Performance, Computing, and Communications, pp. 821–826 (2004)

16. Thompson, P., Champagne, D., Kemp, J., Aarts, R., Bone, N., Castellanos-Zamora, D., Crom, J.M., Kannappan, L., Lindsay-Stewart, A., Maeda, K., Meyerstein, M., Nochimowski, A., Gonzalez, A., Poignet, A., Serret, X., Vanderbeek, J., Vittu, J., Walter, A., Sergent, J., Madsen, P., Cahill, C., Linn, J., Landau, S., Sibieta, P.: Liberty ID-FF Implementation Guidelines - Version 1.2, Available: https://www.projectliberty.org/specs/liberty-idff-guidelines-v1.2.pdf (4th September 2006)

17. Varadharajan, V., Crall, C., Pato, J.: Authorization in enterprise-wide distributed system: a practical design and application. In: Proceedings of the 14th Annual Computer Security Applications Conference, pp. 178–189 (1998)

18. Vimercati, S.D.C.D., Samarati, P.: Access control in federated systems. In: Proceedings of the Workshop on New security paradigms, Lake Arrowhead, CA, USA, pp. 87–99 (1996)

Pre-execution Security Policy Assessment of Remotely Defined BPEL-Based Grid Processes

Klaus-Peter Fischer[1,2,3], Udo Bleimann[2], and Steven Furnell[3]

[1] Digamma Communications Consulting GmbH, Karlstr. 25, 64367 Mühltal, Germany
K.P.Fischer@digamma.de
[2] Aida Institute of Applied Informatics Darmstadt,
University of Applied Sciences Darmstadt, Darmstadt, Germany
U.Bleimann@fbi.h-da.de
[3] Network Research Group, University of Plymouth, Plymouth, United Kingdom
sfurnell@plymouth.ac.uk

Abstract. In this paper results from research on security policy enforcement for cross-domain defined business processes specified in BPEL are transferred to the field of Grid computing, where BPEL is used to define Grid processes. In order to facilitate the assessment of remotely defined BPEL-based Grid processes for compliance with security policies prior to execution, a method for specifying security policies with respect to security-relevant semantic patterns in BPEL is applied. The paper shows the extent to which transfer of the former results was successful and indicates limitations and areas of further research. Where the situation is similar to cooperative business processes, such as in forming dynamic virtual organizations using Grid technology, the results turned out to be transferable with minor modifications, whereas for a transfer to the Grid context in general further investigation is required (in particular with respect to formal specification of security-relevant semantics of Grid services).

Keywords: Business Process Execution Language (BPEL), Grid Processes, Security Policy Enforcement, Information Flow Analysis, Virtual Organizations, Grid Services.

1 Introduction

For the purpose of defining business processes on top of Web services, Business Process Execution Language (WS-BPEL) [1], usually abbreviated BPEL, has emerged as the de-facto standard for Web service composition [26]. In the field of Grid computing, Grid services [24] play a role similar to Web services in the field of business processes. Due to this similarity, BPEL has been found its way to application in Grid context for the specification of long-running processes modeled with BPEL invoking Grid services (*e.g.*, [2,14]). Because of its analogy to using BPEL in collaborative business process (CBP) context, this paper proposes to transfer results of research on security policy enforcement for remotely defined business processes [9,10,11] to a Grid process context.

In a CBP context, availability of BPEL-enabled platforms at every site involved in such a business process could be assumed, since this already is or soon will be

C. Lambrinoudakis, G. Pernul, A M. Tjoa (Eds.): TrustBus 2007, LNCS 4657, pp. 178–189, 2007.

common practice in enterprises engaging in CBPs. Therefore, gaining access to a BPEL-enabled node was not considered a motivation for remotely defining BPEL scripts. Instead, location-dependent access restrictions gave rise to defining business processes displaced from the intended location of execution [9,11]. In a Grid context, however, the lack of access to a BPEL-enabled platform could very well motivate definition of BPEL scripts for remote execution since not every location having the need for defining Grid processes may be assumed to have local access to a BPEL-enabled platform. In particular, having (local) access to such a platform may not be considered a standard situation in small or medium-sized organizations. Therefore, defining BPEL scripts for remote execution might be an interesting amendment of current state of the art of using BPEL in a Grid context.

As indicated in our earlier works [10,11], security issues involved in this way of using BPEL-defined business processes (the same holds for BPEL-defined Grid processes) may impede practical application of this approach. When execution of remotely defined BPEL scripts is requested, there is first of all the uncertainty about the semantics of the process defined with respect to their compatibility with local security policies that gets in the way of executing them without reservation.

Making otherwise inaccessible Web services available to a controlling business process while still observing the security policy with respect to non-disclosure of information gained or access to resources granted by invoking such Web services was discussed in [11]. Since the conditions to be observed with respect to access control could be much more diverse in a Grid context [5], the investigation of generally granting access to otherwise restricted Grid services as the reason for executing remotely defined BPEL scripts is left to further study.

However, the transfer of our results from the CBP context to the Grid context seems to be most obvious for situations where Grid technology is used for forming virtual organizations (VOs) [13]. In this context, the number of partners are limited and controlled by regulations for joining a VO, particularly with respect to authentication and authorization. When remotely defined BPEL scripts are used for controlling Grid processes in VOs, there are many analogies to business processes defined by remotely defined BPEL scripts in the CBP context. As with CBPs, local security policies of an organization offering resources for being used in a VO usually determine access to these resources. These policies will result in restrictions to allowed semantics of remotely defined BPEL scripts that may be accepted for execution from a member of the VO. Such restrictions on allowed semantics may further restrict access to Grid services than access would be restricted by security policies of the sites offering these services alone. Reasons for this could be that allowing invocation of a Grid service in a particular context of a Grid process would violate a security policy such as prevention of generating or relaying mass e-mail from within the domain executing the BPEL script.

In this paper, the method of defining security policies in terms of security-relevant semantics inherent in BPEL in order to facilitate the assessment of compliance with such policies will be transferred from the field of business processes to the Grid context. It will be shown to what extent this attempt is successful and where limitations and issues for further study exist.

A further aspect discussed in this paper is the possibility to delegate the task of assessing compliance of BPEL-defined Grid processes with local security policies. An infrastructure supporting the delegation of this task to one or several dedicated nodes in a network or to specific assessment centers has also been introduced for the CBP context [9]. This possibility may be of even more interest in the Grid context where typically many small to medium size computers, spread over different locations, are involved, not necessarily belonging to a larger organization (as typically encountered in a CBP context) that can afford or provide the effort required for the task of performing the security policy assessment as proposed in this paper.

2 Related Work

Since security in the Grid context plays a paramount role, much research has been dedicated to this field on Grid computing. In particular, research concerned with expressing security policies in the context of VOs are related to our approach presented herein. In [7], for example, a security architecture for peer-to-peer-based Grid computing is proposed where a security layer offering security-related functionality resides between the Grid application layer and the communication infrastructure. This way, applications do not need to implement such functionality on their own. Security requirements may be stated by each member of a VO on a peer-by-peer basis or for groups of peers.

In [27], it is investigated how security functionality can be made available to Grid services, in particular in the context of VOs. A security model for Open Grid Services Architecture (OGSA) [12] specifying security services to provide different security functionality is proposed for this purpose. The authors show how security-related specifications from the field of Web services can be used in the context of this security architecture. In their paper, expressing security policies for using a Web service in terms of WS-Policy [3] specifications and publishing these policies together with the WSDL [6] specification of the service is also addressed.

It should be noted that security policy expressed in terms of WS-Policy deals with the requirements for security mechanisms to be applied or provided for using a Grid service (such as certificates to be required for accessing a service, or encryption methods to be applied when communicating input and output parameters of a service). In a layered architecture for composing new services from existing ones, or for executing processes based on existing services as proposed in [16], these mechanisms are to be provided in layers below the business process layer, since in the business process layer (and particularly in BPEL) there are no means for providing communication security and for exchanging or checking security certificates. The security policies expressed in the two approaches above, therefore, address aspects of policies complementary to those that have to be obeyed in the business process layer when remotely defined BPEL scripts are to be executed (as addressed in our former research [10,11] and in this paper).

Process algebra and language-based research, not dedicated specifically to Web services or Grid services, addressing the relation of programs and programming languages with security policies [8,21] are comparable with the scope of our approach, albeit from a theoretical perspective. Approaches requiring for analysis purposes, that all programming logic is expressed by algebraic formulations such as λ-calculus (*e.g.*, [17]) may be of limited use in the field of Grid processes considering the program size of the execution environment running such processes. However, some insights from these theory-oriented papers might be of interest also in the context of Grid processes. With respect to information flow, for instance, Sabelfeld and Myers [21] emphasize the advantage of static analysis considering all possible execution paths of a program compared to dynamic analysis considering only one instance of program execution. They also explicate the potential existence of so-called covert channels (*i.e.*, means of information transfer exploiting mechanisms not primarily intended for information transfer such as the number of iterations in a loop to leak information via externally observable program behavior) and emphasize the difficulty to detect them during information flow analysis.

Our approach, as described in [9,10,11], tries to keep the assessment of compliance and the methods for analyzing security-relevant semantics of BPEL scripts as simple as possible without requiring profound skills in special formalisms such as algebraic formulation of programming logic. The methods proposed are based on technologies and methods well-known to developers of Web services and business processes as well as of Grid services and Grid processes in order to be comparatively easy to be applied and, therefore, could be attractive to be adopted by practitioners in this fields. The insights from theory-oriented research with respect to information flow analysis and consequences of the considerations with respect to covert channels mentioned above, however, have been taken into account in our approach.

Other related work proposing runtime monitoring as a concept for security policy enforcement in mobile or untrusted code requires access to Java byte code as in [25] or to program code at system level as in [22]. These approaches might also be of only limited use to be applied for analyzing BPEL scripts and the Grid process defined by them for compliance with security policies (since neither Java byte code nor program code at system level is available for instrumentation or monitoring at the level a Grid process is executed on a BPEL-enabled platform).

Since the approach taken in our research allows for assessing compliance of BPEL scripts with security policies prior to execution, the shortcomings of approaches requiring execution of a Grid (or any other) process in order to observe its behavior and to check it for possible violations during execution are neatly avoided. One of these shortcomings is the risk that upon detecting a violation of security policy, the activity causing violation could already have passed a point of no return such that interception would have been exercised too late to prevent security violations from being committed, which can be securely avoided by pre-execution assessment.

3   Security-Relevant Semantic Patterns in BPEL-Based Grid Processes

Based on the results of an analysis of BPEL as a specification language for its potential to define security-critical behavior, security-relevant semantic patterns in BPEL have been identified as combinations of BPEL activities and Web services subject to access or information flow restrictions to and from their parameters as derived from security policies [10]. In order to transfer this concept to the Grid context, the classes of security policy-induced access restrictions found in [10] are converted with respect to Grid services (GS) as shown in Table 1.

Table 1. Classification of access restrictions to Grid services (adapted from [10])

Class	Description of Restriction
1	GS with unrestricted access to all parts of resources or information offered
2	GS with completely restricted access (*i.e.*, GS that are not allowed to be invoked)
3	GS parameters with restricted visibility of output values with respect to specific targets: information returned by these parameters is not allowed to be carried to specific targets (*i.e.*, to specific other GS or to particular parameters of specific GS)
4	GS with restricted write access: some of the input parameters of the GS are not allowed to be used at all
5	GS parameters with restricted set of values allowed in write access: such input parameters of a GS may only be used with particular values
6	GS parameters with values in write access restricted to specific sources: for such input parameters of a GS only values from particular origins may be used, that is, only values returned by a particular GS or a specific parameter of a particular GS
7	GS particularly prone to overload if invoked excessively. For these GS, maximum invocation rates or maximum amount of data passed to it that prevent overloading will have to be observed

Whereas the term 'Web service' had to be replaced by 'Grid service' throughout Table 1, most descriptions could be transferred otherwise unchanged (classes 1, 2, 4, and 5) or nearly unchanged (class 6). Only the description of class 3 was modified to better fit in the Grid context and a new class 7 was introduced.

While in the CBP context the restriction in class 3 was specified in terms of restricted visibility to targets outside the domain executing a BPEL script, this distinction does not always play an important role in the Grid context. Therefore, the definition of class 3 was abstracted from the location where a target resides to generally express restricted information flow to dedicated targets irrespective of their location. Hence, restrictions will be specified in terms of specific Grid services or particular input parameters thereof that are forbidden to receive the values returned from these parameters. In order, for instance, to prevent a list of e-mail addresses returned by a particular Grid service to be used for generating mass e-mail, this output parameter could be restricted not to be used as input parameter of particular other Grid services known to generate an e-mail to each address passed to it. Obviously, the location of the second Grid service (inside or outside the executing site) does not matter in this case.

Unlike in the CBP context, where effective runtime mechanisms for prevention of overloading a Web services could be deemed to be in place (in layers below the business layer) at a platform running these services, this might not, in general, be expected from sites running Grid services. Therefore, a security policy of a site accepting remotely defined BPEL scripts in a Grid context could require that a process running on resources of this site shall not cause overload (running the risk to result in an intentional or unintentional denial of service attack) to specific Grid services known to be prone to overload when invoked in a particular manner. Since, in a Grid context, effective runtime prevention of overloading a Grid service shall not be expected to take place at all sites running these services, semantic patterns of BPEL potentially causing such overload have to be identified and looked for in pre-execution compliance assessment to prevent BPEL scripts including such patterns from being executed.

Table 2. Security relevance of semantic patterns with primitive activities (adapted from [10])

	Primitive Activities	Class 3	Class 4	Classes 5/6	Class 7
`invoke`	invocation of a Grid service	IFA(v)	w	IFA(w/s)	IFA(a)
`receive`	waiting for a message to arrive	IFA(v)	–	–	–
`reply`	sending a reply to a message received	–	w	IFA(w/s)	–
`assign`	assignment of values between two different locations	(relevant in IFA only)			
`wait`	waiting for a specified amount of time	time(v)	–	–	–
`throw`	indication of exceptions such as failures during execution	except(v)	–	–	–
`empty`	no operation	–	–	–	–
`exit`	termination of a process instance	exit(v)	–	–	–

w   = observance of restricted use of input parameters in write access to GS.

IFA = information flow analysis, (v) with respect to visibility of values read from GS, (w) with respect to
      values written to GS,
      (s) with respect to sources of values written to GS, (a) with respect to amount of data written.

There are two types of overload that may be caused to a Grid service: One type is
sending more data in an invocation of a Grid service than can be handled. The other
type is invoking a Grid service at a higher rate than this service can cope with. Therefore, performance-related restrictions related to these types of overload may be indicated for a Grid service falling in this new class 7 in the Grid context.

Table 3. Security relevance of semantic patterns with structured activities (adapted from [10])

	Structured Activities	Class 3	Class 4	Classes 5/6	Class 7
`sequence`	definition of a fixed execution order	–	–	–	FQ
`flow`	parallel execution of activities	–	–	–	FQ
`switch`	branching between several alternate activities depending on conditions	switch cond(v)	–	–	–
`while`	iterative execution, *i.e.*, looping	loop cond(v)	–	–	FQ
`pick`	waiting simultaneously for sev-eral events to occur and procee-ding with the event that occurs first (see note)	IFA(v)	–	–	–
		time(v)	–	–	–

Note: Typically, one of the events is a timeout event, while the other are messages to arrive.

IFA(v) = information flow analysis with respect to visibility of values read from GS.
FQ   = invocation frequency to be checked against maximum.

The security-relevant semantic patterns were adapted from [10] in Tables 2 and 3.
For reasons discussed in [10], no such patterns exist for classes 1 and 2. While all semantic patterns identified in [10] are also relevant in the Grid context and, therefore,
could be transferred by simply substituting the term "Grid service" for "Web service",
some new semantic patterns were added as combinations of BPEL activities and the
new restriction class 7 in the last column of Tables 2 and 3, respectively. Hence, attention has to be paid during compliance assessment to semantic patterns identified as
being capable of generating high invocation frequencies of Grid services (in **while**,
sequence, or **flow** activities, marked 'FQ' in Table 3) or passing large amount of

data to Grid services not designed for coping with such data volumes (in **invoke** activities, marked 'IFA(a)' in Table 2).

From Tables 2 and 3, it can be seen that information flow analysis is required for most of the semantic patterns identified as security-relevant in [10]. It should be noted that the security relevance of the patterns in Table 2 related to restriction class 3 denoted by 'time(v)' (*i.e.*, duration of wait dependent on visibility-restricted value), 'except(v)' (*i.e.*, type of exception thrown dependent on visibility-restricted value), and 'exit(v)' (*i.e.*, termination dependent on visibility-restricted value) as well as in the same column of Table 3 denoted by 'switch cond(v)' (*i.e.*, branching dependent on visibility-restricted value), 'loop cond(v)' (*i.e.*, number of iterations dependent on visibility-restricted value), and again 'time(v)' is a consequence of the requirement to prevent covert channels as mentioned above.

Making, for instance, the condition for choosing alternative flows in a **switch** activity dependent on visibility-restricted information, constitutes a covert channel since this could enable an external observer of the executing process to draw conclusions on the values of such visibility-restricted information from the observation which alternative flow actually is being taken thereby violating the security policy of non-disclosure of this information.

4   Rewriting Security Policies to Support Pre-execution Security Policy Assessment

In [9,10], rewriting security policies in terms of security-relevant semantics has been proposed to support compliance assessment of remotely defined BPEL-based business processes with these policies. An informal checklist for stating allowed and disallowed semantic patterns was introduced in [9] leading to a so-called security policy statement (SPS) when filled in to reflect the security policies of a specific domain. In the CBP context, such an SPS was defined domain-specific with respect to two domains, namely the domain where the security policy is in effect (*i.e.*, domain executing BPEL scripts) and the domain defining and sending BPEL scripts for execution. An XML-based schema for specifying an SPS in machine-readable form which has been the basis for implementing an automatic assessment of BPEL scripts for compliance with security policies expressed by such an SPS has been introduced in [11].

In the Grid context, rewriting security policies in such a way may also prove useful for assessing BPEL scripts with respect to compliance with these policies. Since semantic patterns have been modified (definition of restriction class 3) and supplemented (patterns involving new restriction class 7) compared with those found in [10], the check list as basis of an SPS as well as the XML-based SPS schema for machine-readable versions thereof have to be modified accordingly in order to accommodate this new set of security-relevant semantic patterns.

Unlike in the CBP context, an SPS may not be sensibly defined for a specific foreign domain, since Grid computing is concerned with a potentially large amount of foreign domains that are essentially indistinguishable from the point of view of the domain executing the BPEL-defined Grid processes. Only in a VO environment, when the identities of members and their privileges to execute Grid services are known in advance, defining an SPS for each other member in the VO that is allowed to send BPEL scripts for execution could make sense.

Therefore, with the exception of the latter situation, only one or a few SPSs without any relation to a specific external domain will make sense in the Grid context. If more than one SPS will be specified for a domain, they are expected to be differentiated with respect to different application contexts for which they apply (*e.g.*, computational simulation in a particular field, collection of field-specific data such as in meteorology). Although details of application context-dependent SPSs are left to further study, it is anticipated that such SPSs will be tightly bound to access privileges or roles classifying the sender of a BPEL script.

Specifying security policies in terms of security-relevant semantic patterns identified in section 3 requires an exhaustive list of all Grid services allowed to be invoked by a remotely defined BPEL script. Furthermore, for every Grid service mentioned in this list, the security-relevant semantics of the service and its parameters has to be known in order to determine the access restriction classes appropriate for each of them (cf., Table 1). This requirement may cause additional effort since specification of security-relevant semantics may not be available for Grid services in the first place.

It should be noted that unavailability of semantic specification (at least as far as security-relevant semantics is concerned) may prevent the approach proposed herein from being applied. However, unavailability of such specification may also prevent the application of any other pre-execution approach to assessing compliance of Grid processes with security policies. This holds independently of both the location where a Grid process is being defined and executed, and also the manner in which the process is being specified (*i.e.*, independent of using BPEL or any other means for specifying Grid processes). In case of unavailable semantic specifications, the only way of enforcing security policies is monitoring the execution of a Grid process and interfering in cases when violations of security policy have been detected involving the known shortcomings of such approaches mentioned above.

However, much current research is concerned with describing the semantics of Grid services in order to support identification of matching Grid services for automatic Grid process orchestration (*e.g.*, [18,20]). Bringing the results of this research together with the approach proposed in this paper in order to define a framework for formally specifying security-relevant semantics of Grid services in terms of well-defined (maybe even standardized) categories is expected to be an interesting field of further study.

A further motivation for research in this direction could be the endeavor to facilitate specification of information flow restrictions of output parameters and value or source restrictions for input parameters with respect to particular characteristics of a Grid service by denoting particular semantics bound to this Grid service instead of particular Grid services themselves. Such semantic characteristics could be "returning lists of e-mail addresses" or "causes sending e-mails to addresses passed". Means to specify restrictions this way would eliminate the need to analyze every potentially allowed Grid service for falling into a specific restriction class if, in parallel, Grid services and their parameters would have been specified in terms of such characteristics with respect to their (security-relevant) semantics.

If such classification of Grid services would be available, then, for instance, in order to enforce a security policy of avoiding the generation of Spam emails at a Grid node, one could require that any output parameter with the semantic characteristic "returning a (potentially large) list of email addresses" must not be input to any parameter with the characteristic "causes sending e-mails to addresses passed". Specifying allowed and disallowed semantic patterns with respect to such categories instead of individual Grid services and their parameters obviously would help to shorten the content of an SPS considerably. How far this idea of categorizing Grid parameter semantics for this purpose can be successfully based on or linked with research such as work on semantic Grid services [15], semantic matchmaking of Grid service composition [18], or workflow ontology of Grid services [4] requires further investigation.

Such amendments of addressing semantic characteristics of Grid service parameters in an SPS are expected to involve increased complexity of the assessment task because of required matching of SPS and semantic characteristics of the Grid services actually used in a BPEL script. Even before such amendments are available, it is not obvious and actually will require further investigation whether the assessment of compliance with security policies specified in an SPS is similarly straightforward as it has been shown for the CBP context by implementing a research prototype [11]. In particular, it is expected that covering semantic patterns involving class 7 restrictions in automatic compliance assessment prior to execution will turn out to be complex or even impossible to a certain extent since this class of restrictions addresses dynamic aspects of a BPEL script that obviously are not easy to be analyzed in a static pre-execution assessment.

5 Delegation of Security Policy Assessment

Since, as indicated above, the assessment of compliance with security policies may be more complex in a Grid context requiring specific skills or use of dedicated tools, the motivation to delegate this task to a specific node or an assessment center may be higher in the Grid context than it already was in the CBP context. Delegation of compliance assessment can occur in a variety of ways, as described in the specification of a security infrastructure enabling such delegation [9]. This infrastructure can be transferred to the Grid context in a straightforward manner and some amendments specific for the Grid context are made.

Assessment can be performed against locally or remotely defined SPSs. Such remotely defined SPS may be sent together with the BPEL script as a kind of assertion what the Grid process defined by the BPEL script is going to do or not to do with respect to security-relevant semantics inherent in BPEL and the Grid services involved.

When this approach is taken, means for checking the proper relation and integrity of the SPS and the BPEL script may be provided based on appropriate certificates added to both the BPEL script and the SPS.

A remotely defined SPS provided with a BPEL script may be checked against local security policy requirements. After positive assessment of compliance with these requirements, the local site:

- may decide to trust in the assertion provided by the remote site and, after checking integrity of BPEL script and SPS, execute the BPEL script without any further compliance assessment, or
- may initiate an assessment of compliance in any ways mentioned below.

Besides local or remote definition of SPSs, there is the third alternative that an SPS may be defined centrally (*e.g.,* defined by a central organization within a Grid environment or agreed upon as a standard relevant to a Grid context). In any of these cases, assessment of compliance with security policies expressed in an SPS may be performed in different ways:

- Locally at the executing site itself. The potential problem with this approach as already indicated above could be that performing security policy assessment locally might be too elaborate a task to be conducted by small footprint computers (*e.g.,* stand-alone personal computers) or small organizations that cannot afford specific checking tools or acquire specific skill required for this task.
- Remotely (in an assessment center) on behalf of the site executing the BPEL script. The SPS will be sent together with the BPEL script to the trusted assessment center for checking compliance of BPEL script and SPS-defined security policies. In case of a centrally defined SPS, a reference to this SPS may be sent instead of the SPS itself. The results will be returned to the executing site as certified verdicts (*i.e.,* passed or failed, the latter possibly accompanied by the reason(s) for this verdict).
- (Not applicable for locally defined SPS) Remotely (in an assessment center) on behalf of the site defining the BPEL script with respect to an SPS defined by the remote site or centrally defined. BPEL script and SPS are sent to the assessment center as in the previous case. The results of the assessment may be certified by the assessment center and sent back to the defining site together with the certified (with respect to integrity and identity) BPEL script and SPS. The defining site may then pass the certified BPEL script and SPS to the executing site possibly accompanied by the certified results from the assessment center. If an assessment center adheres to a published policy to only certify BPEL scripts and SPSs that received a passed verdict when checked for compliance, then sending the result from the defining site to the executing site can be abandoned since, in this case, having a certificate from such an assessment center implies the passed verdict for the BPEL script.

From the current point of view, these alternatives seem to be versatile enough to cover the requirements in the Grid context and, therefore, there seems to be no particular need for further research in this area.

6   Conclusions and Further Research

In this paper, the results arising from research into collaborative business processes, defined using BPEL scripts at one site and brought to another side for execution, with respect to assessing their compliance with the security policies effective at the executing site have been transferred to Grid processes. The discussion has identified the extent to which such a transfer can succeed, with or without requiring modifications of the former results and the limitations and areas needing further study.

The insights with respect to compliance with security policies could also be beneficial for security policy enforcement of Grid processes in strictly local environments (*i.e.,* when definition and execution of BPEL scripts occur at the same location in a Grid environment), since reformulating security policies such that the process of compliance assessment is facilitated thereby possibly enabling automatic performance of assessment could also be useful there.

In the attempt to transfer the results from the CBP to Grid context, several issues for further research have been encountered. Amongst them the classification of security-relevant semantics of Grid services and their parameters is deemed to be the most challenging as well as the most promising field for further study.

Investigating how the approaches proposed in this paper could be applied based on Grid environments or Grid middleware such as Globus Toolkit [23] or OurGrid [19], and what adaptation would be required in order to be successful in doing this, is another interesting direction of further research.

References

1. Alves, A., Arkin, A., Askary, S., Bloch, B., Curbera, F., Goland, Y., Kartha, N., Liu, C.K., König, D., Mehta, V., Thatte, S., van der Rijn, D., Yendluri, P., Yiu, A. (eds).: Web Services Business Process Execution Language Version 2.0. In: OASIS, 2006 http://www.oasis-open.org/committees/download.php/18714/wsbpel-specification-draft-May17.htm (last accessed 2007-02-22)
2. Amnuaykanjanasin, P., Nupairoj, N.: The BPEL Orchestrating Framework for Secured Grid Services. In: Proc. International Conference on Information Technology: Coding and Computing (ITCC'05), vol. I, pp. 348–353 (2005)
3. Bajaj, S., Box, D., Chappell, D., Curbera, F., Daniels, G., Hallam-Baker, P., Hondo, M., Kaler, C., Langworthy, D., Nadalin, A., Nagaratnam, N., Prafullchandra, H., von Riegen, C., Roth, D., Schlimmer, J., Sharp, C., Shewchuk, J., Vedamuthu, A., Yalçinalp, Ü., Orchard, D.: Web Services Policy 1.2 - Framework (WS-Policy). In: World Wide Web Consortium (2006), http://www.w3.org/Submission/2006/SUBM-WS-Policy-20060425 (last accessed 2007-02-25)
4. Beco, S., Cantalupo, B., Giammarino, L., Matskanis, N., Surridge, M.: OWL-WS: A Workflow Ontology for Dynamic Grid Service Composition. In: Proc. 1st International Conference on e-Science and Grid Computing (E-SCIENCE '05), pp. 148–155 (2005)
5. Chadwick, D.W., Su, L., Laborde, R.: Providing Secure Coordinated Access to Grid Services. In: Proc. 4th International Workshop on Middleware for Grid Computing (MCG '06), pp. 1–6 (2006)
6. Chinnici, R., Moreau, J.-J., Ryman, A., Weerawarana, S.(eds.): Web Services Description Language (WSDL) Version 2.0 Part 1: Core Language. In: World Wide Web Consortium (2006), http://www.w3.org/TR/2006/CR-wsdl20-20060327 (last accessed 2007-02-22)
7. Detsch, A., Gaspary, L.P., Barcellos, M.P., Cavalheiro, G.G.H.: Towards a Flexible Security Framework for Peer-to-Peer-based Grid Computing. In: Proc. 2nd Workshop on Middleware for Grid Computing (MGC'04), pp. 52–56 (2004)
8. Echahed, R., Prost, F.: Security Policy in a Declarative Style. In: Proc. 7th ACM SIGPLAN international conference on Principles and practice of declarative programming, PPDP'05, pp. 153–163 (2005)
9. Fischer, K.P., Bleimann, U., Fuhrmann, W., Furnell, S.M.: A Security Infrastructure for Cross-Domain Deployment of Script-Based Business Processes in SOC Environments. In: Proc. 5th International Network Conference, INC'2005, pp. 207–216 (2005)
10. Fischer, K.P., Bleimann, U., Fuhrmann, W., Furnell, S.M.: Security-Relevant Semantic Patterns of BPEL in Cross-Organisational Business Processes. In: Proc. 6th International Network Conference, INC'2006, pp. 203–212 (2006)

11. Fischer, K.P., Bleimann, U., Fuhrmann, W., Furnell, S.M.: Security Policy Enforcement in BPEL-Defined Collaborative Business Processes. In: Proc. 1st International Workshop on Security Technologies for Next Generation Collaborative Business Applications (SECOBAP'07), pp. 685–694. IEEE Computer Society, Los Alamitos (2007)
12. Foster, I., Kesselman, C., Nick, J., Tuecke, S.: The Physiology of the Grid: An Open Grid Services Architecture for Distributed Systems Integration, Globus Project (2002), http://www.globus.org/alliance/publications/papers/ogsa.pdf (last accessed: 2007-02-23)
13. Foster, I., Kesselman, C., Tuecke, S.: The Anatomy of the Grid: Enabling Scalable Virtual Organizations. Int. J. High Perform. Comput. Appl. 15(3), 200–222 (2001)
14. Gannon, D., Krishnan, S., Fang, L., Kandaswamy, G., Simmhan, Y., Slominsk, A.: On Building Parallel & Grid Applications: Component Technology and Distributed Services. Cluster Computing 8(4), 271–277 (2005)
15. Goble, C., De Roure, D.: The Grid: An Application of the Semantic Web. SIGMOD Rec. 31(4), 65–70 (2002)
16. Medjahed, B., Benatallah, B., Bouguettayaet, A., Ngu, A.H.H., Elmagarmid, A.K.: Business-to-business interactions: issues and enabling technologies. VLDB Journal 12, 59–85 (2003)
17. Li, P., Zdancewic, S.: Downgrading Policies and Relaxed Noninterference. In: Proc. 32nd ACM Symposium on Principles of Programming Languages (POPL'05), pp. 158–170 (2005)
18. Ludwig, S.A., Reyhani, S.M.S.: Introduction of Semantic Matchmaking to Grid Computing. J. Parallel Distrib. Comput. 65(12), 1533–1541 (2005)
19. OurGrid, http://www.ourgrid.org, (last accessed: 2007-02-23)
20. Ren, K., Xiao, N., Song, J., Chen, T., Zhang, W.: A Model for Semantic Annotation and Publication of Meteorology Grid Services in SMGA. In: Proc. 5th International Conference on Grid and Cooperative Computing Workshops (GCCW'06), pp. 496–503 (2006)
21. Sabelfeld, A., Myers, A.C.: Language-Based Information-Flow Security. IEEE Journal on Selected Areas in Communications 21(1), 5–19 (2003)
22. Sekar, R., Venkatakrishnan, V.N., Basu, S., Bhatkar, S., DuVarney, D.C.: Model-Carrying Code: A Practical Approach for Safe Execution of Untrusted Applications. In: Proc. 19th ACM Symposium on Operating Systems Principles (SOSP'03), pp. 15–28 (2003)
23. The Globus Toolkit, http://www-unix.globus.org/toolkit (last accessed: 2007-02-24)
24. Tuecke, S., Czajkowski, K., Foster, I., Frey J., Graham, S., Kesselman, C., Maquire, T., Sandholm, T., Snelling, D., Vanderbilt, P. (eds.): Open Grid Services Infrastructure (OGSI) Version 1.0", Global Grid Forum (2003) http://www.ggf.org/documents/GWD-R/GFD-R.015.pdf (last accessed: 2006-11-16)
25. Venkatakrishnan, V.N., Perit, R., Sekar, R.: Empowering Mobile Code Using Expressive Security Policies. In: Proc. New Security Paradigms Workshop'02, pp. 61–68 (2002)
26. Wang, H., Huang, J.Z., Qu, Y., Xie, J.: Web Services: Problems and Future Directions. Journal of Web Semantics 1(3), 309–320 (2004)
27. Welch, V., Siebenlist, F., Foster, I., Bresnahan, J., Czajkowski, K., Gawor, J., Kesselman, C., Meder, S., Pearlman, L., Tuecke, S.: Security for Grid Services. In: Proc. 12th IEEE International Symposium on High Performance Distributed Computing (HPDC'03), pp. 48–57 (2003)

Situation-Based Policy Enforcement

Thomas Buntrock, Hans-Christian Esperer, and Claudia Eckert

Technische Universitt Darmstadt
Department of Computer Science
Darmstadt, Germany
{buntrock,esperer,eckert}@sec.informatik.tu-darmstadt.de

Abstract. Current operating systems enforce access control policies based on completely static rules, a method originating from a time where computers were expensive and had to serve several users simultaneously. Today, as computers are cheap, a trend to mobile workstations can be realized, where a single device is used to perform a *dedicated* task under unpredictable, *changing conditions*. However, the static access rules still remain, while their use in mobile environments is limited, because in changing environments, access rights must constantly be adjusted to guarantee data integrity in all situations. With dynamically adjusting rules, in turn, it is not sufficient anymore to check access to data only once; instead, access rights must be revalidated every time data is actually accessed, even if part of that data is cached by an application. In this paper, we present a method to dynamically and retrospectively enforce access control policies based on the context a device is operating in, while tracing data beyond disk accesses.

1 Introduction

Today's computer systems are frequently used in dynamic environments with changing contexts. This is made possible by the increasing mobility and reduced costs of computers.

In dynamic environments data integrity and information confidentiality cannot be verified solely by defining static rules on a per-user basis. Additional factors must be taken into account, such as the location a device is currently operating within. This, in term, demands mobile systems to have according access control enforcement mechanisms.

To enforce access control policies, it is not sufficient anymore to control only disk access. The fact that processes can load data into system memory and operate on it must be taken into account as well. That way, complete control over the data can be provided. The following example will illustrate why it is necessary to trace and control the data at all times.

A service agent working for an insurance company visits customers to discuss treaty details. For this task he has a Laptop which contains the company policies, general treaty details as well as the confidential data of each client. In his office he can work on all data, while when visiting a

C. Lambrinoudakis, G. Pernul, A M. Tjoa (Eds.): TrustBus 2007, LNCS 4657, pp. 190–200, 2007.

client he must only access data that is related to the client. Read access to data, such as general terms and conditions, is granted, while write access to this data should be denied. If the agent leaves his applications opened while he leaves for another client, it must still be ensured that no confidential data is accessible outside that client's house.

Enforcement mechanisms of current operating systems are uncapable of dealing with situations where content suddenly becomes unavailable due to changing access policies.

Many applications load data into local buffers and once the data has been loaded, access to these buffers is no longer controlled. Furthermore, access is only granted based on the accessing user and the accessed resource; the external context is not taken into account. To satisfactorily handle the condition of a dynamically changing environment, access to a particular resource must be controlled at every operation, including operations in locally cached buffers.

An operating system, however, is neither able to determine which data has been loaded into a local buffer, nor it is able to detect whether a process has removed data from a local buffer, as this would require some kind of cooperation between the operating system and the application.

The access control architecture we propose overcomes these shortcomings. We provide a context-based access control scheme, the *Situation-based Access Control (SBAC)*, as well as a method to dynamically prevent unauthorized access to data, for resources that are being opened and read as well as for resources that are already cached by an application.

The next section defines important terms that are used within this work. Section 3 presents the SBAC architecture, SBAC components and the used policy language. Section 4 presents details of the implementation. Section 5 discusses performance issues and section 6 shows limitations of SBAC. In section 7 we will present related work dealing with context-based access control and policy enforcement. Further we present some open issues for future work in section 8 and close this paper in section 9 with a conclusion of our work.

2   Definitions

In order to further describe the SBAC architecture, it is necessary to introduce some terms.

Context *[...] is any information that can be used to characterize the situation of an entity.* [1]
A **situation** is a predefined set of context.
The **current context** is context detected at a given time.
The **current situation** is the situation resulting from the current context.

A context may be defined by many different attributes, such as *time, location, attendees, running processes* and so on. The current situation is determined by the current context. A change in the current situation therefore implies a change in the current context. A change in the current context, however, does not necessarily imply a change of in current situation. For example, the situation `employee_at_work` does not change with time, but the situation `mornings` does. Sensors are required to gather context information and situations must be defined with respect to the available sensors. Using a wireless network sensor and a GPS sensor, the situation `office` could be defined as followed. How exactly a situation is detected – based on sensor input – is out of the scope of this paper.

```
Situation(office):=
  GPS.location=="(49.52365N, 8.30573E)"
  and GPS.radius=="30m"
  and WLAN.ESSID=="TUD"
```

3   Architecture

This section presents the SBAC architecture, that is an add-on to an existing access control scheme – providing a *Mandatory Access Control* – and is capable to dynamically control access to logical resources. Dynamic environments require frequent adjustment of active policy rules. To enforce changing policy rules at all times we apply the concept of complete mediation [2], both to files on disk and to data locally cached in memory by applications.

The current access control architecture of a Linux-based operating system is shown in figure 1a. It only satisfies static access decisions based on static ACLs. The *Common Access Control* performs ACL checks or capability verification and then triggers the *Security Hooks*, which are provided by the *Linux Security Modules* (LSM) [3,4] to allow easy implementation of third-party security extensions.

Figure 1b illustrates our proposed extension that implements the dynamic access control. Combined with the static enforcement this architecture is able to handle dynamic situations, such as the scenario described in section 1.

SBAC introduces the rules *read, write* and *transfer*. Furthermore, in contrast to the classic access control, SBAC guarantees rule compliance at all times, which complies to the principle of *complete mediation* as demanded by Saltzer et al. in [2]. While their proposition only requires disk accesses be checked, we go a step further and demand that memory accesses are checked as well. Current architectures do not support tracing of data fragments once they have been loaded into memory. This functionality cannot be implemented easily, because it would require application cooperation. For our architecture this is not necessary, as a similar effect can be achieved by logging all disk read accesses for each process to keep track of all possibly accessible data. This is sufficient to enforce our proposed access policies.

In order to distinguish between the types of resources, we add an additional attribute to logically describe the content. Currently the content attributes are labels assigned to files and directories. The labels are simply names that are in no relation to one another and do not have any kind of order. A labeled

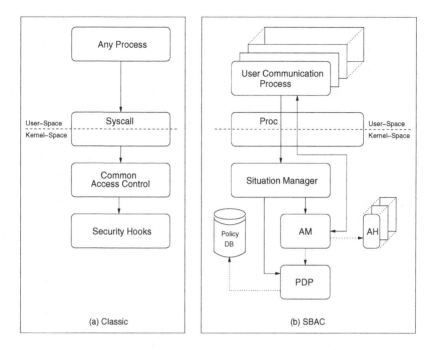

Fig. 1. Classic Access Control Architecture with SBAC

directory is called an SBAC container. Files inherit the label of the container they reside in, unless they are labeled individually, in which case they are treated like a container, but without the ability to bequeath their label to another file or directory.

Figure 2 shows an example of the resource labeling.

The directory /home/buntrock is labeled home_buntrock and defines a container for this label. The file a is not explicitly labeled and therefore inherits the label of the container. File b is specifically labeled file_b and does not inherit the container label. The directory tmp within the container home_buntrock defines a new container labeled buntrock_tmp and the files x and y inherit this label.

```
1. /home/buntrock/        (home_buntrock)
2.          ..      /a
3.          ..      /b      (file_b)
4.          ..      /tmp/   (buntrock_tmp)
5.          ..      .. /x
6.          ..      .. /y
```

Fig. 2. Labeling Example

3.1   Components

The SBAC architecture introduces six entities, of which one is settled in user space and five are settled in kernel space:

Situation Manager (SM): The SM handles the context information and aggregates it to a situation. When a context change leads to a change in the current situation, the SM informs the *Policy Decision Point* and the *Action Manager* of the new situation.

Situation Access Policy Database (SAPDB): The SAPDB states which objects can be accessed in which situations with what rights and whether this access is to be logged.

Access History (AH): Access Histories are memory stored lists. Each AH is attached to one process to log its performed data accesses.

Policy Decision Point (PDP): The PDP decides whether an access is allowed or denied. It uses the information stored in the SAPDB and the access history of the requesting process.

Action Manager (AM): The AM revalidates access rights whenever the SM dictates a new situation. Processes whose access rights should be revoked due to the new situation will be isolated, preventing any kind of data exchange with the rest of the system (incl. the user). The user is offered predefined choices to resolve the violation. The communication between user and AM is handled by the *User Communication Process*.

User Communication Process (UCP): The UCP is an optional user space application that provides the communication between the user and the AM. It can be customized to fit in different environments.

3.2   Policy Language

The SBAC policy language is used to define the access rules for different situations. Figure 3 shows the language syntax.

```
<situation> read|write|rw <container> allow|deny [log]
<situation> transfer from <container> to <container> allow|deny [log]
```

Fig. 3. SBAC rules syntax

situation specifies the situation the rule applies to or ANY, if it applies to all situations.

container specifies the container the rule applies to or ANY, if it applies to any container.

The optional **log** switch causes all accesses matched by the rule to be logged.

More specific rules override general rules; in ambiguous cases denying rules outweigh allowing rules.

A *transfer* is a *write operation* in a container performed by a process that has previously read data from a different container. In addition to the transfer permission, a transfer operation requires *write* permission on the target.

Operation	Required Permissions
`a = readfile('/home/buntrock/a')`	read *home_buntrock*
`writefile('/home/buntrock/tmp/z', a)`	write *buntrock_tmp* transfer *home_buntrock* → *buntrock_tmp*

Fig. 4. Operations with required permissions

Figure 4 shows an example operation with the appropriate rules required for execution. The the according rule configuration syntax is shown in figure 5, assuming the example runs in the `office` situation.

```
office read  home_buntrock allow
office write buntrock_tmp allow
office transfer from home_buntrock to buntrock_tmp allow
```

Fig. 5. SBAC rules configuration syntax

3.3 Behavior

If a change in the *current situation* causes a process to be in violation with one or more access rules, the process will be frozen (SIGSTOP) and remains in that state until it is automatically thawed when the process is no longer in violation with the rules. By user demand, this behavior can be altered. A user can give a process the chance to emergency-safe its data while the process is violating rules. In order for this to be possible without breaching security, a frozen process is completely isolated from its environment, effectively eliminating all means of communication for the process. Upon isolation, the process is thawed and sent a TERM-signal. The process can then save cached data; it cannot modify existing files, but only create new files, which will be marked as *emergency dumps* (see 3.4).

3.4 Object Categories

In SBAC we categorize objects in *ordinary data, emergency dumps* and *temporary files*. Access rights to these files are defined per situation by rulesets consisting of read, write and transfer rules. Emergency dumps are created by processes violating rules of the current situation. The situation the violating process was created in is attached to the emergency dump. Emergency dumps can only be accessed in that situation or in a predefined – so-called *trusted* – situation. Temporary files are associated with the creating process which is granted exclusive rights over them. They are deleted once the owning process dies.

4   Implementation

SBAC is mainly implemented as a kernel module for the linux kernel of the 2.6 series.

The kernel module itself bases upon the linux security module architecture, which allows for easy implementation of security extensions. The SBAC module implements the *Situation Manager*, the *Action Manager*, the *Access History* and the *Policy Decision Point*.

The linux security architecture allows us to hook into the standard security-relevant syscalls like *open*, *read* and *write*. When such a syscall is made, the linux kernel firstly checks the static access policies that have been defined. If they allow access, the kernel calls the SBAC subroutines, passing them relevant data such as the *accessing process* and the *file to be accessed (inode number)*.

The SBAC module then checks if access is to be granted. It notes accesses in the access history and writes appropriate entries into the log file. Control is then returned to the kernel, alongside the access decision.

The labeling database stores labels that were assigned to files or directories. It is kept independent of the filesystem, making no modifications to it necessary. Entries are assigned to files and directories using the (unique) combination of *inode number + device id*

The per-process access history is kept as a linked list that gets directly assigned to a process descriptor.

The per-process access history is temporary and gets deleted once a process dies. The policy and labeling database are stored to disk on a flush proc-call. They are re-read when the module is loaded (i.e. at boot-time) or when a filesystem is mounted. The policy database is kept on the root filesystem, while a labeling database is stored on each supported, mounted filesystem.

SBAC userland configuration utilities communicate with the SBAC kernel module through a proc device.

5   Performance

SBAC brings along a little performance overhead with respect to disk operations. For every disk access the access history of the calling process must be traversed, either to log access (on reads) or to detect a transfer (on writes) and when forking a child the complete access history of the parent has to be copied to the newly created child. We have run performance tests with focus on disk-excessive and non disk-excessive processes.

Figure 6 shows the CPU usage time for the operating system (system time). We have done measures on disk-excessive (figure 6a), on disk- and fork-excessive (figure 6b) and on CPU-excessive processes (figure 6c). The system had 1600 defined labels and the access histories contained 30 entries each.

The *tar*-command in figure 6a unpacked a file and created several new ones. Without SBAC, the permissions had to be checked only once and then a file handle is used to infinitely cache the access permissions. With SBAC, each access

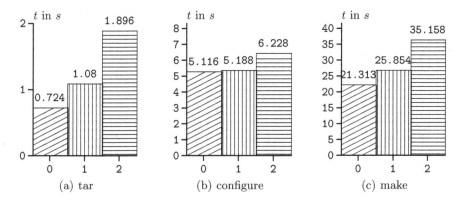

Fig. 6. Process execution time (compiling mplayer on an AMD Athlon 1.3 GHz). 0: without sbac; 1: with sbac; 2: with sbac and logging.

causes a little overhead, because for every disk operation the access history has to be traversed. The tar process performs as many *write* operations as it performs *read* operations.

The *configure*-command in figure 6b is primarily *reading* many small files, a complete file at a time. In addition to that it uses the *fork* syscall extensively. Performance leaps achieved by the file handle concept are negligible for small files.

The *make*-command in figure 6c *forks* many children, who then perform many small *read*- and *write* operations on their part. The *make*-command mainly requires CPU power, instead of disk access.

These tests had been performed with an access history containing 30 entries. In non-laboratory environments it is unlikely for a process to have 30 entries in its access history.

The overhead caused by a change in the situation can be compared with the *write* syscall. The access history of each process must be checked against the SAPDB, however only once for each change.

6   Limitations

The low-level security mechanisms come with a small loss of comfort. While it is possible to detect newly accessible data by monitoring reading disk access, it is not possible to detect discarded data. Thus, the access history of a process can only grow and data that was once accessible is always considered present until the termination of the process.

Labels logically describe the content of an object. Currently we assume that file operations do not change the type of the content. However, when the content is modified, it is possible that the logical base for the label is also altered, e.g. the label "decrypted" is invalid for a file after it has been encrypted. The current container model does not fit such content modifications.

Transfer rules are only checked between the source and the target, thus it may be possible to bypass transfer restrictions, when using an intermediate container. This may happen due to bad policy specification, which is not checked for conflicts.

7   Related Work

In the past years much research has been performed in the area of context-based access control. Kumar et al. [5] use an RBAC [6,7] model, which they have extended by *context filters*. These context filters are applied on the mapping of roles to permissions, restricting the set of permissions based on the context. Hulsebosch et al. [8] also use an RBAC model, but they focus on context determination rather than access policy enforcement. Furthermore, applications need to be modified to fit their requirements. These models provide good methods for single points of authorization.

Moyer and Ahamad introduced the Generalized RBAC (GRBAC) [9] in 2001. Covington et al. [10] use the environment roles from GRBAC for ensuring context-aware access control.

The *Security Enhanced Linux* (SELinux) Project [11,12,13] by the NSA uses Domain-and-Type-Enforcement [14,15] to implement a mandatory access control upon an existing access control scheme. SELinux uses an *access vector cache* to keep track of changes to the ACL of an object. If the ACL changes while the object is being accessed, the access permissions are rechecked and right revocations are immediately enforced. However, Jaeger et al. have analyzed the SELinux policy in [16]. They argue that configuring SELinux with 50 000 and more policy statements is highly error-prone.

Neither of those works provide *complete mediation* [2] throughout the processing cycle of the information they work on. Once data has been cached by an application, this data is out of reach for the access control enforcement. None of these models enforce access permissions retrospectively for applications.

The context toolkit [17,18,1] by Salber et al. could be used for handling the context and thus the situation. The main intention of that project was to provide a framework for developing context-aware applications. Covington et al. use the context toolkit in [10] for their context management. The context toolkit provides widgets, interpreters and aggregators, which can be queried individually.

8   Future Work

The current architecture assumes that the type of a data fragment never changes. However, as the type attribute assigned to data fragments represents the logical type of the data fragment, it is possible that the label has to actually change when the file itself is changed, as the label would be rendered insignificant otherwise. For example, after a data fragment labeled "decrypted_letters" is encrypted, its label is not meaningful anymore and therefore should be changed by the encrypting application to reflect the changed content.

However, as the labels are used by the PDP to make access policy decisions, the parts of the system that change and/or assign new labels to data fragments must be trusted. The easiest way to achieve that is to introduce the concept of trusted processes.

For that to work effectively, it must be possible to assign more than one label to a data fragment. Also, the current label inheritance method would have to be expanded, assigning all labels in a container hierarchy to a data fragment. If, however, data fragments are marked by more than one label, it is necessary to introduce a *weighting* mechanism to distinguish between more/less important labels. How the weighting is handled is determined by the task a device is used for.

Another piece in progress is combining the different policy definitions / specifications. Currently an administrator has to specify access control policies, situation sets and SBAC policies independently. The future goal is to specify policies in one place and derive the mechanism dependent policy from that specification.

9   Conclusions

With SBAC, we present a dynamic access control model to overcome the limitations of static access control systems in mobile environments.

To achieve that, we introduce a way to dynamically define access control rules for logical data fragments, effectively separating data access control rules from the filesystem layer. To keep the rule definition as simple and straightforward as possible, we introduce the concept of *situations*, to separate rule definition from context definition.

By implementing a retrospective policy enforcement, which does not only check disk accesses but handles data that resides in applications' memory space as well, we increase the effectivity of the kernel mode data access control mechanisms, making it reliable for dynamically changing rules and therefore usable for mobile environments.

References

1. Dey, A., Salber, D., Abowd, G.D., Futakawa, M.: The conference assistant: Combining context-awareness with wearable computing. In: 3rd International Symposium on Wearable Computers, San Francisco, California, pp. 21–28 (1999)
2. Saltzer, J., Schroeder, M.: Protection of Information in Computer Systems. Proceedings of the IEEE 63(9), 1278–1308 (1975)
3. Wright, C., Cowan, C., Morris, J., Smalley, S., Kroah-Hartman, G.: Linux Security Modules: General Security Support for the Linux Kernel. In: USENIX Security Symposium (2002)
4. Wright, C., Cowan, C., Morris, J., Smalley, S., Kroah-Hartman, G.: Linux security module framework. In: Ottawa Linux Symposium (2002)
5. Kumar, A., Karnik, N., Chafle, G.: Context sensitivity in role-based access control. SIGOPS Oper. Syst. Rev. 36(3), 53–66 (2002)

6. Ferraiolo, D., Kuhn, R.: Role-based access controls. In: 15th NIST-NCSC National Computer Security Conference, pp. 554–563 (1992)
7. Sandhu, R.S., Coyne, E.J., Feinstein, H.L., Youman, C.E.: Role-based access control models. IEEE Computer 29(2), 38–47 (1996)
8. Hulsebosch, R.J., Salden, A.H., Bargh, M.S., Ebben, P.W.G., Reitsma, J.: Context sensitive access control. In: SACMAT '05: Proceedings of the tenth ACM symposium on Access control models and technologies, New York, NY, USA, pp. 111–119. ACM Press, New York (2005)
9. Moyer, M.J., Ahamad, M.: Generalized role-based access control. In: Proceedings of the IEEE International Conference on Distributed Computing Systems, Mesa, Arizona, USA, pp. 391–398. IEEE Computer Society Press, Los Alamitos (2001)
10. Covington, M.J., Long, W., Srinivasan, S., Dey, A.K., Ahamad, M., Abowd, G.D.: Securing context-aware applications using environment roles. In: Proceedings of the sixth ACM symposium on Access control models and technologies, pp. 10–20. ACM Press, New York (2001)
11. Loscocco, P., Smalley, S.: Integrating flexible support for security policies into the linux operating system. Technical report, NAI Labs, NSA (2001)
12. Loscocco, P., Smalley, S.: Integrating flexible support for security policies into the linux operating system. In: USENIX Annual Technical Conference (2001)
13. Loscocco, P., Smalley, S.: Meeting critical security objectives with security-enhanced linux. In: Ottawa Linux Symposium (2001)
14. Badger, L., et al.: Practical domain and type enforcement for unix. In: IEEE Symposium on Security and Privacy, IEEE Computer Society Press, Los Alamitos (1995)
15. Boebert, W.E., Kain, R.Y.: A practical alternative to hierarchical integrity policies. In: 8th National Computer Security Conference, pp. 18–27 (1985)
16. Jaeger, T., Sailer, R., Zhang, X.: Analyzing integrity protection in the selinux example policy. In: Proceedings of the 12th USENIX Security Symposium (2003)
17. Salber, D., Abowd, G.D.: The design and use of a generic context server. In: Proceedings of the Perceptual User Interfaces Workshop (PUI '98), San Francisco, CA, pp. 63–66 (1998)
18. Salber, D., Dey, A.K., Abowd, G.D.: The context toolkit: Aiding the development of context-enabled applications. In: Proceeddings of the 1999 Conference on Human Factors in Computing Systems (CHI '99), Pittsburgh, PA, pp. 434–441 (1999)

Using Purpose Lattices to Facilitate Customisation of Privacy Agreements

Wynand van Staden and Martin S. Olivier

Information and Computer Security Architecture Research Group
University of Pretoria
Pretoria, South Africa
http://csweb.rau.ac.za/staff/wvs/,
http://www.mo.co.za

Abstract. Protecting the privacy of individuals demands that special care be taken with the handling of an individual's personal information. Either the system should store as little or no user data at all, or it should protect access to the data in cases where it is necessary that data has to be stored. A common approach to the protection of PII (in a privacy aware system) is to associate a set of purposes with the PII which indicates the enterprise's use of the data.

Purposes placed in a hierarchical structure (such as a lattice) can subsume each other, which can provide flexibility in the customisation of a privacy agreement. In this article the customisation of privacy agreements using purposes placed in a lattice is considered. In particular minimal acceptance levels, maximal acceptance levels, validation and invalidation of agreements with respect to purpose lattices are introduced.

1 Introduction

The conducting of day to day business for many enterprise requires the use of data. In particular it requires the use of data that can be linked to an individual, or Personal Identifiable Information (PII). A bank, for example, cannot conduct business without PII. Even so, the collection of PII demands that the enterprise act responsibly with the PII it collects. In order to engender trust, enterprises will publish a privacy policy to state their intent with the collected data.

This can lead to two extreme cases in the management of the PII. Firstly, on the one end of the spectrum there is the data owner (the customer), at the other the enterprise. Both of these parties wish to exert maximal control over the collected data, resulting in a natural conflict of interest. The enterprise publishes their privacy policy, and the customer either accepts the policy, receiving the service, or declines not receiving the service. Business is thus conducted in a "do-or-die" fashion: "either accept our terms or go away."

Oberholzer et al [11] proposes the use of privacy contracts which catagorise agreements in one of four levels, 0 to 3. Level 0 transactions are mandatory, and levels 1 through 3 provide more flexibility in terms of what customers allow an enterprise to do with their data.

C. Lambrinoudakis, G. Pernul, A M. Tjoa (Eds.): TrustBus 2007, LNCS 4657, pp. 201–209, 2007.

This paper considers the use of purpose lattices to facilitate the customisation of privacy policies by facilitating the privacy agreement levels as proposed by Oberholzer et al. In our model, purposes are placed in a lattice, the partial ordering being an indication that some purposes are stronger (better) reasons for accessing data. Any purpose that subsumes a purpose which is associated with a datum can thus be used to gain access to the datum. To allow customisation, the enterprise specifies their most specific (mandatory) purpose, as well as their most general purpose with a datum. Between these two extremes, the customer specifies his personal preferences, allowing easier customisation of the privacy agreement, and finer control over the purposes for which their data will be used.

This paper contributes by showing that purpose lattices can facilitate in the customisation of privacy agreements by allowing the customer to set custom levels per datum at an even finer grained level than that of just privacy agreement levels. This can be accomplished by using compound purposes which are provided by purpose lattices. Customers are also provided with a single view towards privacy level customisation. We further explore how invalidation of the privacy contracts can be accomplished by proposing that the lattices can be versioned and showing that customers can continuously modify their preferences without the need to renegotiate the privacy agreement.

The rest of this paper is structured as follows: Section 2 provides background information, section 3 discusses acceptance levels, section 4 considers agreements and invalidation, and finally section 5 concludes the paper.

2   Background

Business today thrives on data (including data on individuals), and many systems are devoted to the storage and retrieval of this data. It can be, and has been [1,13,4,12] argued that business has a responsibility to protect the privacy of those individuals on which data is stored.

An original proposal by the Organisation for Economic Cooperation and Development (OECD) that any data that is stored by an enterprise has to be used for the published purposes only, has created an explosion of research being to devoted to the protection of the individual's privacy.

Many of these Privacy Enhancing Technologies (PETs) can be categorised as either preserving privacy through providing anonymity, pseudonimity, unlinkability, or untracability [14]. These include anonymous remailers [8], web browsing anonymisers [7,6], to name but a few.

In many cases, however, a system has to store PII in order for the enterprise to conduct business. A privacy aware system will make use of purposes to protect access to the customer's data. An example of such a PET is the hippocratic database [1]. The need to store PII and protect it has also prompted the development of many access control languages such as XACML [10], and EPAL [2].

When recording data the customer has to be informed of the use for the data, such mechanisms (P3P [5], and E-P3P [15]) are well published in research literature. These mechanisms allow an enterprise to state its purpose with data to a potential customer. A back end system like the hippocratic database will ideally take these promises and enforce them.

Using privacy agreement levels [11] allows the customer to customise his agreement with the enterprise. Transactions performed on level 0 are mandatory, and the customer must agree to these. Level 1 exhibits a "do-or-die" approach, a customer can only opt-in or opt-out. Level 2 allows the customer to state the purposes that an enterprise may use his data for, and finally level 3 allows the customer to state not only the purposes for which his data may be used, but also which data may be used for which purposes.

Purposes that are used by the enterprise can be organised in many ways, but it seems as though an informal consensus in research places them all in some hierarchical form [3,2,9]. Work by Fischer-Hübner also places purposes in a lattice [8].

In previous work, the authors have suggested placing purposes in a lattice, and having purposes in the lattice subsume each other [16]. Purposes are organised from a *most general* least upper bound, to a *most specific* greatest lower bound. If purpose x subsumes another purpose y (there exists a path between the purposes) we write $x \geq y$. Access to a datum that is "protected" with y is granted if purpose z is given, such that $z \geq y$.

Purposes from the lattice can also be combined into *compound purposes* using operators [16]. These operators are used to create more expressive purposes by combining existing ones using conjunctions and disjunctions. For example, one can indicate that two purposes x and y are required to access a datum by writing $x \cdot_p y$; or that either one can be presented to access the datum by writing $x +_p y$. A technique for the verification of compound purposes will be reported on elsewhere.

3   Acceptance Levels

Privacy agreement levels may require a large amount of customisation by the customer (selecting all the elements for levels 1,2 and 3). To ease this burden we propose that a single view of privacy agreements are presented to the customer.

To accomplish this customisation the enterprise publishes a minimum set of purposes for which the customer data will be used, known as the Minimal Acceptance Limit (MinAL). For example, the enterprise might state that it will use e-mail addresses for "marketing" **or** "invoicing" (figure 1). A customer who feels that these purposes are too unrestricted, can set his preference levels more restrictive, such as just "invoicing". The enterprise can now no longer use any marketing related purposes to access data, since it may only specify a purpose which is stronger than "invoicing". From figure 1[1], the MinAL is thus $\phi_1 +_p \phi_2$, and the customer's preference is ϕ_2. Note that $\phi_2 \geq \phi_1 +_p \phi_2$.

The obvious problem with this approach is that a customer might be too strict with his preference level, for example the user might set his preference level to

---

[1] The nodes are labelled with an integer, and we will refer to each node from the figure in this paper as ϕ_i, where i is the node's label.

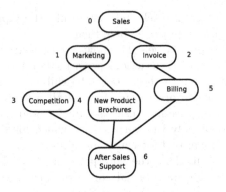

Fig. 1. A small sub-purpose lattice

"Only for access demanded by law" (not shown in the figure). In this case, the enterprise may be unable to conduct business, as it cannot get access to data (for sending out invoices). To prohibit such a draconian approach by the customer, the notion of a Maximal Acceptance Limit (MaxAL) is introduced.

3.1   Maximal Acceptance Limit

A *MaxAL* indicates that set of purposes which marks the most specific reason for using a datum. Any purposes more specific than those purposes will prohibit the enterprise from conducting day to day business.

The enterprise thus associates two sets of purposes with each piece of data, a MinAL and a MaxAL. The customer is allowed to adjust his preferences between these two levels, as long has his preferences are not stronger than the MaxAL, the enterprise will be able to use the data to conduct business.

For example: a company states their MinAL to be ϕ_i, and their MaxAL is ϕ_j. The customer can set his personal preferences ϕ_u anywhere between these limits (inclusive). Thus, $\phi_j \geq \phi_u \geq \phi_i$, must hold.

A small change to the privacy meta data schema as proposed by Agrawal et al [1] will allow the enterprise to record these acceptance limits (table 3) for a particular piece of data.

In cases where the data is imperative for day to day operation, it is still possible for the customer to take an active roll in specifying the uses for his data. He is thus not strong-armed into an agreement. The enterprise also benefits, in that it still has access to the data for normal business functions, it promotes a relationship of trust between the customer and itself, and may receive access to the data for less restrictive purposes.

3.2   Optional Acceptance

In cases where the data submitted by the customer will be used to provide fringe services, the user may be interested in adjusting this level of opt-in as well. Because the data is not necessary to conduct business, the enterprise may not care if the customer states that his data may only be used in very rare occasions, such as in the event of a law-enforced inspection of the database.

In this case MaxAL can be set to the most specific purpose for accessing the data, allowing the user to choose this purpose as his preference. The enterprise still acts in good faith and specifies a MinAL, and allows the user to adjust his preferred acceptance levels. If the purpose for the data is specified as ϕ_i, then the customer's opt-in specification ϕ_u must be such that $\phi_z \geq \phi_u \geq \phi_i$, where ϕ_z is the enterprise's most specific reason for accessing any data.

Table 1. Privacy Meta Data Schema

Table	attributes
Privacy Policies Table	policyID, MinAL,MaxAL
Agreements Table	table, attribute, external recipients, retention ownerID, policyID, Custom Acceptance Level Valid Flag, Version

Table 2. The Privacy Policies Table

policyID	MinAL	MaxAL	Table	Attribute	Ex. Recipients	Retention
1	ϕ_0	ϕ_6	customer name	x		y
2	$\phi_1 \cdot_p \phi_2$	ϕ_6	customer address	x		y
3	ϕ_3	ϕ_4	customer credit card	x		y
4	ϕ_4	ϕ_4	customer credit card	x		y

Table 3. The Agreements Table

dataownerID	policyID	Custom AL	Valid Flag	Version
x_1	1	$\phi_1 +_p \phi_5$	true	y
x_2	3	ϕ_4	false	y

To support the notion of acceptance levels the table schema presented in tables 1 through 3 is presented.

By adjusting MinAL and MaxAL we can effectively employ privacy agreement levels from Oberholzer. For example, by setting MinAL and MaxAL to the same value forces the customer to accept a certain purpose for data, by widening the distance between MinAL and MaxAL we approach levels 1,2 and 3.

4   Agreement Invalidation

Whenever an enterprise changes its privacy policy, a new agreement between it and the customers must be reached. Using the model presented in this paper it is also possible that the customer may decide to adjust his preference levels – a function that should be provided by the enterprise *bona fide*.

4.1   Customer Changes

Changes by the customer means that the enterprise may have more, or less access to the customer's data. Any change in the customer's preferences of course indicates a change in the agreement that is undertaken by the customer and the enterprise. This will result in a new agreement having to be "undersigned" by both parties. However, since the user changes his preferences, and as long as his preferences remain within those allowed by the enterprise (between the MinALs and MaxALs, it can be assumed that the enterprise has a "safe" agreement with the customer to have access to the information which will not hinder day to day business.

From the customer's side, since he is changing the preferences, and since the enterprise is running a PET which will ensure that his data will not be misused, accepting the changing of the agreement can be automated.

4.2   Enterprise Changes

Agreement on changes originating from the enterprise cannot be automated in such an easy way as changes initiated by the customer. Since the enterprise is effectively "borrowing" information from the customer any change in policy has to accepted by the customer first. In such an event the privacy contract between the customer and the enterprise can be "frozen" [11].

In this paper the term "invalidated" will be used, to indicate that the agreement between the enterprise is no longer considered valid, and that the enterprise may no longer use any of the data which falls under the invalidated agreement.

The enterprise can invalidate an agreement in one of several ways. Firstly, they may change their MaxALs for a particular type of data. This means that a customer who set his preference level to the MaxAL may no longer be "protected". Either the MaxALs subsumes the customer's levels, or they are subsumed by the customer's level.

In either case, the agreement cannot be considered valid anymore, as the customer's levels might prohibit the conducting of day to day business. However, the enterprise cannot simply adjust the customer's custom levels, as this would allow them to get access to his data with more general purposes. If the MaxALs subsume the customer's preference levels, then the customer might wish to adjust his levels to the "maximum" allowed again.

Secondly, it is also foreseeable that the enterprise can modify its purpose lattice, and therefore introduce new purposes which subsume the preference levels as set by the customer. Purposes can also be removed from the purpose lattice. To avoid situations where purposes which are present in agreements are removed from the lattice, which will invalidate agreements, a restricted delete can be performed. That is when a purpose is removed from the lattice, the system will first verify that no agreement is subject to that purpose. This technique can typically be used to clean up the purpose lattice and remove purposes that are not used.

A final remark on the deletion of entries in the purpose lattice: it is possible that the enterprise may consider a purpose and all its children as unnecessary.

The system should therefore support a "deep" removal of a purpose from the lattice. Thus the targeted purpose and all its children will be removed.

A "cascaded" removal of a purpose from the lattice is analogous to a cascaded delete from a relational database. Where the database deletion removes the entries that violate integrity, the cascaded delete removes the targeted purposes from the entries in the privacy policy table.

Finally, the enterprise may change their MinALs. An increase or decrease in these levels has to be inspected by the customer before the agreement can be considered valid.

4.3   Versioning of the Policy and Purpose Lattice

Changes to the purpose lattice need not invalidate an agreement. A customer that subscribes to a service provided by an enterprise under a particular agreement may continue to receive services provided by the enterprise, as long as precise details regarding the version of the privacy policy under which the agreement took place is kept.

Since the basis for a privacy policy in the model presented here is the purpose lattice, as long as the purpose lattice can be *versioned*, that is changes to the lattice is recorded, and a particular version can be reconstructed accurately, the privacy policy can be versioned. Versioning of the lattice can be accomplished in much the same fashion as performing a difference calculation between two files. An agreement with a new customer is always done under the latest version of the purpose lattice.

By labeling an agreement, it is possible to version an agreement directly. Consider the fourth entry in table 2: it applies to the same object in the database, but has a different policyID.

4.4   Multiple Agreements

It is of course plausible that the enterprise can have multiple agreements with the customer. For example an agreement between the customer and the enterprise regarding the physical address, and an agreement regarding the customer's credit card details. These agreements can then be grouped under one umbrella agreement. The reason for having many agreements can be easily justified. Suppose for example an enterprise changes its policy regarding credit card details. Such a shift need not invalidate the agreement the enterprise had with the customer regarding his address.

This is especially true in the case where a minor change in the purpose lattice suddenly invalidates a customer's agreements with the enterprise completely, effectively cutting him of from services.

4.5   Invalidation

Whenever a change in policy originates from the enterprise, it can be considered either mandatory or optional. Mandatory changes require that all agreements are invalidated, and optional changes only requires a versioning of the lattice or policy (as recorded in the database).

Requests to access data of invalidated agreements will not be granted, and will result in a "conflict miss". Before data can be accessed the agreement will have to be validated again.

Requests to access data of versioned agreements will result in the appropriate version of the lattice or policy being loaded, after which verification of the access request will take place based on those versions.

5   Conclusion

This article extended the notion of privacy agreement levels by showing that they can be implemented using purposes placed in a lattice, and how the purpose lattice itself can allow for a finer level of customisation. The notion of MinALs and MaxALs was introduced. These elements allows a customer to take control over the use of his data while enabling the enterprise to still have access to the customer's data for day to day business tasks. Purpose lattices, MinALs, and MaxALs sufficiently supports privacy agreement levels and provides even finer grained access control.

It was also argued that agreements need not be invalidated if the different versions of the purpose lattice can be stored.

In order to fully employ this technology it will be necessary to optimise the speed of verification. We are exploring a solution which requires a total ordering of the "agreements table" based on the custom acceptance level. Based on the reason used to access the data searches can be limited to only those customers who have a custom acceptance level weaker than the given reason. Combined with effective search techniques on the agreements table, and query rewriting, speed impact can be kept minimal. Space unfortunately precludes a detailed discussion and our results will be reported on elsewhere.

References

1. Agrawal, R., Kiernan, J., Srikant, R., Xu, Y.: Hippocratic databases. In: Proceedings of the 28th VLDB Conference, 2002, Hong Kong, China (2002)
2. Ashley, P., Hada, S., Karjoth, G., Powers, C., Schunter, M.: Enterprise privacy authorisation language (EPAL 1.1). Technical report, International Business Machines Corporation (2003)
3. Byun, J.-W., Bertino, E., Li, N.: Purpose based access control of complex data for privacy protection. In: SACMAT'05, Stockholm, Sweden, June 2005, ACM Press, New York (2005)
4. Chaum, D.L.: Untraceable electronic mail, retrun addresses and digital pseudonyms. Communications of the ACM 24(2), 84–88 (1981)
5. Cranor, L., Langheinrich, M., Marchiori, M., Presler-Marshall, M., Reagle, J.: The platform for privacy preferences (P3P1.0) specification. Technical report, W3C (2002), Available at http://www.w3.org/TR/P3P/

6. Danezis, G., Dingledine, R., Mathewson, N.: Mixminion: Design of a Type III Anonymous Remailer Protocol. In: Proceedings of the 2003 IEEE Symposium on Security and Privacy, May 2003, IEEE Computer Society Press, Los Alamitos (2003)

7. Dingledine, R., Mathewson, N., Syverson, P.: Tor: The second-generation onion router. In: Proceedings of the 13th USENIX Security Symposium (August 2004)

8. Fischer-Hübner, S.: IT-Security and Privacy: Design and Use of Privacy-Enhancing Security Mechanisms. Springer, Heidelberg (2001)

9. Karjoth, G., Schunter, M.: A privacy policy model for enterprises. In: Proceedings of the 15th IEEE Computer Security Foundations Workshop, June 2002, Springer, Heidelberg (2002)

10. OASIS Access Control TC. OASIS extensible access control markup language (xacml) version 2.0. Technical report, OASIS (February 2005)

11. Oberholzer, H.J.G., Olvier, M.S.: Privacy contracts incorporated in a privacy protection framework. International Journal of Computer Systems Science and Engineering 21(1), 5–16 (2006)

12. OECD guidelines on the protection of privacy and transborder flows of personal data. Technical report, Organisation for Economic Co-operation and Development (1980)

13. Olivier, M.S.: A layered architecture for privacy-enhancing technologies. In: Eloff, J.H.P., Venter, H.S., Labuschagne, L., Eloff, M. (eds.) Proceedings of the Third Annual Information Security South Africa Conference (ISSA2003), Sandton, South Africa, July 2003, pp. 113–126 (2003)

14. Pfitzmann, A., Hansen, M.: Anonymity, unobservability, and pseudonymity: A consolidated proposal for terminology. Draft (July 2000)

15. Schunter, M., Ashley, P.: The platform for enterprise privacy practices. Technical report, IBM (2002)

16. van Staden, W.J.C., Olivier, M.S.: Purpose organisation. In: Proceedings of the fifth annual Information Security South Africa (ISSA) Conference, Sandton, June 2005, Johannesburg, South Africa (2005)

A Pattern-Driven Framework for Monitoring Security and Dependability

Christos Kloukinas and George Spanoudakis

Department of Computing, The City University, London, EC1V 0HB, U.K.
{C.Kloukinas,G.Spanoudakis}@soi.city.ac.uk

Abstract. In this paper we describe a framework that supports the dynamic configuration, adaptation and monitoring of systems that need to guarantee specific security and dependability (S&D) properties whilst operating in distributed settings. The framework is based on *patterns* providing abstract specifications of implementation solutions that can be used by systems in order to achieve specific S&D properties. The focus herein will be on the monitoring aspects of the framework which allow it to adapt to violations of the S&D requirements and changes to the current context.

1 Introduction

Ensuring security and dependability in systems which operate in highly distributed environments and frequently changing contexts (e.g. changing networks and system deployment infrastructures), whilst maintaining system interoperability and adaptability, is one of the major challenges of current research in the area of security and dependability [1], where systems need to adapt to dynamic changes in their context. This necessitates the incorporation of mechanisms that can monitor a system's operation and report violations of S&D requirements that would require the deployment of alternative S&D mechanisms.

In this paper, we present a framework that is being developed as part of the European research project SERENITY[1] to address the above challenges. This framework is driven by S&D patterns which specify reusable architectural solutions for S&D requirements, the contextual conditions under which these solutions are applicable, and rules that need to be monitored at run-time to ensure that the implementation of the pattern behaves correctly. The framework is responsible for selecting the patterns which are appropriate for fulfilling the S&D requirements of a system in specific operational contexts, as well as, activating and integrating the implementations of these patterns with the system at runtime. The framework can also monitor the execution of the system and the implementations of the S&D patterns, and take corrective actions if a violation of rules or contextual conditions of the patterns is identified.

The general architecture and functions of this framework have been introduced in [2]. Our focus in this paper is to describe the support that the framework

---

[1] http://www.serenity-project.org/motivations-&-objectives.php

C. Lambrinoudakis, G. Pernul, A M. Tjoa (Eds.): TrustBus 2007, LNCS 4657, pp. 210–218, 2007.

provides for *system monitoring* at run time and present the use of the S&D patterns in monitoring and the mechanisms that the framework incorporates to support this activity. The rest of this paper is structured as follows. In section 2, we present an example of a system which will be used throughout the paper to illustrate the operations of the framework. In section 3, we present the general architecture of the framework and discuss the S&D patterns and other artefacts which are deployed during monitoring. In section 4, we discuss the monitoring life cycle that is realised by the framework and how it is driven by the dynamic selection, activation and deactivation of S&D patterns. In section 5, we overview related work and, finally, in section 6 we give some concluding remarks and outline plans for future work.

2   Motivating Example

The system that we use to illustrate the function of the S&D framework that we describe in this paper is an *e-healthcare system* whose objective is to support the monitoring, assistance, and provision of medication to patients who have been discharged from hospitals with critical medical conditions [3]. In an operational scenario of this system, a patient does not feel well and sends through his *patient e-health terminal (PHT)* a request for assistance to the *emergency response centre (ERC)*. To establish the cause of the problem, ERC retrieves the patient's medical record from its internal database. From this record, ERC establishes that the patient's doctor is on vacation and contacts an alternative doctor D whose expertise matches with the expertise of the patient's doctor. Doctor D receives this message on her *doctor e-health terminal (DHT)* and replies immediately. ERC verifies D's identity and sends the patient's medical data to DHT. D creates an electronic prescription on her DHT, sends it to ERC, which subsequently forwards it to the *pharmacy system (PhS)* that is closest to the patient's

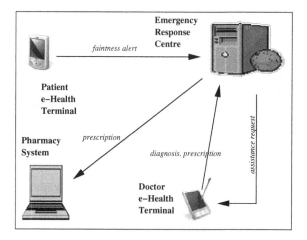

Fig. 1. e-Healthcare system

location. The pharmacy delivers the medicines to the patient, and PhS confirms the dispatch to the ERC.

3   Overview of the Framework

The generic architecture of the S&D framework is shown in Fig. 2. The *S&D configurator* accepts as input the S&D configuration of an external system and the S&D properties that this system wants to realise. Then the S&D configurator selects an S&D pattern which can provide the required S&D properties and also selects a concrete implementation of this S&D pattern which is applicable in the particular setting. Then the S&D configurator sends the rules that need to be monitored for the specific pattern and implementation to the monitoring engine, and activates the implementation.

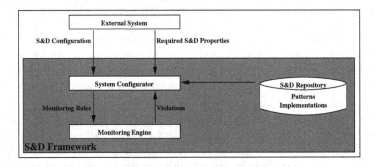

Fig. 2. Architecture of the S&D framework

The *monitoring engine (ME)* gets the rules that should be monitored and starts the monitoring activity. During this activity, the engine gets events concerning the state of the external system and the selected implementation from *event captors* and sends notifications of violations of monitoring rules to the S&D configurator. *S&D implementations* include operational runtime components that can be used to realise the S&D properties of the pattern that they are associated with. They also include event captors which provide the events required for checking the monitoring rules of the S&D patterns. S&D implementations are activated and deactivated dynamically by the S&D configurator through different mechanisms depending on their type.

3.1   The Basic Artefacts

Requirements and Properties S&D requirements of systems are expressed as S&D properties which need to hold. More specifically, a system provides the framework with a configuration file specifying: (i) the required S&D properties, (ii) the part of the system's architecture that each property relates to, and (iii) the *attack/fault model* (*afm* - itself expressed as an S&D property) under which

Properties	True ⇒ Confidentiality, True ⇒ Integrity
Parameters	P_1: { ... }, P_2: { ... }
Components	$Encrypt_1$: { ... }, $Decrypt_1$: { ... }, Filter: { ... }
Architectural Description	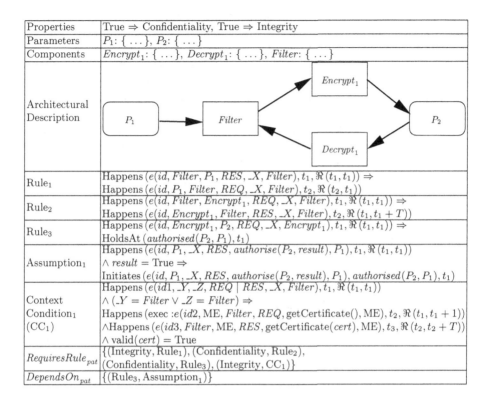
$Rule_1$	Happens $(e(id, Filter, P_1, RES, \_X, Filter), t_1, \Re(t_1, t_1)) \Rightarrow$ Happens $(e(id, P_1, Filter, REQ, \_X, Filter), t_2, \Re(t_2, t_1))$
$Rule_2$	Happens $(e(id, Filter, Encrypt_1, REQ, \_X, Filter), t_1, \Re(t_1, t_1)) \Rightarrow$ Happens $(e(id, Encrypt_1, Filter, RES, \_X, Filter), t_2, \Re(t_1, t_1 + T))$
$Rule_3$	Happens $(e(id, Encrypt_1, P_2, REQ, \_X, Encrypt_1), t_1, \Re(t_1, t_1)) \Rightarrow$ HoldsAt $(authorised(P_2, P_1), t_1)$
$Assumption_1$	Happens $(e(id, P_1, \_X, RES, authorise(P_2, result), P_1), t_1, \Re(t_1, t_1))$ $\wedge\ result = $ True $\Rightarrow$ Initiates $(e(id, P_1, \_X, RES, authorise(P_2, result), P_1), authorised(P_2, P_1), t_1)$
Context Condition$_1$ (CC$_1$)	Happens $(e(id1, \_Y, \_Z, REQ\ \vert\ RES, \_X, Filter), t_1, \Re(t_1, t_1))$ $\wedge\ (\_Y = Filter \vee \_Z = Filter) \Rightarrow$ Happens $($exec $:e(id2, ME, Filter, REQ, $getCertificate$(), ME), t_2, \Re(t_1, t_1 + 1))$ $\wedge$Happens $(e(id3, Filter, ME, RES, $getCertificate$(cert), ME), t_3, \Re(t_2, t_2 + T))$ $\wedge\ valid(cert) = $ True
$RequiresRule_{pat}$	{(Integrity, $Rule_1$), (Confidentiality, $Rule_2$), (Confidentiality, $Rule_3$), (Integrity, CC$_1$)}
$DependsOn_{pat}$	{($Rule_3$, $Assumption_1$)}

Fig. 3. A simplified pattern example of integrity and confidentiality

the property should be guaranteed, in an assume-guarantee type of reasoning: $afm_a \Rightarrow prop_b$. Using (i)-(iii), the S&D framework can select an appropriate pattern for the relevant property.

The properties and attack/fault models are represented abstractly as keywords and their interdependencies as implications, e.g., $prop_a \Rightarrow prop_b$. By doing so, it is easy to dynamically check whether the assumed attack/fault model is more constrained than that of a pattern, i.e., $afm_{sys} \Rightarrow afm_{pat}$, and whether the property required by the system is weaker than the property provided by the pattern, i.e., $prop_{pat} \Rightarrow prop_{sys}$.

Patterns. A simplified[2] example of an S&D pattern (I&C) is shown in Fig. 3. I&C provides two *properties*, integrity and confidentiality, under any attack model. It contains *monitoring rules* for verifying the properties at runtime, *assumptions* which provide extra information about the system behaviour, and *contextual conditions* under which the pattern is applicable. Relation $RequiresRule_{pat}$ helps determine the subset of rules which should be monitored, to avoid wasting resources

---

[2] More details about the contents of S&D patterns and the scheme for describing them can be found in [4].

if we do not need all properties, while relation $DependsOn_{pat}$ indicates which assumptions should be used when particular rules need to be monitored. Finally, the pattern contains an *architectural description* of the offered solution, which describes its *components*, i.e., what the pattern provides for realising the solution, the *parameters*, i.e., partially unknown components of the system which will use the pattern, and the *connectors* which link these together (shown as arrows).

Rules, context conditions and assumptions are specified in Event Calculus (EC) [5]. An event $e(ID, sender, receiver, status, operation, source)$, provides us with its *source*, that is the component from which the occurrence of the *operation* has been captured (may be different from either *sender* or *receiver*), and their *status*, that is whether the *operation* is a request (REQ) or a response (RES). Fluents are represented as relations between objects of the general form: $f(o_1, \cdots, o_n)$.

$Rule_1$ in the I&C pattern describes an integrity constraint, where for each response to an operation call that P_1 receives from *Filter*, there should be a matching earlier call of this operation that was sent from P_1 to *Filter*. $Rule_2$ checks the (bounded) availability of $Encrypt_1$, by asking that *Filter* should respond to an operation $\_X$ within T time units. $Rule_3$ checks if the recipient P_2 of any message $\_X$ from $Encrypt_1$ is authorised by P_1 to receive messages at the time of dispatch of $\_X$. Finally, the context condition (CC_1) examines the validity of the certificate of the pattern every time that an operation is called on/by *Filter*. If the certificate has been revoked between any of these points, then the pattern is no longer applicable and must be deactivated.

4   The Monitoring Lifecycle

The typical operational scenario of the S&D framework involves: (i) the selection of a pattern that can provide the properties required by a system, (ii) the activation of an appropriate implementation for it and the monitoring of the pattern rules, and, (iii) the deactivation of the pattern if it is no longer relevant to the external system of concern or cannot be applied in the current context. In the following, we describe how the S&D framework performs these activities.

Selection of Patterns. Based on the system S&D configuration file, the S&D framework searches its pattern repository, to identify patterns which offer the required properties ($RProp_j$), given the specific attack/fault models (AFM_i). More specifically, it computes the *TolerableAttacks* = {$afm : AFM_i \Rightarrow afm$} and *ProvidedProperties* = {$prop : prop \Rightarrow RProp_j$} and uses these to find the *Candidate Patterns*, which provide the property $afm \Rightarrow prop$. Then the framework finds the *Realisable Candidates* which have currently applicable implementations. At this stage, extra constraints specified by the system configuration are used to sort the set of realisable candidate patterns with respect to how closely they match the user's criteria, e.g. the maximum cost of the provided implementation, the identity of its provider, etc. Then, the closest match is considered for the most difficult part of the search, i.e., selecting a pattern which is *architecturally compatible* with the system. The problem of architectural compatibility is ensuring that the system components which require a property will be correctly assigned to the parameters of the pattern. This architectural match is performed through architectural unification [6]. The selection process ends when the S&D framework has found an architecturally compatible pattern in the ordered set of *Realisable Candidates*. In reference to the example of Fig. 1, we will assume that the configurator has selected the pattern of Fig. 3 as a realisable candidate pattern, using the substitutions $\{P_1 \rightarrow ERC, P_2 \rightarrow DHT, \_X \rightarrow assist(\cdots)\}$, where $assist(\cdots)$ is the operation that the ERC is calling on the DHT.

Activation of Patterns. The activation of patterns by the S&D framework has two major steps with respect to monitoring: (1) the activation of monitoring rules by the monitoring engine, and (2) the attachment of the event collectors to the system/pattern components in order to generate the events required for monitoring.

The activation of monitoring rules happens according to the following steps, using the information that the I&C pattern has been selected for both its properties $SelectedFor_{pat} = \{(Confidentiality, Integrity)\}$:

Computations	Results
$InitRules_{pat} = CC_{pat} \cup$ $\{r : \exists prop \in SelectedFor_{pat} \mid$ $(prop, r) \in RequiresRule_{pat}\}$	$InitRules_{pat} = \{CC_1, Rule_1, Rule_2, Rule_3\}$
$FinalRules_{pat} = InitRules_{pat} \cup$ $\bigcup_{r \in InitRules_{pat}} DependsOn_{pat}(r)$	$\{CC_1, Rule_1, Rule_2, Rule_3, Assumption_1\}$
$ActiveRules_{pat} =$ $substitute(FinalRules_{pat}, substitutionlist)$	$substitutionlist = (P_1 \rightarrow ERC,$ $P_2 \rightarrow DHT, \_X \rightarrow assist(\cdots)))$

Once the monitoring rules of the selected pattern have been instantiated and activated, the event collectors of the respective S&D implementation are activated. This process uses $ActiveRules_{pat}$:

Computations	Results/Comments
$EventsOfInterest_{pat} =$ $\bigcup_{r \in ActiveRules_{pat}} Contains_{pat}(r)$	$EventsOfInterest_{pat} = \{$ $ev(id, ERC, Filter, REQ, assist(\cdots), Filter),$ $ev(id, Filter, ERC, RES, assist(\cdots), Filter),$ $\cdots\}$
$SourceOf_{pat}(e) = c$	$Filter$ (for all events)
Find the event collectors for each event e: $CollectedBy_{imp}(SourceOf_{pat}(e), e)$	*From the the configuration of the selected S&D implementation*

The monitoring engine checks the activated monitoring rules as described in [7]. If a rule is violated, the engine logs the violation and performs the control action which was specified in the system configuration, if any, to notify the system. If the violated rule is part of the pattern's context conditions, then the framework configurator is notified in order to deactivate the pattern and replace it with a new one.

Deactivation of patterns. When a context condition is violated or when the S&D requirements change, e.g., due to legal reasons, then the pattern needs to be deactivated and replaced by another. Replacing a pattern entails the deactivation of the monitoring rules and assumptions, the detachment of the event collectors which collect the events for these rules and the deactivation of its implementation. Even though the $ActiveRules_{pat}$ are easy to deactivate, event collectors should only be deactivated if they are not also being used by other implementations. Therefore, the S&D configurator needs to identify the collectors which are used exclusively by the current pattern and deactivated these only.

5   Related Work

The objective of the framework that we present in this paper is two-fold: (a) to provide runtime support to external systems for the realisation of specific S&D properties, presented in more detail in [2], and (b) to monitor the effectiveness and adequacy of the support that it provides in specific operational contexts. The approach that we advocate for (b) is related to *security monitoring systems*, which can be distinguished into *firewalls* and *intrusion detection systems* [8,9], *intrusion prevention systems* [10,11], and *access control systems* [12,13]. Firewalls control access on packets entering or leaving local networks to protect them from external networks, thus do not consider the application layer and cannot protect against internal threats or monitor general security properties. Intrusion detection systems also aim to detect attacks at the network layer based on models of expected user/system behaviour but do not always have the control capability to prevent attacks. A combination of attack detection and prevention capabilities is provided by intrusion prevention systems. Access control systems aim to restrict access to sensitive information based on pre-assigned rights for accessing specific information objects to different subjects (e.g. system component), the requester's role in an organisation (*role based access control systems*), or access policies combining credentials of users with the context of the system (*context based access control*). Such systems can monitor information access but not other, more general, properties which are supported by our approach. Furthermore, they cannot adapt and integrate complex security solutions to running systems [1].

Our approach also relates to *general purpose runtime monitoring systems*, which focus on the verification of program behaviour against properties specified at some temporal logic or on requirements monitoring, e.g. [14,15]. Many of the former systems focus on runtime verification of Java code [16,17] where events record changes of internal program variable values and/or invocations and returns of program methods. The latter systems express requirements in some high level formal specification language and subsequently assume the refinement and mapping of these requirements onto patterns of events whose occurrence would indicate their violation at run-time. This transformation is the responsibility of system providers, e.g. [14].

The framework that we present in this paper can support the monitoring of general properties for software systems including security properties [18]. Its main difference from existing work is that monitoring is driven by S&D patterns which define the rules that should be monitored at different stages and contexts of a system's operation, in order to ensure specific security properties. Furthermore, the generation of events in this framework is performed by pattern implementations and thus there is no need for explicit code instrumentation or developing other types of event emission methods.

6   Conclusions

In this paper, we described the monitoring-related aspects of a framework [2] that supports the dynamic configuration, adaptation and monitoring of systems that need to guarantee specific security and dependability properties whilst operating in distributed settings. The framework is based on *patterns* [4] providing specifications of implementation solutions that can be used by systems in order to achieve specific security and dependability properties. Patterns identify contextual conditions which need to hold in order to guarantee the effectiveness of the solutions that they describe, and rules that should be monitored at runtime to check that these conditions are satisfied and the offered solutions do indeed comply with the required security and dependability properties.

Based on the security and the dependability properties which are required by external systems, the framework can automatically select patterns and concrete implementations, integrate them with the system, and monitor the behaviour of the integrated entity to check the effectiveness of the adopted solutions in it. The framework can also take certain control actions when there are runtime violations of the monitored rules. These actions may include the selection and activation of other patterns if the current ones fail to meet the requirements, the activation of additional monitoring activities, and the suspension of the system's operation.

Currently, we are working on the introduction of mechanisms for detecting potential threats to S&D requirements and the provision of detailed diagnostic information for the detected violations of the S&D pattern rules and contextual conditions. We are also looking onto mechanisms for the effective distribution of rules onto different monitors in order to optimise the monitoring performance of the framework.

References

1. Maña, A., et al.: Security engineering for ambient intelligence: A manifesto. In: Integrating Security and Software Engineering: Advances and Future Vision, pp. 244–270. Idea Group Publishing (2006)
2. Sanchez-Cid, F., et al.: Software engineering techniques applied to AmI: Security patterns. In: Developing Ambient Intelligence: Proc. of the First Int. Conf. on Ambient Intelligence Developments (AmID'06), Sophia-Antipolis, France, Springer, Heidelberg (2006)
3. Campadello, S., et al.: S&D requirements specification. Deliverable A7.D2.1, SERENITY Project (2006), Available from http://www.serenity-forum.org
4. Maña, A., et al.: Patterns and integration schemes languages. Deliverable A5.D2.1, SERENITY Project (2006), Available from http://www.serenity-forum.org

5. Shanahan, M.P.: The event calculus explained. In: Veloso, M.M., Wooldridge, M.J. (eds.) Artificial Intelligence Today. LNCS (LNAI), vol. 1600, pp. 409–430. Springer, Heidelberg (1999)

6. Melton, R., Garlan, D.: Architectural Unification. In: Proceedings of CASCON'97, Ontario, Canada (1997)

7. Spanoudakis, G., Mahbub, K.: Non intrusive monitoring of service based systems. International Journal of Cooperative Information Systems 15, 325–358 (2006)

8. Axelsson, S.: Intrusion detection systems: A survey and taxonomy. Technical Report 99-15, Dept. of Computer Engineering, Chalmers Univ. (2000)

9. Hofmeyr, S.A., Forrest, S.: Architecture for an artificial immune system. Evolutionary Computation 7, 1289–1296 (2000)

10. Anagnostakis, K., et al.: Detecting targeted attacks using shadow honeypots. In: Proc. of the $14^{t}h$ USENIX Security Symposium (2005)

11. Labbe, K., et al.: A methodology for evaluation of host-based intrusion prevention systems and its application. In: Proc. of the 7th IEEE Work. on Information Assurance (2006)

12. Corradi, A., et al.: Context-based access control management in ubiquitous environments. In: Third IEEE Int. Symp. on Network Computing and Applications, pp. 253–260. IEEE Computer Society Press, Los Alamitos (2004)

13. Hulsebosch, J., et al.: Context sensitive access control. In: Proc. of the Tenth ACM Symp. on Access Control Models and Technologies, SACMAT'05, pp. 111–119. ACM Press, New York (2005)

14. Robinson, W.: Monitoring software requirements using instrumented code. In: Proc. of the Hawaii Int. Conf. on Systems Sciences, 2002, Hawaii, USA (2002)

15. Feather, M., et al.: Reconciling system requirements and runtime behaviour. In: Proc. of 9th Int. Work. on Software Specification & Design (1998)

16. Kannan, S., et al.: Runtime monitoring and steering based on formal specifications. In: Workshop on Modeling Software System Structures in a Fastly Moving Scenario (2000)

17. Kim, M., et al.: Java-MaC: a runtime assurance tool for Java programs. Electr. Notes in Theoretical Computer Science, 55 (2001)

18. Spanoudakis, G., Kloukinas, C., Androutsopoulos, K.: Towards security monitoring patterns. In: ACM Symposium on Applied Computing (SAC07) - Track on Software Verification, Seoul, Korea, vol. 2, pp. 1518–1525. ACM, New York (2007)

Security Aspects for Secure Download of Regulated Software

Sibylle Hick and Christoph Ruland

Institute for Data Communications Systems (DCS), University of Siegen,
Hoelderlinstrasse 3, D-57076 Siegen, Germany
{Sibylle.Hick,Christoph.Ruland}@uni-siegen.de

Abstract. Software can be found in a lot of different infrastructures in our daily life e.g. mobile phones, cars, or ticket machines. Due to always increasing requirements or failures in programs, updates are needed at all times and mean a great cost and time advantage. Not always can the technical possibility to download software components be realized right away because various security issues or legal restraints have to be taken into account. This paper introduces a security architecture for regulated software download that is performed in the area of measuring instruments but can also be applied for other infrastructures. Therefore at first the legal requirements in which the software download is performed – here the liberalized energy market - is introduced. Furthermore different security requirements that are necessary to connect the technical and legal needs are presented. The analysis of the legal situation, the participants, resources, and threads draws a total picture of the system. Starting from these conclusions an infrastructure that supports the different security aspects will be presented.

1 Introduction

Computer systems or control units demand new versions of software in order to provide services that on the one hand control and monitor the hardware and on the other side respond and execute functions that solve different kinds of individual user problems. If the functions that need to be accomplished are not regulated by law or any other requirements it is comparatively easy to implement such an operation at least from the technical side of view. Nevertheless there are situations where the alteration or exchange of software can only be allowed if several preconditions are fulfilled. The requirements and thus restrictions on programs range from legal specifications to security aspects that have to be met.

In the scope of energy meters the restrictions of a technical feasible software download result from the need of obligatory verification. Based on the German Verification Act (Eichgesetz) sec. 2 para. 1 EichG all energy measurement devices that are used in the area of business commerce have to be explicitly approved [1]. In the case of the energy industry software is classified into two groups; legally relevant and non-legally relevant software [2]. In the first case the software includes functions, data and parameters that have to be approved by an appropriate authority. A software

C. Lambrinoudakis, G. Pernul, A M. Tjoa (Eds.): TrustBus 2007, LNCS 4657, pp. 219–227, 2007.

module that needs not to be certified contains functions, data and parameters that are not allowed to have any effect on legally relevant tasks in a measurement instrument [2]. In the following it is focused on the first type of software. After the verification the meter can only be changed directly on location by employees with special legal rights to do so. The possibility to establish a software download over open networks is very advantageous and challenging for measurement device manufacturer. It arises the chance to respond very fast and cost-saving to errors that have been observed, new requirements that are demanded by the customer as well as to changes in legislation. In this paper mainly energy measurement instruments are observed that are described in the annexes MI-001 till MI-004 of the European Measurement Directive [3].

So far software download is not allowed to be performed although it is technical possible. But the recent changes in the energy market open the possibility to pervade the necessary national and international legal requirements. Software modules that are approved and installed in a calibrated measurement device will be able to be altered fully or partly by new components if an appropriate security policy is introduced in the existing infrastructure. Chapter 2 introduces the legal framework that has experienced a lot of changes during the last years and is still in the process of being adjusted to international harmonization. The monopolistic energy market has changed to a liberalized energy market with new participants where so called unbundling has taken place. Section 3 outlines the initial situation without any security mechanisms from a technical and legal side of view. In section 4 the different requirements in the scope of security issues are presented. The WELMEC consortium [4] has already published several documents which include security analyses for measurement instruments (e.g. scales). They address besides other the problem of software download. Experiences from analogy needs are taken also into account. Afterwards an insight how an appropriate security architecture can be designed is given. The infrastructure is expanded by appropriate and selected security mechanisms. The last chapter summarizes the phases of a software download in the energy market and gives an outlook on the next steps.

2 Liberalized Energy Market

The monopolistic energy market in Europe was turned into a liberalized energy market in 1996 when the Electricity Directive (Directive 96/92/EC, Elektrizitätsbinnenmarktrichtlinie) had come into effect through the decision of the European Parliament and of the Council [5]. The purpose was and still is to receive a harmonized legislation in Europe and a market that supports competition between the participants. Before the liberalization the number of participants was rather small and clearly arranged because there were only a few enterprises that offered services related to energy. After the introduction of the new directive the different tasks in the energy industry were separated and assigned to different roles. This concept is called unbundling. The primary idea is to divide up the duties and responsibilities of transmission of energy (compare article 10 Electricity Directive [5]), distribution of energy (compare article 15 Electricity Directive [5]), and the accounts of energy services (compare article 19 Electricity Directive [5]). In Germany the European legislation was becoming effective two years later by the Energy Industry Act (Energiewirtschaftsgesetz - EnWG) [6]. The harmonization was not only limited to electricity but was expanded to gas in 1998 by the Gas Directive 98/30/EC (Erdgasbinnenmarktrichtlinie) [7]. Due to the changes on international legislation (the Electricity Directive was changed again in 2003 [8]) as well as experiences gained in the new market the Energy Industry Act was newly adjusted in 2003 [9] and at last in 2005 [10].

Besides laws in energy the harmonization proceeded in the area of legislation on verification. In 2004 the Measurement Instrument Directive (MID) became effective and lead to wide reorganization in verification [3]. In Germany these changes were determined in February 2007 with the new Verification Act (Eichgesetz - EichG) [1] and Verification Ordinance (Eichordnung - EO) [11]. One major consequence was the partially shifting from several monitoring and approval tasks from the so far established testing laboratories to the meter device manufacturers. Before the MID was introduced there were only testing laboratories in charge of verification and calibration in Germany. They were assigned as "state accredited testing laboratories" based on the Verification Ordinance sec. 57 EO [11]. The MID introduced the conformity assessment based on different modules that are described in [3] via the annexes B, D, F, and H1 and are taken on sec. 7k para. 1 EO [11] in Germany. These modules will be administered not only by the existing approved testing laboratories and the PTB (Physikalisch-Technische Bundesanstalt - national metrology institute) but also by notified bodies. The disestablishment in partitions and the international regulations towards meters yielded further to the fact that new participants had to be introduced. In the case of electricity only distribution system operators (DSO) were afore allowed to maintain the meter and deal with the resulting measurements. When the German Energy Industry Act from 2005 came into force the situation changed. Now the law allows a third party to work as a meter device operator with sec. 21b para. 2 EnWG who performs installation, operation, and maintenance [10] of a meter if certain conditions are fulfilled. Although the possibility to perform the service of measurement was designated to be conducted through a third party according to sec. 21b para. 3 EnWG, it has not been further specified in a valid ordinance yet. Figure 1 gives an overview of the different market participants. Since this paper is concentrating on an infrastructure for secure software download the meter is placed in the middle of the model. It is essential for the security analysis and the design of the following architecture to highlight the instances that have influence on the meter and the within connected legally relevant software.

In this paper we display the market divided into three sub areas. The first group includes the responsible agencies that monitor the market and the competition within. Therefore the Ministry of Economic Affairs and Employment as well as the Federal Network Agency were chosen to do so. Furthermore the PTB, the verification authorities with the connected state accredited testing laboratories and the notified bodies are dealing with the inspection and approval of the meter devices. The participants that offer services related to energy are grouped in a second category. The energy is offered by a producer and transmitted through Transmission System Operators (TSO) as well as Distribution System Operators (DSO). Additional supplier and merchants are shown but do not have a great influence on legally relevant software. Therefore they are not considered in the following architecture any further.

The meter is developed by a manufacturer and can later be used by a DSO or a third party in the role of the Meter Device Operator (MDO). In the third group the energy customer is presented. The consumer can be classified as Access Customer (AC) e.g. a hirer who provides a network connection to the Access User (AU) as a leaser who obtains energy through the circuit. Although so far only the AC has the choice to assign a third party for the services of installation, operation, and maintenance (sec. 21b para. 2 sent. 1 EnWG), the Federal Government has the possibility to publish an ordinance to allow the AU according to sec. 21b para. 3 sent. 2 EnWG to choose a third party for the measuring service. Therefore it is necessary to include the different roles of an energy customer in the security considerations.

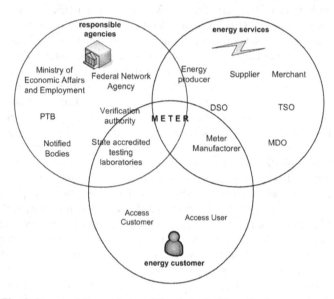

Fig. 1. Survey of the market participants in the liberalized energy market

3   Initial Situation of the Existing Infrastructure

In order to establish a service like secure download of software it is at first necessary to give an overview of the existing system. Chapter 2 has already given an insight in the legal background and the involved participants. It is further essential to identify the connected resources and thereby especially the data that has to traverse several phases until it can be installed and put into operation in a meter. All components are connected through communication that has to occur among them and have therefore to be observed in detail. All the above mentioned information allows a system description before any additional security mechanisms are applied. Afterwards a first abstract use case diagram can be signed.

Figure 1 already showed that the meter is the main component in this scenario and can therefore be identified as the most important resource. A meter is only to be deployed at a customers place if it has afore passed several verification phases. It was mentioned earlier that the meter manufacturer can choose from a list of modules for the conformity assessment. This is usually done by a first examination of a single meter as a reference model for an assembly group unit. Afterwards every single meter in that product line is certified on its own. Latterly this can be done in one continuous process that is drawn through the whole design, development and realization cycle [3]. These considerations display the impact of verification. The meter can later only be changed if permission from the appropriate entity is given and only by a duly accredited agent. For the exchange of software the same requirements have to be applied accordingly. Legally relevant software is to be composed of programs, data and functions that have to be calibrated and to be inspected [2] by the appropriate testing and approval instances. It is created through the meter manufacturer or an assigned organization with different kinds of tools. The executable code has to be provided with additional information so that the connection between the software component and the underlying meter can be made later. An adequate authority has to release the software before it can be written into one or more meters. An energy meter is measuring the consumption of a customer or company and makes the results available for the later accounting. Therefore the measurement values need to be requested by a data acquisition centre. The reading and processing of the information and data is done by management systems. In this scenario a meter is addressed by management systems and the testing and approval instance over open networks for example the internet. The connection can be established e.g. with a modem or GSM (Global System for Mobile Communications).

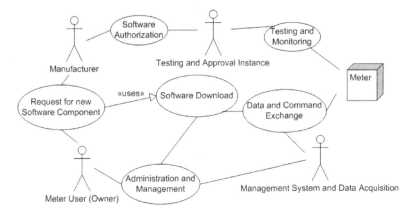

Fig. 2. Use case of a complete software download without security

Figure 2 shows a use case diagram which describes the steps that have to be executed. The process of a complete software download is evaluated only from a technical side of view. So far no security mechanisms have been applied. In the following a rough overview of the required phases of a download process based on the above given use case diagram is presented.

The owner of a meter device requests a software update. New software is implemented by the meter manufacturer due to new requirements of a customer, an error that have been observed, or legal control. The executable code is sent to the testing and approval instance. After appropriate tests the new software component is approved or rejected. In the first case the module can be delivered to the owner of the meter directly or through intermediate entities. Management systems initiate the transportation of the software to the meter. Installation and putting into operation is executed. The meter is working with a new version of application and is monitored by the appropriate instances and the user.

4 Security Requirements and Resulting Architecture

A system environment like the liberalized energy market makes high demands on operations such as e.g. software download. Although the general conditions are altered in some way (here by exchange of software remote over open networks) the goals of consumer protection, measurement assurance, and the trust in measurement results according to sec. 1 EichG has still to be retained [1]. The technical description given in chapter 3 intends that different security issues have to be answered in order to comply with these requirements. Therefore at first the various security aspects that have to be considered are outlined. Based on the requirements that arise from the MID [3] the WELMEC consortium [4] has already released guidelines with [12], [2], and [13] that deal with the security analysis of software and connected resources in particular definitions, description of module concepts, hardware devices, examination, risk analysis, etc. Even though some of the WELMEC documents describe non-automatic Weighing Instruments the analysis results can be applied partially in the scope of meters as well, here especially [13] is referenced. The security analysis has to focus in the first place on the software in the meaning of the legally relevant data, parameters, and functions that are executed within, the meter to which the software component is installed to and operated with, the different people that are connected to the various actions, and the transmission paths. Eligible test scenarios are to be taken into account as well. Thus the use case scenario from section 3 is reviewed under the aspect of necessary security services.

Software Separation. At the beginning of the action a new software component is requested due to new requirements, determined misbehavior of the software in the meter, or new legal specifications. The meter manufacturer creates a new software component and declares the full component as legally relevant or only parts (of course this decision depends on the design on the underlying meter). In the second case he has to support the concept of software separation (compare chapter 8 in [13]). The advantage of software separation goes back to the fact that a manufacturer can modify non-legally relevant parts of software without permission from a higher instance. In this case [13] forces software interfaces that control the interaction among both parts correctly. It is mandatory that the documentation for the specific measuring instrument supporting software separation contains a detailed description how the manufacturer has assured that no effects on legally relevant parts in the meter or to the legally relevant software are possible. This specification has furthermore to be approved by the respective authority.

Software Identification. Since legally relevant software objects do have different states through their life cycle it is necessary that they can be recognized unambiguously by additional information (compare section 3.3 in [12], section 4.2 in

[13]). The introduction of a version number is only one parameter that should be considered here.

Confidentiality. Together with detailed documentation (compare section 12 in [13]) the executable code is committed to the testing and approval authority. This path can be classified as confidential but the manufacturer could choose to use postal delivery. In the first case state-of-the-art security mechanisms like SSLv.3 [14] or TLS [15] can be applied. Cryptographic mechanisms can be used to make a connection between software and manufacturer.

Approval. The certification can be achieved through adequate cryptographic mechanisms that can not be copied for other meters or altered without any notification. If the approval is successful the manufacturer receives the legally relevant software which now consists of three main parts: the software object itself, the software identification, and an electronic approval from the authority that the software is allowed to be used for a special type or the respective assembly group unit.

User acceptance and access control. Requirement B.4 in [12], respectively requirement D5 in section 9 [13] command that only the user can allow and invoke a download to his own measuring instrument. The intension is that a manufacturer can not change the state of the meters' software without explicit permission after it has been sold to a customer. The download authority might receive the software through intermediate entities. Access control has to be established so that the meter can check if the incoming software has been sent by the real owner of the device. Cryptographic mechanisms like the use of digital signatures can be applied here [13].

Secure Transmission. This scenario describes software download over open networks (e.g. the internet). Security mechanisms for authentication, integrity and confidential data have to be added to the legally relevant software module when it is sent from the software management system to the meter.

Authentication and Integrity. Approved Software (through the respective authority and the meter user) can be written into the meter by a software management system. The meter on the other hand must be able to check if the sender of the download command is known as the owner or an authorized body. Authentication (compare requirement D2 of section 9.2 in [13]) is needed not only for the sender of software but also for the data itself. If only the first part is solved a third party could be sending data after a correct authentication of entities. The meter must also recognize if the software component is suitable for the assembly group unit and especially the concrete device. Software that has influence in terms of verification needs to be secured against manipulation (requirement D3 in section 9.2 in [13]). The measuring instrument has at least to be able to identify if software has been changed after approval of the authority. With alteration not only intended changes are covered but also changes that can lead from transmission errors or failure.

Download function. Further requirements concern the installation and operation of software inside the meter (this is described as "Download mechanism" requirement

D1 in [13]). The interfaces in the meter should not allow software download at any time. A special command has to notify the meter that a download will occur in a specified time window. In case the transmission fails or the download is completed the interfaces will be closed directly or after a short timeout. The function that executes the download mechanisms and afore listed requirements in the meter has to be saved in fixed memory so that it can under no circumstances be tampered. It must contain adequate recovery and alarm mechanisms in case the software download is not completed correctly or interrupted in between. If a fault occurs additional requirements depending on the meter type have to be realized. Further information can be found in section 10 of [13]. Requirement D1 in [13] further claims that the principal task of the meter (measuring the consumed energy) should be hold or "be guaranteed" through the download.

Verification scenarios. A software download concept can only be complete if verification scenarios are assimilated. The software module has to be installed by the owner of the measuring instrument but at the same time the testing laboratories need to have mechanisms to check if only approved and correct software has been installed in a meter and is operating like expected (compare D4 in [13]). Figure 3 summarizes the enhancements according to the given legal aspects, presentation of participants, and security analysis in a security architecture.

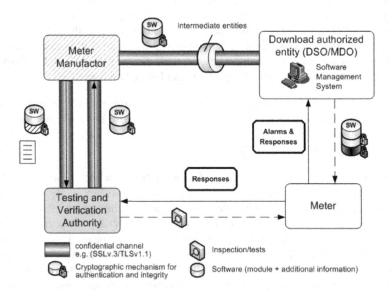

Fig. 3. Security architecture

5 Summary and Outlook

Software download is demanded in different development areas because it offers advantages in the meaning of reduced costs and the possibility to respond very fast to new requirements. In this paper secure software download was described against the background of the liberalized energy market, connected participants, as well as national and international legislation on verification. We showed that a download scenario in the energy industry needs to be expanded by an appropriate security policy that allows fulfilling the different requirements for validation of the regulated software. Therefore security mechanisms have to be integrated in the existing processes. Although the Verification Act and Verification Ordinance were adjusted to the international directives at the beginning of 2007 the legal situation has still not finalized. In the next step a security concept with security mechanisms needs to be described that is able to realize afore introduced requirements.

References

1. Gesetz über das Mess- und Eichwesen (Eichgesetz) vom 08. Februar 2007. BGBl. I 2007, S. 58ff
2. WELMEC - European cooperation in legal metrology. WELMEC 7.1 Issue 2. Informative Document. Development of Software Requirements (May 2005), Available at: http://www.welmec.org/publications/7-1.pdf
3. Directive 2004/22/EC of the European Parliament and of the Council of 31 March 2004 on measuring instruments OJ L 135 30.04.2004, pp. 1–80 (2004)
4. WELMEC – European cooperation in legal metrology. More Information is available at: http://www.welmec.org
5. Directive 96/92/EC of the European Parliament and of the Council of 19 December 1996 concerning common rules for the international market in electricity OJ L 27, 30.01.1997, pp. 20–29 (1996)
6. Gesetz über die Elektrizitäts- und Gasversorgung (Energiewirtschaftsgesetz - EnWG) vom 24. April 1998 BGBl. I 1998, S. 760ff (1998)
7. Directive 98/30/EC of the European Parliament and of the Council of 22 June 1998 concerning common rules for the international market in natural gas OJ L 2004, 21.07.1998, pp. 1–12 (1998)
8. Directive 2003/54/EC of the European Parliament and of the Council of 26 June 2003 concerning common rules for the international market in electricity and repealing Directive 96/92/EC OJ L 176, 15.07.2003, pp. 37–56 (2003)
9. Gesetz über die Elektrizitäts- und Gasversorgung (Energiewirtschaftsgesetz - EnWG) vom 20. Mai 2003 BGBl. I 2003, S. 686ff (2003)
10. Gesetz über die Elektrizitäts- und Gasversorgung (Energiewirtschaftsgesetz - EnWG) v. 07. Juli 2005 BGBl. I 2005, S. 1970ff (2005)
11. Eichordnung – EO v. 08. Februar 2007 BGBl. I 2007, S. 70ff (2007)
12. WELMEC - European cooperation in legal metrology. WELMEC 2.3 Issue 3. Guide for Examining Software (Non-automatic Weighing Instruments) (May 2005) Available at: http://www.welmec.org/publications/2-3.pdf
13. WELMEC - European cooperation in legal metrology. WELMEC 7.2 Issue 1. Software Guide (Measuring Instruments Directive 2004/22/EC) (May 2005) Available at: http://www.welmec.org/publications/7-2en.pdf
14. Freier, A., Karlton, P., Kocher, P. (Transport Layer Security Working Group): The SSL Protocol Version 3.0. Netscape Communications (November 1996), Available at: http://wp.netscape.com/eng/ssl3/
15. Dierks, T., Rescorla, E. (Network Working Group): The Transport Layer Security (TLS) Protocol Version 1.1. (April 2006), Available at: http://www.ietf.org/rfc/rfc4346.txt

Using the Lens of Circuits of Power in Information Systems Security Management

Christos Fragos, Maria Karyda[1], and Evangelos Kiountouzis[2]

[1] University of the Aegean, Department of Information and Communication Systems
Engineering, Karlovassi, Samos, GR 83200, Greece
[2] Athens University of Economics and Business, Department of Informatics, Patission 76,
Athens, GR 10434, Greece
chfragos@hotmail.com, mka@aegean.gr, eak@aueb.gr

Abstract. This paper uses the perspective of power in the study of IS security management. We explore the role of power in the implementation of an information systems security policy, using the Circuits of Power as a Framework for the analysis. A case study research was conducted in a public sector organization that introduced a security policy in order to comply with the law. The authors interviewed members of the organization to explore the different aspects of power relations which were intertwined with the implementation of the policy and used the Circuits of Power to analyze the data gathered. The conclusions derived from the analysis illustrate the role of power in the policy implementation process and indicate that a power perspective provides useful insight in the study of factors affecting the implementation of security policies.

Keywords: power, information systems security management, security policy, Circuits of Power Framework.

1 Introduction

Information systems (IS) are socio-technical systems comprising of data, hardware, software, procedures and humans. The social aspect of IS has been extensively studied [1] by researchers, who often draw insights and theories from social sciences (see for example [2, 3, 4]). In the area of security management, the social element of information systems has been identified as critical for the effectiveness of security measures applied [5].

For most organizations IS security management entails implementing a security policy [6]. Organizations apply a security policy for different reasons: to protect their information infrastructure, because tight competitive conditions make it prohibitive for a company to risk suffering any major security related incident that would damage its reputation and would destroy relations with clients and business partners, because IS security has started to be acknowledged as source of competitive advantage for organizations, even though this very often wears out as a marketing tool and finally, because laws and regulations (in particular those related with personal data protection) may make it mandatory for an enterprise to apply a security policy.

C. Lambrinoudakis, G. Pernul, A M. Tjoa (Eds.): TrustBus 2007, LNCS 4657, pp. 228–236, 2007.

However, and despite the high number of companies enforcing IS security policies, it is considered that only a small fraction of these policies is properly implemented to achieve their objectives. Given the fact that security policies are typically designed and formulated by security experts and that guidelines for designing security polices are widely available, it becomes evident that the reasons for which security policies are not effective have not yet been properly identified or addressed.

This paper explores the interplay between the exercise of power in organizations and the practices of IS security management. The Circuits of Power is used as a theoretical Framework to analyze the implementation of a security policy in a public organization. The goal of this paper is to investigate the applicability of Power Circuits as a theoretical framework for security management and use it to facilitate the understanding of policy application process.

The rest of the paper is organized as follows: section two discusses how the concept of power has been used within IS security management literature; section three describes the research approach followed; section four describes the case study and analyzes research findings; finally section five includes some overall conclusions and indications for future research.

2 Power and Information Systems Security Management

An information security policy is a document that sets the security priorities and contains the measures and practices, including techniques, technologies and procedures, to be used for protecting the information system. Despite the fact that organizations devote significant resources to security management, often the application of a security policy fails to accomplish its goals [5, 6]. According to [7], as high as 80% of the organizations that participated in the research carried out by the National Computing Center (NCC) in the United Kingdom, described the application of their security policy as problematic and ineffective.

Traditionally, the element of power has been studied in the field of sociology and organization sciences. Since the 80's, it has also attracted the attention of researchers in the area of information systems, as the latter is considered a multidisciplinary field. The authors of [8] use the term 'battle metaphor' to denote that an IS implementation process can be portrayed in terms of battles between users and developers. In [1] it is argued that, the question whether the information is beneficial, should be rearticulated as to whom they are beneficial. Information systems have also been reported to function as systems of surveillance and discipline [9, 10]. In [11] the exercise of power by IT professionals over users is studied and an analysis of the types of power exercised over users is provided. The author of [2] explored the exercise of power in systems implementation focusing on user resistance; while in [4] power and resistance in the case of a medical management information system are studied to demonstrate the usefulness of the concept of power in explaining organizational changes resulting from the implementation of large information systems. In [3] an adaptation of the Circuits Framework is employed to study the institutionalization of information systems through a longitudinal case study. It is argued that information systems are both the product and the source of power [3].

In general, IS researchers use the concept of power in multitude ways. In [12] 82 IS papers studying power are examined and different conceptualizations used are identified, concluding that power is better viewed and understood by multiple aspects.

While power has been studied extensively in the IS field, only few references can be found within IS security management literature, possibly because most researchers focus on the technological aspect of security [13]. However, it is argued that IS security research should expanded to cover all aspects of information systems [14, 15, 16]. In [17] the role of power in shaping the notion and application of privacy is explored. In [5] it is argued that the concept of power can be useful for security management research as it can explain why users fail to apply security rules. It is also suggested that many security policy application failures can be attributed to the fact that security specialists are no longer perceived to be gurus; thus they lack power and their role is disputed [18]. The authors of [16] argue that the greatest difficulty in IS security management is not resolving technical issues, but rather achieving consent among stakeholders. Furthermore, it has been found that some organizations consider security measures as conferring too much power to the systems security group [19].

It is also reported that, some employees perceive the security policy as 'barrier to progress' in their effort to perform efficiently their tasks [5, 18]. Finally, it has been argued that the adoption of the security policy is depended on the way the content in the document is communicated to the users [6]. These findings indicate that both end users and managers need to be convinced for the benefits that derive from applying a security policy.

3 Research Approach

The Circuits of Power Framework [20], drawing form sociology and organizational studies [21, 22, 23, 24, 25] has been used in the study of power in the institutionalization of information systems [3] and in the development of an international information systems security standard [26]. Its theoretical strength derives from the fact that it integrates different views and perspectives of power which are dynamically connected. The 'circuits metaphor' emphasizes that power has a relational nature in contrast with the idea that power can be owned. Power 'circulates' through social relations, working practices and discipline techniques [26] providing stability to social systems [3].

The Circuits of Power Framework emphasizes the context in which power is exercised by taking into account institutional and environmental factors as well as technological artifacts. It comprises of three Circuits: the Episodic Circuit; the Social Circuit; and the Systemic Circuit; each describing a different type of power (Figure 1). The three circuits are integrated into an Obligatory Passage Point, which represents what entity A wants entity B to do.

The *Episodic Circuit* represents *causal power*. Causal power is the power exercised by entity A over entity B, when A makes B do something B otherwise would not do. This Circuit allows explain how two entities, A and B, compete in the process of achieving their goals. For instance, security specialists strive to safeguard the information system, while end users interests lie in protecting their privacy.

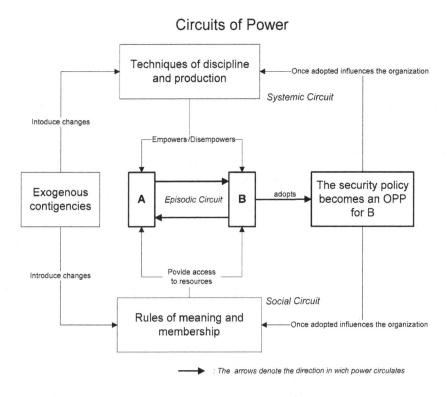

Fig. 1. The Circuits of Power Framework (adapted from [20, 26])

The *Social Circuit* focuses on rules of meaning and membership in organizations, which provide access to resources. For example, management may see the security policy as a means for protecting the information system, while the employees may see it as a document, which adds overhead and sets constrains. Power resources include status, authority, social relations and alliances which exist in the formal and informal structure of the organization. This Circuit represents *dispositional power*, which corresponds to the case where entity A, drawing on these resources, exercises power over entity B.

Under the perspective of the *Systemic Circuit*, power is viewed as a facilitator for producing and achieving collective or individual goals. The concept of *facilitative power*, which draws on production means and discipline, describes how B's compliance can be facilitated and enabled. For instance, a system monitoring employees' tasks facilitates managers to control them.

Finally, *Exogenous Contingencies* introduce changes into the Circuits by affecting the rules of meaning and membership or the techniques of discipline and production. These contingencies include laws, regulations or innovations from competitors. These factors may, in some cases, introduce a new Obligatory Passage Point.

4   Case Study

We explored the application of a security policy in a public organization, which we call the INDA (Independent Agency). INDA is an independent organization, located in Greece and supervises the application of specific legislation. It was inaugurated in 1997 but did not fully function until 1999. It is directed by its President and the Management Board, which consists of six members. All Board members are individuals of high standing and experience in their field. Employees are divided in the Auditors department, the Public Relations department and the Financial department. There are also two employees working for the IT Department. Overall, at the time of our research, INDA employed a little over 30 individuals.

In 1998 INDA acquired an ERP system developed by a private software company, which was not fully operated until 2000. Since it handled sensitive data, INDA was obliged, under the national law on data protection, to develop a security policy and implement adequate security controls. For this reason, the Management Board outsourced the risk analysis project to a group of external security consultants, who designed the security policy in cooperation with INDA members. One of the Board members, having a relative academic background, championed the adoption of the security policy under the President's authorization. The President, however, retained all decisions concerning personnel management. Following the development of the policy, part of the hardware and software were replaced; also security related software (a firewall, antivirus and back up applications) were purchased and installed.

Research reported in this paper took place a few years after INDA had implemented the policy. The authors conducted semi-structured interviews with INDA's employees from all departments and the Board member, who had been given the authority to supervise all issues related to the application of the policy. We also interviewed one of the external consultants who had been involved in the policy design.

In most organizations, information security issues are considered sensitive and employees are reluctant or even unwilling to discuss about them with outsiders. This disinclination grows stronger when the research agenda includes power relations, since this involves answering questions about relationships between colleagues. Employees find it hard to express their true opinion about politics in the organization. In a relatively small organization such as the INDA, however, politics and relations can be easier observed and analyzed by a researcher.

4.1   The Circuit of Social Integration

From a social integration perspective, the employees appeared to be "divided" both by their academic education (specialty) and by the department they belonged to. Especially employees in the Financial department seemed to be isolated from the rest; perhaps due to the fact that they were overloaded with work due to staff shortage. Based on the answers we recorded, collisions and competition among employees existed at all levels and among all hierarchical levels. Complaints about the job allocation between the departments were also recorded.

The implementation of the security policy was faced with opposition by employees whose access to information resources was restricted, as a result of the application of a need-to-know policy. Moreover, some employees commented that the policy regulated the functions of the information system, thus changing the division of work. In general, however, security controls introduced by the policy were positively viewed by most of the employees. The majority of the personnel embraced the necessity of protecting the information system and thus complied with the policy. The security controls were, however, warily viewed by INDA's President, who, being of older age and judicial, had limited understanding of technology.

4.2 The Circuit of Systemic Integration

The implementation of access control measures that was provisioned in the policy deprived employees working for the Relations department from access to information resources they previously had, which resulted in complains. On the other hand, IT personnel were provided with access to more resources, resulting to an increase of the related budget. The implementation of the policy involved monitoring log files and setting rules for creating and managing passwords.

Thus, IT personnel were empowered, since they could control user's access to information resources. However, they themselves felt that they were at the same time disempowered, as they had more work to do without any increase in their salary. Finally, there were no provisions of disciplinary actions in the case of policy violation, nor were any reward policies introduced.

4.3 The Episodic Circuit

Since causal power is directly related to the use of resources, it is critical to understand how means and resources were controlled in INDA. The President, who is appointed by a parliament committee, controls resources and allocates responsibilities; thus acquiring his support is critical for employees who compete for it. On a departmental level, the Relations department depends on IT personnel for managing their applications and on the Audit department for having access to information.

With regard to resistance, there was not notably exercise of power. A few isolated reactions were affectively handled. These reactions originated from employees lacking technical knowledge that could not understand security issues and considered that restricting their access rights was meant to "downgrade" them or add them extra workload. Exogenous environmental contingencies in this case, take the form of national legislation on personal data protection which forced the organization to develop a security policy.

The analysis showed that there was a "negative" exercise of power by the President, who did not use his influence to enforce the policy, even though the Board acknowledged the need of implementing it. On the other hand, there was also a non effective exercise of power by the member of the Board who championed the security policy. This member admittedly failed to convince the President to employ a security specialist to control the application of the security policy. The Board member, having a part time contract with INDA, lacked the authority to enforce the policy, since he had no adequate resources and chances to exercise power over users.

It should also be noted that, on a personal level, the Board Member and the President were on friendly terms but frequently disagreed. This low social integration, from a Circuits of Power point of view, can be attributed to the fact that their worldviews were significantly different: the Board member has the attitude of a technocrat whereas the President that of a legal person.

4.4 Obligation Passage Points

Balance between the Circuits is achieved through an OPP. In the case of INDA, the security policy plays the role of the OPP for the members of the organization. While all the interviewees estimated that the security of the information system was a very important issue, however the security policy failed to be adopted in its whole extend, besides the implementation of some technical controls. This can be attributed to the lack of management support, from the President's side, due to his lack of understanding with regard to information systems security issues and to the low degree of power exercised by the Board member who championed the adoption of the policy. As a result, no awareness and training programs on security were implemented. Most importantly, the role of the security manager was assigned to an IT administrator, instead of employing a person with relevant qualifications.

4.5 Discussion

Conclusively, we found that low levels of power were exercised with regard to the implementation of the security policy; competition among employees was mostly contained on a personal level. Power was exercised by a member of the Management Board, who used his influence on making employees comprehend the significance of implementing a security policy. However, this was not effective enough to persuade the President to champion the adoption of the security policy. The member of the Board did not manage to circulate power through Social and Systemic Circuits to support his vision. The majority of the employees considered the Board member as an "isolated exogenous individual", who could not exercise any power over the users and who lacked the power to affect the politics inside the organization, as the analysis of the Circuit of Causal Power indicates.

Besides that, the introduction of the security policy restricted access to data resources for some employees groups (which was interpreted as loss of power by them) and provided access to more resources to other employees, especially to the information systems administrator group, since they could now claim more funding on the basis of applying security controls for securing the information system.

The role of power in the INDA case has been twofold: in the first place the security policy was introduced to comply with a legal obligation, which is an example of an Exogenous Contingency while, later, individual power was exercised for the adoption of the policy. The introduction of the policy did influence the power structure, though not extensively, through empowering/disempowering certain employees' groups. The security policy was not either accompanied with any control mechanisms or supported by the President. As a result, its adoption was limited.

Using the Circuits Framework we were able to analyze the complex role of power in the case of INDA by combining multiple views of power. However, there are some limitations in adopting the Circuits of Power as a theoretical tool; the most important of which is that it requires a large amount of data to be gathered [3]. For this reason, it is mostly applied in longitudinal case studies. The case of INDA was studied within a relatively short period; however the small size of the organization and the personal interviews provided us with a good insight of the organization. Furthermore, since the focus of the analysis is the implementation of the security policy, the interviews were directed to related issues.

Another limitation of the approach employed in this paper is the element of subjectivity. Our analysis and conclusions have been based on the data collected through the interviews, which merely reflect the interviewees' understanding, or interpretation, of what has happened.

The purpose of this paper is not to provide general conclusions as to the relationship between power and the process of implementing a security policy. The Circuits of Power Framework helped us understand and analyze the complex phenomenon of power relations with regard to the policy implementation.

5 Conclusions and Further Research

The Circuits of Power Framework allowed us explore the application of a security policy from different perspectives and acquire an in-depth insight of the implementation and adoption process. Power appears as one of the factors affecting the adoption of a security policy and thus researchers need to be able to understand the process that governs power [26].

The contribution of this paper is twofold: it informs security researchers and practitioners that power relations should be taken into account in information security management and especially in the processes of security policy development and implementation; it also shows that security research can benefit from employing theoretical tools that originate in the social science field. The social aspect of information systems requires that suitable theories and tools are used. This paper showed that the Circuits of Power Framework can be a useful analysis tool for security management.

However, an even broader research approach is needed to fully explore the dynamics of security policies application. Power appears to be one of the factors affecting the effective adoption of a security policy; thus it could be combined or embedded within a broader research framework that explores social as well as technical issues, such as the one provided by Actor Network theory [27]. Furthermore, such an approach would ideally require a longitudinal or ethnographic research approach. It would also be useful if, more than one, large organizations were studied, so as to collect a larger set of data. In this way, all three Circuits of Power could by analyzed in depth, especially since the Circuit of Causal Power demands longitudinal observation to detect and study the conflicts arising between actors.

References

1. Avgerou, C.: Information systems: what sort of science is it? Omega 28, 567–579 (2000)
2. Markus, L.: Power, Politics, and MIS Implementation. Communications of the ACM 26(6), 430–444 (1983)
3. Silva, L., Backhouse, J.: The Circuits-of-Power Framework for Studying Power in Institutionalization of Information Systems. Journal of the Association for Information Systems 4(6), 294–336 (2003)

4. Doolin, B.: Power and resistance in the implementation of a medical management information system. Info Systems J. 14, 343–362 (2004)
5. Karyda, M., Kiountouzis, E., Kokolakis, S.: Information systems security policies: a contextual perspective. Computers and Security 24(3), 246–260 (2005)
6. Hone, K., Eloff, J.: What makes an effective security policy? Network and Security 6, 14–16 (2002)
7. Goodwin, B.: Companies are at risk from staff ignorance. Computer Weekly, 00104787, 1/27/2004 (2004)
8. Hirschheim, R., Newman, M.: Symbolism and Information Systems Development: Myth, Metaphor and Magic. Information Systems Research 2(1), 29–62 (1991)
9. Zuboff, S.: In the age of the smart machine, New York, Basic Books (1988)
10. Sewell, G., Wilkinson, B.: 'Someone to watch over me': surveillance, discipline and just-in-time labour process. Sociology 26, 271–289 (1992)
11. Markus, L., Bjorn-Andersen, N.: Power over users: Its exercise by system professionals. Communications of the ACM 30(6), 498–504 (1987)
12. Jasperson, J., Carte, T., Saunders, C., Butler, B., Croes, H., Zheng, W.: Review: Power and Information Technology Research. MIS Quarterly 26(4), 397–459 (2002)
13. Dhillon, G., Backhouse, J.: Current directions in IS security research: towards socio-organisational perspectives. Information Systems Journal (11), 127–153 (2001)
14. Karyda, M., Kokolakis, S., Kiountouzis, E.: Redefining Information Systems Security: Viable Information Systems. In: The Proceedings of the 16th IFIP International Conference on Information Security (SEC 2001), Paris, France, June 2001, pp. 453–467. Kluwer Academic Publishers, Dordrecht (2001)
15. Lipson, H., Fisher, D.: Survivability – a new technical and business perspective on security. In: The proceedings of the New Security Paradigm Workshop, June 1999, Canada (1999)
16. Dhillon, G., Backhouse, J.: Information System Security Management in the new Millennium. Communications of the ACM 43(7), 125–128 (2000)
17. Introna, L., Pouloudi, A.: Privacy in the Information Age: Stakeholders, Interests and Values. Journal of Business Ethics 22, 27–38 (1999)
18. Wood, C.: An unappreciated reason why security policies fail. Computer Fraud and Security 10, 13–14 (2000)
19. Wood, C.: Information systems security: Management success factors. Computer and Security 6, 314–320 (1987)
20. Clegg, S.R.: Frameworks of power. Sage Publications, London (1989)
21. Callon, M.: Some elements of sociology of translation: Domestication of the scallops and the fishermen of St Brieuc Bay. In: Law, J. (ed.) Power, Action and Belief, pp. 196–233. Routledge and Kegan Paul, London (1986)
22. Latour, B.: Science in Action. Harvard University Press, Cambridge, MA (1987)
23. Foucault, M.: Power/Knowledge: Selected interviews and other writings 1972-77. Harvester Press, Brighton, UK (1980)
24. Lukes, S.: Power: A radical view. The Macmillan Press Ltd, London (1974)
25. Giddens, A.: The constitution of society. Polity press, Cambridge, UK (1984)
26. Backhouse, J., Hsu, C., Silva, L.: Circuits of Power in Creating de jure Standards: Shaping an International Information Systems Security Standard. MIS Quarterly 30, 413–438 (2006)
27. Latour, B.: Reassembling the Social: An Introduction to Actor-Network-Theory. Oxford University Press, Oxford (2005)

Fuzzy Service Selection and Interaction Review in Distributed Electronic Markets

Stefan Schmidt, Robert Steele, and Tharam Dillon

Faculty of IT, University of Technology, Sydney, Australia
{sschmidt,resteele,tharam3}@it.uts.edu.au

Abstract. Today, the Internet provides an alternative platform where service consumers and service providers can exchange goods and services at electronic marketplaces (e-Markets). In second generation e-Markets consumers and providers have the opportunity to use autonomous agents to act on their behalf to discover, select, and negotiate with potential business partners. Agents can close contracts, make payments, monitor and review contract compliance. Information about the trustworthiness, reputation and the credibility of services, service providers, retailers, and entire business domains is crucial for the assessment of business partners during the service selection process in marketplaces. Agent owners expect their agents to follow social principles and values found in traditional marketplaces. In this paper we discuss the *DEco Arch* framework which enables autonomous agents to evaluate social information which is then used for service selection. Furthermore, agents will are able to review ongoing or completed business interactions for the benefit of peers and their own future decisions. We simulate how the service selection process progresses through new information drawn from reviews of past business interactions.

1 Introduction

Consumers will only be truly comfortable with services and products offered in e-Markets if they are able to evaluate these services or products in the same way they are evaluating them in real life scenarios today. Several factors such as cost, risk, and service need, trustworthiness and reputation influence such decisions. Similarly, service providers and retailers have an interest to evaluate the trustworthiness of consumers for high value transactions.

Semantic overlay networks provide the underlying technology to store and exchange social information about services, service providers, retailers, and business domains among peers. The biggest obstacle to the establishment of trust and reputation in distributed environments is the ambiguity and subjectivity involved in the evaluation of these social values. Furthermore, the establishment of trust in a potential service or service provider is a result of complex subconscious calculations by a human being. Often, we use a combination of past experiences, referrals from friends and associates as well as common sense to select the optimal service or product.

C. Lambrinoudakis, G. Pernul, A M. Tjoa (Eds.): TrustBus 2007, LNCS 4657, pp. 237–247, 2007.
© Springer-Verlag Berlin Heidelberg 2007

The reputation of service providers or manufacturers, retailers, or complete contexts such as 'health services' or 'car sales', we refer to these as *'business domains'*, are combined to find an overall business value. This business value is then used to decide which service or product best suits our requirements and select the most suitable service or product to purchase it. After the business interaction we then evaluate the outcome of our decision based on criteria such as service quality, service satisfaction, on time delivery, etc. The review outcome for each criterion is then associated with the respective business entity. For example, on time delivery is associated with the retailer, service quality is associated with the manufacturer or service provider, and product suitability is associated with the service rankings themselves. All this information contributes to our experience and can be shared with others upon request.

The *DEco Arch* framework provides a flexible architecture to translate these evaluation and review processes into modules to be used by autonomous agents during their service selection and contract review activities. The integration of social values into the decision making process of autonomous agents has been widely recognized in the research community. Some researchers have proposed measures for trustworthiness or reputation values; however most do not address the complex nature of this integration process. Agents can not just rely on one of these values for their decisions, but need to take several aspects such as cost, service suitability, service need, and risk factors into account.

Fuzzy logic provides the underlying mathematical concept that integrates rule-based expert knowledge into calculations undertaken by the agent. All fuzzy rules are expressed in natural language. Measures for social values such as trustworthiness, reputation or credibility are not expressed through binary logic based on 'true' and 'false' statements but instead through continuous values or categories such as 'very good', 'good', ..., 'very bad'. Fuzzy logic is designed to cope with partial or imprecise inputs and is therefore suited to simulate human thinking. Agent owners can incorporate their domain knowledge by composing natural language-based rules in the form of *'if* x *and* y *then* z'. As an alternative to composing custom rule bases for the various fuzzy inference engines incorporated into the *DEco Arch* framework, the agent owner is provided with a set of predefined rulebases.

Agents act on behalf of their owners and therefore follow their interests rather than the community around them. They may provide outdated, inconsistent or even misleading opinions to other agents when asked. To provide incentives for agents to share their opinions and provide truthful information we use the *credibility* value. This value is assigned to every agent in the network which shares opinions about other agents. The credibility value represents the ability or willingness to give a correct opinion and, thus, represents the trustworthiness of the opinion. The *reputation* of an agent or service is the aggregation of past opinions from opinion providing agents in response to the trusting agent's reputation query about the quality of an investigated agent. Finally, following Chang et al. [1], we define trust as the belief the trusting agent has in the trusted agents willingness and capability to deliver a mutually agreed service in the given context and in a given time slot.

2 Business Partner Selection

The selection of a business partner p_b is influenced by a combination of very different aspects such as monetary factors $\chi(p_b)$, context-dependent service suitability $\varphi(p_b)$, service need v and trustworthiness of businesses $\tau(p_b)$. We define a business partner p_b as a composite structure consisting of a service $p_{b(s)}$, a service provider $p_{b(p)}$ and a service retailer $p_{b(r)}$. In some cases service providers directly market and sell their services and therefore $p_{b(r)}$ is optional. The trustworthiness of a business itself consists of reputation opinions which are obtained from recommending peers p_r about $p_{b(s)}$, $p_{b(p)}, p_{b(r)}$. Furthermore, business domain memberships $p_{b(d)}$ and the private opinion $p_{b(i)}$ of the trusting agent p_t play an important role for the evaluation of the trustworthiness of a business partner p_b.

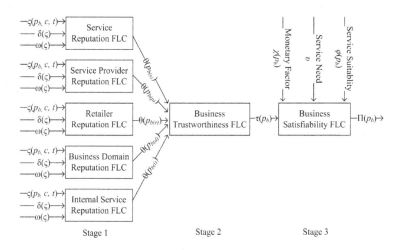

Fig. 1. 3 Stage FLC in *DEco Arch* Framework

In order to select the optimal business partner the trusting agent p_t calculates an overall business satisfiability value $\Pi(p_b)$ for every potential business partner p_b which he previously discovered. The business partner which scores the highest satisfiability value is selected by the trusting agent. The *DEco Arch* framework provides several fuzzy logic controllers (FLCs) to support the trusting agent p_t during the calculation of $\Pi(p_b)$ for each potential business partner. The FLCs make up a three stage system, as depicted in Fig. 1, and are arranged hierarchically to divide the task of calculating $\Pi(p_b)$ into sub tasks and therefore reduce the complexity of the FLC. This is due to the observation that with a growing number of variables per FLC the number of rules increases exponentially [2]. In stage one p_t calculates individual reputation values $\theta(p_{b(s)})$, $\theta(p_{b(p)})$, and $\theta(p_{b(r)})$ for the potential business partner as well as the reputation value for the business domain $\theta(p_{b(d)})$ and an internal reputation value $\theta(p_{b(i)})$ from past interactions with p_b. The reputation values are calculated from opinions delivered by recommending peers p_r as a response to the reputation request $\varsigma(p_b,c,t)$ where c is the business context and t is the time slot of interest for the reputation request. While all available reputation data is included in the calculation of the weighted reputation value, more recent information is provided with higher (exponentially) weighted factors w_i (see expression (1)).

$$\varsigma(p_b,c,t) = \sum_{i=1}^{N}(w_i * r_i) \text{; where } w_i = \frac{e^{-\frac{(n-m_i)}{(n-m_1)*\alpha}}}{\sum_{i=1}^{N}e^{\frac{(n-m_i)}{(n-m_1)*\alpha}}} \tag{1}$$

The collection of reputation opinions (with size N) is normalized and scaled, numbered (with the label i) and sorted by its timespots. n denotes the current timespot, m denotes the timespot of the reported reputation value. α is a user adjustable denominator to alter the shape of the exponential function which characterizes the rate of decay of reputation opinions over time. w_i represents the exponential weight factor and, finally, r_i represents the normalized reputation opinion which was obtained from an recommending agent p_r. The classification we use for the reputation value is closely related to the work presented by Chang et al [1]. The reputation value is represented as a fuzzy set with five fuzzy variables (see Fig. 2a) namely, '*very bad reputation*', '*little reputation*', '*some reputation*', '*good reputation*', and '*very good reputation*' where the Universe of Discourse (UoD) is between 0 and 5 as discussed in [1].

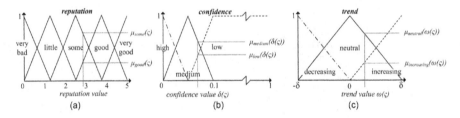

Fig. 2. Distributions of membership functions for stage 1

The second input variable for all stage one FLCs is the reputation confidence $\delta(\varsigma)$ which quantifies the significance of the reputation value. We represent the confidence as the standard error of the mean of reputation values $\bar{r}$ (see expression (2)). The more reputation data is available for the calculation of the overall reputation value the smaller is $\delta(\varsigma)$. The smaller $\delta(\varsigma)$ the higher our confidence in the reputation information about an entity. More specifically, the size $\delta(\varsigma)$ is inversely proportional to the square root of the dataset size N. The confidence value is translated into a fuzzy set with three variables '*low confidence*', '*medium confidence*', and '*high confidence*' where the UoD is in the range between 0 and 1. Our simulations show that the standard error of the mean is not larger than 10% in most cases. The value ranges for the fuzzy sets are adjusted accordingly, see Fig. 2b.

$$\delta(\varsigma) = \frac{s}{\sqrt{N}} \text{; where } s = \sqrt{\frac{\sum r_i - \bar{r}}{N}} \tag{2}$$

The third input variable is the reputation trend value $\omega(\varsigma)$ which indicates whether the reputation of an entity has been improving or deteriorating lately. The reputation trend value $\omega(\varsigma)$ is calculated with expression (3a). We determine the relative changes of the sorted reputation value collection and multiply these values with the exponential weights w_i. The calculation of the exponential weights is analogous to the calculation of the previously discussed weighted reputation value from expression (1). The trend value is translated into a fuzzy set with three variables '*decreasing*', '*neutral*', and '*increasing*' where the UoD is in the range between $-\delta$ and δ. δ represents the maximum change between two adjacent reputation values plus an additional factor β which extends the UoD of the trend variable. β can be chosen from experience, or trial and error (see Fig. 2c).

$$\omega(\varsigma) = \sum_{i=1}^{N}\left(w_i * \left(r_i - r_{i-1}\right)\right) \tag{3a}$$

$$\delta = \max\left(\left|r_i - r_{i-1}\right|\right) + \beta \tag{3b}$$

Using these input variables the trusting agent p_t is able to calculate the individual reputation values $\theta(p_{b(s)})$, $\theta(p_{b(p)})$, and $\theta(p_{b(r)})$ for the potential business partner as well as the reputation value for the business domain $\theta(p_{b(d)})$ and an internal reputation value $\theta(p_{b(i)})$ derived from past interaction data with p_b.

These reputation values serve as an input for stage 2 of the *DEco Arch* framework where p_t calculates an overall trustworthiness value $\tau(p_b)$ for every potential business partner. For the business trustworthiness FLC the same fuzzy variables and distributions as for the reputation membership functions as depicted in Fig. 2a are chosen. $\tau(p_b)$, then, serves as an input to the business satisfiability FLC in stage 3 of p_t's calculations. Again the fuzzy variables and their distributions for $\tau(p_b)$ are similar to the ones depicted in Fig. 2a. The service suitability $\varphi(p_b)$ factor is another input to the stage 3 FLC. $\varphi(p_b)$ indicates the matching level between the user-defined business requirements and the actual service description that the potential business partner offers. The third input to the stage 3 FLC is the service cost $\sigma(p_b)$ factor which indicates the cost of the evaluated service relative to the price offered by competing businesses which are evaluated as part of the business selection process. The service need υ is the final input to the stage 3 FLC. The service need is a user-defined variable which indicates the necessity for the use of the service. The membership functions for $\varphi(p_b)$, $\sigma(p_b)$ and υ are modeled as fuzzy sets with three variables '*low*', '*medium*', and '*high*' where the UoD is between 0 (low) and 1 (high).

The result of stage 3 is $\Pi(p_b)$ which indicates the satisfiability of a potential business partner p_b in the given context c and the given timeslot t. $\Pi(p_b)$ is then compared to other satisfiability values calculated for competing business partners. The trusting agent p_t will select the business partner p_s with the highest satisfiability value and begin its contract negotiations, service payments, etc.

3   Interaction Review

The trusting agent p_t has several incentives to review the ongoing or finalized business interaction with the selected business partner p_s. Firstly, p_t can adjust his own opinion about p_s and, therefore, increase its calculation accuracy for future trustworthiness calculations which involve this business partner. Secondly, p_t can adjust its credibility ratings [3] for all recommending agents p_r which contributed reputation opinions about the business partner p_s. Third, p_t can share its review results with other peers in the form of opinions. The offering of such opinions to its peer agents will increase the credibility of p_t given that the provided information is truthful and correct. As previously discussed, a business partner is composed of a service $p_{s(s)}$, a service provider $p_{s(p)}$ and a retailer $p_{s(r)}$. Consequently, p_t needs to evaluate reputation values for these business elements individually, whereas the reputation of a business domain $p_{s(d)}$ and the internal reputation values $p_{s(i)}$ for p_s are simply calculated as an average of $p_{s(s)}, p_{s(p)},$ and $p_{s(r)}$.

We use the methodology known as CCCI (Correlation, Commitment, Clarity, and Influence) [4] to review the business interaction between p_t and p_s. The central objective of this methodology is the measurement of the correlation between the criteria or conditions both agents agreed to in the business contract. The business contract was negotiated and agreed upon before the business interaction. Every criterion specified in the contract is assigned to one or more elements which constitute the business partner.

Table 1 illustrates an example where p_t is commissioned to find and subscribe to broadband internet service with the following conditions:

Table 1. Example service conditions, responsibilities, and influence and clarity metrics

	Criterion	Expected Value	Actual Value	Influence	Clarity	Responsibility
cr_1	download speed	> 512 kbps	~ 480 kbps	4.5	4	$p_{s(p)}, p_{s(s)}$
cr_2	service availability	> 350 days per year	~ 354 days	3	4.5	$p_{s(p)}$
cr_3	allowed data transfer volume	> 10 GB per month	~ 12 GB per month	3.5	3.5	$p_{s(p)}$
cr_4	DNS lookup speeds	high (200ms - 350ms)	~ 450ms	2.5	2	$p_{s(s)}$
cr_5	payment installments	monthly	fortnightly	3	3	$p_{s(r)}$

The agent owner initially specifies a number of criteria (cr). p_t then searches several electronic market platforms to discover potential business partners whose offerings match the given criteria to a high degree. After selecting the most satisfying business partner p_s as described in the previous section, p_t negotiates a business contract with p_s which includes the quality measurement criteria upon which p_s will be assessed during or after the business interaction. The contract furthermore provides detailed information about the responsibilities of the individual elements of p_s. For example, the service provider $p_{s(p)}$ will be held responsible for the criteria 1, 2 and 3. p_t reviews the performance of $p_{s(p)}$ by comparing expected and actually delivered service conditions (commitment) and weights them by their influence and clarity as specified in the contract with the following expression [4]:

$$Correlation(p_{s(p)}) = \frac{\sum_{i=1}^{3} Commitment_{cr(i)} \cdot Clarity_{cr(i)} \cdot Influence_{cr(i)}}{\sum_{i=1}^{3} Max\_Comm_{cr(i)} \cdot Max\_Clarity_{cr(i)} \cdot Max\_Infl_{cr(i)}} \quad (4)$$

This correlation value is then compared to the initially calculated reputation value $\theta(p_{s(p)})$. If both values differ significantly the reputation value for $p_{b(s)}$ is adjusted as discussed in [5]. This new reputation value $\varsigma(p_{b(p)},c,t)$ is then fed back into its own reputation FLCs for future calculations (as depicted in Fig. 3). Furthermore, it is used to adjust credibility values for all p_r which contributed their opinions about p_s during the service selection calculations and it is used to provide opinions about p_s to other peers.

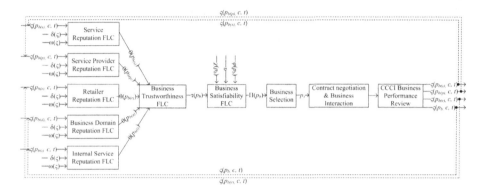

Fig. 3. CCCI review results are fed back into initial reputation FLCs

4 Experiments

As part of the *DEco Arch* framework research we have implemented an environment which simulates business selection, business interaction and the business interaction performance review process. Initially, we generate $n \geq 1$ peers $p_1,...,p_n$ as java processes. From this pool of agents we randomly draw m ($1 \leq m \leq n$) recommending agents $p_{r1},..., p_{rm}$ and assign ≥ 1 reputation opinions about o ($1 \leq o \leq n$) business partner elements $p_{b1},..., p_{bo}$. Reputation opinions about a particular p_b are generated from individually generated Gaussian distributions where mean and standard deviation are drawn randomly within the reputation value space of 0 to 5. Using this distribution a number of values is randomly drawn and scaled to the reputation value space. Furthermore, each of these values is assigned with a timestamp t and a parameter set s. t is drawn randomly from a preset time period between now and t_{max}, and s is drawn randomly from the service parameter label space $\Delta\{A, B,...,H\}$. In a next step, all generated reputation opinions for a particular p_b are sorted by their timestamps.

A business partner is composed of a service, a service provider and a service retailer. Therefore, $p_{b1},..., p_{bo}$ are clustered in groups of three were the highest matching level of s is the determining factor for the selection of group elements. Service elements within the business partners are assigned with a random price tag. The trusting agent p_t is then generated with random parameters from Δ which represent its business requirements. Moreover, p_t is assigned with a service need value v ($0 \leq v \leq 1$) and a service cost value χ_{max}. A search query in over all business partners is issued and all business partners with a matching level of $\varphi(p_b) \geq 75\%$ are included in the business partner satisfiability calculation process. To increase the flexibility of the FLCs the simulation environment is equipped to process four fuzzy rulebases for each FLC. Three rulebases are predefined as '*low risk*', '*medium risk*', and '*high risk*' and a fourth rulebase can be freely defined by the user.

Once p_t has selected the most satisfiable business partner $p_s=max(\Pi(p_b))$ with respect to v, $\varphi(p_b)$, $\chi(p_b)$, and $\tau(p_b)$, the simulation of the business interaction process between p_t and p_s is initiated. The business interaction simulation assigns performance values to $p_{b(s)}$, $p_{b(p)}$, and $p_{b(r)}$ which designate the relationship between the expected value as indicated by the previously calculated reputation values $\theta(p_{s(s)})$, $\theta(p_{s(p)})$, and $\theta(p_{s(r)})$ and the actual outcome of the business interaction. The actual business interaction results are drawn from a Gaussian distribution where the previously calculated reputation values are used as mean values. After calculating the correlation between expected and actual values by using CCCI metrics [4] p_t adjusts the reputation values according to [5] and propagates these back as additional input values for the stage one FCLs as depicted in Fig. 3. This process is then repeated for k rounds.

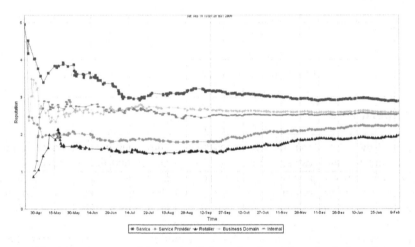

Fig. 4. Development of Reputation Information for a selected p_s in Stage 1

The simulation results for one of selected the business partners p_s are depicted in Fig. 4. As initial settings the following values where selected; $n=1000$, $m=700$, $o=300$, $k=60$, and $t_{max}=300$ days.

Due to the exponentially smoothed averages as discussed in equation (1) all reputation values stabilize over time as more opinions from recommending agents and CCCI review results are added to the calculations for all stage one FLCs. In this simulation it is apparent that some elements of p_s such as the retailer reputation value $\theta(p_{b(r)})$ and the service provider reputation value $\theta(p_{b(p)})$ gradually increase over time during our simulation rounds. The reputation of the business domain $\theta(p_{b(d)})$ and the internal reputation $\theta(p_{b(i)})$ records maintain a stable level while the reputation of the service decreases somewhat. Observations from further simulations show that in most cases all reputation values tend to converge over a large number of simulation rounds. Furthermore, our simulations show that the choice of generally lower risk rulebases for stage 1 and stage 2 FLCs results in a more restricted service selection process as fewer business partners fulfill reputation, trustworthiness and credibility requirements. With fewer business partners to choose from, the price of the selected service seems to increase in most cases. On the other hand, when selecting more permissive (higher risk) rulebases the selected business partner is likely to offer lower prices. However, in such cases, one should expect higher deviations from the expected outcome of the business interaction.

5 Background

A number of calculation methodologies for social values such as trustworthiness, reputation and credibility for various activities in distributed environments have been proposed so far. For example trust measures are often used to address the negative impact of deception during information exchange in distributed systems [6, 7]. Trust is often regarded as a highly subjective and delicate measure. Recovery from breach of trust through deception takes considerable time. Resnick et al. [8] outline common problems of existing reputation systems in e-Market systems such as eBay [9], Yahoo Auctions, and Amazon which use simplistic rating measures which fail to provide the consumer with the complete picture. For example, it is often not clear how credible people are who contribute to ratings. Also, many users of such systems may refrain from providing negative feedback due to fear for retribution. Finally, it is hard to establish how honest a particular rating is as users or agents could collaborate to improve their ratings, or, to discredit competition.

Kamvar et al. [10] propose the Eigentrust algorithm which improves the quality of service in P2P file share systems. They employ a probabilistic approach to compute trust values. In a similar approach Whitby et al. [11] propose a filtering system to address unfair ratings. In the *DEco Arch* framework [12] we use Fuzzy logic as a mathematical means to compute reputation ratings as well as an overall business value which is used for service selection. Fuzzy logic is ideal for the evaluation of imprecise information such as trustworthiness opinions delivered by peer agents while being transparent and configurable to the agent owner. Carbo et al. [13] propose reputation management systems using fuzzy sets and compare their approach to existing systems. Similarly, Rubiera et al. [14] propose a fuzzy logic based approach. These approaches are quite different from ours with regards to suitability for e-Market environments. The establishment of trust is not the only decision factor for autonomous agents as discussed above. Furthermore, in e-Markets we need to distinguish between different reputation values which not only involves the seller or retailer but also the service provider, the service or product itself as well as the business domain.

6 Conclusion

In this paper we have discussed details of the *DEco Arch* framework which equips autonomous agents with modules to support the selection of a business partner based on user defined requirements. We have shown that this selection process is non trivial due to the need to evaluate a number of social criteria such as reputation, trustworthiness and credibility of a business partner. A business partner itself is a composite structure which is composed of a service, a service provider and (possibly) a retailer. Other criteria such as risk, service need, service suitability and cost are also an integral part of the business partner selection process. We use several hierarchically arranged fuzzy logic controllers (FLCs) to simulate human thinking and to cope with partial or imprecise opinions an agent receives from its peers. A second module supports the business interaction review process of the autonomous agent. This process enables the agent to adjust its own trustworthiness ratings about the business partner, to evaluate the quality of opinions delivered by peers and adjust their credibility values if needed, and to share its review results with interested peers in order to improve its own credibility ratings. We use CCCI metrics for the calculation of the correlation of the expected and the actual outcome of the business interaction as part of the review process.

We have shown how the service selection, business interaction, and the business interaction review processes progress over numerous simulation rounds. Reputation values which are initially calculated from opinions provided by peer agents are complemented by review results after simulation rounds start. Reputation values stabilize over time and tend to converge. The simulations produce plausible results.

References

[1] Chang, E., Hussain, F., Dillon, T.S.: Trust and Reputation for Service-Oriented Environments: Technologies For Building Business Intelligence And Consumer Confidence. J. Wiley & Sons, Chichester (2005)

[2] Raju, G.V.S., Zhou, J.U.N., Kisner, R.A.: Hierarchical fuzzy control. International Journal of Control 54, 1201–1216 (1991)

[3] Schmidt, S., Steele, R., Dillon, T., Chang, E.: Fuzzy Service Quality Review in Service Oriented Architectures. In: IEEE World Congr. on Comp. Intelligence. Vanc., Canada (2006)

[4] Chang, E., Hussain, F.K., Dillon, T.: CCCI metrics for the measurement of quality of e-service (2005)

[5] Schmidt, S., Steele, R., Dillon, T., Chang, E.: Building a fuzzy trust network in unsupervised multi-agent environments. In: Intl. Workshop on Web Semantics, Agia Napa, Cyprus, pp. 816–825 (2005)

[6] Standifird, S.S.: Reputation and e-commerce: eBay auctions and the asymmetrical impact of positive and negative ratings. Jnl. of Management 27, 279–295 (2001)

[7] Schweitzer, M.E., Hershey, J.C., Bradlow, E.T.: Promises and lies: Restoring violated trust. Organizational Behavior and Human Decision Processes 101, 1–19 (2006)

[8] Resnick, P., Kuwabara, K., Zeckhauser, R., Friedman, E.: Reputation systems. Communications of the ACM 43, 45–48 (2000)

[9] Resnick, P., Zeckhauser, R.: Trust Among Strangers in Internet Transactions: Empirical Analysis of eBay's Reputation System. The Economics of the Internet and E-Commerce 11 (2002)

[10] Kamvar, S.D., Schlosser, M.T., Garcia-Molina, H.: The Eigentrust algorithm for reputation management in P2P networks. In: Proceedings of the twelfth international conference on World Wide Web, pp. 640–651 (2003)

[11] Whitby, A., Jsang, A., Indulska, J.: Filtering out unfair ratings in bayesian reputation systems. In: Proceedings of the 7th Intl. Workshop on Trust in Agent Societies (2004)

[12] Schmidt, S., Steele, R., Dillon, T.: DEco Arch: Trust and Reputation Aware Service Brokering in Digital Ecosystems I. In: IEEE Intl. Digital Ecosystems and Tech. Conf., Cairns, Australia (2007)

[13] Carbo, J., Molina, J.M., Davila, J.: Trust management through fuzzy reputation. International Journal of Cooperative Information Systems 12, 135–155 (2003)

[14] Rubiera, J.C., Lopez, J.M.M., Muro, J.D.: A fuzzy model of reputation in multi-agent systems. In: Proceedings of the fifth international conference on Autonomous agents, pp. 25–26 (2001)

X316 Security Toolbox for New Generation of Certificate

Rachid Saadi[1], Jean Marc Pierson[2], and Lionel Brunie[1]

[1] LIRIS lab, INSA de Lyon, France
{rachid.saadi,lionel.brunie}@liris.cnrs.fr
[2] IRIT lab, University Paul Sabatier Toulouse, France
jean-marc.pierson@irit.fr

Abstract. Most of industrial or public domains involve a trusted and distributed infrastructure which provides individuals digital credentials and certificates. These latter allow their owner to authenticate herself, prove her rights and gain access inside trusted organizations. The certificate usability scope is extended to contain more and more information, where someones can be considered as sensitive. Contrary to existing certificate standards, we aim to provide a flexible format of certificate enabling to disclose, to blind and to cipher any authorized part of a certificate according to the user context, environment and willing. In this paper, we define and describe a new certificate model called: "X316"[1] and we supply a security toolbox (i.e. X316 Signature, X316 Encryption and X316 Context) allowing its owner for managing her certificate freely according to contextual situation.

1 Introduction

Increasingly, organizations and sites provide individuals with digital identity certificates representing the means of participating and pertaining to their company. Among this domain actors are telecommunication organizations, secure web transaction, health care providers, mobile service providers, financial institutions, state and federal governments, etc.

Actually all distributed systems (grid, pervasive etc.) are based on a certification model that embeds in the certificate more and more user information such as: name, birthday, role, public key identifier etc. Each certificate can thus be used freely by its owner anywhere in the environment.

When a certificate is presented to an organization, this should read only relevant information from the certificate. Let's illustrate this by an example:

Bob obtains from his home site a certificate containing his electronic identity with: name, photo, birth-date, marital status, Social Security number, health insurance, job title, and employer. When Bob would like to shop online, he will present from his certificate only needed information (e.g. name) and would not disclose his marital status, birth-date or job information. When Bob visits a

---

[1] X316: [13]Morph [1]Access [16]Pass. "A" is the first letter of the alphabet...

C. Lambrinoudakis, G. Pernul, A M. Tjoa (Eds.): TrustBus 2007, LNCS 4657, pp. 248–258, 2007.
© Springer-Verlag Berlin Heidelberg 2007

doctor he has to provide his name, health insurance information, SS number, etc., but will not declare his job status. Similarly, when Bob wants to buy an alcoholic drink he must prove his age(older than eighteen). So he presents his certificate, showing only his photo and his birth-date and hides all other information. *The problem is: How the certificate format can be adapted according to user and environment context?*

In the paper we define some security tools to provide trust signature, privacy and contextual adaptation of certificates.

This paper is organized as follows. Section 2 presents related works. Next, in Section 3, we describe the X316 certificate. We define the X316 morph signature in Section 4. In Section 5 and 6 we define the X316 encryption and context modes. In section 7, we discuss benefits and the scalability of our certification model. Finally we conclude this paper and we suggest future directions.

2 Related Works

2.1 Certification Mechanism

The Certification mechanism is a service based on digital signature. It uses the concept of Public Key Infrastructure (PKI) to provide a security privilege based on the trust accorded to the signatory. This mechanism is implemented to authenticate contents of the certificate and to implement a distributed system based on trust.

In the literature, some certification models are standardized and formalized e.g. PGP(Pretty Good Privacy) [1], SPKI [2], Sygn [3], X509 [4], Akenti [5].

X509 is the most used standard. However, it has first been designed as an identity certificate, and its last extension proposed to extend its scope to attribute certificate. Unfortunately, the usability of the new extension is deemed to be too complex and requires adaptations (depending on security policies e.g. RBAC), like in PRIMA [11] and PERMIS [10] which adapt the X509 attribute format to extend its capabilities.

SPKI was proposed to become an alternative to X509, SPKI focuses on authorization certificates more than identity certificates. The objective of SPKI is simplicity. Unlike the X509, which is based on ASN 1.0 [6] format, SPKI certificate is described in S-expression [16] offering more flexibility and readability.

These last models of certification have some drawbacks. In fact, all of them identify one user only with her public key using a challenge-response mechanism [17]. But, each nomadic user owns multiple devices with different capacity (computing power) and capabilities (biometric identification,...). One certificate should embed more than one identification offering to user different means to authenticate her certificates. Furthermore, on one hand, the certificate contains more and more information (sensitive or public) and, on the other hand the context is very important in new environment framework. The certificate contents should be adapted according to context.

2.2   Morph Mechanism

We define the morph mechanism to perform the certification contextual adaptation. It represents the ability to hide some attributes on a signed message according to context. Steinfeld and al [18] define this property as CES (Content Extraction Signature): "*A Content Extraction Signature should allow anyone, given a signed document, to extract a publicly verifiable extracted signature for a specified subdocument of a signed document, without interaction with the signer of the original document*".

The most used approach divides the messages into fragments, then signs each one separately. Micaly and Rivest [7] is the first work which introduces the concept of transitive signature. In their algorithm, giving a signature on two graph edges Sig(x,y) and Sig(y,z) (where x, y and z represent subdocuments), a valid signature Sig(x,z) can be computed to hide "y" without accessing the secrete key. Johanson and al [8] have introduced some improvements by enabling a homomorphic signature. Let a signature Sig(x). Anyone can compute a signature Sig(w) on any subpart w of x obtained by rubbing out some position of x.

[9] is the first work which uses homomorphic function property to define a new signature algorithm for morphing certificates.

All previous approaches have a drawback; they define a new algorithm to perform the certificate adaptability, instead of using the existing standard.

[18] exposes a modification of the RSA computing algorithm. Their approach is based on the homomorphic property of RSA, i.e. $h_1^d h_2^d mod N = (h_1 h_2)^d mod N$. This algorithm multiplies the RSA sub-messages$_i$ signatures ($h_i^d mod N$), and checks whether the result is the signature of the hash values products. Their approaches are very useful. However, they are based on mathematical proprieties that address only a specific class of signature algorithm. This constraint reduces the usability scope.

The World Wide Web Consortium "W3C" standard: "XML Digital signature"(XMLDSig) [12] offers the capability to sign different parts of documents. [19] add some elements to the XMLSignature standard to perform the certificate adaptability. These last methods are very attractive, but it is not appropriate in a certificate model. They treat certificates as any documents, where each one is decomposed into several sub-documents. Consequently, the user is free to disclose or blind any part(e.g certificate identifier). In the contrary, credential or certificate does not consist of distinct parts, but composed of a single bloc, which contains two sort of fields: **Static field** (e.g. certificate identifier, issuer identity, time of validity...) and **Dynamic field** (e.g. user name, user rights...).

3   X316: Morph Access Pass Certificate

In this paper, we define a new certificate structure called X316: Morph Access Pass Certificate. The "X316" can be seen as a passkey, allowing its owner to roam and gain access in the environment [13]. Our contribution has an objective to define a very flexible model of certification. It is inspirited by the W3C standards: "XML Digital signature"(XMLDSig) and "XML Encryption" (XMLEnc) [15].

The X316 is designed for a nomadic user. In fact by defining specific tags to delimit the dynamic parts, this certificate acquires the capability to transform and to morph easily its content according to context, situation, and environment.

The X316 [2] certificate is composed of four parts as follow: Header, Right, Authentication and Signature

HEADER: It identifies the certificate, and is mainly composed of the issuer and the subject.

RIGHT: It is a variable part of a certificate, depending on the site's policy. This part contains information about user's profile (e.g. role or access level) and user capabilities (e.g. delegation).

AUTHENTICATION: This part permits to identify the owner of the X316. The authenticators are numerous, and related to the variety of devices used in the pervasive environment (PDA, mobile phone, terminals). Facilitating certificates management could be fulfilled by embedding some authenticators according to the device's authentication capabilities and the site's security policy. Two ways of authentication have been identified, remote and local authentication [14].

SIGNATURE: This part contains the information about the public cipher key and the result of the certificate's signature.

4   X316 Signature (The Morph Capability)

All standards (e.g. X509 and PGP) use a hash algorithm to obtain a residual value from the certificate data. This value is signed by a private key of the certification authority. Consequently if the content of the certificate is modified, the residual result will be erroneous. In this case, the user can't adapt her certificate by masking any information inside.

In our solution we use a single certificate that mainly contains the user profile, all user access rights and some authentication systems. Yet we define in this model a specific signature method using specific tags. The user can manage and morph her certificates according to the specific transaction or context (see fig1). However some authorized information can be freely masked by the certificate owner far from her home company. In this manner each user is able to extract a sub-certificate from the original one, which only contains needed information for each specific situation.

Thus, the challenge is: How each user can customize her static certificates according to a contextual situation? To solve this problem, we must distinguish The Dynamic Part from the Static Part.

The Static Parts: is composed of mandatory and non changeable data (ex: the ID of the certificate, the time of validity, signature...). These data set up the identity of the certificate.

---

[2] The X316 is represented in XML. In the rest of this paper, we use the W3C syntax definition to describe each X316 parts, where "?" denotes zero or one occurrence; "+" denotes one or more occurrences; "*" denotes zero or more occurrences; and "W3C definition" denote the same syntax of the W3C standard.

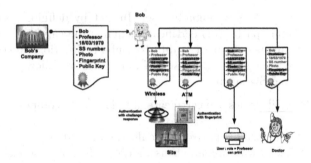

Fig. 1. Morph certificate: In this figure Bob roams in the environment and according to context he discloses only needed information e.g his role to use a printer or his "SS number" to see a doctor

The Dynamic Part: provides sensitive information (e.g. the user name profile, telephone...) and a contextual information (e.g. the device capability, security context...).

To perform the X316 signature algorithm, all dynamic parts in the certificate must be delimited.

We define two types of tags:

DP tag : delimits the dynamic part, each dynamic part can also contain another DPs;

DPDigest tag: delimits the corresponding digest value of the DP part. The signature hash algorithm is used to compute the digest value.

We apply a new algorithm (Morph_Body) to generate the X316 certificate as follows(see figure 2):

1. Transform the source Body B to a Morph Body MB, by replacing all dynamic parts "DP" with the corresponding digests values (DPDigest).
2. Apply a hash function to the Morph Body MB to obtain a Digest D.
3. This residue D is encrypted (by the private key of signatory) to obtain the signature of the document S.
4. Finally, according to context, the dynamic parts can be put or masked (replaced by their corresponding digest value) then moved to signature certification float part.

To verify the authenticity of this certificate, the remaining dynamics parts are replaced by their corresponding hash values before checking signature. Moreover, each DP can contain some DP. In this manner the user has the possibility to mask all the DP parts or some sub-parts inside the DP part. Consequently before computing the global DP part, the digest of all sub DP parts must be computed recursively.

The user has therefore two kinds of certificates: The Source certificate Cert(B,S): It is composed of the source body and the signature. The Sub-certificates SubCert:

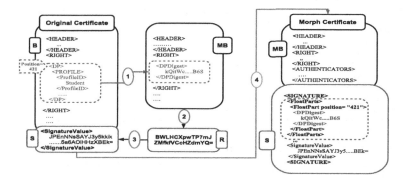

Fig. 2. X316 Signature

The user is able to creates some versions of her certificate. She only selects the required information for a specific context (C) and blinds all other ones.

When the blinded DP parts are selected, the corresponding DPDigest parts are computed and moved to the float part in the signature. This helps to keep clarity in the certificate (see figure 2 step 4). The FloatPart contains all DPDigest parts and their positions in the original certificate. The position field is mandatory to rebuild the morph body for checking the signature.

5   X316 Encryption

X316 certificate may be transfered along the user trip among different sites, where some are trusted and others are not.

Alice want to access target site. For her request she must send some sensitive information held in her certificate to the site administrator. Unfortunately she consider the communication protocols not safe.

One solution consists to encrypt these information. If one section in the certificate is ciphered, the scope of the certificate will be limited, allowing only the site that has the cipher key to check the signature.

The morph certificate can solve this problem allowing each user to make safe any information as long as it is delimited by a DP tag. If the certificate is to be transferred to several sites, Alice ciphers the different sensitive information with different keys. Each user can manage her certificate freely; she can cipher any dynamic part, if this one is considered as sensitive.

Therefore, the X316 encryption is defined to allow user to make confidential any dynamic part inside the certificate. X316 encryption operates like XMLEncryption, with differences. Indeed, the certificate must still be checkable even if some parts are ciphered.

The X316 encryption allows to cipher only the dynamic part. The idea is to put in the cipher part the corresponding hash value of the plain text part. This hash value allows anyone to check the validity of the certificate without

knowing the actual content. In fact the morph transform algorithm replaces all
EncryptedDP parts by the corresponding DPDigest of its plain text.

5.1 X316 Encryption Syntax

```
00  <EncryptedDP>                            03      <KeyInfo>
01    <DPDigest>                             04      <ec:CipherValue>
02    <ec:EncryptionMethod Algorithm=/>      05  </EncryptedDP>
```

5.2 EncryptedDP Description

"DPDigest" (Line 01) contains the digest value of the plain text part. When the
X316 encryption is used, DPDigest must appear. Indeed the certificate must be
checkable by anyone not only the recipient.

"EncryptionMethod Algorithm" (Line 02) defines the algorithm used to perform the encryption task. It is defined following W3C recommendation.

The X316 encryption allows using the symmetric and the asymmetric encryption. The difference between these modes is in the "KeyInfo" parameter.

KeyInfo Syntax

```
                                 04      <ec:EncryptionMethod Algorithm=/>
                                 05      <KeyInfo>
00  <KeyInfo>                    06      <ec:CipherValue>
01    <ds:KeyID id= />?          07      </EncryptedKey>)?
02    <ds:KeyValue>?             08  </KeyInfo>
03    (<EncryptedKey>
```

KeyInfo Description. The keyInfo contains the description of the key used to
cipher the DP part. We define two types of encryption:

Symmetric encryption: In this case, only the KeyId (Line 01) is informed as
W3C definition. This identifier allows to recognize and retrieve the used key.

Asymmetric encryption: This mode computes with two keys, a public key and
a session key (symmetric key). This method of encryption ciphers the plain text
with a session key, then, it ciphers it with the public key. Thus, "EncryptedKey"
(lines 03-07) are required to inform of the ciphered session key; the line 04
defines the Asymmetric encryption algorithm following W3C recommendation;
"KeyInfo" in line 05 defines the public key that is used to cipher the session key.
It contains the KeyID (line 01) or the KeyValue (line 02); the 05 contains the
encrypted session key.

Example: In the next example, we describe an asymmetric encryption using
RSA(line 09) with AES(line 05).

```
Asymmetric encryption:              09      ...Algorithm=".. xmlenc#rsa-1_5"/>
                                    10      <KeyInfo>
00 <EncryptedDP>                    11      <ds:KeyId Id="YrQkh1zr.2SsoKE1M="/>
01  <DPDigest>                      12      </KeyInfo>
02   kQitWcHqiq6rcZopVVpmm/bB6S=    13      <ec:CipherValue>xizrbc</ec:CipherValue>
03  </DPDigest>                     14    </EncryptedKey>
04  <ec:EncryptionMethod           15   </KeyInfo>
05   ...Algorithm="..#aes128-cbc"/> 16   <ec:CipherValue>
06  <KeyInfo>                       17    G5LyRhgvjChfoOSYiPGWxwPW2
07   <EncryptedKey>                 18   </ec:CipherValue>
08    <ec:EncryptionMethod          19 </EncryptedDP>
```

As the "DPDigest" part the "EncryptedDP" part is placed into the signature float part.

The signature is checked by moving the corresponding "DPDigest" parts to their original positions. Consequently any entity is able to verify the authenticity of the certificate without reading the ciphered part. The entity having the corresponding key can solely decrypt the "CipherValue" part and compare the hash result with the "DPDigest" value to check the containing validity.

6   X316 Context

In the X316 framework, the user is allowed to manage her certificate. This procedure is difficult because she must manually choose the corresponding dynamic parts according to context. To help the user we introduce the concept of X316 context. It defines the context profile e.g. Buying, Selling, Delegation etc.

Each context profile defines its corresponding parts and indexes the essential parts in the source certificate.

6.1   X316 Context Syntax

```
00 <X316_Context ID=>              09        (<Encryption Digit=>
01   <Cx_Profile>                  10          <Subject>
02   <Certificates>                11        </Encryption>)*
03    (<Certificate>               12      </Privacy>
04     <ID>                        13    </Mask>
05     <Issuer>                    14   </Certificate>)+
06     <Mask>                      15 </Certificates>
07       <Value>                   16 </X316_Context>
08       <Privacy>
```

6.2   X316 Context Description

Each X316 context is defined by a Profile (line 01). Some certificates (lines 02-14) are selected for each context. Each certificate is defined by its ID and a Mask.

The Mask represents the certificate stamp. It is composed of a series of digits (bounded between 0 and n) separated by points, where the nth Mask digit corresponds to the nth DP part (i.e. with respect to its position and order in the certificate) as following:

$$Mask\ digit = \begin{cases} 0 & \text{If the corresponding DP must be blinded} \\ 1 & \text{If the corresponding DP must be disclosed} \\ \geq 2 & \text{If the corresponding DP must be ciphered} \end{cases}$$

In one certificate some DPs parts can be ciphered with different keys. In this case a Mask digit can take several values between 2 and n, where each value(lines 09-12) identifies the entity (subject: line 10) that be able to decipher the encrypted parts.

Example

This example defines a transaction among three actors:
Buyer="Alice", Seller ="Bob" and his Bank.

- HEADER: ID="1234" Issuer="Buyer:Alice" Subject="Seller:Bob"
- RIGHT :
  - Bob_Profile="Seller"

- Capability= Transfer from
  * Alice account **CreditCardNumber="5487..."** to
  * Bob account BankAccount="USA ..."
  * the DUE="400$" for
  * the **OBJECT="PDA HP HX4700"**.
- AUTHENTICATION: Alice PUBKEY="RSA 1024".

This certificate must be checked by both Bob and his Bank, but neither Bob should be able to read the Alice 'CreditCardNumber', nor the Bank should be able to read the transaction 'OBJECT'. Therefore in this certificate we define the 'CreditCardNumber' and the 'OBJECT' as Dynamic Parts "DPs". In this manner these fields can be secured using the X316 Encryption. The corresponding X316 Context for this transaction is as following:

```
00 <X316_Context ID="3AE456">              09        <Subject>Seller's Bank</Subject>
01 <Cx_Profile> Buying transaction </Cx_Profile> 10   </Encryption>
02 <Certificates>                          11        <Encryption Digit="3">
03  <Certificate>                          12          <Subject>Seller</Subject>
04   <ID>1234</ID>                          13        </Encryption>
05   <Issuer>Alice</Issuer>                 14      </Privacy>
05   <Mask>                                 15    </Mask>
06     <Value>2.3</Value>                   16   </Certificate>
07     <Privacy>                            17  </Certificates>
08       <Encryption Digit="2">             18 </X316_Context>
```

As illustrated in the X316 context, the first DP "CreditCardNumber" having the first Mask digit="2"(line 05 and lines 07-09) must be ciphered with the seller's bank key (e.g. Bank's public key. The second DP "OBJECT" corresponding to the mask digit="3" (line 05 and lines 10-12) must be ciphered with the Seller key (e.g. The session key defined by both Alice and Bob to securely communicate).

7   Discussion and Test

The X316 presents a number of advantages. The new computing signature algorithm and the morph characteristic gives to the certificate the ability to be

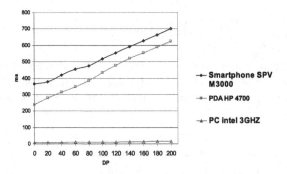

Fig. 3. Test and evaluation

adapted to context with respect to authentication, non repudiation and privacy. Our contribution is inspirited by XML Signature, but adapted to certificate format. The X316 signature is more efficient than other approach. The delimitation of removable parts is fulfilled easily allowing to discern static fields from removable ones. Some tests were implemented to verify the scalability of the X316 morph characteristic. We used an XML file of 20KByte (it is already a large size for a certificate), and computed the elapsed time to verify the signature by varying the number of dynamic parts (DPs) from 0 to 200. For these tests we have used three devices: a smartphone "SPV m3000" (195MHZ CPU), a PDA "HP HX4700"' (624MHZ), and a PC intel (3GHZ). As shown in the figure 3, even the SPV M3000 can compute the X316 signature within less than 1 second.

8   Conclusion and Future Work

The certification model is the basis of the authentication in distributed environment. In this paper we define a new model of certification (X316) which allows a broad user access when this latter is roaming. We have also introduced a new signature computing method to enrich the certificate scope.

The X316 is declined into three categories: X316 Signature to generate a flexible certification model; X316 Encryption to make safe any dynamic part in the certificate; X316 Context to define how each certificate can be automatically adapted according to defined contexts.

One of the new system generation challenges is the fluency of the interaction between the environment and the user. Indeed when the user wants to access a target site, her device should perform the following actions autonomously: Select the corresponding certificate which helps user to gain a maximum access in the target site. Select the corresponding certificate subparts which are essential for this access according to the context, and hide others.

Thus, we will integrate our team works on ontologies and context description [20] to the X316 framework, giving the user device the capacity to manage and adapt the certificate dynamically with respect to context without soliciting any user intervention.

References

1. Zimmermann, P.R.: The Official PGP User's Guide. MIT Press, Cambridge, MA, USA (1995)
2. ITU-T Simple public key infrastructure (SPKI) charter, http://www.ietf.org/html.charters/OLD/spki-charter.html
3. Seitz, L., Pierson, J.M., Brunie, L.: Semantic Access Control for Medical Applications in Grid Environments. In: A International Conference on Parallel and Distributed Computing, pp. 374–383 (August 2003)
4. Adams, C., Farrell, S.: RFC 2510: Internet X.509 Public Key Infrastructure: Certificate Management Protocols (March 1999)
5. Thompson, M.R., Essiari, A., Mudumbai, S.: Certificate-based authorization policy in a PKI environment. ACM Trans. Inf. Syst. Secur. 6, 4, 566–588 (2003)

6. ITU-T Rec. X.680, ISO/IEC 8824-1:2002 (2002), http://asn1.elibel.tm.fr/en/standards/index.htm
7. Micali, S., Rivest, R.: Transitive Signature Schemes. In: Proceedings of the the Cryptographer's Track At the RSA Conference on Topics in Cryptology, Computer Science, February 2003, vol. 2271, pp. 236–243 (2003)
8. Johnson, R., Molnar, D., Song, D., Wagner, D.: Homomorphic signature schemes. In: Preneel, B. (ed.) CT-RSA 2002. LNCS, vol. 2271, pp. 244–262. Springer, Heidelberg (2002)
9. Brands, S.: A technical Overview of Digital Credentials. Research Report (February 2002)
10. Chadwick, D., Otenko, A.: The PERMIS X.509 Role Based Privilege Management Infrastructure. In: Proceedings of the 7th ACM Symposium on Access Control Models and Technologies, June 2002, pp. 135–140. ACM Press, New York (2002)
11. Lorch, M., Adams, D., Kafura, D., et al.: The PRIMA System for Privilege Management, Authorization and Enforcement. In: Proceedings of the 4th International Workshop on Grid Computing (November 2003)
12. Bartel, M., Boyer, J., Fox, B., LaMacchia, B., Simon, E.: XML-encryption syntax and processing. In: W3C Recommendation (February 2002), http://www.w3.org/TR/2002/REC-xmldsig-core-20020212/
13. Saadi, R., Pierson, J.M., Brunie, L.: (Dis)trust Certification Model for Large Access in Pervasive Environment. JPCC International Journal of Pervasive Computing and Communications 1(4), 289–299 (2005)
14. Saadi, R., Pierson, J.M., Brunie, L.: Authentication and Access Control Using Trust Collaboration in Pervasive Grid Environments. In: Proceedings of the International Conference in Grid and Pervasive Computing (to appear, 2007)
15. Imamura, T., Dillaway, B., Simon, E.: XML-signature syntax and processing. In: W3C Recommendation (December 2002), http://www.w3.org/TR/2002/REC-xmlenc-core-20021210/
16. Orri, X., Mas, J.M.: SPKI-XML Certificate Structure Internet-Draft, Octalis SA (November 2001), http://www.ietf.org/internetdrafts/draft-orri-spki-xml-cert-struc-00.txt
17. Challenge-response authentication From Wikipedia, the free encyclopedia, http://en.wikipedia.org/wiki/Challenge-response_authentication
18. Steinfeld, R., Bull, L., Zheng, Y.: Content Extraction Signatures. In: Proceedings of 4th International Conference of Information Security and Cryptology, December 2001, pp. 285–2004 (2001)
19. Bull, L., Stanski, P., Squire, D.M.: Content extraction signatures using XML digital signatures and custom transforms on-demand. In: Proceedings of the 12th international Conference on World Wide Web, May 2003, pp. 170–177 (2003)
20. Ejigu, D., Scuturici, M., Brunie, L.: CoCA: A Collaborative Context-Aware Service Platform for Pervasive Computing. In: The proceedings of the IEEE/CS International Conference on Information Technology: New Generations (to appear, May 2007)

Detecting Malicious SQL

José Fonseca[1], Marco Vieira[2], and Henrique Madeira[2]

[1] ESTG-ISUC, University of Coimbra, Portugal
`josefonseca@mail.telepac.pt`
[2] CISUC, University of Coimbra, Portugal
`{mvieira,henrique}@dei.uc.pt`

Abstract. Web based applications often have vulnerabilities that can be exploited to launch SQL-based attacks. In fact, web application developers are normally concerned with the application functionalities and can easily neglect security aspects. The increasing number of web attacks reported every day corroborates that this attack-prone scenario represents a real danger and is not likely to change favorably in the future. However, the main problem resides in the fact that most of the SQL-based attacks cannot be detected by typical intrusion detection systems (IDS) at network or operating system level. In this paper we propose a database level IDS to concurrently detect malicious database operations. The proposed IDS is based on a comprehensive anomaly detection scheme that checks SQL commands to detect SQL injection and analyses transactions to detect more elaborate data-centric attacks, including insider attacks.

Keywords: Web applications, Security, Intrusion Detection.

1 Introduction

Web applications are extremely popular today because they are ubiquitous and can be easily maintained and updated. Users access the interface via a web browser and send requests to the web server, which in turn translates these requests to database SQL commands and, using the results of those commands, generates the response that is sent back to the browser for final presentation to the user.

A major problem is that web applications are often insecure. In fact, web application developers are normally not specialized in security and the usual time to market constraints direct the effort on satisfying the user's requirements, causing security aspects to be easily neglected. Additionally, rapid application development (RAD) environments (e.g., VS.NET, Eclipse, PHP-Nuke, Drupal, osCommerce) frequently used to build web applications may generate code with vulnerabilities, even when the developer follows the best security practices.

SQL-based attacks, such as SQL injection, are an important class of attacks in web applications as can be confirmed by innumerous vulnerabilities daily reported in specialized sites (e.g., www.securityfocus.com) [1]. SQL-based attacks basically exploit unchecked input fields at user interface to change the SQL commands that are sent to the database. Although some flaws could be mitigated by means of simple operations (e.g., using bind variables, using correctly implemented stored procedures, granting the minimum privileges needed for every action, restricting the input character set,

C. Lambrinoudakis, G. Pernul, A M. Tjoa (Eds.): TrustBus 2007, LNCS 4657, pp. 259–268, 2007.

using escaping quotes, etc.), theses aspects are frequently disregarded. The altered commands may give the attacker access to unauthorized data (read, change or delete), access to privileged database accounts or even permission to execute server side commands (e.g., database stored procedures).

Typical intrusion detection systems (IDS) at network or operating system level cannot detect SQL-based attacks. Although they can be applied to prevent the use of some common malicious strings like "union", "or 1=1", they are quite restrictive, not exhaustive and can be evaded easily. Even traditional database security mechanisms cannot detect these attacks, as they are perceived as authorized commands executed by authorized users. End to end encryption is also useless to stop these attacks because commands are executed by users who have been granted with the appropriate application access privileges.

In this paper we defend that the best way to detect SQL-based attacks that exploit web application code vulnerabilities is to place an additional intrusion detection layer at the database level. At this level, malicious SQL can be detected independently from the web application that has been exploited to launch the attack. In addition, insider attacks launched by malicious users can also be detected.

In spite of all the classical database security mechanisms, current Database management Systems (DBMS) are not well prepared for assuring high privacy and confidentiality [2], especially in what concerns to intrusion detection features [3]. In fact, very few IDS for databases have been proposed so far [4, 5, 6, 7, 8, 9] and, to the best of our knowledge, there is no DBMS that offers intrusion detection as a security feature. It is worth noting that the only mechanism available today to detect malicious database actions is the analysis of database audit trails. However, as this analysis is done offline, audit trails can only be used for diagnosis purposes after attacks.

Recent works have addressed concurrent intrusion detection and attack isolation in DBMS. Valeur et al [4] presented an IDS for SQL injection attacks using several detection models for the different types of attacks. In [5] the authors use the audit logs to derive user profiles that describe typical behavior of users in the DBMS, using the notion of distance measure and most frequent item sets. In [6] a real-time intrusion detection mechanism based on the profile of user roles and three levels of precision in the definition of the data is proposed. In Vieira et al. [7] and Chung et al. [5] the detection of malicious DBMS transactions was addressed with the assumption that the transaction profiles was known in advance and provided manually to IDS.

In this paper we propose an IDS composed of a comprehensive anomaly detection scheme based on automatic learning of SQL commands and transaction profiles. The proposed IDS uses intrinsic characteristics of database applications that allow the definition of an abstraction of the utilization of the database using two levels of detail: 1) *SQL commands* to detect SQL injection attacks and 2) *database transactions* to detect more elaborate data-centric attacks, including insider attacks. These two levels actually represent a fingerprint of every web database application.

The structure of the paper is as follows. Section 2 presents the proposed IDS mechanism. Section 3 presents a two level definition of profiles. Section 4 presents the evaluation of the proposed mechanism using the TPC-W standard benchmark and real database applications. Section 5 concludes the paper and introduces future work.

2   Intrusion Detection at Database Level

Web applications normally rely on a back-end database where the information is processed and stored. Typically the database is located inside a LAN and benefits from the enterprise network security systems. Although security mechanisms at network and operating system level are essential, many web applications have vulnerabilities that allow SQL-based attacks that cannot be detected by IDS at operating system (OS) and network levels. Additionally, database attacks may also come from inside the organization where the attacker has physical access to terminals or even to the database server machine. In this case the network security mechanisms are overridden and useless because the user is already inside the network containment barrier. Thus, we believe that it is important to provide additional intrusion detection capabilities at the DBMS level aimed to cover specifically SQL-based attacks.

General methods for intrusion detection in computer systems are based either on pattern recognition or on anomaly detection. Pattern recognition is the search for known attack signatures. Anomaly detection is the search for deviations from an historical profile of good behavior. To use the pattern recognition approach we need the signatures of known attacks. The problem is that new attacks related to web-based database applications are discovered every day (and it is trivial to change an attack slightly) and the creation of new signatures in a daily basis requires a substantial investment. On the other hand, anomaly detection is able to detect both known and unknown attacks whenever there is a deviation from the expected behavior profiles.

2.1   IDS Architecture

The IDS proposed in this paper includes comprehensive anomaly detection at SQL command and at database transaction level and comprises two phases: a learning phase, where SQL commands and transaction profiles are extracted and a detection phase, where learned profiles are used to concurrently detect SQL-based attacks.

The architecture of the proposed IDS is shown in Fig. 1. The Database Interface intercepts the data flow between the application and the database server, and is used for both the learning and the detection phases. During the *learning phase* the Command Capturing component logs the SQL commands executed by each user. Commands are parsed (by the Parsing component) in order to remove the data variant part (if any) of SQL commands and a hash code is generated to uniquely identify each command. The Learning component examines the SQL command sequence, learns the execution flow (including branches and loops), and generates a list of hash codes of the commands executed and a directed graph representing database transactions profiles for each database user. Different database users will have their own collection of profiles. Although the number of the application users may be quite large, the number of database users is usually restricted corresponding to the several types of users of the application. During the *detection phase* the commands and transaction profiles previously learned are used to detect intrusions. When a potential intrusion is detected the Action component performs an automatic predefined function (e.g., killing the attacker session, warning the database administrator).

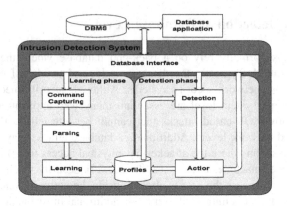

Fig. 1. IDS building blocks and workflow

2.2 Database Profile Learning

The SQL commands and transactions learning curve depends on the utilization profile of the database application. Many database applications include functionalities that are only executed from time to time, for example at the end of the week or end of the month. Until the Database Administrator (DBA) is not confident with the learned profile the Detection component should not act drastically on the session (e.g., should not kill sessions that are considered as intrusion). Instead the DBA should analyze those situations first and, possibly, add the detected transaction to the learned profile. In a real database application, the DBA knows exactly when there is an upgrade and when new functionalities are added to the application. When this happens it is common to have new transactions and, after a short period they would be learned by the IDS mechanism. The set of transactions remains stable, as long as the database application is not changed. There are two ways to obtain the new profiles automatically: concurrently during normal utilization of the applications and by running application tests. In addition to profile learning, some other alternatives could be considered, such as manual gathering and static analysis. Manual gathering of profiles assumes that database transactions are well documented and, usually, this is not the case. Static analysis of the source code could also be used [10, 11]. However this is a complex task and fails when dynamic SQL is used, which is usually the case.

3 Database Utilization Profiles

In a typical web application the code includes the sequence of SQL commands organized as database transactions. When a user connects to the DBMS and establishes a session, the user starts the first transaction. That is, the user cannot escape to the transaction mechanism, as all the commands executed always belong to a transaction. When one transaction ends a new transaction begins. Although the SQL commands can be generated dynamically by the application, users cannot execute pure ad hoc SQL commands. The set of transactions and corresponding SQL commands hard-wired in a web application code represent a well defined set, which allow an exhaustive learning of all commands and transactions. For example, in a banking web application users have only access to the functionalities available at the interface (e.g., withdraw money, balance check account, etc) and no other operation is allowed.

The proposed IDS is based on a set of security constraints defined at two abstraction levels: *command level* and *transaction level*. Intrusion detection activity starts at the lowest level (command level). If no intrusion is detected at this level, the detection continues at the next level (transaction level). If no restriction is violated after having passed both levels, the command is considered valid.

3.1   Command Level Abstraction

SQL commands represent the basic data needed to generate the information required at the two abstraction levels. SQL commands also represent the entry data used to feed the IDS in both the learning and detection phases.

The basic information on each command required for intrusion detection is the following: 1) name of the user who executes the command; 2) identification of the session established when the client application connects to the database server; 3) full text of the SQL command executed; 4) time stamp of the execution of the command.

An important aspect is that the information stored by the IDS does not represent the exact command text, since commands may differ slightly in different executions, while keeping the same structure. For example, in the command *"SELECT * from EMP where job like 'CLERK' and SAL >1000"*, the job and the salary in the select criteria (job like ? and sal > ?) depend on the user's choices. This way, instead of considering the full command text, we just represent the invariant part of it. After removing the variant part of each command it is possible to calculate the command signature using a hash algorithm. These signatures are used at both abstraction levels to represent the command in a compact form.

To perform an SQL injection the attacker alters the structure of the SQL command in order to exploit an unchecked input in an application page. Usually as a first step the attacker adds a condition in the where clause of the SQL command to gain privileged access. Then the attacker executes SQL commands returning valuable information (usually using a union clause with the malicious select), changing the database (performing inserts, deletes or updates) or even performing OS commands. Command level abstraction can be used for detection in both the first and the second steps of the SQL injection attack as both steps require a change in the structure of the query.

The command level abstraction is not sensitive to attacks that do not alter the structure of the SQL commands. In order to execute malicious actions without being detected the attacker has to execute the authorized commands by changing the criteria values in a way that makes the altered command useful for his purposes. In [4] the authors parse the SQL commands and one of the models used is the string model where the strings present in the SQL commands are analyzed. However this approach has a limited detection capacity and inevitably it increases the false positives rate because of the difficulties in modeling most of the string variations. To overcome this problem we propose another level of abstraction: the transaction level.

3.2   Transaction Level Abstraction

At transaction level, our intrusion detection mechanism uses the profile of the transactions implemented by database applications (authorized transactions) to identify user attempts to execute unauthorized transactions. The profile of a database transaction is represented as a directed graph describing the different execution paths (sequences of selects, inserts, updates, and deletes) from the beginning of the transaction to the commit or rollback commands that terminate the transaction. The nodes in the graph represent commands and the arcs represent the valid execution sequences. Depending on the data being processed, several execution paths may exist for the same transaction and an execution path may include cycles representing the repetitive execution of sets of commands (a typical example of cycles in a transaction is the insertion of a variable number of lines in a customer's order).

This command level IDS can be used to detect, among others, attacks from inside the organization. In this kind of attacks the user knows very well and already has access to the database application. The attacker may use his own account or he can impersonate another user and may use a SQL terminal to access the database instead of using the application. The attacker could mimicry a SQL command because of the privileged access to information. However it would still be difficult to mimicry the transactions in order to override the transaction level of the IDS.

To bypass this level a malicious user has to execute SQL commands in the correct order inside the transaction. To execute malicious actions without being detected he must choose and execute adequate dummy commands (commands that have no particular interest for the attacker, except to dodge the IDS) in the correct order and change the criteria in one of them in a way that makes the command useful for him.

4   Database IDS Evaluation and Experiments

We consider the following typical IDS evaluation metrics: 1) *false positives rate*: number of valid commands that are seen as malicious by the IDS over the total number of commands; 2) *coverage*: represents the percentage of malicious commands detected of all the malicious commands; 3) *impact on server performance*: represents the decrease in database performance due to the presence of the IDS; 4) *latency*: time between the execution of a malicious command and its detection.

Key points in assessing these metrics is how the attacker is modeled, which weakness of the system will be used, what commands will be executed and in what order. Another important issue to be addressed is how we can test unknown attacks. In the evaluation experiments we consider that the attacker knows exactly how the IDS works. Before starting the attack the adversary spends some time analyzing the system looking for the weakest point and the right moment. Relying on the ignorance of the attacker seems to be unrealistic. If the database under sight is widely deployed it may be possible that the attacker knows their commands and transactions.

4.1   Experimental Setup

In the present work the IDS was built as a SQL command sniffer that can be used independently of the target DBMS. However, the proposed IDS could also have been included inside the DBMS. In this case, the IDS can use standard DBMS functionalities such as SQL parser, transaction control, and data dictionary access, which would simplify its implementation.

As we want to test our mechanism with real database applications and independently of the target DBMS we have to setup the IDS using the least intrusive manner.

The sniffer approach is the best option because the IDS can be placed in the local network near the database server or it can be placed inside the database server machine. One clear limitation of the sniffer approach is the need of clear network packets (or having access to the decryption function). Because we are focusing our work on the database IDS itself and not on the topology and related questions about its setup we are not going to discuss some well-known technical issues about network IDS, like packet splitting and Host-Based IDS vs Network-Based IDS [12].

The experimental setup consists of a Database Server, a Client Computer and an IDS Computer (where the IDS acting as a sniffer is installed) connected through a fast-Ethernet network. We used the following database application scenarios, running Oracle: 1) a well-known database performance benchmark, the *TPC-W* [13], which simulates the activities of an e-commerce business oriented transactional web server; 2) an academic and financial management application of the University of Coimbra, the *Pk_2005*; 3) a real (and large) hospital database application, the *SCE* (Central Service of Sterilization) currently in use in Coimbra University Hospitals.

4.2 Results Discussion

To evaluate both the learning and detection phases of the IDS and its response to two different kinds of synthetic attacks (exploring command and transaction levels) we used the TPC-W. All the experiments using the TPC-W are based on a training data obtained by a 180 minutes learning phase where 51126 commands were executed. The last transaction profile, as well as the last SQL command, were learned 140 minutes after the beginning of the experiment, which corresponded to the execution of 40419 commands. To test the completeness of the profiles learned the detection phase of the IDS was used with an eight-hour execution of TPC-W, corresponding to the execution of 137233 SQL commands. During this test all the commands and transactions were considered valid, hence no false positives were observed. This means that the learning phase was exhaustive. The TPC-W profiles could be completely covered by the learning algorithm in a couple of hours because of the specific nature of a benchmark. The results should be similar in a real application when application tests are used to exercise the application during the learning phase.

Next we evaluated the IDS against a battery of malicious commands and transactions. A well informed attacker (for example an insider) will not just execute a random collection of SQL commands easily detected by the IDS presented in this paper. Instead, the attacker will try to be stealthy by executing commands similar to those of the application. Thus, the commands that are used to simulate SQL-centric attacks should be based on variations of the SQL commands that are actually generated by the application in order to simulate plausible (and hard to detect) attacks. Random tests are also used for the sake of completeness. To exercise the IDS more thoroughly, both in the command level and in the transaction level, we developed an application to automatically create and inject the attacks.

We executed 14 types of attacks for the command level IDS (Table 1). For each test an input file was created containing 100 SQL commands that were executed in the TPC-W database while the IDS was using the command level abstraction. The IDS detected every command as malicious except for the "Alter the text inside the strings and the values in the where clause" test. As we already expected this test would fail, because we developed the IDS in such way that ignores what is inside the strings and values, so the SQL commands that are exactly as expected, but with different information on the variable parts are not detected as malicious. Note that processing the variable parts is an error prone approach because it is extremely difficult to guarantee that learning algorithm will cover all the possible range of values. The "Place another SQL command at the end of the current command" test could not be executed because the TPC-W implementation used was built in Oracle and it does not allow these kinds of commands, unlike other database engines (SQL server, Mysql).

Table 1. Command level attack tests

Command Test	# attack commands	# false positives
Random queries	100	0
Delete fields from select statements	100	0
Scramble the order of the fields in the select statement	100	0
Insert fields (may be functions) in select statements	100	0
Delete tables from select statements	100	0
Scramble the order of the tables in the select statement	100	0
Insert tables in select statements.	100	0
Delete conditions from the where clause	100	0
Scramble the order of the conditions from the where clause	100	0
Insert conditions from the where clause	100	0
Create an SQL anonymous block	100	0
Create a compound SQL query using UNION, UNION ALL, INTERSECT and MINUS	100	0
Place another SQL command at the end	-	-
Alter the text inside the strings and the values in the where clause	100	100

To exercise the transaction level IDS we have executed 6 tests (Table 2). All the malicious transactions where spotted as soon as the erroneous command was executed.

The learning phase is a critical step that was tested with two real applications (the Pk_2005 and the SCE) during their normal use. The Pk_2005 executed 731438 SQL commands during one week (left side graphic in Fig. 2). The last transaction was learned after the 731373 command and the last different command was learned after the 731327 command. As shown in Fig. 2, there were some bursts of learning during this week test, which is related to some new procedures executed in those occasions.

The SCE executed 753699 SQL commands during 64 days (right side graphic in Fig. 2). The last transaction was learned after the 728424 command and the last

Table 2. Transaction level attack tests

Transaction Test	# attack transactions	# false positives
Random transactions	100	0
Delete SQL commands from the transaction	100	0
Scramble the order of the SQL commands in the transaction	100	0
Insert SQL commands in the transaction	100	0
Commit the transaction before its end	100	0
Rollback the transaction before its end	100	0

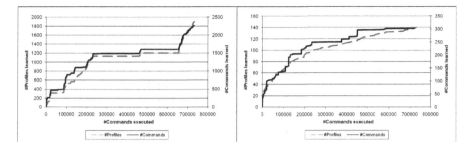

Fig. 2. Pk_2005 (on the left) and SCE (on the right) learning curves

different command was learned after the 718265 command. Like the Pk_2005, the SCE shows bursts of learning, confirming the conclusion of some procedures being executed only in certain times of the day, week, month, etc. The learning phase is considered complete only when the number of new profiles and commands stabilizes.

From the analysis of the results in Fig. 2 we can see that the learning period for the command level and for the transaction level are similar, showing that different transactions are usually made of different commands. We can also conclude that an intrusion detection mechanism based on learning the profiles while the application is in production may take a long time. If the application could be exercised by automatic test procedures or with users executing the applications functions specifically for the IDS the learning period would be drastically reduced.

Because we used the IDS as a network sniffer it introduces no load in the database server and we experienced no packet drop during the experiments. For the sake of completeness we also measured the load impact on server performance for the case where the IDS is located in the DBMS machine. This was done with the TPC-W database and, in the worst scenario, the IDS caused a degradation of almost 11% in the number of transactions executed per minute. By reducing the load to 50%, the impact in the performance decreases to only 5%, and below 40% load it is less than 0.1%. The analysis of these results must take into account that the IDS application tested has not been thoroughly revised for speed as a commercial application should be.

The latency observed is less than 2ms. In most of our tests the malicious commands were detected even before the DBMS could send the responses back to the client. This is a very important reference value because it indicates that a malicious action can be stopped right in the first malicious command, thus preventing the spread of attack consequences. Implementing the IDS inside the DBMS core allows the detection to be made before the SQL command ever reaches the database server. In this case there is a tradeoff between the detection latency and the server response time.

5 Conclusion

This paper presents an intrusion detection system targeted for web-based database applications. It uses the anomaly detection approach and a two level definition of profiles (SQL commands and transactions) to represent the normal utilization.

Our implementation of the IDS was evaluated using a standard benchmark for database systems and two production databases. The detection coverage observed for the nineteen types of attacks tested was 100%, except for one of them. There is no relevant performance penalty using the IDS as a network sniffer.

The experiments show that the learning times can be significant if only normal usage of the application is considered for profile identification. The automatic or manual execution of existing tests or application functions may be used to shorten this period. Both SQL command learning and transaction learning require similar periods of training, but transaction level detection can be used with a wider range of attacks.

References

1. Acunetix, available at: http://www.acunetix.com
2. Anton, A., Bertino, E., Li, N., Yu, T.: A roadmap for comprehensive online privacy policies. CERIAS Technical Report (2004)
3. Agrawal, R., Kiernan, J., Srikant, R., Xu, Y.: Hippocratic databases. In: proc. VLDB (2002)
4. Valeur, F., Mutz, D., Vigna, G.: A Learning-Based Approach to the Detection of SQL Attacks. In: DIMVA 2005 (2005)
5. Chung, C., Gertz, L.: DEMIDS: A Misuse Detection System for Database Systems. In: proc. of Third International IFIP TC-11 WG11.5 Working Conference on Integrity and Internal Control in Information Systems, Kluwer Academic Publishers, Boston (1999)
6. Bertino, E., et al.: Intrusion detection in RBAC-administered databases. In: ACSAC 2005 (2005)
7. Vieira, M., Madeira, H.: Detection of malicious transactions in DBMS. In: PRDC 2005 (2005)
8. Lee, S.Y., Low, W.L., Wong, P.Y.: Learning Fingerprints For A Database Intrusion Detection System. In: Gollmann, D., Karjoth, G., Waidner, M. (eds.) ESORICS 2002. LNCS, vol. 2502, Springer, Heidelberg (2002)
9. Low, W.L., Lee, J., Teoh, P.: DIDAFIT: Detecting Intrusions in Databases Through Fingerprinting Transactions. In: International Conference on Enterprise Information Systems (2002)
10. Viega, J., Bloch, J.T., Kohno, Y., McGraw, G.: ITS4: A static vulnerability scanner for C and C++ code. In: Computer Security Applications Conference (2000)
11. Bergeron, et al.: Static Detection of Malicious Code in Executable Programs. In: SREIS (2001)
12. Internet Security Systems: Network- vs. Host-based Intrusion Detection (1998)
13. TPC Benchmark W (2002) available at: http: //www.tpc.org/tpcw

Trusted Code Execution in JavaCard*

Antonio Maña and Antonio Muñoz

Computer Science Department
University of Málaga. Spain
{amg,amunoz}@lcc.uma.es

Abstract. Some important problems in information security such as software protection, watermarking and obfuscation have been proved to be impossible to solve with software-based solutions. By protecting certain actions in order to guarantee that they are executed as desired, trivial solutions to those problems can be implemented. For tamperproof hardware devices such as smart cards to serve this purpose they must provide the capability to execute code on-the-fly. This paper presents mechanism to allow dynamic code execution in Java Card in order for these cards to be used in software protection problems. However, the solution can be used in other applications.

1 Introduction

There are important problems in information security that have been proved to be impossible to solve with software-based solutions. Among these, we find problems such as software protection, watermarking, obfuscation, production of digital signatures, etc. [1-5]. For other problems, such as auditability, anonymity, or fair exchange, existing cryptographic solutions are very complex and inefficient. However, those problems would have trivial and fast solutions if we could assume that certain actions are protected in such a way that guarantees that they are executed as desired and that the function performed can not be determined.

Therefore, for all these problems, solutions must be based in the use of a "trusted element" that can perform the protected actions [6]. Tamperproof hardware devices and external entities (usually known as trusted third parties) are the most frequent "trusted elements". Although required, the use of trusted elements in the solution is not sufficient to guarantee a good solution. In the optimal solution the amount of trust in these elements must be minimal, while the amount of protection is maximal. The problem is that, usually, these two criteria are conflicting and we need to find a balance among them.

In order to increase the level of trust, it is possible to obtain independent certifications of the behaviour of trusted hardware, especially in the case of simpler hardware. This certification is not possible in the case of trusted third parties (TTPs), which therefore require a higher amount of trust and are not able to provide high

* Work partially supported by E.U. through projects SERENITY (IST-027587) and GREDIA (IST-034363) and by Junta de Castilla la Mancha through MISTICO-MECHANICS project (PBC06-0082).

C. Lambrinoudakis, G. Pernul, A M. Tjoa (Eds.): TrustBus 2007, LNCS 4657, pp. 269–279, 2007.

levels of protection. Consequently, we support the use of tamperproof hardware elements for this purpose. Additional reasons for this claim are:

- TTPs are intrinsically not multipurpose (there are specific TTPs for specific problems). Therefore every user has to deal with multiple TTPs, which complicates the trust and certification schemes.
- Many environments require that the trusted element performs certain actions in representation of the user. TTPs require more trust because they could potentially use the knowledge of these actions and the data involved for illicit purposes.
- TTPs do not provide better protection than tamperproof hardware because, after all, they must use computing systems, which are usually easier to attack.
- TTPs require an online connection that introduces performance and availability problems. For many applications this requirement is a serious inconvenient. TTPs cannot be used in offline applications.

Among other tamperproof hardware elements, we claim that secure general coprocessors, such as PCI coprocessors (for instance IBM's 4758 PCI Cryptographic Coprocessor and other similar products from nCipher, Baltimore Technologies, etc.) or smart cards, which are able to collaborate with the standard unprotected processor are necessary [7]. Simpler hardware elements, such as protected memory tokens, or fixed-functionality processors are not able to fulfil our requirements. In order to guarantee that certain software elements are protected as previously defined, the secure coprocessors used must be capable of receiving the protected code and executing it on-the-fly, a feature that we call dynamic code execution.

2 Background and Related Work

Several mechanisms for secure code execution, and their properties have been proposed in the literature. A classification of these approaches is included below discussing their deficiencies. From this discussion we conclude that a trusted element is needed to achieve a secure code execution.

2.1 Different Mechanisms Related to Secure Execution of Code

A classification of the different approaches to the software protection problem is presented in this section. We focus on security, convenience and practical applicability, more extensive reviews of the state of the art in software protection can be found in [7-8].

Some protection mechanisms are oriented to the protection of the computer system against malicious software. Among these SandBoxing is a popular technique to create a secure execution environment which should be used to run non trusted codes. A sandbox is a container that limits, or reduces, the level of access its applications have, and controls the interaction between them. SandBoxing has been an important technique in research since a long time: Butler Lampson in his paper entitled "Protection", back in 1971 defined the antecedents of the SandBoxing technique.

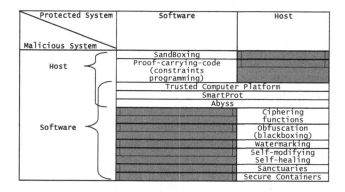

Malicious System \ Protected System	Software	Host
Host	SandBoxing	
	Proof-carrying-code (constraints programming)	
	Trusted Computer Platform	
	SmartProt	
	Abyss	
Software		Ciphering functions
		Obfuscation (blackboxing)
		Watermarking
		Self-modifying Self-healing
		Sanctuaries
		Secure Containers

Fig. 1. Classification of the different approaches regarding malicious-protected systems

Proof Carrying Code refers to a general mechanism to verify that part of code can be executed in a host system in a secure way. This strategy requires that every code fragment is associated to a detailed description on how security policy is satisfied, the host just has to verify that the description is correct and the code fits properly. This strategy shares some similarities with Constraints Programming. Both are based on a code that is able to perform a limited set of operations. Furthermore both Proof Carrying Code and Constraints Programming have several problems mainly caused due to the faculty of determining the set of operations permitted. Also in many cases it is difficult to determine restrictions that preserve the semantic integrity. There are Variants of this strategy, such as Proof-referencing-code, do not carry code proofs explicitly [9].

Other mechanisms are oriented to defend software against malicious servers. A example of such mechanism is the concept of Sanctuary [10] for agents. A Sanctuary is a site where a mobile agent can be securely executed. An important precedent, although not directly related with software are Cryptolopes [11-12], developed by IBM. A Cryptolope is a container that includes all management information needed, such as terms and access condition, digital signatures to protect the authenticity, etc. A Similar alternative is Digibox, later named Rights System Platform [13] both of them developed by Intertust, based on contents which are protected even when resold within this system. This platform is designed for high-value digital contents. Due to this, they are not suitable for content commerce environments such as newspaper or information portals for which the value of each element is much reduced. Furthermore this platform only is able to support three different formats (PDF for texts, MPEG for video and MusicMatch for audio).

Several techniques can be applied to software in order to verify self-integrity. Anti-tamper techniques, such as encryption, cryptographic checksumming, anti-debugging, anti-emulation and some others [5] are in this category. Some schemes are based on self-modifying code, and code obfuscation [15]. A related approach is represented by software watermarking techniques [8]. In this case the purpose of protection is not to avoid analysis but to detect whether the software has been copied or modified. The relation between these techniques is strong. In fact, it has been demonstrated that neither perfect obfuscation nor perfect watermark exists [1]. All of these techniques provide short-term protection; therefore, they are not applicable for our purposes.

Many protection systems are based on checks. In these systems the software includes "checks" to test whether certain conditions are met. We can distinguish solutions based exclusively on software, and others that require some hardware component. However, in both types of schemes, the validation function is included into software. Therefore, reverse engineering and other techniques can be used to discover it. Theoretic approaches to the formalization of the problem have demonstrated that a solution exclusively based on software is unfeasible [15]. By extension, all autonomous protection techniques are also insecure.

In some scenarios, such as agent-based ones, the protection required is limited to some parts of the software (code or data). In this way, the function performed by the software, or the data processed, are hidden from the host where the software is running. An external offline processing step is necessary to obtain the desired results. Among these schemes, the most interesting approach is represented by function hiding techniques. In [16] the authors present a scheme that allows evaluation of encrypted functions. The fundamental idea is to establish an homomorphism between the spaces of plaintext and encrypted data, with the objective of evaluating a certain function on some data without revealing them. The case of online collaboration schemes is also interesting. In these schemes, part of the functionality of the software is executed in one or more external computers. The security of this approach depends on the impossibility for each part to identify the function performed by the others. This approach can be appropriate for distributed computing architectures such as agent-based systems or grid computing, but presents the important disadvantage of the impossibility of application to off-line environments.

Finally there are techniques that establish a two-way protection, such as the Trusted Computer Platform, with recent appearance of ubiquitous computing has raised a needed of a secure platform. Therefore this approach consists of a platform with a trusted component, frequently built-in hardware, which is used to create a foundation of trust for software processes [17]. Another alternative is the ABYSS architecture [18]. Some processes of the software to be protected are substituted by functionally equivalent processes in this system, which runs inside a secure coprocessor. Processes are encrypted while outside of the secure coprocessor. Additionally, the SmartProt mechanism is based on the division of an application's code between a trusted and an untrusted processor in such a way that is not possible to run the application without the collaboration of the trusted processor [19].

2.2 Smart Cards

Smart cards represent a qualitative advance in the way to practical information security. Until the introduction of smart cards, the ability to produce digital signatures and other cryptographic primitives was limited by the necessity of using a provable secure and trusted computing environment. In practice, this requirement was very difficult to fulfil, especially in environments with a high degree of mobility. Smart cards solve this problem because they are secure, tamperproof and portable computing devices capable of storing sensible information (such as cryptographic keys or biometric profiles) and performing computations required in digital signatures and other cryptographic primitives.

Programmable smart cards, such as Java Card, facilitate the development of specific applications and provide tools to achieve security properties that can not be supported by cryptographic protocols and algorithms alone. These cards allow the issuer to control the information that they contain. In this sense, the combination of the physical security and the fact that the software that they execute is under control of the issuer, are the key to achieve those security properties.

Two main problems have traditionally hindered the widespread use of these devices: (i) the difficulty of integration of smart card applications in personal computing environments and, (ii) the reduced data transmission speeds between cards and hosts. The new dual-interface smart cards open the door to the solution of both problems because they make use of two contacts "reserved for future use" in the ISO7816 standard to provide a USB interface in addition to the ISO7816.

Although the amount of memory, computing power, communication speed and physical protection of devices such as PCI coprocessors is higher, smart cards offer several advantages over PCI coprocessors. The most important are:

- Smart cards are portable and can be kept under control of the owner.
- Smart cards circuits are simpler and this facilitates the analysis of possible weak points or hidden traps.
- The level of standardization of smart cards is much higher making them much more interoperable. There are open operating systems for smart cards.
- Smart cards are cheaper.
- Smart cards are multipurpose and can be used in different devices.

Regarding the performance, semiconductor industry has achieved important advances in the development of smart card processors. Among these, we must highlight the availability of RISC processors, the integration of USB controllers in the smart card chip, and the implementation of the Java Card virtual machine in hardware. As an example of the power of current smart card designs, the ST22 family of processors from ST Microelectronics has 32 bits RISC CPUs, with hardware support for most of the Standard Java Card 2.1 virtual machine instructions, as well as a proprietary native code. Some of them include a hardware USB controller.

2.3 Hard Security Properties

Nowadays in systems development is relevant to take into account some security properties desirable to be reached. These security properties are hard to get mainly due to the lack of suitable and efficient solutions instead of which we have only partial solutions to these problems. Moreover, in most cases those solutions are difficult to be applied and can be used under restricted conditions or in concrete environments. Finally, it is very usual that solutions to these problems involve the necessity of any kind of trusted device such as Trusted Third Parties (TTPs). These properties we named Hard Security Properties.

These properties are very relevant in order to solve some problems that we find in today applications. Especially relevance we find in web applications and e-commerce applications related. Some properties that we can mention are non-repudiation, fair exchange and secure payment.

We highlight the fair exchange case, because no satisfactory solution exists to solve this problem. Another important issue to note is that almost all existing fair exchange systems base their security in additional security elements such as Trusted Third Parties (TTPs). Furthermore, it is important to mention that today fair exchange solutions put too much confidence in the TTPs.

Similarly in Secure Payment systems, there are a big number of different solutions which are incompatible in most cases. This fact goes in the opposite sense to reach a standardisation in order to consolidate businesses electronic commerce based.

Non-repudiation problem happen some similar fact. In general security solutions applied by different vendors are: each vendor uses a different software-hardware platform. This heterogeneity of platforms is suitable to be reduced dramatically if we arrange of a common platform to perform all security related operations. Obtaining these properties can be easily achieved in case we have a secure element to perform dynamic code execution on-the-fly as part of the runtime environment.

In this paper we highlight the advantages of including on-the-fly code execution capabilities in the Javacard Virtual Machine (JCVM). This new capability of the JCVM enables the development of simple solutions for the aforementioned problems.

3 Dynamic Code Execution in JavaCard

The basic idea of the trusted code execution scheme is that some sections of the software to be protected can be substituted by functionally equivalent sections to be processed in the secure device. In this way, the protected software is divided and will not work unless it cooperates with the appropriate device. Code modification attacks will not succeed in this case and the only possible attack is to analyze the data transmitted to and from the device trying to guess the functions that it performs. By including a large enough number of functions, with enough importance in the main code, and enough complexity, the attack described can become impractical.

Consequently, for the trusted code execution mechanism to be used in different applications and for different purposes, allowing the implementation of simple and secure solutions to the aforementioned problems, the secure device must support dynamic (i.e. on-the-fly) code execution. The dynamic code execution mechanism is inspired on standard Java applets. An applet is a program written in Java that can be included in a web page. When you use a Java technology-enabled browser to view a page that contains an applet, the applet's code is transferred to your system and executed on-the-fly by the browser's Java Virtual Machine (JVM).

In the previous discussion we have highlighted the advantages of smart cards versus other secure hardware devices. The popularization of smart cards and their evolution in storage and processing capacity have lead us to consider them the most appropriate choice for the implementation of our scheme. However, our design does not depend on this technology and, consequently, our solution can be implemented using any similar hardware token (for example, some hardware keys and some tokens that integrates smart card and reader functionalities).

Among the different technologies currently available on the smart card market, Java Card represents one of the best alternatives for building a prototype of our dynamic code execution scheme because it provides features that are useful for this purpose. Java Card standard defines mechanisms for dynamic code loading, but as we will show later, these mechanisms are not enough to support trusted code execution. Other limitations of the current Java Card specification have important impact in our implementation. The most significant are: the lack of file management capabilities, the lack of flexibility in the code loading mechanisms, the lack of code authentication mechanisms; and the lack of dynamic memory management.

Because the basic idea is to execute part of the application code in the smart card, some additional objectives for the code execution mechanism can be established:

- Secure coprocessors (smart cards in this case) must be identified by the protected software. Mechanisms must exist for the code to authenticate the secure coprocessor in order to identify it as a trusted coprocessor.
- Protected software sections must be identified by the secure coprocessor. Mechanisms must exist for the secure coprocessor to authenticate the protected code sections in order to identify them. This is necessary in order to avoid a type of "Trojan horse" attack based on the substitution of some of the authentic protected sections by other fake sections produced by a malicious user. For instance, such a false section could try to extract data of the protected application stored in the card.
- Code must be encrypted while outside of the secure coprocessor. This, in turn, means that the coprocessor must be capable of decrypting the code on-the-fly before execution.
- It must be possible to execute several protected applications at the same time. This does not mean that the coprocessor must support multitasking, but it requires the coprocessor to keep separate memory spaces for each application.
- Enforcement of actions, such as payment, associated to the execution of the protected software must be possible.

3.1 Structure of the Virtual Machine and Execution Environment

The current implementation of the dynamic code execution mechanism is based on a single Java Card applet. Fig. 2 shows the conceptual structure of this applet and highlights the fact that these components are built on top of the Java Card virtual machine. However, applications at this level have limitations (for example, they are isolated by firewalls) and performance constraints.

Therefore, our aim is to propose the implementation of those functions at a lower level in order to obtain better performance and to facilitate the deployment of other applications that can take advantage of the dynamic code execution infrastructure.

The dynamic part of this applet represents the memory assigned to the applet during its installation. The amount of memory reserved for the different purposes (code, application data and optional licenses) can be defined when the applet is loaded into the card. Java Card does not support dynamic memory allocation. For this reason the Runtime Manager component allows protected applications to use this memory in a dynamic way.

The static part is permanently loaded in the card. This static part includes the card-specific data (keys, etc.) as well as these components:

A License Manager that performs all operations directly related to licenses, such as installation, transfer, backup, etc. It also implements the operations required by the license management protocols.

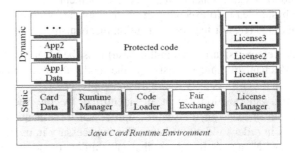

Fig. 2. Logical structure of the card components

A Code Loader that creates the internal representation of the protected code sections when they are downloaded to the card. The Code Loader must then locate the corresponding license and decrypt, translate and create a representation of this section suitable for being executed by the Runtime Manager. The format of this specific code is described in next section. The APDU (Application Protocol Data Unit) used to download the code into the card has three parameters: (i) the license identifier, which is required in order to locate the license and to decrypt the section; (ii) an array of encrypted code; and (iii) an array containing the data required by this section, which can be specified either explicitly or by reference. In the latter case, the actual value of the data is determined at runtime, possibly depending on the results of previously executed sections of the same application.

The most important goal of the Runtime Manager is to overcome the lack of dynamic memory management in Java Card. It is responsible for executing the code, for dynamic allocation/deallocation of memory and for keeping separate memory spaces for different applications. When memory is deallocated it is always overwritten to avoid that other application can try to use it illegitimately. An optional Fair Exchange component, which has been specifically designed to provide a generic fair exchange service that can be used for payment as well as for other purposes.

3.2 Representation of the Dynamic Code Fragments

The lack of mechanisms that allow dynamic code execution in the standard Java Card has forced us to define a specific virtual machine and an associated language.

Regarding the language, our basic objective has been to achieve a compact, yet powerful and flexible representation of the instructions to be executed in the card. Because the main performance bottleneck of smart cards applications is the communication with the card, we have defined a compact format for the external storage and transmission to the card. The Code Loader decrypts the protected code using the corresponding license and then translates into an internal format designed to overcome the problems associated to the lack of file management functionality in Java Card. We have defined the Instruction class in the Java Card language in order for the instructions of the virtual machine to be self-contained and to achieve an easy referencing between instructions. Together with the aforementioned components, this class constitutes the core of the dynamic code execution mechanism. This representation integrates the interpreter in the Instruction class, which in turn results in greater flexibility because it allows the definition of different interpreters without changing the supporting components.

When loaded into the card the code is converted into an array of Instruction objects. The execution is then as simple as calling the Execute method of the first object of the array. Each instruction is linked to the next one(s) to be executed.

```
public class Instruction
{
    final static byte addType= (byte)1;
    final static byte ...
    public instruction next, gotoTrue;
    public S result, op1 ,op2;
    public byte instType;

    //simple constructor
    public Instruction()
    {
        next=null;
        gotoTrue=null;
        type=nullType;
    }

    //alternative constructor
    public instruction(byte myType=nullType,
            S myResult, S myOp1, S myOp2,
            instruction myNext=null,
            instruction myGotoTrue=null)
    {
        instType=myType;
        result=myResult;
        op1=myOp1;
        op2=myOp2;
        gotoTrue=myGotoTrue;
        next=myNext;
    }
}
```

```
//assign
public void assign (byte myType=nullType,
        S myResult, S myOp1, S myOp2,
        instruction myNext=null,
        instruction myGotoTrue=null)
{
    instType=myType;
    result=myResult;
    op1=myOp1;
    op2=myOp2;
    gotoTrue=myGotoTrue;
    next=myNext;
}

//execute
public void execute()
{
    switch(instType)
    {
        //add
        case addType:
            result.myShort=((short)
                (op1.myShort + op2.myShort));
            next.execute(); break;
        //other types
        ...
    }
}
```

Fig. 3. Summary of Instruction class

The lack of file management in Java Card has been solved by (i) Structuring the code in a way that is easily managed by the standard Java Card (that is the reason why the Protected Code memory is defined as an array of Instruction objects) and (ii) using our own software for the management of the instructions. The aforementioned Code Loader is responsible for this second functionality. When the Code Loader has created the Instruction objects that represents the protected code it calls the execute method of the first object in the array. There are jump and loop instructions that open new execution branches. This process goes on until a final instruction is reached, which finalises the execution of the current branch. The execution of the protected section ends when the main branch ends.

4 Applications

The mechanism that provides trusted code execution in JavaCard has a great impact on the ability to solve difficult security problems as explained before. Furthermore, applications using this concept provide a further justification of the previous assertions. Some of these applications are briefly explained below.

An interesting application of dynamic code execution based on our JavaCard implementation has been developed to protect and distribute audio files in mp3, wma and CD-audio formats. Our system uses dynamic code execution to decrypt and play protected audio files. Moreover, the protection mechanism enables the free distribution audio files. The JavaCard applet cooperates with Java executed in the player device to perform decryption and reproduction. This applet requires to playing audio file a card specific license to be produced for each audio file. This prevents unauthorized use of the file.

A related work consists of a secure platform for pay-TV through the Internet. Pay-per-view platform uses different technologies such as Java Media Framework, Real Transport Protocol, and Video Streaming to provide a fine-grained timeslot model for video distribution. In this case trusted execution code is used to implement a variant of forward secrecy schemes. The ability to execute code dynamically us the key to the controlled generation of time-limited keys for the player device.

A secure framework for digital newspaper distribution named EC-GATE was developed and obtained the gold award in the e-Gate Open International Contest. This application is based on the following idea: The security requirements of all processes related to the secure transmission and commerce of information can be fulfilled if we guarantee that the software running at the other side of the communication line is protected. This solution is based on the notion of "secure container", a protected package of data and administrative information. Opposed to other proposals we use "active" instead of "passive" containers (we use software instead of data) in order to avoid some problems of the latter. The dynamic code execution capability is used to guarantee that decryption and payment operations are performed inside the smartcards as an atomic operation, therefore providing a fair payment mechanism.

The SmartProt scheme [19] is designed to protect software elements from analysis and to ensure that they are executed as desired by its creator. The system works in different phases starting with a card setup phase. The dynamic code execution mechanism presented in this paper is used in SmartProt in order to prevent code modifications attacks. Main goals of these attacks are to produce an unprotected copy of the protected software.

5 Conclusions

An infrastructure to allow dynamic code execution in Java Card has been presented. We have shown the relevance of this functionality for some important information security problems and have discussed how other approaches are less suitable. The infrastructure presented is based on creating a specific virtual machine on top of Java Card. However, applications at this level have limitations (for example, they are isolated by firewalls) and performance constraints. Therefore, our aim is to propose the implementation of those functions at a lower level in order to obtain better performance and to enable the deployment of other applications that can take advantage of the software protection infrastructure.

References

[1] Barak, B., Goldreich, O., Impagliazzo, R., Rudich, S., Sahai, A., Vadhan, S., Yang, K.: On the (Im)possibility of Obfuscating Programs. In: Kilian, J. (ed.) CRYPTO 2001. LNCS, vol. 2139, pp. 1–18. Springer, Heidelberg (2001)

[2] Maña, A., Matamoros, S.: Practical Mobile Digital Signatures. In: Bauknecht, K., Tjoa, A.M., Quirchmayr, G. (eds.) EC-Web 2002. LNCS, vol. 2455, pp. 224–234. Springer, Heidelberg (2002)

[3] Pagnia, H., Gartner, F.C.: On the impossibility of fair exchange without a trusted third party. Darmstadt University of Technology, Department of Computer Science Tech. Rep. TUD-BS-1999-02 (1999)

[4] Spalka, A., Cremers, A.B., Langweg, H.: Protecting the creation of digital signatures with trusted computing platform technology against attacks by Trojan Horse programs. In: Proceedings of the 16th International Conference on Information Security (IFIP/SEC 2001), Kluwer Academic Publishers, Dordrecht (2001)

[5] Schaumüller-Bichl1, I., Piller, E.: A Method of Software Protection Based on the Use of Smart Cards and Cryptographic Techniques. In: Beth, T., Cot, N., Ingemarsson, I. (eds.) Advances in Cryptology. LNCS, vol. 209, pp. 446–454. Springer, Heidelberg (1985)

[6] Herzberg, A., Pinter, S.S.: Public Protection of Software. ACM Transactions on Computer Systems 5(4)-87, 371–393 (1987)

[7] Maña, A.: Protección de Software Basada en Tarjetas Inteligentes. PhD Thesis. University of Málaga (2003)

[8] Hachez, G.: A Comparative Study of Software Protection Tools Suited for E-Commerce with Contributions to Software Watermarking and Smart Cards. PhD Thesis. Universite Catholique de Louvain (2003) http://www.dice.ucl.ac.be/hachez/thesis_gael_hachez.pdf

[9] Gunter Carl, A., Peter, H., Scott, N.: Infrastructure for Proof-Referencing Code. In: Proceedings, Workshop on Foundations of Secure Mobile Code (March 1997)

[10] Yee, B.S.: A Sanctuary for Mobile Agents. Secure Internet Programming (1999)

[11] Cryptolope link. http://ei.cs.vt.edu/wwwbtb/book/chap8/sect2/cryptolope.html

[12] Garcia-Molina, H., Ketchpel, S., Shivakumar, N.: Safeguarding and Charging for Information on the Internet. In: Proceedings of the Intl. Conf. on Data Engineering (1998)

[13] Intertrust Technologies. Intertrust Technologies Home Page, http://www.intertrust.com/

[14] Collberg, C., Thomborson, C.: Watermarking, Tamper-Proofing, and Obfuscation - Tools for Software Protection. University of Auckland Technical Report #170 (2000) http://www.cs.auckland.ac.nz/collberg/Research/Publications/CollbergThomborson2000a/index.html

[15] Goldreich, O.: Towards a theory of software protection. In: Proc. 19th Ann. ACM Symp. on Theory of Computing, pp. 182–194. ACM Press, New York (1987)

[16] Sander, T., Tschudin, C.F.: On Software Protection via Function Hiding. In: Aucsmith, D. (ed.) IH 1998. LNCS, vol. 1525, pp. 111–123. Springer, Heidelberg (1998)

[17] Pearson, S., Balacheff, B., Chen, L., Plaquin, D., Proudler, G.: Trusted Computer Platforms. Prentice Hall PTR 2003, Englewood Cliffs (2003)

[18] White, S., Commerford, L.: ABYSS: An Architecture for Software Protection. IEEE Transactions on Software Engineering 16(6) (1990)

[19] Maña, A., López, J., Ortega, J.J., Pimentel, E., Troya, J.M.: A Framework for Secure Execution of Software. International Journal of Information Security (to appear, 2004)

How to Use ISO/IEC 24727-3 with Arbitrary Smart Cards

Detlef Hühnlein[1] and Manuel Bach[2]

[1] secunet Security Networks AG,
Sudetenstraße 16, 96247 Michelau, Germany
detlef.huehnlein@secunet.com
[2] Federal Office for Information Security,
Godesberger Allee 185-189, D-53175 Bonn, Germany
manuel.bach@bsi.bund.de

Abstract. The forthcoming ISO/IEC 24727 series of standards defines application programming interfaces for smart cards and is expected to provide a major contribution to the global interoperability of smart cards and card-applications. However it assumes in part 2 [8] that certain information concerning the capabilities of the card and its (cryptographic) applications is stored *on the card* itself. As already issued smart cards do not provide the required structures, the significance of ISO/IEC 24727 for billions (see [5]) of "legacy cards" seems to be questionable. In order to overcome this problem, the present paper introduces an alternative approach, which does *not require any specific information on the card* but provides the information which is necessary to map generic requests to card-specific APDUs to the middleware in form of XML-based `CardInfo`-files.

1 Introduction and Motivation

The forthcoming ISO/IEC 24727 series of standards [7,8,9,10] defines application programming interfaces for smart cards. As this standard – unlike existing cryptographic APIs like PKCS #11 [20] – allows a fine granular access to card-applications and covers aspects of card-application management, it promises to provide a major contribution to the global interoperability of smart cards and card applications. In this architecture (see figure 1) a client-application uses a card-application via two layers (the Service Access Layer defined in [9] and the Generic Card Access Layer defined in [8]). For this purpose the client-application sends some Action Request to the Service Access Layer, which in turn sends a Generic Request to the Generic Card Access Layer. This layer "knows" about the specific capabilities of the card and finally sends a Specific Request to the card-application, which performs some operation and gives back the response through the different layers.

The development of the ISO/IEC 24727 standards was stimulated by the US Government Smartcard Interoperability Specification [17], which defines a virtual card edge interface, which can be supported by cards with a file system according to [12] as well as by Java-cards [16]. In a similar fashion, the

C. Lambrinoudakis, G. Pernul, A M. Tjoa (Eds.): TrustBus 2007, LNCS 4657, pp. 280–289, 2007.
© Springer-Verlag Berlin Heidelberg 2007

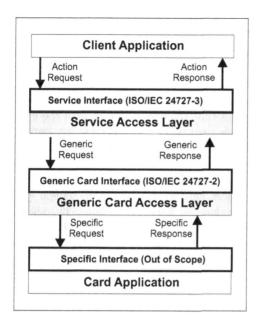

Fig. 1. ISO/IEC 24727 Architecture

Generic Card Interface [8] defines a subset of functions standardized in [12,14] and two files, which may contain further information about the capability of the present card. The Card Capability Description (CCD) tells the Generic Card Access Layer what card applications and predefined Cryptographic Information Application (CIA) profiles according to [11] are present on the card and how some generic request can be mapped to a specific request for the given card. In a similar fashion, the Application Capability Description (ACD) provides such mapping information for application specific requests.

While this approach, just like the virtual card edge from [17], makes it possible that cards with ISO-file system and Java-cards may be accessed using the same interface, it has a major drawback, which seriously limits the applicability of it in (current) practice.

The problem is that the ISO/IEC 24727-2 standard frankly assumes that the *card itself* carries all information (i.e. CCD, ACD and CIA), which is necessary to map some Action Request to the Specific Request for the present card (e.g. consisting of appropriate APDU-sequences referencing a specific file or key on the card).

As the ISO/IEC 24727 series of standards is currently developed it is not surprising that there are no issued cards yet, which comply to this standard and provide the necessary CCD and ACD files. Furthermore, there seem to be very few smart cards in the field, which internal structure is *completely* described by an appropriate CIAInfo-structure according to [11]. This may in part be due to the fact that this structure requires some additional storage on the card and saving storage is still a concern – at least in large volume smart card projects.

Because the card does not provide the required information, it is necessary that the smart card middleware (i.e. some software between the client-application and the card-application) is able to "recognize" a given card type and "knows" how to map a generic call on the Service Interface to card-specific APDUs. The naive but common way to realize this in practice is that the specific features and personalization of some card type are directly coded into the smart card middleware. As this implies that the executable code of the middleware needs to be changed if there are new card types which need to be supported, this clearly renders smart card interoperability more difficult and the maintainance of the smart card middleware turns out to be a major cost factor, especially if the system is to be evaluated according to Common Criteria [6]. Furthermore it is very hard to successfully implement card-application management systems as the middleware would need to be changed if there is a change in some card-application on a supported card. While it is possible to choose a modular middleware design as in [19,1,15] in which only a certain part of the middleware – the "card-provider" – needs to be updated, the problem is not entirely solved as there are still changes to the executable code, which would require some re-evaluation according to [6].

In order to overcome these problems, the present paper introduces an alternative to ISO/IEC 24727-2, in which the necessary information to map a generic Action Request to a Specific Request for the present card (e.g. card-specific APDUs) is provided to the middleware in form of an XML[1]-based configuration file and hence it is *not* necessary to change the executable code of the middleware but it is sufficient to provide a new `CardInfo`-file. This configuration file may be viewed as an an off-card variant of the CCD-, ACD- and CIA-files which otherwise would need to be present on the card itself.

The rest of the paper is structured as follows: Section 2 introduces an alternative to ISO/IEC 24727-2 and explains the major content of the `CardInfo`-files as well as its use to recognize a card type and to map generic requests to card-specific APDUs. We conclude this work in section 3 and sketch how our approach may be embedded in a comprehensive framework for electronic identity cards [3] as it is used for the implementation of the eCard-strategy of the German government.

2   A Generic Alternative to ISO/IEC 24727-2

In this section we present an alternative to ISO/IEC 24727-2, which allows to use the Service Interface according to [9] with cards which do *not* provide CCD-, ACD- and CIA-files and hence are not compliant to [8].

This section is structured as follows: In section 2.1 we will sketch the main ideas of our approach in which the middleware is fed with so called `CardInfo`-files, which describe how to recognize the card type and allow to translate generic

---

[1] It would also be possible to use ASN.1-based `CardInfo`-files. As the files are not supposed to be stored on the card, tools for handling XML-based data tend to be more widespread than similar tools for ASN.1 and XML serves as basis for the definition of web service interfaces, it seems to be the canonical choice here.

requests to card-specific APDUs. How the middleware may recognize the card type is explained in section 2.2. Section 2.3 sketches how the middleware is able to perform the mapping from a generic request to card-specific APDUs. Section 2.4 explains the structure of the CardInfo-files, which are at the heart of our approach, in more detail.

2.1 Outline of the Approach

As our aim is to support *arbitrary* cards via the generic Service Interface defined in ISO/IEC 24727-3 [9], it is necessary that the middleware "knows" how to perform the mapping from a generic request to card-specific APDUs. In order to achieve this goal the middleware is fed with CardInfo-files which allow to perform the following steps:

1. *Recognition of the card type*
   As soon as the card is captured by an interface device, the middleware must be able to "recognize" the type of the card in order to identify the appropriate CardInfo-file which allows to perform the mapping of generic requests to card-specific APDUs.
2. *Mapping the generic requests to card-specific APDUs*
   When the client-application sends a generic Action Request to the Service Interface the middleware must look into the appropriate CardInfo-file in order to translate the generic request to card-specific APDUs.

These two steps are explained in the following subsections.

2.2 Recognition of the Card Type

In this step the middleware must be able to "recognize" the type of the presented card in order to determine the applicable CardInfo-file. For every card type there is a unique CardInfo-file, which contains a set of CharacteristicFeature-elements which are used to recognize the type of a given card. A characteristic feature is described by a pointer to a (part of a) file on the card and a reference value, which is compared to the answer provided by the card. As depicted in figure 2 the set of CardInfo-files accessible by the middleware is used to build at runtime a "decision tree", which is traversed upon reset of the card.

After the reset of the card the middleware reads the "application directory file" (EF.DIR) at adress '2F00' and checks whether there is a match with one or more CharacteristicFeature-elements given by the set of CardInfo-files. As we assume in our simple example (which is currently the case in practice) that the presence of certain card applications on a card uniquely determine the card type (e.g. AID='A0 00 00 03 08 00 00 10 00 01 00' would make clear that the card is a Personal Identity Verification (PIV) card [18] and AID='4F 06 D2 76 00 00 01 02' would make clear that the card is a German electronic Health

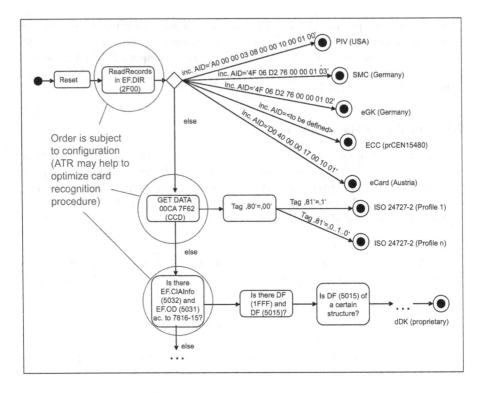

Fig. 2. An example for a decision tree to recognize the card type

Card (elektronische Gesundheitskarte, eGK) [4]) the recognition process would already stop in an acceptable state in which the card type is uniquely determined. If the analysis of EF.DIR in our example would not lead to a match, the next request to the card would check whether the Card Capability Description (CCD) is present at adress '7F62' and so on. This process will finally determine the card type or end up with an error message which states that the presented card is not among the supported card types determined by the CardInfo-files. Note that the order of the calls to the card determines the efficiency of the recognition step and hence should be optimized for a certain user environment such that card types which are more likely to occur are tested first.

2.3 Mapping the Generic Requests to Card-Specific APDUs

As soon as middleware has determined the type of a card, it can use the information provided in the CardInfo-file in order to map a generic Action Request at the Service Interface according to [9] to a Specific Request (e.g. consisting of card-specific APDUs) for the present card.

This step will be explained by a simple example as depicted in figure 3.

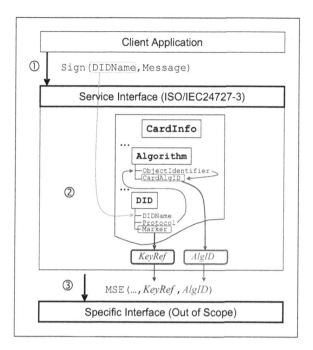

Fig. 3. Mapping of a generic request to card-specific APDUs

Suppose that a client-application wants to sign some message with a key stored on the card. Then it would roughly[2] invoke the **Sign**-function at the Service Interface with the two parameters **Message** and **DIDName**. The parameter **DIDName** is the logical name of a key-structure (called "Differential-Identity" (DID) in [9]), which is used for authentication and other cryptographic purposes. A DID comprises at least the following information:

- **DIDName** – is the logical name of the DID.
- **Protocol**[3] – specifies the cryptographic protocol, for which the DID can be used in form of an object-identifier OID. This OID must be among the algorithms supported by the card (see figure 3).
- **Marker** – may be
    - a PIN / password
    - a symmetric key
    - an asymmetric key, which may be used to generate digital signatures
    - a card-verifiable certificate

---

[2] As [9] is card-application oriented it may be necessary to connect to a specific card-application first.

[3] In the current draft of [9] this parameter is called **Authentication Protocol**. As a DID can also be used in other cryptographic primitives (e.g. for decryption or signature generation) it would be advisable to change the name of this parameter to **Protocol**.

- a biometric image or template
- a pair of symmetric keys (one for encryption and one for message authentication)

Typically a marker will be a reference to a key on a card (see figure 3).

In order to compute a digital signature the following steps are necessary:

1. *Manage Security Environment (MSE)*
   In the first step the middleware will use the MSE command (see [12, Section 7.5.11] and [14, Section 10]) to prepare the card for the computation of a digital signature with a certain key (identified by a card-specific key reference, $KeyRef$) and a certain algorithm (identified by a card-specific algorithm identifier, $AlgID$).
   As depicted in figure 3 the $KeyRef$ is found in the Marker-element of the DID referenced by DIDName. The $AlgID$ is found by looking into the description of the algorithm with the same object-identifier as the Protocol element in the DID referenced by DIDName.
2. *PSO: Compute Digital Signature (PSO:Compute DS)*
   In the second step the middleware will call the Perform Security Operation: Compute Digital Signature command (see [14, Section 11.7]) and send the data to be signed (DTBS) to the card.

In this way the middleware is able to map all generic requests defined in [9] to card-specific APDUs.

2.4   The Structure of the CardInfo-Files

At the heart of our approach are the CardInfo-files, which allow to recognize the type of a given card (cf. section 2.2) and map generic requests to card-specific APDUs (cf. section 2.3).

A CardInfo-file consists of the following four elements:

- CardType
- CardIdentification
- CardCapabilities
- ApplicationCapabilities

The main content of these elements is explained in the following. Full details may be found in [3].

CardType. This element contains a unique identifier for the card-type and optionally further useful information, like the name of the specification body or issuer (e.g. "CEN" in the case of a European Citizen Card according to [2]), the name of the card-type (e.g. "European Citizen Card"), the version and date of the specification and further references to specification documents (e.g. a URL where the specification documents [2] of the European Citizen Card may be downloaded).

CardIdentification. This element is used to identify the card-type and an individual card of this type. It consists of the following elements:

- ATR – may be used to specify a boolean mask of the ATR/ATS which is specific for the card-type. This information may be used to determine an appropriate starting point in the decision tree (cf. figure 2) which is traversed within the card-recognition procedure (cf. section 2.2).
- CharacteristicFeature – contains a sequence of characteristic features which are checked in order to recognize the card-type. A CharacteristicFeature-element consists of a reference to a (part of a) file (FileRef) on the card and a Value-element, against which the answers from the card are compared. Note that the set of CharacteristicFeature-elements in all CardInfo-files available to the middleware and their order determines the structure of the decision tree (cf. figure 2).
- ICCSN – may contain a reference to a (part of a) file, which contains a unique serial number of the card (e.g. an Integrated Chip Card Serial Number (ICCSN) or a Primary Account Number (PAN)), which allows to distinguish individual cards of a given type.

CardCapabilities. This element contains information about the general capabilities of the given card. It contains the following elements:

- ISO7816-4-CardCapabilities – contains information about the minimum requirements concerning the basic capabilities of the card according to [12, Section 8.1.1.2.7]. If the specification of the card-type does not define such minimum requirements, this element may be omitted.
- ExtendedLength – possibly contains a pointer to a (part of a) file on the card, which specifies the extended length supported by the card.
- CryptoCapabilities – contains information about the cryptographic capabilities of the card. If there is a CIAInfo-file according to [11] on the card, which *completely* describes the cryptographic capabilities and keys of the card, it is sufficient to set the boolean element ISO7816-15-CompliantCard to TRUE. If not this element contains the equivalent information. This means that it contains information about the profiles and card flags according to [11] and the supported algorithms of the card. This includes the object-identifier of the algorithm and the card-specific algorithm-identifier, which are necessary to map the generic requests to card-specific APDUs (cf. figure 3).
- BiometricCapabilities – may contain information about the biometric capabilities of the card.

ApplicationCapabilities. This element contains information about the card-applications available on the card. For every card-application this contains the following information:

- ApplicationID – is a unique identifier of the card-application. This identifier may be a registered card-application according to [13] or a unique value which is defined by the creator of the CardInfo-file.

- ApplicationName – may contain a user-friendly name of the card-application which only serves for informational purposes.
- DocumentationReferences – may contain references to the specification of the card-application.
- CardApplicationServiceSet – contains information about the services supported by the card-application, the respective access control information (cf. [9, Section 5.4.3]) and optionally (a reference to) code to be executed if the card is a Java Card [16].
- DIDInfo – contains for every Differential-Identity (DID) on the card the information which is necessary to map the generic requests to card-specific APDUs (cf. section 2.3) together with the related access control information. Given this access control information the middleware knows what kind of authentication steps (using other Differential-Identities) are necessary to access a particular DID.
- DataSetInfo – contains information about the data sets present on the card and the related access control information. For a card with file system according to [12] a data set is a directory file. A data set consists of a sequence of information about data structures for interoperability (DSI) (cf. [9, Section 8]) and associated access control information. A DSI is referenced by a logical DSIName and contains a reference to a (part of a) file on the card and optionally further information which describes the MIME-type and the encoding of the stored data. This DSIDescription may be used by a generic client-application (card browser) to visualize arbitrary data stored on the card.

3   Conclusion

In this paper we introduced a generic alternative for ISO/IEC 24727-2 [8] which allows to use the Service Interface defined in ISO/IEC 24727-3 [9] with arbitrary smart cards. While the Service Interface provides comprehensive functionality for accessing card-applications, this interface alone is often not sufficient. In particular the experiences gathered in [3] suggest that it is beneficial to have a related interface underneath these layers to access card terminals and another interface above the ISO/IEC 24727-3-interface which supports services for identity management and advanced electronic signatures. While there have been first steps towards standardizing an Interface Device API in [10] it remains to be seen, whether the interfaces in the "Identity Layer" will be standardized within the scope of ISO/IEC 24727 and/or CEN TS 15480.

References

1. German Signature Alliance. SigAll-API - Specification of the Application Programming Interface to the Signature Card. Version 1.0 (2004)
2. Comité Européen de Normalisation (CEN). Identification card systems – European Citizen Card. CEN proposed Standard prCEN15480 (Working Drafts) (2006)

3. Federal Office for Information Security (Bundesamt für Sicherheit in der Informationstechnik). eCard-API-Framework (Part 1-6). Technical Directive (BSI-TR-03112), Draft, A copy of the documents may be obtained from the authors (2007)
4. Gesellschaft für Telematikanwendungen der Gesundheitskarte (gematik). The Specification of the German electronic Health Card eHC – Part 2: Applications and application related structures. Version 1.1.1, 2006-03-23, (2006), http://www.gematik.de/upload/gematik_eGK_Specification_Part2_e_V1_1_1 _516.pdf
5. IMS Research Group. The Worldwide Market for Smart Cards and Semiconductors in Smart Cards–2006 edn. Research Report # IMS9654 (May 2006), http://www.electronics.ca/reports/ic/smart_cards.html
6. ISO/IEC 15408: Information technology – security techniques – evaluation criteria for it security (part 1-3). International Standard (2005)
7. ISO/IEC 24727-1: Identification cards – Integrated circuit cards programming interfaces – Part 1: Architecture. Final Draft International Standard (2006-08-25) (2006)
8. ISO/IEC 24727-2: Identification cards – Integrated circuit cards programming interfaces – Part 2: Generic Card Interface. Final Committee Draft (2006-07-30) (2006)
9. ISO/IEC 24727-3: Identification cards – Integrated circuit cards programming interfaces – Part 3: Application programming interface. Committee Draft (2006-09-07) (2006)
10. ISO/IEC 24727-4: Identification cards – Integrated circuit cards programming interfaces – Part 4: API Administration. Working Draft (2006-06-26) (2006)
11. ISO/IEC 7816-15: Identification cards – Integrated circuit cards – Part 15: Cryptographic information application. International Standard (2004)
12. ISO/IEC 7816-4: Identification cards – Integrated circuit cards – Part 4: Organization, security and commands for interchange. International Standard (2005)
13. ISO/IEC 7816-5: Identification cards – Integrated circuit cards – Part 5: Registration of application providers. International Standard (2005)
14. ISO/IEC 7816-8: Identification cards – Integrated circuit cards – Part 8: Commands for security operations. International Standard (2004)
15. Microsoft Inc.: Cryptography API: Next Generation, http://msdn2.microsoft.com/en-us/library/aa376210.aspx
16. Sun Microsystems. Java Card Technology, http://java.sun.com/products/javacard/
17. United States of America National Institute for Standards and Technology (NIST). Government Smart Card Interoperability Specification – Version 2.1 (July 2003), http://csrc.nist.gov/publications/nistir/nistir-6887.pdf
18. United States of America National Institute for Standards and Technology (NIST). Interfaces for Personal Identity Verification. NIST Special Publication 800-73-1 (March 2006), http://csrc.nist.gov/publications/nistir/nistir-6887.pdf
19. Open Card Consortium. OpenCard Framework Version 1.2, http://www.opencard.org/docs/1.2/index.html
20. RSA Laboratories. PKCS #11: Cryptographic Token Interface Standard - Version 2.2. Public Key Cryptography Standards – PKCS #11 (June 2004), ftp://ftp.rsasecurity.com/pub/pkcs/pkcs-11/v2-20/pkcs-11v2-20.pdf

Author Index

Lecture Notes in Computer Science

For information about Vols. 1–4565

please contact your bookseller or Springer

Vol. 4612: I. Miguel, W. Ruml (Eds.), Abstraction, Reformulation, and Approximation. XI, 418 pages. 2007. (Sublibrary LNAI).

Vol. 4611: J. Indulska, J. Ma, L.T. Yang, T. Ungerer, J. Cao (Eds.), Ubiquitous Intelligence and Computing. XXIII, 1257 pages. 2007.

Vol. 4610: B. Xiao, L.T. Yang, J. Ma, C. Muller-Schloer, Y. Hua (Eds.), Autonomic and Trusted Computing. XVIII, 571 pages. 2007.

Vol. 4609: E. Ernst (Ed.), ECOOP 2007 – Object-Oriented Programming. XIII, 625 pages. 2007.

Vol. 4608: H.W. Schmidt, I. Crnkovic, G.T. Heineman, J.A. Stafford (Eds.), Component-Based Software Engineering. XII, 283 pages. 2007.

Vol. 4607: L. Baresi, P. Fraternali, G.-J. Houben (Eds.), Web Engineering. XVI, 576 pages. 2007.

Vol. 4606: A. Pras, M. van Sinderen (Eds.), Dependable and Adaptable Networks and Services. XIV, 149 pages. 2007.

Vol. 4605: D. Papadias, D. Zhang, G. Kollios (Eds.), Advances in Spatial and Temporal Databases. X, 479 pages. 2007.

Vol. 4604: U. Priss, S. Polovina, R. Hill (Eds.), Conceptual Structures: Knowledge Architectures for Smart Applications. XII, 514 pages. 2007. (Sublibrary LNAI).

Vol. 4603: F. Pfenning (Ed.), Automated Deduction – CADE-21. XII, 522 pages. 2007. (Sublibrary LNAI).

Vol. 4602: S. Barker, G.-J. Ahn (Eds.), Data and Applications Security XXI. X, 291 pages. 2007.

Vol. 4600: H. Comon-Lundh, C. Kirchner, H. Kirchner (Eds.), Rewriting, Computation and Proof. XVI, 273 pages. 2007.

Vol. 4599: S. Vassiliadis, M. Berekovic, T.D. Hämäläinen (Eds.), Embedded Computer Systems: Architectures, Modeling, and Simulation. XVIII, 466 pages. 2007.

Vol. 4598: G. Lin (Ed.), Computing and Combinatorics. XII, 570 pages. 2007.

Vol. 4597: P. Perner (Ed.), Advances in Data Mining. XI, 353 pages. 2007. (Sublibrary LNAI).

Vol. 4596: L. Arge, C. Cachin, T. Jurdziński, A. Tarlecki (Eds.), Automata, Languages and Programming. XVII, 953 pages. 2007.

Vol. 4595: D. Bošnački, S. Edelkamp (Eds.), Model Checking Software. X, 285 pages. 2007.

Vol. 4594: R. Bellazzi, A. Abu-Hanna, J. Hunter (Eds.), Artificial Intelligence in Medicine. XVI, 509 pages. 2007. (Sublibrary LNAI).

Vol. 4592: Z. Kedad, N. Lammari, E. Métais, F. Meziane, Y. Rezgui (Eds.), Natural Language Processing and Information Systems. XIV, 442 pages. 2007.

Vol. 4591: J. Davies, J. Gibbons (Eds.), Integrated Formal Methods. IX, 660 pages. 2007.

Vol. 4590: W. Damm, H. Hermanns (Eds.), Computer Aided Verification. XV, 562 pages. 2007.

Vol. 4589: J. Münch, P. Abrahamsson (Eds.), Product-Focused Software Process Improvement. XII, 414 pages. 2007.

Vol. 4588: T. Harju, J. Karhumäki, A. Lepistö (Eds.), Developments in Language Theory. XI, 423 pages. 2007.

Vol. 4587: R. Cooper, J. Kennedy (Eds.), Data Management. XIII, 259 pages. 2007.

Vol. 4586: J. Pieprzyk, H. Ghodosi, E. Dawson (Eds.), Information Security and Privacy. XIV, 476 pages. 2007.

Vol. 4585: M. Kryszkiewicz, J.F. Peters, H. Rybinski, A. Skowron (Eds.), Rough Sets and Intelligent Systems Paradigms. XIX, 836 pages. 2007. (Sublibrary LNAI).

Vol. 4584: N. Karssemeijer, B. Lelieveldt (Eds.), Information Processing in Medical Imaging. XX, 777 pages. 2007.

Vol. 4583: S.R. Della Rocca (Ed.), Typed Lambda Calculi and Applications. X, 397 pages. 2007.

Vol. 4582: J. Lopez, P. Samarati, J.L. Ferrer (Eds.), Public Key Infrastructure. XI, 375 pages. 2007.

Vol. 4581: A. Petrenko, M. Veanes, J. Tretmans, W. Grieskamp (Eds.), Testing of Software and Communicating Systems. XII, 379 pages. 2007.

Vol. 4580: B. Ma, K. Zhang (Eds.), Combinatorial Pattern Matching. XII, 366 pages. 2007.

Vol. 4579: B. M. Hämmerli, R. Sommer (Eds.), Detection of Intrusions and Malware, and Vulnerability Assessment. X, 251 pages. 2007.

Vol. 4578: F. Masulli, S. Mitra, G. Pasi (Eds.), Applications of Fuzzy Sets Theory. XVIII, 693 pages. 2007. (Sublibrary LNAI).

Vol. 4577: N. Sebe, Y. Liu, Y.-t. Zhuang, T.S. Huang (Eds.), Multimedia Content Analysis and Mining. XIII, 513 pages. 2007.

Vol. 4576: D. Leivant, R. de Queiroz (Eds.), Logic, Language, Information and Computation. X, 363 pages. 2007.

Vol. 4575: T. Takagi, T. Okamoto, E. Okamoto, T. Okamoto (Eds.), Pairing-Based Cryptography – Pairing 2007. XI, 408 pages. 2007.

Vol. 4574: J. Derrick, J. Vain (Eds.), Formal Techniques for Networked and Distributed Systems – FORTE 2007. XI, 375 pages. 2007.

Vol. 4573: M. Kauers, M. Kerber, R. Miner, W. Windsteiger (Eds.), Towards Mechanized Mathematical Assistants. XIII, 407 pages. 2007. (Sublibrary LNAI).

Vol. 4572: F. Stajano, C. Meadows, S. Capkun, T. Moore (Eds.), Security and Privacy in Ad-hoc and Sensor Networks. X, 247 pages. 2007.

Vol. 4571: P. Perner (Ed.), Machine Learning and Data Mining in Pattern Recognition. XIV, 913 pages. 2007. (Sublibrary LNAI).

Vol. 4570: H.G. Okuno, M. Ali (Eds.), New Trends in Applied Artificial Intelligence. XXI, 1194 pages. 2007. (Sublibrary LNAI).

Vol. 4569: A. Butz, B. Fisher, A. Krüger, P. Olivier, S. Owada (Eds.), Smart Graphics. IX, 237 pages. 2007.

Vol. 4568: T. Ishida, S. R. Fussell, P. T. J. M. Vossen (Eds.), Intercultural Collaboration. XIII, 395 pages. 2007.

Vol. 4566: M.J. Dainoff (Ed.), Ergonomics and Health Aspects of Work with Computers. XVIII, 390 pages. 2007.